OXFORD ENGLISH MONOGRAPHS

On Sympathy

SOPHIE RATCLIFFE

CLARENDON PRESS · OXFORD

OXFORD

UNIVERSITY PRESS

Great Clarendon Street, Oxford OX2 6DP

Oxford University Press is a department of the University of Oxford.
It furthers the University's objective of excellence in research, scholarship,
and education by publishing worldwide in

Oxford New York

Auckland Cape Town Dar es Salaam Hong Kong Karachi
Kuala Lumpur Madrid Melbourne Mexico City Nairobi
New Delhi Shanghai Taipei Toronto

With offices in

Argentina Austria Brazil Chile Czech Republic France Greece
Guatemala Hungary Italy Japan Poland Portugal Singapore
South Korea Switzerland Thailand Turkey Ukraine Vietnam

Oxford is a registered trade mark of Oxford University Press
in the UK and in certain other countries

Published in the United States
by Oxford University Press Inc., New York

British Library Cataloguing in Publication Data

Data available

Library of Congress Cataloging in Publication Data

Ratcliffe, Sophie, 1975–
On sympathy / Sophie Ratcliffe.
p. cm.— (Oxford English monographs)
Includes bibliographical references.
ISBN–13: 978–0–19–923987–0
1. English literature—History and criticism—Theory, etc. 2. Sympathy in literature.
3. Authors and readers. 4. Literature and morals. 5. Reader-response criticism.
6. Books and reading—Philosophy. I. Title.
PR149.S95R37 2008
820.9'353—DC22 2007051453

Typeset by SPI Publisher Services, Pondicherry, India
Printed in Great Britain
on acid-free paper by
Biddles Ltd, King's Lynn, Norfolk

ISBN 978–0–19–923987–0

1 3 5 7 9 10 8 6 4 2

For my mother, Rel,
with love and thanks,
and for Andrew, always.

i.m. A. J. Ratcliffe (1943–1988)

Acknowledgements

Miranda—The Tempest, by J. W. Waterhouse is reproduced with the permission of Christie's Images Ltd. Extracts from the following copyrighted material are used in this work: *The Sea and the Mirror*, copyright © 1976 by Edward Mendelson, William Meredith and Monroe K. Spears, Executors of the Estate of W. H. Auden, 'Shorts', copyright © 1974 by The Estate of W. H. Auden, 'Ode to Terminus', copyright © 1968 by W. H. Auden; 'The Watchers', copyright © 1976 by Edward Mendelson, William Meredith, and Monroe K. Spears, Executors of the Estate of W. H. Auden; *The Age of Anxiety*, copyright 1947 by W. H. Auden and renewed 1975 by the Estate of W. H. Auden, 'The Dark Years', 'Their Lonely Betters', copyright 1951 by W. H. Auden; 'At the Grave of Henry James', copyright 1940 and renewed 1969 by W. H. Auden; *For the Time Being*, copyright 1944 and renewed 1972 by W. H. Auden; 'New Year Letter', copyright 1941 and renewed 1969 by W. H. Auden; from *Collected Poems* by W. H. Auden, copyright © 1976 by Edward Mendelson, William Meredith and Monroe K. Spears, Executors of the Estate of W. H. Auden, used by permission of Random House, Inc and Faber & Faber Ltd; lines from 'Christmas 1940', copyright © 1941 by W. H. Auden and 'The Creatures', © 1935 by W. H. Auden are reprinted with permission of Curtis Brown Ltd and Faber & Faber Ltd; four lines from 'Elegiac Stanzas on a visit to Dove Cottage' from *Collected Poems* by Geoffrey Hill (Penguin Books, 1985) first published in *For the Unfallen* (1959), copyright © Geoffrey Hill, 1959, 1985; five lines from 'Huntress, no, not that Huntress' from *Speech! Speech!* (Viking, 2001), copyright © Geoffrey Hill, 2001; 'Just a Smack at Auden' (four lines) from *The Complete Poems of William Empson*, edited by John Haffenden (Allen Lane: The Penguin Press, 2000), copyright © Estate of William Empson, 2000, reproduced by permission of Penguin Books Ltd. Quotations from Samuel Beckett's *How It Is* (London: John Calder, 1964) and Becketts *Complete Dramatic Works* (London: Faber, 1986) are reproduced with the permission of Faber & Faber Ltd. Aside from this, every reasonable effort has been made to contact and acknowledge the owners of copyright material, and care has been taken to ensure that all quotations fall within the definition of fair dealing for the purposes of criticism.

This book was developed from a doctoral thesis, funded by the Arts and Humanities Research Council. It was completed during my time as a Postdoctoral Research Fellow appointed by the British Academy. An additional research grant from the British Academy enabled me to pay the permission fees to reproduce material that appears in this book. I thank both bodies for their generous support. Many thanks, also, to the three Oxford colleges in which the work for this book was carried out—Hertford, Jesus, and Keble—and to my colleagues there.

I have been lucky enough to have wonderful teachers. For his insight, intellectual rigour, humour, and kindness, I cannot thank Christopher Butler, who supervised the original thesis, enough. I am hugely grateful to have worked with him. My thanks also to Eric Griffiths and Adrian Poole; their teaching, over a decade ago, formed the seeds of some of the ideas in this book. Many thanks to Andrew McNeillie, Jacqueline Baker, Valerie Shelley, and Alice Jacobs at OUP for all their help and advice, and to Rowena Anketell and Cyril Cox for their careful editing. A number of people have been kind enough to read parts of this book in various forms, or to discuss the ideas it contains with me. My thanks to Rachel Buxton, Matthew Creasy, Steven Connor, Valentine Cunningham, Robert Douglas-Fairhurst, Mina Gorji, John Kelly, Peter McDonald, Ronan McDonald, Andrew Schuman, Helen Small, Bharat Tandon, Shane Weller, and Christopher Woodard. I have also gained from speaking to many students and former students. Thanks, in particular, to Joe Hickey, Anastasia Tolstoy, and Kirsty Martin. Only the errors are entirely mine.

For their support as I have been writing this work, or even thinking about writing about it, my thanks to Erin Blondel, David Bradshaw, Paddy and Rebecca Bullard, Richard Butchins, Lindsay Duguid, Ralph Hanna, Xander Cansell, Peter Carroll, Clive James, Claudia Fitzgerald, Nicholas Hallam, Alan Jenkins, Jeri Johnson, Rhodri Lewis, Frances Neale, Diane Purkiss, Chris Ratcliffe, Ellie Ratcliffe, David and Jenny Rhymes, Alan Schuman, Amy Shindler, Emma Smith, Joanna Walsh, Miranda Ward, and Jenny Wheeldon. I wish it were possible to thank Anthony Levi and Anthony Nuttall; I hope that they might have approved of some of what is written here. My greatest debts are reflected in the dedication.

S. R.

Contents

Note on Short Titles, Texts, and Names

Full citations are provided for works when they first appear and abbreviated versions thereafter. The following works, more frequently cited, are referred to throughout by abbreviations. When Shakespeare's characters are re-written by other authors, I specify the author in question, with the exception of Auden. Audenesque Shakespearean characters are given in capitals, as is the case with all the characters in the text of his longer poems. All references to the Bible are taken from the text given in the King James version. Unless otherwise stated, quotations from Shakespeare are taken from the text given in *The Riverside Shakespeare*, ed. G. Blakemore Evans (Boston: Houghton Mifflin Company, 1974).

ABBREVIATIONS

ACP	W. H. Auden, *Collected Poems*, ed. Edward Mendelson (London: Faber, 1976)
BCP i, ii	Robert Browning, *The Poems*, 2 vols., ed. John Pettigrew (Harmondsworth: Penguin, 1981)
CDW	Samuel Beckett, *The Complete Dramatic Works* (London: Faber, 1986)
DH	W. H. Auden, *The Dyer's Hand and Other Essays* (New York: Random House Inc., 1962)
EA	*The English Auden: Poems, Essays and Dramatic Writings 1927–1939*, ed. Edward Mendelson (London: Faber, 1977)
HII	Samuel Beckett, *How It Is* (London: Calder, 1964)
ISIS	Samuel Beckett, *Ill Seen Ill Said* (London: Calder, 1982)
Kintner, i, ii	*The Letters of Robert Browning and Elizabeth Barrett Browning 1845–1846*, ed. Elvan Kintner, 2 vols. (Cambridge, Mass.: Belnap Press of Harvard University Press, 1969)
LOS	W. H. Auden, *Lectures on Shakespeare*, ed. Arthur Kirsch (Princeton: Princeton University Press, 2002)
LV	George Eliot, *The Lifted Veil: Brother Jacob*, ed. Helen Small (Oxford: Oxford University Press, 1999)
MPTK	Samuel Beckett, *More Pricks than Kicks* (London: Calder, 1993)

OED	*The Oxford English Dictionary*, 2nd edn., ed. J. A. Simpson and E. C. S. Weiner (Oxford: Oxford University Press, 1989, repr. 1991)
Prose, i, ii	W. H. Auden, *Prose*, ed. Edward Mendelson, i. *1929–1938* (London: Faber, 1996); ii. *1939–1948* (London: Faber, 2002)
SW	W. H. Auden, *Secondary Worlds: The T. S. Eliot Memorial Lectures Delivered at Eliot College in the University of Kent at Canterbury October 1967* (London: Faber, 1968)
T	*The Beckett Trilogy: Molloy; Malone Dies; The Unnamable* (London: Calder, 1994)
TRB	Robert Browning, *The Ring and the Book*, ed. Richard D. Altick (Harmondsworth: Penguin, 1971). References are to book and line numbers followed by page ref.
W	Samuel Beckett, *Watt* (London: John Calder, 1988)

Men owe us what we imagine they will give us. We must forgive
  them this debt.
To accept the fact that they are other than the creatures of our
  imagination is to imitate the renunciation of God.
I also am other than what I imagine myself to be. To know this is
  forgiveness.

Simone Weil, Gravity and Grace

> I have looked upon those brilliant creatures,
> And now my heart is sore.
>> W. B. Yeats, 'The Wild Swans at Coole'

Miranda—The Tempest, J. W. Waterhouse, 1916 Oil on Canvas, 100.4 × 137.8 cm (39 × 54 in)
Private Collection

Introduction

Late in 2006, a painting by the Pre-Raphaelite artist John William Waterhouse was rediscovered, having been missing for over a century. Attached to the back of the picture, a quotation in Waterhouse's handwriting confirmed its subject:

> *Tempest* Act I Scene II[1]
>
> *Miranda*   O, I have suffered
> With those that I saw Suffer! a brave vessel
> Who had, no doubt, some noble creature in her
> Dash'd all to pieces. O, the cry did knock
> Against my very heart. Poor souls they perished.

The figure of Miranda haunted the painter throughout his career. He sketched a new composition of the scene in pencil in 1903–4, and, just before his death, produced two more paintings of her in the same pose. The earlier one was exhibited at the Royal Academy's Summer Exhibition in 1916 (see Figure). A further *Miranda*, echoing the composition of the 1916 version, was among the final works completed. The painting's theme might reveal actual as well as fictional pains; as he returned to this subject at the height of the war, Waterhouse was suffering from terminal cancer.

Critics often praise Waterhouse for his skill in capturing the emotion and passion of his subjects. He is, a contemporary writes, 'a man who thinks tenderly... in a spirit always sympathetic'.[2] When it comes to

---

[1] *Miranda* was exhibited at the 1875 Summer Exhibition at the Royal Academy. I replicate the precise quotation as given on the painting. See Peter Trippi's 'Essay' in 'Sale 14218: 19th Century Paintings and Watercolours, 14 November 2006', *Bonham's Catalogue*, <http://www.bonhams.com/cgibin/public.sh/pubweb/publicSite.r?s Continent = EUR&screen=lotdetailsNoFlash&iSaleItemNo=3180526&iSaleNo=14218 and http://www.johnwilliamwaterhouse.com/pictures/newly-discovered-waterhouse-paintings-miranda.html>. Unless otherwise stated, I use *The Tempest*, ed. Frank Kermode (London: Routledge, 1964). All further line references will be given in the text.

[2] Unsigned, 'Some Drawings by J. W. Waterhouse, R.A.', *Studio*, 44/86 (1908), 247–52, at 250.

Miranda, however, the spirit is reticent. In all three of the paintings based on *The Tempest*, he holds back, offering not his characteristic 'Waterhouse girl', with her 'yearning flower-like face', but her merest edge, a *profil perdu* rarely seen in his work.[3] The pose may not appear to give much away, but it captures something important—it directs us to the difficulty of finding an appropriate expression for compassion.

Scores of other artists and writers, from Dryden to Coover, have shown concern for *The Tempest*'s 'life of afterlife'.[4] Its 'goodly creatures' appear to haunt the imagination, inspiring many adaptations, and, in this way, the play provides a sympathetic creative link between generations of artists.[5] Adaptation and adapting also form the thematic centre of the work. From the misshapen Caliban to the villainous Antonio, each of the figures in the play undergoes an ethical shift, analogous to the 'sea-change' described in Ariel's song, and such transformations extend outwards at the play's end when both author and audience seem implicated in *The Tempest*'s metamorphosis.

The thought that we may change by or through our encounters with art is both tempting and terrifying. For T. S. Eliot, it is the reason for writing. A poet, he argues, has only one struggle: 'to transmute his personal and private agonies into something rich and strange.'[6] It is a great hope and, as he alludes to *The Tempest*, Eliot enacts what he describes. The echo allows him, for a moment, to stand on the edge of elsewhere, speaking in a way that is neither personal nor private, but strangely, and perhaps sympathetically, extended towards a voice from the past.

The four chapters of this book, and its epilogue, trace the ways in which we think about ethics and sympathetic understanding, ranging from the manner in which people comprehend each other, to the ways in which they think about God. The book focuses, in particular, on the

[3] The description is Trippi's. See his *J. W. Waterhouse* (London: Phaidon, 2004), 125. My thanks to Julia Kerr and Andrew Schuman for their help with researching Waterhouse.

[4] Beckett writes of 'The life of afterlife' in the '*Summary*', which comprises the final, epilogic chapter of *Mercier and Camier* (repr. London: Calder, 1999), 123.

[5] The phrase 'goodly creatures' is Miranda's. See *The Tempest*, v. i. 182. See Dryden and D'Avenant, *The Tempest: or, the Enchanted Island, a Comedy* (1676; London: Cornmarket, 1969) and Robert Coover's 'The Magic Poker' in *Pricksongs & Descants* (New York: Dutton, 1967), 20–45.

[6] See 'Shakespeare and the Stoicism of Seneca' (1927), in T. S. Eliot, *Selected Essays* (London: Faber, 1969), 137. Eliot writes about 'escape from personality' in 'Tradition and the Individual Talent' (1919), ibid. 21.

work of Browning, Auden, and Beckett, paying close attention to their dramatic monologues that allude to *The Tempest*: Browning's 'Caliban upon Setebos; or, Natural Theology on the Island' (1864), Auden's *The Sea and the Mirror* (1942–4), and Beckett's *How It Is* (1964).

As this is a book about relating and relationships, the tracing of literary connections is central, and the use of allusion forms a crucial part of this study. The chain of remembrance, in which writers reinflect the same words or stories, is analogous to the difficulty of understanding others. While the echoes of Shakespeare within these works are similar, they are never quite the same and, in this way, allusions allow us to see the ideals and the fractured actualities of feeling and understanding. For, while allusion may be seen as a form of sympathy, it is also a form of obligation. Acts of allusion alert us to the way in which one may move towards a new world, while still feeling for the past. With this in mind, these allusive monologues form the basis for a study of these authors' concerns about dependence (especially theological dependence), their thoughts on sympathy, and the way in which both of these matters come to bear on their stylistic development.

The difficulty of recognizing another's point of view is central to the problems that one encounters when dealing with any literary work. Once the nuances of the spoken, live voice are lost, we, as readers or performers, may become engaged in acts of imagination, attempting to reconstruct the voice and intentions of an absent person. One of the voices that seems to be missing, or most missed, in *The Tempest* is the voice of Shakespeare. And, just as the play lends itself to theological speculation—when Prospero appears to deal in a godlike way with the isle's visitors—the search for Shakespeare's intentions has become, in a sense, analogous to a religious quest. Browning, Auden, and Beckett take their part in this, responding not only to the play but also to the ways in which the play has been received before them. For early critics, such as Schlegel, Heine, and De Quincey, *The Tempest* was seen in relation to the Neoplatonic concept of ideal forms.[7] By the late nineteenth century it was also being read as a personal allegory, with Prospero standing, as Edward Dowden puts it in 1875, for Shakespeare 'passing from his service as artist'.[8] Others, meanwhile, have seen the play as an allegory for man's relation to God.

---

[7] A. D. Nuttall, *Two Concepts of Allegory: A Study of Shakespeare's 'The Tempest' and the Logic of Allegorical Expression* (London: Routledge & Kegan Paul, 1967), 3–5, 10.
[8] Edward Dowden, *Shakspere: His Mind and Art* (London: Kegan Paul, 1897), 423.

The presence of this chain of allegorical readings is an important part of understanding *The Tempest*, and of understanding my chosen authors' attractions to the play. We turn to analogical modes of thought and allegorical modes of storytelling because there are limits to our sympathetic comprehension; our recourse to such metaphorical means of understanding might be said to stem from the sense of our mental confinement. Beckett, Browning, and Auden are all too aware of their own limits, and repeatedly consider the difficulties and pleasures of analogical thought. But here, too, they are working allusively, remembering those who have thought about these questions before their own life's span. Therefore, before considering individual texts, this book will look further back, making a general survey of the relationships between analogy, allegory, sympathy, and theology from which Browning, Beckett, and Auden work.

This analysis of poetic form and poetic thought will show how these authors use the dramatic monologue itself to question the possibility of development, in terms ranging from the shaping of individual morality through human and textual encounters, to the ethical evolution of the human species. My interest is, therefore, philosophical and generic, as well as chronological. In considering the dramatic monologue form, I aim to question critical assumptions about sympathetic engagement and ethical progress which have, so far, characterized discussions of the genre. In this sense, my argument takes issue with Langbaum's seminal work, *The Poetry of Experience* (1957)—a work that depends on what may now be seen as a very simple association of the dramatic monologue with a transparent sympathetic understanding, and its simplistic relationship to moral judgement.[9] Such questions of sympathetic understanding are themselves currently under review. While a critic such as Martha Nussbaum has followed Langbaum's line in recent years, cognitive philosophers such as Noël Carroll, Murray Smith, and Gregory Currie have introduced new and influential thoughts about the means by which we engage with fictional characters.[10] Their claims about the

[9] See Robert Langbaum, *The Poetry of Experience: The Dramatic Monologue in Modern Literary Tradition* (1957; London: Chatto & Windus, 1972).

[10] See Noël Carroll, *Beyond Aesthetics: Philosophical Essays* (Cambridge: Cambridge University Press, 2001); *A Philosophy of Mass Art* (Oxford: Clarendon Press, 1998); *The Philosophy of Horror* (New York: Routledge, 1990); Gregory Currie and Ian Ravenscroft, *Recreative Minds: Imagination in Philosophy and Psychology* (Oxford: Oxford University Press, 2002); Gregory Currie, *The Nature of Fiction* (Cambridge: Cambridge University Press, 1990); Murray Smith, *Engaging Characters: Fiction, Emotion and the Cinema* (Oxford: Clarendon Press, 1995).

way in which we relate to other minds, not so much through 'identification' as with a complex understanding of a situation, challenges the
common perception of the dramatic monologue as the location for the
'*tension* between sympathy' (which Langbaum defines variously as 'romantic projectiveness', '*Einfühlung*', and 'empathy') and 'judgment'.[11]

Any attempt to engage with literary works requires tact—a quality
which one might see as related to sympathy, involving both a 'sensitivity
of critical touch', a good ear for tone, and a consciousness of one's own
limits in understanding or influencing others.[12] Tactful readings are
made particularly difficult when encountering *poems* such as these that
are based upon a *dramatic* work. The generic shift makes readers even
more conscious of their distance from the spoken voice, as they attempt
to reimagine the tones of these creatures who will always seem 'but air';
insubstantial in the light of their performed dramatic counterparts.[13] In
preferring the page to the stage, these are texts that have a peculiar tact of
their own—a resistance to what might be seen as the dramatic mode,
both as a genre, and as a sensibility. In sympathy with this resistance, this
book argues for a vision of poetry that resists dramatic claims. At the
time of writing, there is something of a 'vogue for empathy'; a fuzzy but
general assumption that expressing sympathy or empathy, and engaging
in purportedly 'empathetic' literary encounters, may encourage civic
virtue and liberal humanitarianism.[14] To say that this is unlikely is to say
nothing new. However, by involving us in difficult creative acts of
imagining, the writers discussed raise important questions about sympathy, reading, and faith. Not least, they question the faith we should
place in reading.

[11] Langbaum, 'Preface', *Poetry of Experience*.
[12] Valentine Cunningham, 'Fact and Tact', *Essays in Criticism*, 51/1 (2001), 119–38, at 132–3.
[13] Prospero refers to Ariel as 'but air' when he asks 'Hast thou, which art but air, a touch, a feeling | Of their afflictions?' v. i. 21–2.
[14] Suzanne Keen, *Empathy and the Novel* (Oxford: Oxford University Press, 2007), p. vii.

1

Understanding Sympathy and Sympathetic Understanding

Are you unable to give me your sympathy—you who read this? Are you unable to imagine this double consciousness at work within me, flowing on like two parallel streams that never mingle their waters and blend into a common tune?[1]

Midway through 'The Lifted Veil', George Eliot's narrator turns on his audience. A man with a 'sensitive, unpractical' nature, Latimer presents himself as suffering from a peculiar illness (*LV*, 7). He is, he claims, cursed with a 'double consciousness'—an ability to participate in the minds of others. Paradoxically, the imposition of others' feelings makes him feel thoroughly isolated:

I began to be aware of a phase in my abnormal sensibility, to which, from the languid and slight nature of my intercourse with others since my illness, I had not been alive before. This was the obtrusion on my mind of the mental process going forward in first one person, and then another, with whom I happened to be in contact: the vagrant, frivolous ideas and emotions of some uninteresting acquaintance . . . would force themselves on my consciousness like an importunate, ill-played musical instrument, or the loud activity of an imprisoned insect. (*LV*, 13)

For Latimer, this telepathic state manifests itself as a sort of emotional tinnitus, 'like a preternaturally heightened sense of hearing, making audible to one a roar of sound where others find perfect stillness' (*LV*, 18). It is characteristic of Eliot to find similitudes for feeling by describing one sense of the world through the means of another sense. Latimer's ear for the perils of intimacy echoes, in its content and its phrasing, both her vision of an author who may teach 'by giving us his higher sensibility as a medium, a delicate acoustic . . . instrument' and the narrator in *Middlemarch*, for whom 'a keen vision and feeling of all human life'

---

[1] George Eliot, 'The Lifted Veil', repr. In *The Lifted Veil; Brother Jacob*, ed. Helen Small (Oxford: Oxford University Press, 1999), 21. Henceforth *LV*.

would be like 'hearing the grass grow and the squirrel's heart beat'. For them, as for Latimer, this sensitivity is something to fear. If we possessed it, 'we should die of that roar that lies on the other side of silence'.²

The story itself, however, was seen as out of character for Eliot. She was a writer who repeatedly 'articulated a project for the cultivation of the reader's sympathetic imagination'.³ With its terrifying vision of minds meeting, 'The Lifted Veil' contrasts with the ideas expressed in Eliot's letters—the conviction that, for a writer, 'true morality' is the 'active participation in the joys and sorrows of our fellow-men ... in a word, in the widening and strengthening of our sympathetic nature', or that an author's role is to 'call forth tolerant judgment, pity, and sympathy' in her readers'.⁴

This is perhaps why Eliot described the story as being of an 'outré kind', and her publisher, Blackwood, expressed some concern about its 'unsympathising, untrustworthy' hero.⁵ 'I wish the theme had been a happier one', he wrote, 'and I think you must have been worrying and disturbing yourself about something when you wrote.'⁶ The story is, indeed, disturbing. It highlights Eliot's feeling for some difficult questions. How can one find oneself 'giving sympathy' when it is, at heart, a concept that is not fully understood? Are the explanations of sympathy gained through knowledge missing something crucial? And, as Helen Small points out, '[w]ould sympathy necessarily accompany keenness of insight?' Given all this, Small argues, 'there are moments of recognition in Eliot's novels that sympathy may, after all, be an inadequate basis for a moral code'.⁷

Such questions relating to the interplay between 'knowledge', 'explanation', 'understanding', and 'sympathy' haunt 'The Lifted Veil'. Eliot was well aware that her own descriptions of sympathetic nature

---

² George Eliot, '[*Westward Ho!* and *Constance Herbert*]' (July 1855), in *Essays of George Eliot*, ed. Thomas Pinney (New York: Columbia University Press; London: Routledge and Kegan Paul, 1963), 123–36, at 126; George Eliot, *Middlemarch; A Study of Provincial Life*, ed. David Carroll (Oxford: Oxford University Press, 1989), 189.

³ Keen, *Empathy*, 38.

⁴ George Eliot, 'Worldliness and Other-Worldliness: The Poet Young' (Jan. 1857), repr. in *Essays and Leaves from a Notebook* (Edinburgh: William Blackwood, 1884), 1–78, at 63; GE to John Blackwood, 18 Feb. 1857, in *The George Eliot Letters*, ed. Gordon S. Haight, 9 vols. (New Haven: Yale University Press, 1954–78), ii. 299.

⁵ GE to John Blackwood, 31 Mar. 1859; JB to GE, 8 July 1859, in *George Eliot Letters*, iii. 41, 112.

⁶ *George Eliot Letters*, iii. 67.

⁷ My discussion of this text is indebted to Small's excellent introduction. See Small, 'Introduction' to *LV*, p. xiii.

would have struck her readers in different ways. While Latimer's notion of a 'double consciousness' would, for many Victorian readers, have summoned the idea of mesmerism, the words 'had a different meaning for Victorian researchers of the organic structure of the brain'. For them, 'double consciousness' signified a clash of the brain's separate cerebra that resulted in insanity: 'the intermixture of two synchronous trains of thought', depriving the 'discourse of coherence or congruity'.[8] In this sense, the ambiguity of the phrase 'double consciousness' allows Latimer's plight to hover between diagnoses. By one turn, he is capable of participating in the minds of others. The second opinion blights him with a delusion that this condition is possible. In either case, Latimer's request for sympathy is as contrary as his temperament. He requires a sympathetic leap on the part of the reader in order to understand his predicament, and simultaneously casts doubt on the possibility and value of mental closeness.

For a contemporary critic, as for Eliot, one of the main challenges when writing about the idea of sympathy is the vagueness that surrounds the term itself. The confusion begins on the level of definition, with the difficulties of distinguishing 'sympathy' from a number of cognate terms. The first is 'empathy', coined from the German 'Einfühlung' by Vernon Lee.[9] Used by Lee in 1904 to describe the experience of relating to a work of art, it has now come to 'designate imaginative reconstruction of another person's experience'. For some, this reconstruction is seen to be 'without any particular evaluation of that experience'.[10] The second is the idea of 'pity', which was once related closely to the idea of 'sympathy' or 'compassion', but which 'has recently come to have nuances of condescension and superiority to the sufferer'.[11] Meanwhile, 'sympathy' itself is 'frequently used in British eighteenth-century texts to denote an emotional equivalent' to what some contemporary critics would term 'compassion' or 'empathy'.[12] Such a definition is found in Johnson's *Dictionary*, which gives 'to sympathize' as 'to feel with another; to feel

    [8] See Small, 'Introduction', p. xviii; Arthur Ladbroke Wigan, *A New View of Insanity: The Duality of the Mind* (London: Longman, Brown, Green and Longmans, 1844), 28–9.
    [9] Vernon Lee and Clementina Anstruther-Thomson, *Beauty and Ugliness and Other Studies in Psychological Aesthetics* (London: John Lane, the Bodley Head, 1912), 241–350, at 337.
    [10] The definition is Martha Nussbaum's, *Upheavals of Thought: The Intelligence of the Emotions* (Cambridge: Cambridge University Press, 2001), 301–2.
    [11] Ibid. 301.
    [12] Ibid. 302.

in consequence of what another feels; to feel mutually' and 'sympathy' as 'Fellowfeeling; mutual sensibility; the quality of being affected by the affection of another'.[13] As Isobel Armstrong elaborates, 'in eighteenth-century discussions of the psychology of ethics . . . Sympathy was the faculty of sharing and understanding the situation of another person by being able to change places with him in imagination':

> For [Adam] Smith our moral sense is derived from being the attentive spectator of the action of others and from the resulting development of judgements which we then apply to our own conduct. But we cannot test the moral validity of anything except 'by changing places in fancy' with the person we are judging: 'we enter as it were into his body, and become in some measure the same person with him, and thence form some idea of his sensations, and even feel something which, though weaker in degree, is not altogether unlike them'. The morality of a society will be created by a series of delicately reciprocal acts of imagination in which each person is able to call up an 'analogous emotion' in response to the feeling of another and is therefore able to check both his companion's conduct and his own.[14]

Isobel Armstrong claims that this idea of sympathy is no longer common: the 'notion . . . has completely lost its richness and dense moral weight for us'.[15] This is not exactly true. My argument sets out to look at the ways in which 'sympathy' has been understood in both the nineteenth and twentieth centuries, and how it weighs in the moral balance.

SYMPATHY, EMPATHY, AND COGNITION

There is some disagreement as to whether 'empathy' is necessary for sympathy or compassion to be present, as well as the question of whether empathy or sympathy do, in fact, promote altruistic behaviour.[16] Furthermore, while it is generally given that 'sympathy' is imagined as a state in which one develops an understanding of the emotional states of others, such a definition begs the question of what it means

---

[13] Samuel Johnson, *A Dictionary of the English Language* (London: Times Books, 1983).

[14] Isobel Armstrong, *Victorian Scrutinies* (London: Athlone Press, 1972), 9–10. She quotes from Adam Smith, *The Theory of Moral Sentiments*, ed. Dugald Stewart (London: Henry G. Bohn, 1853), 4, 5.

[15] Armstrong, *Scrutinies*, 9.

[16] See Keen, *Empathy*.

to 'understand' an emotional state. After all, 'understanding' is a word that operates in two ways, invoking both ideas of knowledge and of emotional feeling. There are, moreover, further questions as to whether 'sympathy' should be understood as an emotion (or feeling) in and of itself—or as a cognitive position achieved through processing judgements of emotional states.

This is a debate that has its own ethical ramifications. Humanist literary critics have taken Smith's definition of sympathy as an act of judgement as paradigmatic. However, as Brigid Lowe points out, 'Smith's conception of sympathy is something of a retreat within the sentimental tradition', and a correction of the idea that Hume promoted in his *Treatise of Human Nature* (1739–40). In the *Treatise*, Hume's ideal of sympathy was one through which one 'receive[s] by communication' the 'inclinations and sentiments' of another, 'however different from, or even contrary to our own'.[17] As Lowe rightly argues, 'Smith seeks to replace Hume's celebration of sympathy as a fundamental principle of radically intersubjective communication . . . with a model of sympathy as distance, spectatorship, impartiality, control and subjective consolidation'.[18]

The important differences between Hume's early idea of sympathy and the ideal that he and Smith later champion continue to resonate in debates about emotion. The uncertainty as to whether 'sympathy' exists as a somatic feeling in itself or as a state of mind resulting from an act of cognition persists through the nineteenth and twentieth centuries, with terms and ideas from scientific discourses drifting into literary works and vice versa. A work such as George Henry Lewes's 1859 *Physiology of Common Life* wrestled with the distinction between thinking and feeling, drawing both on the metaphysics of William Hamilton and on the metaphors of George Eliot, while the poems of Browning's *Men and Women* were received not simply as works of art, but as 'portraits in mental psychology' contributing to the debate itself.[19] While Charles Darwin's 1872 *The Expression of the Emotions in Man and Animals* tackled the emotions' evolutionary and physiological origins,

[17] David Hume, 'Of the Love of Fame', in *A Treatise of Human Nature* (Sterling: Thoemmes Press, 2000), II. ii. xi. 73.

[18] Brigid Lowe, *Insights of Sympathy* (London: Anthem, 2007), 9–10.

[19] See *Quarterly Review*, 118 (July–Oct. 1865), 77–105. An account of the relationship between the emerging psychology and the dramatic monologue is given in Ekbert Faas, *Retreat to the Mind: Victorian Poetry and the Rise of Psychiatry* (Princeton: Princeton University Press, 1988), 3–33.

the emerging sciences (and pseudo-sciences) of psychology and psychiatry, hovered variously between views of emotion, and emotional imbalances, as either somatic states or illnesses, or as the result of errors of cognitive processing and judgement. As behaviourist models of emotion emerged in the early twentieth century, Darwin's contributions to our understanding of emotion as instinct were 'largely overlooked', although his findings were partially channelled into psychoanalytic models of emotional understanding.[20]

By the time Auden was writing, Pinel's disciple, Freud, had created a 'whole climate of opinion' (*ACP*, 275). However, as Auden notes, to 'trace...the influence of Freud upon modern art...would not only demand an erudition which few... possess, but would be of very doubtful utility'.[21] While both Freud and Jung influenced Auden's and Beckett's conceptions of sympathetic understanding, they also put psychoanalytical theory under scrutiny. Beckett's contemporaries were quick to place him on the couch, with later critics following suit, but his own relationship with such theories was driven by parody and suspicion.[22] Browning, Beckett, and Auden were all interested in philosophical and psychological models of thought, but they were also wary of the ways in which such models could become 'a means of escape', offering the illusion of easy moral progress.[23] They were also aware of the ways in which theories of emotion may not simply explain our emotional repertoire, but may take their part in forming it.[24] For a constructivist such as Rom Harré, the question is not what sympathy is, but rather how the word 'sympathy' is used in differing social and cultural contexts.[25]

There is much to be said for the constructivist view. It directs us to the ways in which our senses of our emotions may have shifted as a

[20] See e.g. John B. Watson and B. F. Skinner, *The Behavior of Organisms* (New York: Appleton-Century-Crofts, 1939); Stanley Schachter and Jerome Singer, 'Cognitive, Social and Physiological Determinants of Emotional States', *Psychological Review*, 69 (Sept. 1962), 379–99. I quote Robert C. Fuller, *Wonder: From Emotion to Spirituality* (Chapel Hill: University of North Carolina Press, 2006), 18.
[21] See Auden's 'Psychology and Art Today' (1935), in *EA*, 332.
[22] See Phil Baker, *Beckett and the Mythology of Psychoanalysis* (Basingstoke: Macmillan, 1997), p. xi. For a recent example of a psychoanalytic reading of Beckett see John Robert Keller, *Samuel Beckett and the Primacy of Love* (Manchester: Manchester University Press, 2002), and my review of it, *Review of English Studies* 55 (2004), 301–3.
[23] Auden, 'Psychology and Art', 332.
[24] Mendelson, *Later Auden* (London: Faber, 1999), 92. Mendelson refers to Auden's 'Jacob and the Angel' (1939), *Prose*, ii. 37–9.
[25] Rom Harré, *The Social Construction of the Emotions* (Oxford: Blackwell, 1986).

result of the opportunities for researching, expressing, and analysing them. The differing atmospheric discourses which surround the experiments of Charles Mesmer and James Braid, the early analysis of Pinel and Freud, and the confessional culture of Jerry Springer and Oprah Winfrey offer various means of perceiving and describing emotion and may, in turn, affect the emotions one perceives. As John C. Fuller has described, by the 1980s, we have seen a return to the more Darwinian approach to the emotions, with neuroscientific researchers such as Richard LeDoux and Edward Rolls offering analyses of the way in which, in spite of a 'cognitive overlay', emotions are 'biological functions of the nervous system', with our genes specifying 'the kind of nervous system we will have, the kinds of mental processes in which it can engage, and the kinds of bodily functions it can control'.[26] The discovery of 'mirror neurons' in the brain—neurons which become active when witnessing the actions of others—has led some to argue for 'a very specific, limited version of empathy located in the neural substrate'.[27] Despite the temptation to see this mirroring as biological proof of 'empathy', there is no reason that a mirroring of cellular neural activity actually connotes a mirroring of the same emotional feeling. Nor does this cellular mirroring, as Michael Arbib points out, necessarily 'constitute "understanding" the action'.[28] Ultimately, for LeDoux, 'the exact way we act, think, and feel in a particular situation is determined by many other factors and is not predestined in our genes . . . Some, if not many, emotions do have a biological basis, but social, which is to say cognitive, factors are also crucially important.'[29]

So while the 'evolutionary-adaptive' framework for the emotions has, Fuller argues, been generally accepted, '[d]ebates still rage over fundamental issues entailed in defining precisely what an emotion is. How . . . does an emotion differ from a feeling or a mood? Which . . . emotions are innate . . . and which are learnt? How many emotions are there—and what criteria might distinguish between distinct emotions and feeling

[26] Joseph LeDoux, *The Emotional Brain* (New York: Simon and Schuster, 1996), 137.

[27] Keen, *Empathy*, p. viii. Keen cites Vittorio Gallese, ' "Being Like Me": Self-Other Identity, Mirror Neurons, and Empathy', in S. Hurley and N. Chater (eds.), *Perspectives on Imitation: From Cognitive Neuroscience to Social Science* (Boston: MIT Press, 2005), 101–18 and Sandra Blakeslee, 'Cells that Read Minds', *New York Times*, 10 Jan. 2006, F1: F4.

[28] See Michael Arbib, ' "From Mirror Neurons to Understanding": Discussion of Vittorio Gallese's "Intentional Attunement: The Mirror Neuron System and its Role in Interpersonal Development" ', <http://www.interdisciplines.org/mirror/papers/1/2#_2.>

[29] LeDoux, *Emotional Brain*, 137.

states composed of one or more of these distinct emotions.'[30] As Aaron Ben-Ze'ev comments, 'the nature, causes, and consequences of the emotions are among the least understood aspects of human experience. It is easier to express emotions than to describe them, and harder, again, to analyze them.'[31] It is a statement that, in terms of the emotion of 'sympathy', is in itself complicated by the fact that 'understanding' can be perceived as both an aspect of cognition and as a feeling. Is 'understanding' a form of sympathy itself? Moreover, does 'knowing' something involve 'understanding' it?[32]

SYMPATHY AND THE LIMITS OF THE COGNITIVE-EVALUATIVE VIEW

Despite their name, most cognitive-evaluative psychological theories do not ignore the emotional aspects of the mind. Leda Cosmides and John Tooby note that 'one cannot sensibly talk about emotion affecting cognition because "cognition" refers to a language for describing all of the brain's operations, including emotions and reasoning'.[33] In many ways, the theory of sympathy as described by Adam Smith, which has been generally championed by literary critics such as Wayne Booth and Robert Langbaum, and literary philosophers such as Martha Nussbaum, is in line with the cognitive-evaluative view. Nussbaum sees emotions not as 'animal energies or impulses' but as 'intelligent responses to perceptions of value'.[34] 'Emotions', she argues, 'are not just the fuel that powers the psychological mechanism of a reasoning creature, they are parts, highly complex and messy parts, of this creature's reasoning itself.'[35] Nussbaum's is not in itself a Stoic view. In fact, her argument is in complete opposition to the idea of a life lived in an attempt to detach

---

[30] Fuller, *Wonder*, 24.
[31] Aaron Ben-Ze'ev, *The Subtlety of the Emotions* (Cambridge, Mass.: MIT Press, 2000), p. xiii.
[32] See Roger Scruton, 'Emotion, Practical Knowledge and Common Culture', Amélie Oksenberg Rorty (ed.), in *Explaining Emotions* (Berkeley and Los Angeles: University of California Press, 1980), 519–36.
[33] Leda Cosmides and John Tooby, 'Evolutionary Psychology and the Emotions', in Michael Lewis and Jeanette M. Haviland-Jones (eds.), *Handbook of Emotions* (New York and London: Guilford Press, 2000), 91–5, at 98.
[34] Nussbaum, *Upheavals*, 1.
[35] Ibid. 4.

oneself from the emotions. However, her conception of the emotions 'has its antecedents in the ancient Greek Stoics', holding that

emotions are appraisals of value judgments, which ascribe to things and persons outside the person's own control great importance for that flourishing ... It thus contains three salient ideas: the idea of *cognitive appraisal* or *evaluation*; the idea of *one's own flourishing* or *one's important goals and projects*; and the idea of the *salience of external objects as elements in one's own scheme of goals*.[36]

As Nussbaum rightly points out, 'a theoretic account of emotions is not only that: it has large consequences for the theory of practical reason, for normative ethics, and for the relationship between ethics and aesthetics'.[37]

Such an account also has a particular effect on how we perceive the idea of sympathy. For if sympathy is seen as an aspect of human intelligence, derived from an emotional experience, which is in turn based on evaluating and appraising objects, one can deduce that it is a state which can be changed, developed, augmented, or manipulated, depending on those beliefs and judgements. This is why cognitive theories of emotion have been seen by literary philosophers as particularly important: in their terms, reading is a way of developing our cognitive judgements about our emotions.

One of the weaknesses of cognitive arguments about sympathetic responses, as adopted by literary critics, is the way in which they handle the triangulation of three separate ideas: the ideas of sympathy as an emotion, of understanding, and of knowledge. As described, Nussbaum argues that we have knowledge and cognition of the world because our emotions are 'intelligent'; that is to say they are eudaimonistic 'intelligent responses to perceptions of value'. We feel the emotion of sympathy or compassion towards, for example, our mother, when she is sad, because we possess the knowledge that she is valuable to us in some way, and her sadness threatens this value. (Nussbaum notes that this 'does not mean that the emotions view these objects simply as tools or instruments of the agent's own satisfaction ... But what makes the emotion center around this particular mother ... is that she is *my* mother, a part of my life.')[38] Similarly, we feel the emotion of sympathy or compassion towards someone we read about who has lost their mother because we possess a general belief, in our scheme of goals and aims, that a mother is 'a type of person that it would be good for every human being who has

---

[36] Nussbaum, *Upheavals*, 4.   [37] Ibid. 3.   [38] Ibid. 31.

one to cherish', and that the loss of such a good will, therefore, be painful to us.[39] In some ways, then, Nussbaum allies herself with the view put forward by Richard Lazurus and Robert Plutchik. While she argues that thinking and feeling are entwined, for her 'cognition is always entailed in, and actually precedes, human emotion'.[40]

The problem with this position is that it requires this cognitive 'knowledge' or 'judgment of value' about, for example, the importance of mothers to be in some way pure. As Simon Blackburn comments:

the cognitive view needs more than an equation between feelings towards things on the one hand, and judgments of value on the other. It also requires that the judgments of value are themselves pure cognitions, representing aspects of the world. And this is highly dubitable, since a judgment of value is itself an expression of attitudes, stances, and feelings towards things.[41]

Blackburn's distinction is an important one because viewing sympathy as a cognitive mapping, based on a judgement of value, is highly dependent on the question of what one views to be a self and what one views as an object (not to mention a valuable object) in the first place. Nussbaum would concur. In fact, this is why she encourages the reading of literary texts. For Nussbaum, reading about characters in books that resemble people in life who are quite different to us might 'encourage' us to expand our view of 'valuable' objects.[42]

Nussbaum's own view of valuable objects is not, in fact, very expansive. Throughout her *œuvre*, she sees our relations with literary texts in a particularly narrow way. She also chooses to talk about literary texts that might be considered to have realist, mimetic ambitions. This could be because she requires the text to offer readers the opportunity for what she sees as straightforward identification, in order to live better lives, and to extend their sense of valuable objects. Nussbaum's own most valued object, however, and the one which she holds on to most emphatically, is her own post-Freudian, rationalist view of the 'human self', which she

[39] Ibid. 53.
[40] I quote R. C. Fuller, *Wonder*, 25. See Robert Plutchik, 'The Circumplex as a General Model of the Structures of Emotion and Personality', in Robert Plutchik and Hope Conte (eds.), *Circumplex Models of Personality and Emotions* (Washington DC: American Psychological Association, 1997), 17–46 and Richard Lazarus and Bernice Lazarus, *Passion and Reason: Making Sense of Our Emotions* (New York: Oxford University Press, 1994), 129.
[41] Simon Blackburn, 'To Feel and to Feel Not', rev. of Martha Nussbaum, *Upheavals of Thought*, *New Republic*, 13 Dec. 2001, <http://www.phil.cam.ac.uk/swb24/reviews/Nussbaum.htm.>
[42] Nussbaum, *Upheavals*, 2.

has elsewhere referred to as 'our neutral and natural condition'.[43] She finds herself 'alarmed', for example, at certain sorts of belief, such as the 'insistent otherworldly direction' of Augustine; she affirms that one should direct 'compassion altogether toward the theatre of history and not at all toward the shadowy and uncertain realm that may or may not lie outside it'.[44] As Diana Fritz Cates rightly notes, Nussbaum's 'worldly' beliefs seem to have an influence on the way she reads emotion:

Nussbaum maintains that emotions are thoughts that 'mark our lives as uneven, uncertain, and prone to reversal'. She does not say, simply, that emotions give us the *impression* that our lives are uneven, uncertain, and prone to reversal; she says that our lives are really like this, and emotions help us to acknowledge this. However, people who live within different worlds of religious imagination might quarrel with Nussbaum even at this point: in what respects, for example, is life uncertain? Is it uncertain in the most important respects? What *are* the most important respects?

And as Cates concludes: 'developing a theory of the emotions requires delving extensively into questions about what is really (and not only apparently) real.'[45]

SYMPATHETIC ALTERNATIVES

Nussbaum's vision of compassion as 'our species' way of hooking the good of others to the fundamentally eudaimonistic (though not egoistic) structure of our imaginations and our most intense cares' is a workmanlike explanation of one sort of interaction that takes place between humans, and between humans and non-humans.[46] However, both the eudaimonism and the object-based drive of Nussbaum's argument poses problems. First, it garners counter-arguments from the anticompassion tradition. Secondly, it does not seem to quite capture what many others might understand by sympathy.

The 'antipity' or 'anticompassion' tradition, whose main exponents have included Plato, the Stoics, Spinoza, and Kant, entails the belief that a good person cannot be harmed, and that compassion towards those

---

[43] Martha C. Nussbaum, *Love's Knowledge: Essays on Philosophy and Literature* (New York: Oxford University Press, 1990), 309.

[44] Nussbaum, *Upheavals*, 552.

[45] Diana Fritz Cates, 'Conceiving Emotions: Martha Nussbaum's *Upheavals of Thought*', *Journal of Religious Ethics*, 31/2 (2003), 325–41, at 340.

[46] Nussbaum, *Upheavals*, 388.

who are suffering is based on 'false beliefs about the value of external goods'.[47] The anticompassionist would also raise the objection that 'compassion is an affront to one's dignity, that it leads to softness or incompetence, and that it is related in a close and discreditable way to revenge and anger'.[48] The strong anticompassionist debate now has few followers, and it is generally given in circles of moral philosophy that compassion is an important virtue—arguments are less against compassion, as against seeing compassion as a primary virtue, in contrast to mercy or generosity. However, one aspect of the Nussbaumian model of compassion revives the debate. Namely, her vision of individuals and society is based on a psychoanalytical view of humans as 'imperfect and needy', and society as that which must provide a 'facilitating environment'.[49] As Lester Hunt points out, '[t]he idea that human beings have physical needs, or even, to go further, that every human perfection has . . . a natural basis' differs from the one that holds that 'one of the most important characteristics of human beings is that they are "needy", nor does it imply that the best metaphor for the ideal society is a nursery or a hospital'.[50]

A second problem with Nussbaum's argument is not so much her support of sympathy and compassion as a virtue, as the way in which she defines it. While Nussbaum's conception of sympathy is dependent on eudaimonism, there is an alternative and less discussed perception of the idea, or ideal of sympathy, which dwells on its mystery. Such characterization might be associated less with knowledge, in terms of cognitive 'understanding', than with the idea of wonder, echoing the name of Shakespeare's heroine Miranda. For Schopenhauer, the avoidance of scepticism and the victory over 'egoism' was to be regarded in such a way. For him, it comes through what he sees as the natural omnipresence of compassion, in which the 'weal and woe' of another person directly constitute our own motive:

for this to be possible, I must in some way or other be identified with him; that is, the difference between myself and him, which is the precise *raison d'être* of my Egoism, must be removed at least to a certain extent . . . The process here analysed is not a dream, a fancy floating in the air; it is perfectly real, and by no means infrequent. It is, what we see every day,—the phaenomenon of

[47] Ibid. 356.

[48] Lester Hunt, 'Martha Nussbaum on the Emotions', *Ethics*, 116 (Apr. 2006), 552–77, at 568.

[49] Ibid. 567; Nussbaum, *Upheavals*, 558.

[50] Hunt, 'Martha Nussbaum', 571.

Compassion; in other words, the direct participation, independent of all ulterior considerations, in the sufferings of another.[51]

This 'direct participation' in the suffering of others is, he notes, a matter for, and of, wonder: 'astonishing, indeed hardly comprehensible ... In fact, it is the great mystery of ethics; it is the primary and original phaenomenon of ethics ... the boundary stone, past which only transcendental speculation may dare to take a step.'[52]

Despite her conviction in the importance of the 'untheological mind', George Eliot seems to share the sense that sympathy extended to a feeling beyond both her and other selves.[53] She wrote in an 1860 journal entry that '[o]ne great deduction to me from the delight of seeing world-famous objects is the frequent double consciousness which tells me that I am not enjoying the actual vision enough'.[54] Eliot may have tended towards sceptical rather than transcendental wondering. But such an entry suggests that she too seemed conscious of the ways in which knowledge-based theories of sympathy might have their limits. For her, 'double consciousness' could exist, not simply as a medical condition, or an enlarged mental capacity, but as a sense that there might be a larger understanding, beyond her own vision. It is a distinction that G. H. Lewes noted in relation to 'The Lifted Veil' itself; that there is a difference between 'the one-sided knowing of ... in relation to the self', and 'whole knowledge because "tout comprehendre [*sic*] est tout pardonner" '.[55]

Nussbaum does find the eudaimonistic cast of her argument somewhat problematic, especially when it comes to discussing the idea of sympathy. She notes at two points that she will 'qualify the eudaimonism of the account of her emotions' with a discussion of the emotion of 'wonder'. However, even in her discussion of 'the least eudaimonistic emotion', Nussbaum holds on to her object-based philosophy. '[W]onder', she notes, 'may take a very general object (the moral law) or a highly concrete object (some instance of natural beauty).'[56] 'Wonder' is an emotion which has been seldom considered in Western

---

[51] Arthur Schopenhauer, *The Basis of Morality*, trans. Arthur Broderick Bullock (London: Swan Sonnenchein & Co. Ltd., 1903), 168–70.

[52] Ibid. 170.

[53] George Eliot, *Essays*, 3755.

[54] George Eliot, *The Journals of George Eliot*, ed. Margaret Harris and Judith Johnson (Cambridge: Cambridge University Press, 1998), 336, quoted in Small, 'Introduction' to *LV*, p. xxii.

[55] Eliot, *Letters*, ix. 200.

[56] Nussbaum, *Upheavals*, 54, 73.

scientific thought, and it is a telling omission. John Fuller rightly notes that, as the 'principal emotion that can lift us beyond the pursuit of immediate self-interest', it is 'intimately linked with compassion'.[57] Nussbaum's brief mention is crucial, but it is also crucial that she does not give it enough room to demonstrate how it may potentially disrupt her argument.

While Nussbaum argues that we look to literature to see, in Aristotle's terms, 'such things as might happen' (that is, 'what is likely to occur'), it is also possible to think of literature as pointing towards an ideal.[58] The effect of this relation between human eudaimonism and ideal sympathy may be precisely that which George Eliot hints at, and which has been analysed in more detail by theologians such as Schleiermacher and Otto. In this sense, contemporary views of sympathy might include the idea of sympathy as an ideal emotion or understanding based on a lack of knowledge, and the presence of wonder. In the end, such a view could involve a sense, not of having 'object-relations', but of being, perhaps, something nearer to an object oneself. It might comprise not only a realization that we ourselves may be the object of other people's feelings and emotions, but in realizing that our world-view is not necessarily definitive, that it may be one which is bedevilled with prejudgements, and that there may be other worlds, if only worlds of ideals and imaginations.

In using the term 'sympathy', I use it with the understanding that, as Geoffrey Hill puts it, 'etymology is history'.[59] While recognizing that a distinction between 'sympathy' (feeling for) and 'empathy' (feeling with) is made in both philosophical and psychological texts, 'sympathy' in its common vernacular usage still includes the notion of feeling *with* another person. I also use 'sympathy' with an awareness of the more mystical and ideal notions of sympathy that appear, implicitly, in seemingly rational discussions of the term.

My argument with the cognitive-evaluative view of sympathy has a number of implications. It expands ideas of why, how, and if we sympathize with literary texts. It also unsettles the question of what sort of relationship aesthetic engagement might have with altruistic action, and with our ideas about the world outside the text.

---

[57] R. C. Fuller, *Wonder*, 14.

[58] See Hunt, 'Martha Nussbaum', 561; Nussbaum, *Upheavals*, 238, 240.

[59] See John Haffenden, *Viewpoints: Poets in Conversation with John Haffenden* (London: Faber, 1981), 88.

For some, such as William James, sympathy is more a matter of worlds. It is 'as if there were in the human consciousness a *sense of reality, a feeling of objective presence, a perception* of what we may call "something there" ... a sense of present reality more diffused and general than that which our special senses yield'.[60] Such a feeling may be at odds with some of the humanist and realist theories currently in critical play, but it is notable that they still bear its traces. While this book does not attempt to resolve the question of what sympathy is, it tries to demonstrate that a history of the term must extend to consider the emotional complexities which concern our ideas of other worlds, as well as those that concern other minds. It is such concerns and complexities that *The Tempest* explores.

ART AND ANALOGY

The Tempest doesn't end when Prospero excuses himself. His final address calls upon what Coleridge called 'the moved and sympathetic imagination' of the audience, by asking them for prayer, applause, and to put themselves in his place.[61]

> *Now my charms are all o'erthrown,*
> *And what strength I have's mine own,*
> *Which is most faint: now, 'tis true,*
> *I must be here confin'd by you,*
> *Or sent to Naples. Let me not,*
> *Since I have my dukedom got,*
> *And pardon'd the deceiver, dwell*
> *In this bare island by your spell;*
> *But release me from my bands*
> *With the help of your good hands:*
> *Gentle breath of yours my sails*
> *Must fill, or else my project fails,*
> *Which was to please. Now I want*
> *Spirits to enforce, Art to enchant;*
> *And my ending is despair,*
> *Unless I be reliev'd by prayer,*

---

[60] William James, *The Varieties of Religious Experience* (Cambridge, Mass.: Harvard University Press, 1985), 55, 59.

[61] Coleridge speaks of the 'moved and sympathetic imagination' in relation to *The Tempest*. See *Coleridge's Shakespearean Criticism*, ed. Thomas Middleton Raysor (London: Constable & Co. Ltd., 1930), 133.

> *Which pierces so, that it assaults*
> *Mercy itself, and frees all faults.*
> *As you from crimes would pardon'd be,*
> *Let your indulgence set me free.*

Exit.[62]

As the play draws to a close, the 'profoundly satisfactory' octosyllabics compose a number of questions about the precise nature of Prospero's charms, and the reasons for his need for mercy.[63] Any conceivable answers are less satisfying. Indeed, one of the reasons why *The Tempest* haunts the artistic imagination is that it raises so many key ethical issues, and contains so many interpretative ambiguities. For Samuel Schuman, the 'notion of the artist and the artistic process' in this epilogue 'implies the analog of the divine creator, whose work of art is the universe'.[64] However, the darker side of Prospero's character, the heartless experimenter, is troubling for those who see this play as a personal or theological allegory. The magician's playful resignation might be seen to signal Shakespeare's farewell to art, but his bitter tones also hint at a divine farewell to humanity, or human feeling. For Auden, as for many who read the play, Prospero seems 'like the Duke in *Measure for Measure* in his severity'.[65] But as Auden himself admitted, 'we may severally mean very different things by "like"' and the question of who, or what, Prospero resembles—so central to *The Tempest*—needs careful attention.[66] The possible allegorical readings, or likenesses, that the play has attracted have a number of implications; the presence of this mode of thought might be seen to bear on the history of our ideas about sympathy and theological truth.

Harry Berger Jr. expresses some reservations about critics who have seen this speech as uplifting, standing for 'Prospero's own discovery of an ethic of forgiveness' in tune with 'the lovers' discovery of a world of wonder'. He claims instead that

This is his final and most telling gesture, not only of delay, but also of scene stealing ... the first impression is that of drained energy; literally of collapsed

---

[62] See the 'Epilogue' to *The Tempest*.

[63] See Frank Kermode's 'Notes' to *The Tempest*, 134.

[64] Samuel Schuman, 'Man, Magician, Poet, God—An Image in Medieval, Renaissance, and Modern Literature', *Cithara: Essays in the Judaeo-Christian Tradition*, 19/2 (May 1980), 40–54, at 51.

[65] W. H. Auden, *Lectures on Shakespeare*, ed. Arthur Kirsch (Princeton: Princeton University Press, 2000), 300. Henceforth *LOS*.

[66] W. H. Auden, 'Mimesis and Allegory' (1940), *Prose*, ii. *1939–1948*, ed. Edward Mendelson (London: Faber, 2002), 79. Henceforth *Prose*, ii.

spirits. And this is of course essential to bring out the true strains of feeling under his exhilaration in the final act; a strain which might otherwise have been visible only in his aside to Miranda's 'Brave new world': ''Tis new to thee'. But the epilogue is not easy to make out, because so much is packed into it.

Prospero, Berger notes, 'asks the audience to pray for him, pardon him from a bondage which sounds more ethical than theatrical'.[67]

Berger's sense for the ethical appeal being made in the epilogue centres on the meaning of 'indulgence'. It is, as Eric Griffiths points out, a 'scare word', placed within an ambiguous couplet.[68] Griffiths might also be noticing that 'indulgence' is a Janus-faced term; it can stand for an action 'of being indulgent', and for the instance of this 'action'. 'Indulgence' is a word that bridges two worlds. One of its most common meanings is a kindness or favour, or a 'privilege granted' (*OED* 1.b). With this sense, Prospero's appeal conveys the idea that it is 'a duty to pray for others in this world, declaring "the mutual charity that we bear one towards another"', taking into account the phrasing of 'As you from crimes would pardon'd be' which echoes the Lord's Prayer. 'Indulgence' also has specific religious connotations, and would have suggested to an audience the Catholic practice of praying for the departed.[69] Griffiths argues that Shakespeare's echo back to the 'past imagery' of Catholicism is touching: 'a nostalgia for something he had never known.' However, because the practice of indulgences was, by 1600, seen as suspect (they were employed by ecclesiastics as a means of pecuniary gain), the word is more grasping than touching, suggesting a mercenary relationship between the playwright and his audience: the entrance fee that they have paid is funding his life. Instead of charity's pure grace, the couplet calls the possibility of a free exchange of mercy into question, casting a shadow over Prospero's character.

---

[67] Harry Berger Jr., 'Miraculous Harp: A Reading of Shakespeare's *Tempest*', *Shakespeare Studies*, 5 (1969), 253–83, at 282. He is citing Madeleine Doran, *Endeavors of Art* (Madison: University of Wisconsin Press, 1964), 327.

[68] Eric Griffiths, 'And That's True Too', rev. of *Shakespeare's Language* by Frank Kermode, and *Shakespeare* by Park Honan, *Times Literary Supplement*, 1 Sept. 2000, 3–4, at 3.

[69] 'Actions accompanied by prayer that have been specified by the Church as an acceptable "remission before God" of the debt of "temporal punishment for sins" that remains due after forgiveness has been pronounced in the sacrament of penance,' *New Catholic Encyclopedia*, vii (Farmington Hills, Mich.: Gale, 2003), 436.

These doubts make readers wonder whether the magician might want to give up his art, ask forgiveness, steal this show, or finance the next one; they are worth unpacking, as the sorts of tensions between art, sympathy, and theology that are evident in this scene are central to this book. By stepping out of the framework of the play, declaring that he lacks 'art to enchant', and asking for the audience's mercy, Prospero raises questions about whether the artist's powers can function within a spiritual realm. His breaking of his magic wand is 'his comment on the relation between art and life . . . Prospero seems to be saying that the enchanted island is no abiding place, but rather a place through which we pass in order to renew and strengthen our sense of reality'.[70] Drawing together the idea of the magician's 'enchanted isle' and the idea of the play, Langbaum, here, reflects on Prospero's speech in Act IV in which he declares that 'actors' are 'melted into air, into thin air', and, with a nod to his theatre's own name, that 'the great globe itself, | . . . shall dissolve' (IV. i. 148–9, 153–4). Crucially, Prospero's epilogue is itself an artful construct. It asks us to consider whether art itself has the power to persuade the audience to feel sympathy with the character of Prospero, as an artist.

If we look upon the play as an allegory for (or analogically related to) more general questions about art, sympathy, and life, then it is certain that no clear answers have been reached. What is more, while the play itself is full of such allegories (the banquet that Prospero sets for the travellers (III. iii. 20–60) acts as a practical exercise to teach them not to grasp after sensual pleasure, the masque he sets up for the lovers is a civilizing vision), the extent to which one *can*, or *should*, read this play as an allegory, is never clear.[71] *The Tempest* repeatedly provokes questions about the dangers of moving between fictional and real worlds, and the complexities of mapping fictions onto reality; even Prospero's masque places the idea of allegory under scrutiny. Its necessary interruption signals, to Prospero, the dangers of getting immersed in art. As he watches the reapers engage in a dance with the nymphs to '*celebrate* | *A contract of true love*' (IV. i. 132–3), he '*starts suddenly and speaks*': '(*Aside*) I had forgot that foul conspiracy | Of the beast Caliban and his confederates | Against my life. The minute of their plot | Is almost

[70] Robert Langbaum, '*The Tempest* and Tragicomic Vision', in *The Modern Spirit: Essays on the Continuity of Nineteenth and Twentieth Century Literature* (London: Chatto & Windus, 1970), 199.

[71] For resonances of the masque see *The Tempest*, ed. Stephen Orgel (Oxford: Oxford University Press, 1987), 45–50.

come. (*To the Spirits*) Well done! avoid! no more!' (IV. i. 139–42).
As Stephen Orgel admits, here 'Prospero finds himself once again
relinquishing his power to the vanities of his art'.[72] Furthermore, the
pun on 'plot' as both malign intention and narrative drive makes even
this self-reproach appear to inhabit two worlds, as it slips into the
aesthetic realm. Prospero's final appeal to the audience is perhaps the
most difficult example of allegory at work. The lines 'As you from
crimes would pardon'd be, | Let your indulgence set me free' project
his own situation as an allegory or parable for their spiritual state. That
is to say, he asks for grace from the audience to be conceived in a similar
way to the manner in which they might ask for pardon from their fellow
men, or from God. This 'As' carries a great deal of pressure, for Prospero
does not exist in quite the same way as his audience. In a unique
moment in Shakespearean drama he has declared 'himself not an
actor in a play but a character in a fiction'.[73]

As has been seen in this section, *The Tempest* is possessed by a sense of
allegorical and ontological confusion. This is why, as I will show in the
chapters to come, it captured the imagination of my chosen authors. This
questioning of allegory within the play has not stopped (and has perhaps
even encouraged) the numerous allegorical readings of the play itself. The
two most popular see Prospero as the author, or as God—and often go
hand in hand. The first to make an 'allegorical connection between
Prospero and Shakespeare', Nuttall suggests, is Thomas Campbell, who
with his 1838 *Remarks on the Life and Writings of William Shakespeare*
'stands at the head of a tradition which is to run through Montégut,
Dowden and Raleigh'.[74] As Dowden writes, *The Tempest* 'has had the
quality, as a work of art, of setting its critics to work as if it were an
allegory; and forthwith it baffles them, and seems to mock them for
supposing that they had power to "pluck out the heart of its mystery".
A curious and interesting chapter in the history of Shakespearean criticism might be written', he notes, 'if the various interpretations were
brought together of the allegorical significance.'[75] However, it was
Edward Russell, in 1876, who explicitly claimed the most 'audacious
theological allegory...Prospero is God': 'A man perfectly wise and gra-
cious, scarcely distinguishable in purity and benevolence from what we
believe of God, and endowed by magical studies...with superhuman

[72] Orgel *Tempest*, 50.
[73] Ibid. 55.   [74] Nuttall, *Concepts*, 5.   [75] Dowden, *Shakspere*, 424–5.

power. Prospero, by this happy fiction of magic lore, is put, without profanity, almost in the place of Deity.'[76]

Nuttall notes that Russell's 'seminal' reading provides the basis for over a century of critics 'searching the play for a solution to the Problem of Evil'.[77] Meanwhile, the 'Platonic' approach to the play continued, emerging, in particular, in German criticism of Shakespeare between the 1760s and 1820s which used 'art and characterisation as servants of abstract knowledge'.[78] Nuttall picks out Schlegel's 1811 lecture on the comedies in *A Course of Lectures on Dramatic Art and Literature* and Heine's 1838 observations *Shakespeares Mädchen und Frauen*, while, in America, James Russell Lowell gives another instance of this Platonic approach when he asks if 'ever the Imagination has been so embodied as in Prospero, the Fancy as in Ariel, the brute Understanding as in Caliban' while 'Miranda is mere abstract Womanhood'.[79] A century later, Rawdon Wilson claims that the play demands to be read allegorically, as a 'god-game'.[80] The term, coined by John Fowles, refers to a 'mode of illusion in which one character (or several) is made a victim by another person's superior knowledge and power' and derives from a literary mode that is, as Rawdon Wilson notes, transhistorical, but 'essentially baroque in origins'.[81] The 'god-game', he argues:

signifies a gamelike situation in which a *magister ludi* knows the rules (because he has invented them) and the character player does not ... The entrapped character becomes entangled in the threads of (from his point of view) an incomprehensible strategy plotted by another character who displays the roles of both a game-wright and a god. The master of the game is godlike in that he exercises power, holds an advantageous position, will probably be beyond detection (even understanding), and may even be, like Oberon, or Ariel in Shakespeare's play, invisible. In this respect, the god of the godgame recalls the callous behaviour of the gods toward human victims in certain ancient myths.[82]

[76] Edward R. Russell, 'The Religion of Shakespeare,' *Theological Review*, 55 (Oct. 1876), 482–3, quoted in Nuttall, *Concepts*, 9.

[77] Nuttall, *Concepts*, 10.

[78] See Augustus Ralli, *A History of Shakespearean Criticism*, i (London: Oxford University Press, 1932), 125.

[79] See Nuttall, *Concepts*, 2, 4; James Russell Lowell, 'Shakespeare Once More', in *Among My Books* (London: Macmillan & Co., 1870), 191.

[80] R. Rawdon Wilson, *In Palamedes Shadow* (Boston: Northeastern University Press, 1990).

[81] Ibid. 123; Wilson, 'Spooking Oedipa: On Godgames', *Canadian Review of Comparative Literature*, 4 (1977), 186–204, at 187.

[82] Wilson, *Palamedes*, 123–4.

Rawdon Wilson claims that god-games like *The Tempest* work upon us because they act as allegories for the human condition. The power of the mode is in its 'archetypal overtones', and in the way that this archetype strikes the reader: '[b]eneath every literary godgame there lies a situation that recalls (while evoking the appropriate feelings) the common human intuition of being made a victim, a scapegoat, or a sacrifice, and of being deluded by someone, a *they* set over and against oneself . . . it plays upon, and calls forth, the essential human fear of puniness: of being weak, entrapped, depersonalized.'[83]

However, in his edition, Stephen Orgel resists readings that rely 'too heavily' on such 'allegorical explanations'.[84] His aversion is telling, because the idea of reading allegorically itself was, and still is, philosophically and theologically charged. Orgel is not the only editor of *The Tempest* to distance him or herself from allegorical readings. After outlining various allegorical interpretations, Frank Kermode claims that he will read the play not as an allegory, but as an 'analogous narrative'.[85] 'The practice of allegorical criticism', as Nuttall notes, may be 'alien to many of us today', but when considering much recent writing it is important to think back to this lost practice, and to the lost vision from which it sprang.[86] For the possibility of writing and reading allegories depends, as Auden notes, upon a faith that 'an ultimate and intelligible unity' embraces 'all the diversity of existence'.[87] It was during the sixteenth century, the years when the figures of *The Tempest* were in embryo, that a faith in 'this unity, or rather in its intelligibility' was shattered. '[T]he characteristic medieval method of demonstrating the unity of particulars and the relation of the invisible to the visible by *analogy* began to seem too easy to be true':[88]

Their intellectual weakness was an oversimple faith in the direct evidence of their sense and the immediate data of consciousness, and oversimplification of the relation between the objective and subjective world. Believing that the individual soul was a microcosm of the universe and that all visible things were signs of spiritual truths, they thought that to demonstrate this, it was enough simply to use one's eyes and one's powers of reflection to perceive analogies.[89]

---

[83] Wilson, 'Spooking Oedipa', 203, 204.   [84] Orgel, *Tempest*, 13.

[85] Kermode, *The Tempest*, p. lxxxiii.   [86] Nuttall, *Concepts*, 1.

[87] See Auden's 'Introduction' to *Poets of the English Language: Langland to Spenser* (London: Eyre & Spottiswoode, 1952), pp. xv–xxx, at p. xxviii.

[88] Ibid., p. xxix.   [89] Ibid.

It is clear, therefore, that analogy is important to religious understanding, for as Aquinas argued, a person speaking of God's goodness, or his wisdom, or his love, is 'using words not univocally (in one sense) or equivocally (in different senses) but *analogically*'.[90] However, after the sixteenth century, Auden claims, allegory appeared to be on the decline, as analogical ways of understanding seemed increasingly problematic.

Browning, Auden, and Beckett were well aware of these problems, and questions about them repeatedly emerge in their works. The first of these might be said to be intellectual, for as God is not a human being, to speak about him as if he *were* like a human being is misleading. However, while such egocentric processes of analogy do make an understanding of the divine 'seem too easy to be true', without such processes the theist is lost. He or she is forced 'into a position of total agnosticism, capable of knowing nothing as to the *meaning* of his words-about-God, or Truth, or goodness'.[91] Therefore, for a religious writer, it seems that the activity of making analogies 'is essential to human perception as much to argument'.[92] It is, as Gillian Beer notes, our way of imputing 'a pattern upon the universe', without which we are liable to lose our sense of a beneficent Designer. The 'power' of the analogical mode, then, 'is felt in part because it is *precarious*'. In a description of analogy which chimes nicely with Prospero's conjurings, Beer comments that its 'shifty, revelatory quality... aligns it to magic. It claims a special virtue at once incandescent and homely for its achieved congruities.'[93] In historical terms, it seems that such revelatory, analogous thought, as Auden describes, could not be sustained, and when 'the break came it was drastic. Luther denied any intelligible relation between faith and works. Allegory became impossible as a literary form, and the human Amor seemed no longer a parable of the Divine Love but its blasphemous parody.'[94] The break may have been drastic, but it was not complete. In their variations on *The Tempest*, Browning, Auden, and Beckett continue to think about this 'impossible' form, and, in their own ways, to explore the possibility of 'blasphemous', parodic imitation.

The second related problem or concern about allegorical thought affecting my chosen writers involves its metaphysical implications.

---

[90] A. J. Kenny, *Aquinas* (Oxford: Oxford University Press, 1980), 9.
[91] F. Ferré, *Language, Logic and God* (London: Eyre & Spottiswoode, 1962), 68–9.
[92] Gillian Beer, *Darwin's Plots: Evolutionary Narrative in Darwin, George Eliot and Nineteenth-Century Fiction* (Cambridge: Cambridge University Press, 2000), 74.
[93] Ibid. 78.
[94] Auden, *Langland*, p. xxx.

As Maureen Quilligan argues, allegory would 'not exist as a viable genre' without a ' "suprarealist" (rather than nominalist) attitude toward words; that is, its existence assumes an attitude in which abstract nouns . . . name universals that are real'.[95] While some may find the presence of these transcendental universals reassuring, others may find thinking their way through these ontological levels disturbing. There is, for some, little hope of escaping from the thought that it 'is we who are the shadows'.[96] Prospero's request for charity is an example of this sort of shadow play; his punning on the practice of 'indulgence' as remission of sins, gestures both towards the world of sacrament, and to the idea that our acts in this world are signs of the 'divine' world beyond. The Catholic overtones even suggest that their applause and prayer is not simply a symbol, but a sacrament, participating in another sphere. *The Tempest*, as a whole, however, seems haunted by the idea that one's life story might be simply that—a tale in which people who consider themselves to be real are merely 'such stuff as dreams are made on' (IV. i. 157). This concern is seen again in *Waiting for Godot*, as Vladimir gnostically wonders if the world that he considers real may simply be a dream ('At me too someone is looking, of me too someone is saying, he is sleeping, he knows nothing, let him sleep on'), and by Auden's CALIBAN, who ponders the terror of existence where all are 'merely elements in an allegorical landscape' (*ACP*, 440).[97]

While Vladimir may feel uncertain about the presence of a mind that is superior to his, and a world more real than his own, the possibility of allegory and of analogical thought is still overwhelmingly attractive to those implicated in theological concerns. This is why, W. David Shaw argues, the 'Victorians try to rehabilitate doctrines of analogy', and this is also why my chosen authors find themselves returning to these modes of thought.[98] And just as it is important for Prospero to recognize that

---

[95]   Maureen Quilligan, *The Language of Allegory* (Ithaca, NY: Cornell University Press, 1979), 156.

[96]   I quote from Eric Auerbach's *Scenes from the Drama of European Literature: Six Essays* (New York: Meridian Books, 1959), 2.

[97]   *Samuel Beckett: The Complete Dramatic Works* (London: Faber, 1986), 84–5. Unless otherwise stated, all further references to Beckett's plays will be from this edition. I also quote from W. H. Auden, *Collected Poems*, ed. Edward Mendelson (London: Faber, 1976), 649. Unless otherwise stated, all further references to Auden's poetry will be to this edition, or to *The English Auden: Poems, Essays and Dramatic Writings 1927–1939*, ed. Edward Mendelson (London: Faber, 1977). Page numbers will be given in the text.

[98]   W. David Shaw, *The Lucid Veil: Poetic Truth in the Victorian Age* (London: Athlone Press, 1987), 188.

behind the 'fringed curtains' of Miranda's eye lie memories of a time
before him (she remembers that 'Four or five women once tended' her
(I. ii. 411, 47)), it is crucial that as readers of these poets in what is often
regarded as a secular age, we, like they, retain a 'fringe of uncertainty'
about our readings.[99]
    For Browning, Beckett, and Auden, the question of whether allegory
acts as an analogical route to a transcendental signified, or whether they
are condemned to an infinity of analogues, is crucial, because, as religious
writers, they are all concerned with presence or absence of 'abstract' or
'Platonic' entities such as 'Goodness' and 'Truth'. They are also concerned, as writers, with the way in which they may make these presences
felt. As Auden notes, 'the poet's activity in creating a poem is analogous
to God's activity in creating man after his own image'.[100] Beckett,
Auden, and Browning are all acutely aware that such analogous action
means creating allegories and drawing analogies with the greatest of
delicacy, and a sense for the 'real richness of ontology'; the 'quality of
such equivalences', as Nuttall rightly points out, 'is haunting, mysterious, or it is nothing'.[101] For the substance of such allegories need not be
regarded as a Coleridgean 'phantom proxy'; as Borges writes, when
speaking of *The Divine Comedy*, the best allegory relies on 'a peculiar
sentiment, an intimate process' *between* worlds.[102] The most important
questions, for my chosen authors, concern the moral effects of paying
attention to these conflicting, analogous worlds. It is to the question of
art and goodness that I now turn.

INDULGING IN ART

Prospero's mentioning of 'indulgence', as Berger and Griffiths sense,
sounds suspect. To a modern reader it suggests that by watching the play
the audience has played a part in the performance itself, one that is in
need of pardoning. There is a hint (though no more than a hint) at the
personal greediness that fictional consumption may involve, '[m]oment

---

[99] Nuttall, *Openings*, 72.
[100] W. H. Auden, *The Dyer's Hand and Other Essays* (New York: Random House Inc.,
1962), 70.
[101] Nuttall, *Openings*, 72; Nuttall, *Concepts*, 32–3.
[102] S. T. Coleridge, *The Statesman's Manual* (1816), in *Lay Sermons*, ed. R. J. White
(London: Routledge & Kegan Paul, 1972), 30; Jorge Luis Borges, *Other Inquisitions,
1937–1952*, trans. R. L. C. Simms (Austin: University of Texas Press, 1964), 51–2.

by glutton moment'.[103] While the editors of *The Tempest* do not draw
on this sense, the *OED* notes that the first clear use of 'indulgence' as the
'action of indulging (desire, inclination, etc.); the yielding to or gratifi-
cation of some propensity' (*OED* 1) appears in 1638—and there is a
strong possibility that this alternative sense of 'indulgence' is present in
Prospero's speech. 'Indulgence', then, could therefore be seen as one of
Empson's 'complex words'.[104] Indeed, the sense that Prospero's closing
words are meant to cast doubt upon the value of art is reinforced by his
rejection of his books. The triple sense of indulgence touches on the
multiple ambiguities of Prospero's epilogue. He uses art to appeal to the
sympathetic good-nature of the audience, implying that they can touch
both his world and a world beyond, and simultaneously suggests that
our relation with art is essentially unsympathetic.

The ambiguities implicit within Prospero's epilogue encompass two
approaches of a long tradition of apologies for, and attacks upon, poetry,
and upon the relationship between poetry and the idea of 'sympathy'
and 'goodness', such as Philip Sidney's *A Defence of Poetry* (1579–80).
One criticism of poetry, which Sidney addresses, derives from misread-
ings of Platonic and Neoplatonic philosophy, in which poetry is described as 'a third remove from reality'.[105] Here, then, we see an anxiety
about the relationship between the allegory and the allegorized. The
Platonic argument that in sympathizing with a fictional character we
abandon ourselves to emotional excesses which weaken our better
nature—that by unreflective imitations literature stirs up our feeling
to the 'detriment of reason' (605b)—has been seen as tongue in cheek.
(Iris Murdoch claims that 'Plato is a great artist attacking what he sees as
bad and dangerous art'.[106]) Nevertheless, the edicts of *The Republic*
persist; take Levinas, who argues against those who are optimistic about
the uses of art, warning of 'the play of lights and shadows . . . the mystery
that comes from behind the curtains'.[107] Levinas is engaging with
Plato at a remove here, through figures such as Heidegger and Sartre.

---

[103] I quote from Beckett's, *Ill Seen Ill Said* (London: Calder, 1982), 12.
[104] As Empson notes, 'two meanings may exist in a word for a long time, it seems to
me, without anyone seeing any point in connecting them', *The Structure of Complex
Words* (Harmondsworth: Penguin, 1995), 83.
[105] *The Republic*, trans. Desmond Lee (Harmondsworth: Penguin, 1955), bk. 10,
597e, 425.
[106] Iris Murdoch, *Metaphysics as a Guide to Morals* (Harmondsworth: Penguin,
1993), 13.
[107] Emmanuel Levinas, 'Reality and Its Shadow', in *Levinas Reader*, ed. Sean Hand,
trans. Alphonso Lingis (Oxford: Basil Blackwell, 1989), 46.

As Robert Eaglestone describes, 'for Heidegger art "worlds" the world, it brings us into closer ontological contact with a more real reality. For Levinas, art bewitches us into involvement . . . with non-being.'[108]

This Neoplatonic wariness about being absorbed in fiction extends to the Brechtian tradition for which, as Murray Smith writes, 'emotional responses to fiction of an "empathic" kind lock us into the perspective of individual characters, blocking a more interrogatory relationship with characters and the narrative as a whole': 'Rather than transforming our understanding of the world, emotive ("Aristotelian") narratives divert our critical attention away from the world, by providing a safe, protected sphere in which we can experience sorrow, anger, outrage—and congratulate ourselves on our sensitivity—without having to act on these emotions.'[109] Some, like Lakoff, Johnson, and Mark Turner, might argue that our relationships with the world are intrinsically bound to such narratives in any case, reliant as we are on metaphor in our daily lives.[110] The literary mind, Turner argues, is 'not a separate kind of mind'—it 'is the fundamental mind', drawing on C. S. Lewis's observations about parable.[111] Our use of the projected parable (which is in itself an extended metaphor) 'helps us make sense of another . . . The projection of one story onto another is *parable*, a basic cognitive principle that shows up everywhere, from simple actions like telling time to complex literary creations like Proust's *A la recherche du temps perdu*.' Turner adds, 'We interpret every level of our experience by means of parable'.[112]

However, even these tiny linguistic fictions are frowned upon by a writer such as Alain Robbe-Grillet, who, clearly seeing them as 'indulgent', warned, in 1958, of the 'never innocent figure of speech':

To say that the weather is 'capricious', or a mountain 'majestic', to speak of the 'heart' of the forest, of the 'merciless' sun, of a village 'crouching' in the hollow of a valley is to some extent to describe the things themselves—their form, their dimensions, their situation, etc. But the choice of an analogical vocabulary, however simple it may be, in itself goes beyond the mere description of purely

108 Robert Eaglestone, *Ethical Criticism: Reading After Levinas* (Edinburgh: Edinburgh University Press, 1997), 105.

109 M. Smith, *Engaging*, 55.

110 See George Lakoff and Mark Johnson, *Metaphors We Live By* (Chicago: University of Chicago Press, 1980).

111 Mark Turner, preface, *The Literary Mind* (New York: Oxford University Press, 1996). See C. S. Lewis, *Allegory of Love*, 44.

112 M. Turner, preface, *Literary Mind*.

physical data, and this further context cannot simply be credited to the art of literature. The height of the mountain, whether one likes it or not takes on a moral value, the heat of the sun becomes the result of someone's intention . . . In practically all our contemporary literature these anthropomorphic analogies are too insistently, too coherently, repeated, not to reveal a whole metaphysical system.[113]

Brian Wicker also argues that metaphorical attribution 'is never disinterested, for it stems from a dangerous yearning for reassurance that the world I inhabit is conformable to my designs upon it, that it has the meaning I want it to have'.[114] For Robbe-Grillet, it seems, metaphorical thinking is a way of imposing one's own views upon the world. One such mode of metaphorical thinking might, for example, be to see Prospero as a metaphor for God.

Post-structuralist readings of texts (which are triggered, in part, from the sorts of concerns about solipsistic metaphorical interpretation expressed by Robbe-Grillet) are not immune to solipsism. In setting out to uncover and unsettle received metaphorical interpretations of texts, these critics are still remaking works in their own image. Christopher Butler points out the perils of this interpretative mode when he asks 'what are the "rules" for this play of meaning? Do they simply depend upon the whim and ingenuity of the interpreter? And further, do these two consequences, taken together, imply that interpretation itself must be involved in a perpetual and solipsistic regress, as our playful determinations of the play of the text are themselves seen to be subject to a Derridean critique?'[115]

Concomitant upon the Derridean point of view is the concern that it is impossible to sympathize *with* a fictional character because there is no such thing. Edward Branigan's view suggests that if one were to take a Lacanian post-structuralist reading of *The Tempest*, one would have to 'redefine traditional notions of (literary) character'. It is 'no longer a stable unity . . . but a function in the text which is constantly being split, shifted and reformed elsewhere . . . Character is a construction of the text, not *a priori* and autonomous. It is not a "first fact" for literary criticism through which the remainder of the text is interpreted, made

[113] Alain Robbe-Grillet, 'Nature, Humanism and Tragedy' (1958), in *Snapshots and Towards a New Novel*, trans. Barbara Wright (London: Calder & Boyars, 1965), 78.

[114] Brian Wicker, *The Story-Shaped World: Fiction and Metaphysics: Some Variations on a Theme* (London: Athlone Press, 1975), 2.

[115] Christopher Butler, *Interpretation, Deconstruction and Ideology: An Introduction to Some Current Issues in Literary Theory* (Oxford: Oxford University Press, 1984), 62.

intelligible.'[116] Therefore, on these terms, even if it were possible to make a (stable) reference between the external world and the text (which, on the post-structuralist premiss, it is not, as 'the human subject is racked by contradictory drives from different conscious and unconscious levels') there would be no 'characters' to identify with, merely textual constructs which are, Willemen notes, the 'product of a desire to make a desire recognized'.[117] This mutation of literature into 'system' and 'pattern', where character, in C. H. Rickword's terms, is 'the term by which the reader alludes to the pseudo-objective images he composes of his responses to the author's verbal arrangements', has had a heavy impact upon Shakespearean criticism through the years. Character, for L. C. Knights, is 'merely an abstraction...brought into being by written or spoken words'.[118]

Scepticism is another possible obstacle to the idea of sympathizing with these putative literary protagonists. This 'radical doubt about the possibility of reaching any kind of knowledge, freedom, or ethical truth, given our containment in the world and the impossibility of creating ourselves from scratch' means that arguing over whether identifying with others in fiction or life is good for us would be of little consequence, because we are all functioning from relative points of view, and cannot gain sympathetic access to one another.[119] From such a relativistic standpoint there would be no such thing as a universal 'good' anyway; Simon Blackburn notes that the view 'that there is nothing to show that one view or another is right, or nothing in virtue of which an ethical remark can be true' can have a devastating effect on notions of sympathy, goodness, and ethics.[120] As Thomas Nagel describes, the problem of 'how to combine the perspective of a particular person inside the world with an objective view of that same world, the person and his viewpoint included . . . faces every creature with the impulse and

---

[116] Edward Branigan, *Point of View in the Cinema: A Theory of Narration and Subjectivity in Classical Film* (Berlin: Mouton Publishers, 1984), 12.

[117] Ibid. 12; Willemen, 'The Fugitive Subject', in *Raoul Walsh*, ed. Phil Hardy (Edinburgh: Edinburgh Film Festival, 1974), 72–5, at 74, quoted in Branigan, *Point of View*, 12.

[118] C. H. Rickword, 'A Note of Fiction', in *Towards Standards of Criticism*, ed. F. R. Leavis (London: Wishart, 1933), 3; L. C. Knights, *How Many Children Had Lady MacBeth? An Essay in the Theory and Practice of Shakespeare Criticism* (Cambridge: Minority Press, 1933), 64.

[119] See Thomas Nagel, *The View from Nowhere* (New York: Oxford University Press, 1986), 7.

[120] Simon Blackburn, *Being Good* (Oxford: Oxford University Press, 2001), 29.

the capacity to transcend its particular point of view and to conceive of the world as a whole . . . It is the most fundamental issue about morality, knowledge, freedom, the self, and the relation of mind to the physical world.'[121]

This mire of competing subjectivities, and modes of reading, has been seen to have led to a marked turn towards the ethical in recent literary and philosophical studies. Steven Connor comments that 'the replenishment of ethical and evaluative discourse in philosophy and cultural theory has been echoed and amplified in recent years by the steadily deepening concern among literary critics with the relations between value, ethics and the literary text . . . Indeed, the word "ethics" seems to have replaced "textuality" as the most charged term in the vocabulary of contemporary literary and cultural theory.'[122] Meanwhile, Daniel R. Schwarz argues that 'we are in the midst of a humanistic revival or at least a neohumanist burst of energy'.[123] Notable figures in this revival who have, 'turned . . . back to the "human" concerns of fiction', could be said to include Wayne C. Booth, James Wood, Barbara Herrnstein Smith, Charles Taylor, Martha Nussbaum, Richard Rorty, and Alasdair MacIntyre.[124] Admittedly, words such as 'humanist' and 'humanism', as Tony Davies comments, have a 'very complex history, and an unusually wide range of possible meanings'.[125] For my purposes, I refer to a critic as humanist when he or she has claimed to believe that 'literature speaks to and of the human world, not some merely textual or fictional world; that literature's relation to life is essentially, if variously, a moral one; that "aesthetics" has no autonomy from the life-world; that literature creates and reflects interpersonal "communities"; that literature synthesizes thought and feeling; and that the greatest literature is essentially liberal and democratic in spirit, even if it serves as a modern and secular version of religion'.[126] Booth is

---

[121] Nagel, *View from Nowhere*, 3.

[122] Steven Connor, 'Honour Bound?', *Times Literary Supplement*, 5 Jan. 1996, 24–6, at 25.

[123] Daniel R. Schwarz, 'A Humanistic Ethics of Reading' in Todd F. Davis and Kenneth Womack (eds.), *Mapping the Ethical Turn: A Reader in Ethics, Culture and Literary Theory* (Charlottesville and London: University Press of Virginia, 2001), 3–15, at 3.

[124] Connor, 'Honour Bound?', 25.

[125] See Tony Davies, *Humanism* (London: Routledge, 1997), 2.

[126] I quote from Geoffrey Galt Harpham's article, 'The Hunger of Martha Nussbaum', *Representations*, 77 (2002), 52–81, at 58. Harpham refers to Nussbaum's 'unmoderated humanism', 57.

such a critic, claiming that his 1988 book *The Company We Keep* 'aims . . . to restore the full intellectual legitimacy of our commonsense inclination to talk about stories in ethical terms, treating the characters in them and their makers as more like people than labyrinths, enigmas, or textual puzzles to be deciphered'.[127] Nussbaum, in turn, argues that novels 'can play an important role in the articulation of an Aristotelian morality . . . they ask us to imagine the possible relations between our own situations and those of the protagonists, to identify with the characters and/or the situation, thereby perceiving those similarities and differences. In this way, their structure suggests, as well, that much of moral relevance is universalizable'.[128]

While recognizing the positive intent behind these critical approaches, it often appears that some of the theories about reading championed by this particular wave of humanist critics, simplify both what is going on when we read, and the concerns that we have about ideas of identification and understanding other minds. Admittedly, some of us find the notion of scepticism more threatening than others. For Rorty, '[t]he Problem of the External World and the Problem of Other Minds' is something that is used to 'sucker freshmen' into philosophy courses.[129] However, for a critic such as Peter Lamarque, the problem is 'not merely an idle philosophical thought experiment to raise all-embracing or "world-consuming" doubts but something we "live", something distinctively and unavoidably human'.[130] This attitude seems close to that of Browning, Beckett, and Auden. These are writers who are repeatedly concerned with the possible repercussions of sceptical and the relativistic thought—which explains their repeated return to allegorical modes of reading and writing, and their interest in how to read the other mind of God. It is an interest which manifests itself in Browning's preoccupation with natural theology and the Higher Critics, as exemplified in 'A Death in the Desert' and 'Caliban upon Setebos', as he wonders whether God is 'altogether such a one as' himself.[131] It appears, too, in Beckett's work, particularly in the prose poetry of *How It Is*, while

---

[127] Wayne Booth, *The Company We Keep: An Ethics of Fiction* (Berkeley and Los Angeles: University of California Press, 1988), p. x.

[128] Nussbaum, *Love's Knowledge*, 95.

[129] See Thomas Nagel, 'Go with the Flow', *Times Literary Supplement*, 28 Aug. 1998, 3–4, at 3.

[130] This is Lamarque's description of Cavell in *Fictional Points of View* (Ithaca, NY: Cornell University Press, 1996), 151.

[131] See the epigraph to 'Caliban upon Setebos' from Psalm 50: 21. I discuss this in more detail in Chapter 2.

Auden also groped towards the possibility of art as a tool for understanding others. As Arthur Kirsch notes 'Auden . . . like many critics before and since, understood *The Tempest* as a skeptical work. When he wrote that "The Sea and the Mirror" was his Art of Poetry, "in the same way" he believed *The Tempest* to be Shakespeare's, he added, "ie I am attempting something which in a way is absurd, to show in a work of art, the limitations of art".'[132] For Browning, Beckett, and Auden, the idea that they could not reach out of their own minds in order to understand God, and that art would be of little help to them, was a prime concern. For them, as for Stanley Cavell, 'scepticism, in particular about other minds, is a kind of tragedy' and 'tragedy is . . . obedient to a sceptical structure'.[133] But to understand such concerns about scepticism, we must, at least, recognize the desire for things to be otherwise. This leads to the question of other minds, particularly the minds of the authors.

THE SEARCH FOR THE AUTHOR

MIRANDA   O, wonder!
   How many goodly creatures are there here!
   How beauteous mankind is! O brave new world,
   That has such people in't!
PROSPERO   'Tis new to thee.

(v. i. 181–4)

Miranda's final exchange with Prospero brings such sceptical difficulties centre stage on a smaller scale. The father–daughter wrangle touches on the difficulties of conceiving another's point of view. It shows how hard it is to recognize that someone else is not just a carbon copy of ourselves.

It is hard to let go, and Prospero hangs upon his daughter's words as she steps forward in a world of her own, for he has lost much already. Despite the company of the isle's strange beasts, Ariel and Caliban, he has already spoken bitterly of the more conventional 'creatures that were mine', the suitors of the Milanese court 'new created' by his usurping brother.[134] Miranda's speech shows her to be her father's daughter still,

---

[132] 'Introduction' to W. H. Auden, *The Sea and the Mirror: A Commentary on Shakespeare's* The Tempest, ed. Arthur Kirsch (Princeton: Princeton University Press, 2003).
[133] Lamarque, *Fictional Points of View*, 151.
[134] *The Tempest*, I. ii. 82.

inhabiting his lexicon—but her verbal shifts towards 'mankind' hint that she is his 'precious creature' no more, now conscious of a life and a language beyond, in a world beyond Prospero's control.[135] His ''Tis new to thee' could be taken, too, to be a wry reflection on the uselessness of the moral education that he has tried to give her upon the island. In terms of allegory, Prospero's attempt to explain the 'fall' of man to her, through stories, has failed—she has not managed to draw an analogy between the things he has told her, and the life that lies before her.

The difficulties of recognizing another's point of view can be usefully thought about by considering some of the problems that one encounters in dealing with a printed text. Prospero's comment could be a world-weary sigh, the stresses falling upon the iambs of the line, ''Tis *new* to *thee*'. Alternatively, he might be leaning solely on the final syllable, making this an ironic aside. Finally, perhaps, it is a recognition of her vision, the stress falling on the first syllable, ''*Tis* new to thee', as if seeing her anew, and newly separate.[136] Prospero's echo of his daughter's speech speaks of this difference. His intonation will always be different from hers; our illocutionary redescription will never recover his. The ambiguities that surround this line are the stuff of the printed page, and the following chapters are concerned with the ways that we try, and fail, to simulate intentions that are lost in print. Editors and directors of the play have debated how this line should be played—as an affectionate aside, a moment of revelation, or a disenchanted, pessimistic sigh. In his introduction to the play, Stephen Orgel notes that those facing 'serious problems with the figure of Prospero' have shown a tendency to ignore the text's 'ambivalences', 'to sweeten and sentimentalize' it.[137] Indeed, this has involved the addition of warmer shades of emotion through editorial and typographic intervention. 'May there not be in this comment of Prospero's somewhat of a sad irony?' asks George Allen in 1864, while Arthur Quiller-Couch, in his 1921 edition, adds the stage direction '(*smiling sadly*)' to keep Prospero's humanity in the forefront, creating a balance between fondness and distance.[138]

---

[135] Ferdinand terms Miranda a 'precious creature', 'So perfect and so peerless, are created | Of every creature's best!,' III. i. 25, 47–8.

[136] I am grateful to Eric Griffiths and Bharat Tandon for their discussion of these lines with me. My comments are indebted to Tandon's account in *Jane Austen and the Morality of Conversation* (London: Anthem Press, 2003), 170.

[137] Orgel, *Tempest*, 10.

[138] *Minutes of the Shakspear Society of Philadelphia* for 1864–5 quoted in *The Tempest: A New Variorum Edition of Shakespeare*, ed. H. H. Furness, ix (Philadelphia, 1892), 253; *The Tempest*, ed. Sir Arthur Quiller-Couch and J. Dover-Wilson (Cambridge: Cambridge University Press, 1921), 73.

The question of whether an authorial presence can be located in a text is crucial to the work of Browning, Auden, and Beckett, for the idea that there is a fixed vocal intention which can be located within a text is related to the more general concern about the ways in which we understand all other minds, and whether these minds can be understood through their works. In the last forty years, Browning has been subject to a certain amount of deconstructive criticism. Stefan Hawlin cites the work of Herbert Tucker, Warwick Slinn, and John Schad as examples of deconstructive readings of Browning.[139] He could also include W. David Shaw, who claims that Browning, in *The Ring and the Book*, 'seems to be writing and reading simultaneously like a Victorian Derrida'.[140] Such approaches, which do not just use 'theory to reread the poetry' but 'the poetry to reread the theory', have their virtues.[141] As Schad notes, Victorian poetry is a reflexive mode; it was driven to 'the cultural margins by the double assault of Utilitarianism and the novel' and in this sense 'forced to occupy a critical, or metatextual, space'.[142]

However, while considering the anachronistic nature of an approach like Shaw's (who claims that 'Browning's canon, unlike the New Testament's, is never closed') or Schad's (who yokes together both 'Browning and Derrida' as 'characteristically' seeking or describing 'a movement away from the authority of reason, truth and, of course, origin') it is important not to forget the ways in which Browning, for his readers, was most *unlike* Derrida.[143] Many Victorian readers encountering Browning's verse were determined to locate the authorial presence. Robert Bell, in 1864, for example, comments on that way in which 'Browning's genius' manifests itself in *Dramatis Personae*:

Nothing, it seems to us, is more remarkable in his poetry than the steady determination shown by the writer to regard things from their best side, to look with lenience on human frailty and shortcoming, and to get as much good out of human character as possible . . . He does justice to everybody . . . he shows glimpses of the divine . . . In fact, he finds something to like everywhere, but he

---

[139] Stefan Hawlin, *The Complete Critical Guide to Robert Browning* (London: Routledge, 2002), 127.

[140] W. David Shaw, *Victorians and Mystery: Crises of Representation* (Ithaca, NY: Cornell University Press, 1990), 319.

[141] John Schad, *Victorians in Theory: From Browning to Derrida* (Manchester: Manchester University Press, 1999), 2.

[142] Ibid.

[143] Ibid. 319, 79.

never likes without a reason and his extraordinary sympathy with humanity in general makes him as much at his ease in Petticoat Lane as in Belgravia.[144]

Brimley, meanwhile, comments on the way in which Browning makes it his business 'to enter by sympathy into the lives, characters and conduct of others'.[145] Bell's emphasis on the 'glimpses of the divine' in Browning's poetry shows him to be an author who was seen as fit to be placed beside Shakespeare, one who managed to focus on the individual state of characters. In conceiving of Browning as a simultaneously sympathetic and comprehensible authority, like one of 'those Life Assurance Societies that only take up the rejected cases of all the rest', these critics frame a firm authorial presence, who can provide a domesticated analogy to their vision of the divine.[146] Such reading practices are part of a more general desire within the period to view the author as magus. Dickens, as Nina Auerbach notes, also 'assumed a semi-divine status'. The 'iconography... generated during his life... is a host of tiny characters springing from the brain of a large central figure':

Sometimes, as in Hablot K. Browne's frontispiece to *Martin Chuzzlewit*, the creator is himself a character in the novel, further purging character of its taint of mortality... In other variations, such as Robert W. Buss's 'Dickens's Dream', Dickens... becomes the central dreaming creator... The double deification of this iconography, whereby Dickens is supernaturally endowed in his godlike role as creator of character as well as in his implied beatification by these characters dramatizes... the quickening of the religious imagination artistic images of literary character excited.[147]

The comforting humanist aesthetic gives a clear idea of an author whose intentions are of importance, and conforms, at least, with the possibility of a sympathetic society, and to an extent, with the idea of a benevolent God.

Like those of Browning, the works of Auden and Beckett find themselves subjected to similarly conflicting modes of interpretation, as critics question the extent to which an authorial voice, and an original intention, can be located. It is a question that Auden appears to have wrestled with, perhaps most obviously in his 1959 prose poem 'Dichtung und

---

[144] Robert Bell, *The St. James's Magazine* (July 1864), quoted in Boyd Litzinger and Donald Smalley (eds.), *Browning: The Critical Heritage* (London: Routledge & Kegan Paul, 1970), 223–8, at 223–4.

[145] G. Brimley, *Fraser's Magazine*, Jan. 1856, quoted ibid. 176.

[146] From an unsigned review, *Athenaeum*, 4 June 1864, ibid. 219–21, at 220.

[147] Nina Auerbach, *Women and the Demon: The Life of a Victorian Myth* (Cambridge, Mass.: Harvard University Press, 1982), 200.

Wahrheit': 'Expecting your arrival tomorrow, I find myself thinking *I love You*: then comes the thought:—*I should like to write a poem which would express exactly what I mean when I think these words*' (*ACP*, 649). Auden's 'mean' here is deliberately ambiguous, as it sets up a conflict between what he 'means', as in signifies, against what he 'means', as in what he intends—an example of what H. P. Grice termed natural, and non-natural, meaning.[148] The writer goes on to declare that while he desires that his own poems should be 'genuine, recognizable ... as having been written, for better or worse, by me', he is not concerned if, in a poem by someone else, there is a discrepancy between text and biography (i.e. the matching of non-natural and natural meaning is not important for Auden as a reader, it seems). But the irony of the poem rests in the fact that one is left asking whether (encouraged by the title taken from Goethe's autobiography) we should take this poem as the feelings of Auden, or of a fictional writer. Even if we do take it as the former, as the writer has admitted, words rarely match up to feelings. Faced with such apparent barriers between truth and poetry, and confusions over intentionality, Paul Hendon claims that Auden's poetry 'willingly and effortlessly meshes with a post-structuralist treatment'. He cites Stan Smith as an example of a critic who claims that 'a poet is simply a bundle of texts' and that in encountering Auden's poetry there 'is no original meaning that we can recover, only the play of language in our own moment of history, interlocking with the play of language of texts'.[149] Smith emphasizes what he terms the 'doubleness of the text, which is both a historical product, subject to all the pressures on language of its originating moment, and yet a discourse that floats free of its origins ... in a perpetually open-ended play of history and signification'. His approach to Auden's poetry seems to continually favour the idea of the free-floating poem, severed from its origin, over that of the historical product. His reading of Auden's 'Making, Knowing and Judging' is an example:

Speaking for myself, the questions which interest me most when reading a poem are two. The first is technical: 'Here is a verbal contraption. How does it work?' The second is, in the broadest sense, moral: 'What kind of guy inhabits the poem? What is his notion of the good life or the good place? His notion of

---

[148] See e.g. 'Meaning', *Philosophical Review*, 64 (1968), 377–88.
[149] Paul Hendon, *The Poetry of W. H. Auden: A Reader's Guide to Essential Criticism* (Cambridge: Icon, 2000), 33; Stan Smith, *W. H. Auden: Rereading Literature* (Oxford: Basil Blackwell, 1985), 2, 5.

the Evil One? What does he conceal from the reader? What does he conceal even from himself?'[150]

Smith argues that the 'play between "technical" and "moral" places the emphasis on the constructed "I" of the poem, which in turn constructs a reader to decipher this "I" from the workings of what, after all, is no more than a "verbal contraption". Both "guy" and "reader" are effects of the text.'[151] However, Smith's reading of Auden's views on the author is partial; his argument is weakened by the fact that it relies on the very 'effects of the text' that he locates. What is more, much of his deconstructive argument is epistemological. It investigates how much (or how little) we can know about, and make of, the intentions and meanings of a text. It leaves to one side the ethical. Even if a writer is to be considered as lost within an intertextual maze, this can (and must) have moral implications.

Criticism of Beckett is involved in similar confusion. Ruby Cohn sees Beckett as a writer who 'questions the boundary between art and life', and she is one of a school of critics who write about his work from the humanist side of the fence. Cohn is determined that Beckett is an ethical writer who helps us understand our own 'deepest humanity', and deals with, as Martin Esslin puts it, 'human experience at its most specific and concrete'.[152] However, critics of the post-structuralist persuasion have challenged such views. Judith Dearlove, for instance, posits a Beckett for whom 'no relationships exist between the artist, his art, and an external reality'.[153] Beckett's writing itself, as Iain Wright notes, is part of 'that decentring activity' which constantly questions the relations between the author and his text.[154] Such issues have a bearing on whether Browning, Beckett, or Auden can be seen as having a version of moral authority, or responsibility; a question that is related to the thematic consistency of these *Tempest*-based texts, all of which revolve around the idea of the ethics of fiction, and the responsibilities of the artist.[155]

---

[150] *DH*, 50–1.   [151] S. Smith, *Auden*, 3.

[152] Ruby Cohn, *The Comic Gamut* (New Brunswick, NJ: Rutgers University Press, 1962), 296; Martin Esslin, 'Introduction' to id. (ed.), *Samuel Beckett: A Collection of Critical Essays* (Englewood Cliffs, NJ: Prentice Hall Inc., 1965), quoted in P. J. Murphy et al. (eds.), *Critique of Beckett Criticism: A Guide to Research in English, French, and German* (Columbia, SC: Camden House, 1994), 19.

[153] J. E. Dearlove, *Accommodating the Chaos: Beckett's Nonrelational Art* (Durham, NC: Duke University Press, 1982), quoted in Murphy et al. (eds.), *Critique*, 30.

[154] Iain Wright, '"What Matter who's speaking": Beckett, the Authorial Subject and Contemporary Critical Theory', *Southern Review*, 16/1 (Mar. 1983), 5–30, at 18.

[155] For a discussion of the responsibilities of the author and reader, see Booth, *Company*, 125–55.

   The matter of whether an authorial presence can be located in a text has both secular and theological implications. Indeed, it bears on every reading and religious experience. For the purposes of this book, however, it might be thought about with reference to Prospero's final speech. Did Shakespeare intend us to view Prospero as God, leaving his world? And if so, is this 'God' feeling sorrowful about his departure? Are we, in fact, to care what Shakespeare meant us to think of Prospero and his feelings? What is more, can either Shakespeare's meaning, or Prospero's 'feelings' be talked about at all? Harold Bloom discusses these questions briefly in *Caliban*, part of his series on 'Major Literary Characters'. Anticipating objections to the series' theme, Bloom notes that if one follows the critical schools of Barthes and Foucault in which one believes in the 'demise of the literary author' then it follows that 'there are no fictional personages, presumably because literature does not refer to a world outside language'.[156] Hélène Cixous puts this argument more clearly when she explains that the 'concept' of the character in fiction is the '*porte-parole* of sense... bound up with the authority of the author'—it is a 'social sign'—and works as part of an 'identification circuit' between reader and author.[157] If authority is challenged, then 'character' no longer carries its privileged position. It must, Cixous argues, give way to a 'subject' which 'flounders in the exploded multiplicity of its states', in both life and text.[158] As Seymour Chatman explains, '[c]haracters do not have lives. We endow them with "personality" only to the extent that personality is a structure familiar to us in life and art', following, here, the Proustian idea that in reality, each reader reads only what is in him or herself.[159]

   This post-structuralist approach to character might seem depressing. Along with the possibility of fictional identification, one must give up the idea of certainty, truth, and other metaphysical solaces outside the self. To compensate, one is at least offered the consolation of what

---

[156] Harold Bloom, *Caliban*, Major Literary Characters (New York: Chelsea House Publishers, 1982), p. ix.

[157] Hélène Cixous and Keith Cohen, 'The Character of "Character"', *New Literary History*, 5/2 (Winter 1974), 383–402, at 385.

[158] Ibid. 388.

[159] Seymour Chatman, *Story and Discourse: Narrative Structure in Fiction and Film* (Ithaca, NY: Cornell University Press, 1978), 138; 'mon livre n'étant qu'une sorte de ces verres grossissants comme ceux que tendait à acheteur l'opticien de Combay; mon livre, grâce auquel je leur fournirais le moyen de lire en eux-mêmes', Marcel Proust, *A la recherche du temps perdu*, iii, ed. Pierre Clarac et André Ferré (Paris: Gallimard, 1954), 1033.

Christopher Norris calls an 'enlightened or emancipatory interest'. At its worst, however, as Norris points out, the 'postmodern-pragmatist malaise' of Baudrillard, Fish, Rorty, and Lyotard offers the possibility of endless, playful, polysemic acts of interpretation which cannot be seen as emancipatory because they block the possibility of any certainty as to quite what enlightenment or emancipation might be.[160] John Schad shows some discomfort about the playfulness of his 'transhistorical' approach to Browning: '[t]here are...occasions when I am discussing figures, texts, or tropes which only become apparent as an effect or trick of the unique dynamics of the specific pairing, or dialogue, that I have set up...each chapter is unnerved by an apprehension that it is...in some sense a trick of interpretive ingenuity.'[161] Schad frames his poststructuralist approach in almost Faustian terms here. His use of 'trick', 'set up', and 'ingenuity' implies that his approach might be overly masterful—the negative of the idea of approaching a work and reading for, or sympathizing with, the author. We stand, then, at what has been seen as a 'theoretical crossroads', between what might be seen as Schad's 'rough magic', and Nussbaum's confident sympathy.[162] Such conflicts between liberal humanist and deconstructionist approaches to ideas of character and author can be clarified by a consideration of recent work on cognitive theories of sympathy and identification.

LITERATURE, IDENTIFICATION, AND THE QUESTION OF THE TEXT

As has been discussed, a number of the liberal humanist approaches to literature are highly dependent on the idea of identification, an idea which might be seen to have its roots in an eighteenth-century model of sympathy. According, for example, to Adam Smith's model, a member of an audience would both change places 'in fancy' with Prospero, and attempt to measure Prospero's actions against their own, thus developing their own 'moral sense'. This hypothetical process involves a combination of cognitive activities that Langbaum later sees as 'sympathy'

---

[160] Christopher Norris, *What's Wrong with Postmodernism: Critical Theory and the Ends of Philosophy* (Hemel Hempstead: Harvester Wheatshead, 1990), 5.

[161] Schad, *Victorians*, 4.

[162] 'But this rough magic | I here abjure,' v. i. 50–1; P. J. Murphy writes that 'the English contribution [to Beckett criticism] has, in many fundamental aspects, reached a theoretical crossroads', see *Critique*, 1.

(in the sense of empathy) and 'judgment'.[163] However, this model can be significantly expanded and (perhaps) clarified by looking at it in relation to two cognitive activities currently under debate—the idea of simulation and that of theory-theory.

Advocates of theory-theory, such as Daniel Dennett, Stephen Stich, and Shaun Nichols, argue that we do not empathize with others, or at least we never wholly do so. Rather, we possess, innately, 'knowledge of . . . principles . . . like the principles of grammar' which are 'articulated from a third-person viewpoint'.[164] That is to say—we develop theories about the ways other people behave, and use these theories to predict their behaviour. Simulation theory, is, on the other hand, 'proposed as an alternative to the Theory Theory . . . it argues that when we want to predict or understand the behaviour of others, we put ourselves in their shoes'.[165] Whether we can simulate the experience of another without having a theory about them first might have a bearing on the way in which we respond to literary characters. Take Prospero's appeal. Do we *either* change places 'in fancy' with him—or do we try to conjure something in our imagination that might be seen to be analogous to the fate of a usurped Duke with magical powers? Does he fit into our theoretical world, or are we transported into his?

Robert M. Gordon is generally recognized as the philosopher who first argued for the idea that we depend upon simulation in order to understand and predict the actions of others.[166] However, he notes that a number of earlier philosophers, such as Collingwood, G. H. von Wright, and A. Schutz 'claimed that interpersonal understanding depends on a procedure resembling what I call simulation', while Gregory Currie adds Adam Smith to the term's ancestry.[167] Gordon argues that within 'a close-knit community, where people have a vast common fund of "facts" as well as shared norms and values', only a

[163] Langbaum, 'Preface', *Poetry of Experience*.

[164] 'Introduction' to Martin Davies and Tony Stone (eds.), *Folk Psychology: The Theory of Mind Debate* (Oxford: Blackwell, 1995), 9. See Stich and Nichols, 'Folk Psychology: Simulation or Tacit Theory?', in Davies and Stone (eds.), *Folk Psychology*, 123–58.

[165] Carroll, *Mass Art*, 344–5.

[166] Along with Jane Heal, 'Replication and Functionalism', in J. Butterfield (ed.), *Language, Mind and Logic* (Cambridge: Cambridge University Press, 1986) and Arthur Ripstein, 'Explanation and Empathy', *Review of Metaphysics*, 40 (1987), 465–82. See Currie and Ravenscroft, *Recreative Minds*, 50 ff.

[167] Robert M. Gordon, 'Folk Psychology as Simulation', in Davies and Stone (eds.), *Folk Psychology*, 60–73, at 64. See also Alvin Goldman, 'Interpretation Psychologized', in Davies and Stone (eds.), *Folk Psychology*, 74–99.

small amount of simulation would be called for. However, a 'person transplanted into an alien culture might have to do a great deal' in order to 'explain and predict the behaviour of those around him'. It is crucial for Gordon's case that he argues that while 'one might eventually learn to *begin* all attempts at explanation and prediction with a stereotypic set of adjustments' or 'generalizations' about the alien culture, 'practical simulation ... does not essentially involve (as one might think) an implicit *comparison to oneself*'.[168]

In this sense, George Eliot's ideal of 'active participation' could be seen as a precursor to 'simulation'. As Carroll notes, for philosophers, the 'grain of truth in what is informally called "identification" is, *ex hypothesi*, the process of simulation'.[169] The concept of simulation has, then, been adopted by Gregory Currie as a way of thinking about literary engagements, and it has, Brigid Lowe argues, 'an overwhelming, though as yet unrealized, appeal for the literary critic'.[170] Currie argues that '[w]hat is so often called audience identification with a character is best described as mental simulation of the character's situation by the audience who are then better able to imagine the character's experience'.[171] For a literary philosopher like Martha Nussbaum, the possibility of simulation, and engagement with the author's intention, is crucial. She is joined by Gregory Currie, Susan Feagin, and Murray Smith, in her attempt to translate the idea of simulation in life into a literary context. For all these critics, simulation is a key factor, which confirms the positive moral values associated with reading or viewing fictional works. Nussbaum focuses, in her writing, on the 'ability to imagine what it is like to live the life of another person' for '[n]ovels ... in general construct and speak to an implicit reader who shares with the characters certain hopes, fears, and general human concerns, and who for that reason is able to form bonds of identification and sympathy with them'.[172]

Such a view has a number of problems, and opponents. What must be noted is that the 'overwhelming ... appeal' of simulation theory derives from the fact that it chimes with the notion that literary

---

[168] Gordon, 'Folk Psychology as Simulation', 65–6.
[169] Carroll, *Beyond Aesthetics*, 306.
[170] Lowe, *Victorian Fiction*, 112.
[171] Gregory Currie, 'The Moral Psychology of Fiction,' *Australasian Journal of Philosophy*, 73/2 (June 1995), 250–9, quoted in Carroll, *Beyond Aesthetics*, 306–7.
[172] Martha Nussbaum, *Poetic Justice: The Literary Imagination and Public Life* (Boston: Beacon Press, 1995), 5, 7.

responses are, in some way, morally enlarging, rather than pleasurable; that is to say, that our 'simulation' of literary characters allows us to practise simulating more generally, which makes us more able to function empathetically in everyday life. In fact, it seems highly likely that simulation cannot function without some sort of theorizing, or comparison with the self, taking place.[173] What is more, as both Noël Carroll and Christopher Butler point out, the 'simulation' argument does not ride well with the actual experience of reading. As Butler argues, the reader frequently does not seem to share the experience of the fictional other. 'In the case of suspense, for example, we can care for the prospects of protagonists who are not even aware of the danger they are in, and the asymmetry here is obvious.'[174] In this sense, it is more salient to see the reader as a 'side-participant', recognizing aspects of a character's experience and considering the situation as an onlooker, in order to augment their existing moral framework.[175] In this way, Carroll convincingly argues that identification, and its philosophical cognate, simulation, are not necessarily important activities when we relate to fiction—preferring the concept of 'clarificationism'. As he points out, often 'the emotional state' of the audience 'does not replicate the emotional state of characters'.[176] In this case, one might substitute the idea of 'understanding', in the sense of understanding and empathizing with a fictional character, with the idea of understanding a situation. As Christopher Butler argues 'our pleasurable emotional responses are in general far more likely to be tied to the processes of understanding of a situation, than in our empathetic response to a person'.[177]

The question how we encounter, say, the character of Prospero (be it through theory-theory or simulation or clarificationism) is made more complicated by the fact that he is a fictional and selectively presented, textual entity. As Robert Eaglestone notes, the 'idea of emotional

[173] See Daniel Dennett, *The Intentional Stance* (Cambridge, Mass.: MIT Press, 1987), 101. Although they favour simulation even Currie and Ravenscroft cannot commit to the idea that we engage with others purely through this process. See Currie and Ravenscroft, *Recreative Minds*, 2.

[174] Christopher Butler, *Pleasure and the Arts* (Oxford: Oxford University Press, 2004), 41.

[175] Carroll writes, 'I think that quite clearly as consumers of fiction we are typically in the position of outside observers, or, as Richard Gerrig and Deborah Prentice call it, side participants', Carroll, *Mass Art*, 350.

[176] Carroll, *Philosophy of Horror*, 91. For Carroll's extended argument as to why we do not simulate the experience of fictional characters see ibid. 88–96.

[177] C. Butler, *Pleasure*, 40.

response through identification (with fictional characters) is open to question on both a *critical* and philosophical level' (my emphasis). Indeed, these two approaches to other minds have a bearing on what might be seen to be our motives about, and desires for, our reading of texts. Those who believe that simulation is possible could be aligned with those who favour the traditional, character-based humanist approach to texts, which aims to recover authorial intention. Denis Donoghue terms this approach 'epi-reading'—a mode of textual engagement that 'is predicated on the desire to hear... the absent person; to hear oneself in that person'.[178] Theory-theory, in contrast, could be seen to form part of a reading framework that necessitates poststructuralist critique, for if every reading starts anew, every text is subject to the reader's own theory of reading, in a 'perpetually open-ended play of history and signification'.[179] Furthermore, an extreme theory-theorist might argue that an experience of reading cannot be seen to further our sympathetic understanding of other minds, as we do not meet 'characters' or 'authors' when reading—we only ever meet our own mind, and theory, when encountering the text. 'Characters' are simply marks on a page that we may constitute or deconstruct at will by theory. (If true, this interpretative freedom might be said to be equally possible when a theory-theorist encounters the real world.) Carroll's theory of clarification, which relies, partially, on simulation (if only on the idea of simulating the position of an observer), hovers somewhere between the two. In this sense, the work of Carroll, Butler, Feagin, and Nussbaum is important not only for the arguments they contain, but for the desires they reveal. Each claims that although 'the situations of characters are known to be made up', emotional responses and connections *are* made by the reader with characters in the text.[180]

This is a point of view that has found itself, critically, out of favour. As Murray Smith notes, any supposition of such relations between fictional characters and readers is, today, treated with suspicion by a number of literary critics: '[t]he confluence of Brechtianism with the modernist literary tradition ... has led to a theoretical orthodoxy for which treating characters in any way as if they were real, especially by responding emotionally to them, is regarded as at best naïve and at worst pernicious.'[181] Eaglestone attacks Nussbaum on these grounds, claiming that

---

[178] Denis Donoghue, *Ferocious Alphabets* (London: Faber, 1981), 146.
[179] S. Smith, *Auden*, 5.   [180] Carroll, *Mass Art*, 356.
[181] M. Smith, *Engaging*, 4.

she is suffering from what Donoghue has termed 'a nostalgia for the human'; she 'continually passes over the textual nature of a literary work' in her attempt to advance the cognitive claims of reading.[182] This, he argues, 'forms her crucial blindness... It is her unquestioning acceptance of the idea that literature is to be read through to a "life beyond the text"' which underlies Nussbaum's critical approach and leads to a reductive understanding of reading.[183]

One of Nussbaum's blind spots is certainly her treatment of identification, compassion, and readerly relations with literary characters. As Geoffrey Galt Harpham argues, no other writer calls us so strongly to 'refashion our lives on the model of fictional characters'. She 'insistently blurs the distinction between books and life... Texts may represent alien or distant worlds, but the texts themselves help readers overcome that distance.'[184] In this sense, Harpham argues, her 'relation to literature, and to the world of the mind in general, appears to have been based on the most "primitive" of all readerly responses, identification with fictional characters'.[185]

Harpham's view of Nussbaum's primitivism is well argued, but perhaps unfair. As Murray Smith points out, the concept of character as handled by Nussbaum 'has taken a beating at the hands of both writers and narrative theorists in the twentieth century', it is still 'everywhere assumed in everyday discourse about narratives'.[186] Consider the critic Richard Rorty (a critic who writes specifically about the contingency of selfhood) who refers to the way in which '[b]y identification with Mr. Casaubon in *Middlemarch* or with Mrs. Jellyby in *Bleak House...* we may come to notice what we ourselves have been doing'.[187] Or take Harold Bloom, who devotes an entire series to 'characters' such as Caliban, Holden Caulfield, and Isobel Archer, arguing that while recent 'fashions in literary criticism have reduced "character" in literature to a matter of marks upon a page', the enterprise of analysing 'literary character... will survive every vagary of critical fashion'.[188] This is borne out even by a work such as Leo Bersani's 1978 book on 'character'

---

[182] Donoghue, *Ferocious Alphabets*, 200.
[183] Eaglestone, *Ethical Criticism*, 46–7.
[184] Harpham, 'Hunger', 54. See Nussbaum, *Love's Knowledge*, 390.
[185] Harpham, 'Hunger', 59.
[186] M. Smith, *Engaging*, 17.
[187] Richard Rorty, *Contingency, Irony and Solidarity* (Cambridge: Cambridge University Press, 1989), 141. See Rorty's chapter on the 'Contingency of Selfhood', 23–43.
[188] Bloom, *Caliban*, p. xiv.

and 'desire' in literature—*A Future for Astyanax*. Although Bersani investigates the possibilities of an 'exuberant indefiniteness about our own identity', it would, he argues, 'be impossible to eliminate all fixed character structures. To live entirely without sublimation and psychic continuities is unthinkable . . . even in the "imaginary", "irresponsible" spaces of literature, psychic coherence inevitably reappears.'[189] There is, as Smith, Bloom, and Bersani agree, something 'salient' about the Victorian ideal of the character. Nevertheless, Bharat Tandon rightly locates the problem with Nussbaum's approach in the way in which she 'elides the distance between reading and life' so that 'analogies between readerly and artistic perception frequently become less tenable, direct mappings'.[190]

The answer, perhaps, lies both in a more complex understanding of what happens when we relate to literature characters—as suggested by Butler and Carroll. However, it also lies in a more complex understanding of what, exactly, we are being asked to relate to, an understanding which may be reached by examining literary, as well as theoretical works.

THE CHARACTER OF CREATURELY UNDERSTANDING

Beckett, Browning, and Auden rely heavily on literary allusion and write about emotional attachments to literary figures in their texts. In reimagining Shakespeare's Caliban, for example, they show a fascination with the ways in which more or less sympathetic products of the imagination might live on, beyond their author, and the way in which they might exercise some semblance of autonomy. *The Tempest* is just one of the hundreds of literary texts, from Racine to Johnson to Henry James, that find their way into their work. Attachments to fiction can be comforting. A 'part remains, of one's classics, to help one through the day', as Beckett's Winnie puts it (*CDW*, 164). But such attachments can also verge on the disturbing. Take Krapp's adoration for the heroine of Fontane's novel *Effie Briest*:

---

[189] Leo Bersani, *A Future for Astyanax* (London: Marion Boyars, 1976), 314.
[190] Tandon, *Jane Austen*, 52, 51.

Scalded the eyes out of me reading *Effie* again, a page a day, with tears again. Effie.... (*Pause.*). Could have been happy with her, up there on the Baltic, and the pines, and the dunes. (*Pause.*) Could I? (*Pause.*) And she?   (*CDW*, 222)

In pondering this literary romance, Krapp is setting himself up for a quixotic fall. Woody Allen's hero, Kugelmass, who comes to a sticky end after entering a copy of *Madame Bovary*, might serve as a warning.[191] Both Krapp and Kugelmass certainly desire their fictional women—and so much so that they imagine (or in Kugelmass's case achieve) a tryst. However, there is no sense in which Krapp or Kugelmass appear to simulate the feelings of, or to identify with, their lovers. Indeed, Krapp's wistful afterthought, 'And she?', is telling. While he might enjoy getting under Effie's covers, we may guess that she might not be so happy about hearing his spools. Effie, for Krapp, has a seductive power beyond the confines of her fictional world. Nevertheless, as Carroll points out, there is no reason that being attracted to (or even believing in) a fictional character necessarily means simulating their experience. Many moments in the works of Beckett, Browning, and Auden resonate with such overlappings of worlds, and make us wonder about fictional feeling. Steven Connor might be taking Krapp's intertextual experience to an extreme when he wonders, with reference to Beckett's drama, 'whether we are reading the work or whether it is reading us'.[192] However, this book argues that these authors' allusive practices invite such extreme questions. They demonstrate a concern for the ways in which imaginative creations might be witnessed, rescued, or even save themselves, persisting in time and space. This is an interest, to use a metaphor from *The Tempest*'s world, in textual salvage.

Humanist critics and readers have been attacked for such acts of salvage. For a critic like Colin Radford it is difficult to comprehend how 'people can be moved by fictional suffering given their brute behaviour in other contexts where belief in the reality of suffering described or witnessed is necessary for the response'. In his essay 'How can we be moved by the fate of Anna Karenina?' Radford examines a number of possibilities as to why we should respond to the death of Shakespeare's Mercutio, or Tolstoy's Anna, but concludes that emotional reactions to fictional occurrences involve us 'in inconsistency and incoherence', because there can be no reason why we react with

---

[191] See Woody Allen's *Side Effects* (London: New English Library Ltd., 1981), 45–65.
[192] '*Waiting for Godot' and 'Endgame*', ed. Steven Connor (Basingstoke: Macmillan, 1992), 14.

grief to a fictional circumstance.[193] However, as Michael Weston notes, such emotional reactions to fictional happenings cannot be so easily dismissed. Addressing Radford's concerns, he claims that '[i]t is not that our sadness at Mercutio's death is the same, though wrongly inspired, feeling as our sadness at the death of a real young man, but that the similarities and differences between the feelings are connected to the similarities and differences between their objects. And this, of course, raises questions about the *kind of coherence* our feelings about fictional characters have.'[194] It is worth adding that the similarities and differences between our feelings about the death of a real young man, and our feelings about the death of Mercutio, raise questions about the '*kind of coherence*' that fictional 'characters' themselves (and therefore *their* feelings) might have. Here I use coherence in the sense of solidity of structure, rather than the possession of logical connection. In this section, I will be thinking about the terms by which we refer to these fictional protagonists, and what this tells us about how substantial we feel that they are, as well as the logical coherence of our feelings towards them.

Murray Smith rightly argues that we must preserve the idea of the coherent protagonist in narrative. Despite the imaginative nature of fictional entities such as Prospero, and the possibility that we may deconstruct, and reconstruct, them we *may* still develop a theory about them, and it is as salient for us to regard them as having some sort of integrity as it is for us to regard our mothers or fathers or children in such a way. Manfred Jahn may argue that talking of 'voices in written texts' may involve 'a certain amount of metaphorical slippage', but we involve ourselves in such acts of metaphorical thinking every day.[195] In the case of theorizing about Prospero stepping out of a play, we have to stretch our usual modes of analogy further, perhaps, than wondering how our own father or daughter is feeling in the real world. But all our wondering depends on these analogies—and living on the same plane as someone else is no guarantee of understanding them. However, the term 'character' that Smith and Nussbaum rely on, and upon which Smith's book *Engaging Characters* depends, needs reassessment. Smith

---

[193] Colin Radford, 'How can we be moved by the fate of Anna Karenina?', *Proceedings of the Aristotelian Society*, suppl. vol. 49 (1975), 67–80, at 78.
[194] Michael Weston, 'How can we be moved by the fate of Anna Karenina?', *Proceedings of the Aristotelian Society*, suppl. vol. 49 (1975), 81–93, at 93. My emphasis.
[195] Manfred Jahn, 'The Cognitive Status of Textual Voice', *New Literary History*, 32/3 (2001), 695–7.

begins to investigate this idea when he notes that any 'talk about characters as plausible and possible persons presupposes that we know what a person is. But the nature of the human subject is of course a highly contested issue among contemporary thinkers.'[196] Despite Nussbaum's emphasis on the importance of 'character' (she notes, for example, that 'we read a novel like *Hard Times* with the thought that we ourselves might be in the character's position'), she never quite establishes what she thinks character might be in either human or fictional terms.[197] Her descriptions of the 'dignity and mystery of humanness', which is 'something mysterious and extremely complicated', and 'the mystery and complexity within each life . . . in its attempt to grapple with the mysterious and awful fact of its own mortality', can confuse.[198] This poetic hedging is 'characteristic' of Nussbaum, and, in this sense, she might recognize herself in Gabriel Marcel's description of a mystery as 'a problem which encroaches on its own data'.[199]

Some light might be shed on the 'problematic of the subject' by considering what it means to refer to a protagonist as a 'character'. Amélie Rorty notes that it is worth paying attention to these differences for our 'vocabulary for describing persons, their powers, limitations and alliances is a very rich one. By attending to the nuances of that vocabulary we can preserve the distinctions that are often lost in the excess of zeal that is philosophic lust in action.'[200] She goes on to note that ' "[h]eroes", "characters", "protagonists", "actors", "agents", "persons", "souls", "selves", "figures", "individuals" are all distinguishable. Each inhabits a different space in fiction and in society . . . Our philosophical intuitions—the intuitions that guide our analyses of criteria for personal identity—have been formed by all these notions.' The word 'character'—in its sense of 'a person regarded in the abstract as the possessor of specified qualities; a personage, a personality' (*OED* 16.a.) connotes some sort of psychological consistency or core. As W. J. Harvey notes, when 'in real life, we try to describe a person's character we generally speak in terms of a discrete identity. We think of

---

[196] M. Smith, *Engaging*, 20. Smith is quoting James Phelan, *Reading People, Reading Plots* (Chicago: University of Chicago Press, 1989), 11.

[197] Nussbaum, *Poetic Justice*, 91.

[198] Ibid. 34, 27, 23.

[199] Gabriel Marcel, *The Philosophy of Existentialism*, trans. Manya Harari (New York: Citadel Press, 1967), 19.

[200] Amélie O. Rorty, 'A Literary Postscript: Characters, Persons, Selves, Individuals', in *The Identities of Persons* (Berkeley and Los Angeles: California University Press, 1976), 304, 303.

it as something unique and separable.'[201] Kupperman notes that 'it is the moral overtones of the word "character" that make it of such great interest to ethical philosophers', while Rorty argues that '[t]he qualities of characters are the predictable and reliable manifestations of their dispositions: and it is by these dispositions that they are identified. The elements of character tend to become stoic rather than elemental forces . . . To "have character" is to have reliable qualities, to hold tightly to them through the temptations to swerve and change.'[202]

Character is not always seen as entirely discrete and fixed. Wayne Booth considers, for instance, the ways in which literature can be character-*building* for the reader, allowing their character to be changed by outside influences. However, even Booth's idea of this ever-forming character is cushioned by a sense that he is at heart a socialized human being with a 'mental or moral constitution' and some sort of free, individualized, moral choice (*OED* 17.a, 11). A fictional mimesis of this sort of 'character' then, as 'a personality invested with distinctive attributes and qualities by a novelist or dramatist', has, by implication, an implicit moral aspect. This accords with the theory that readers may exercise their own moral sense in identifying with imaginative worlds. Booth claims to have a close involvement with the texts he writes about, to the point of phrasing himself in fictional terms. He writes that 'as a character I am a kind of focal point in a field of forces . . . or, as we used to say, a creature made in the image of God and hence essentially *affiliated*, joined to others'.[203] He adds that lines can often be merged between self and other: 'I discover that there are no clear boundaries between the others who are somehow both outside and inside me and the "me" that the others are "in".' This lack of division can be traumatic—he notes the way in which we 'all find ourselves "thrown", as Heidegger famously puts it . . . into a world we never made, and confronted with a multiplicity of beings that if *fully* attended to, would threaten to obscure all relationship with Being'. However, Booth also claims that this multiplicity can be beneficial:

To open ourselves deliberately to the conflicting invitations that our narrative heritage offers does not provide in any easy way the standards for choosing among roles. It can free us, however, from the anxiety of influence . . . that

---

[201] W. J. Harvey, *Character and the Novel* (London: Chatto & Windus, 1965), 31. See also Joel Kupperman, *Character* (Oxford: Oxford University Press, 1991), 7.
[202] A. Rorty, *Identities*, 304.
[203] Booth, *Company*, 239–40.

plagues those who attempt to find their being by *resisting* influence. Though I still can suffer anxieties when I accept influences as the very source of my being, my energy will be more likely to go to a careful appraisal of particular invitations than to a futile cursing of my fate as an essentially conditioned creature struggling to deny my condition.

Booth can only be happy about his thoughts of the way in which one might be 'joined to others' in life and narrative because he has put thoughts of being 'a creature' behind him, arguing that the 'Christian ideal of universal love escapes us . . . as it escapes Aristotle; literary criticism cannot build itself on the hope for a world of saints'. He settles instead for a secularist compromise—the idea that one might choose 'humanly well'.[204] But while Booth may see himself as a post-Christian 'character', his choice of terms to describe his sense of self are not free from theological overtones. Take the slide in his comment that he sees himself 'as a character . . . or, as we used to say, a creature made in the image of God'; or the way in which he slips, without explanation, from discussion of readers as 'characters, social creatures by origin' to the 'torn creatures' in fiction, and concludes by discussing the 'problematic creatures' of 'works in themselves'.[205]

The word 'creature' is that 'which is produced by, or owes its being solely to, another thing' (OED 4. *Fig*) and it has a narrower, though more ambiguous, sense of sociological and moral determination than that of 'character'. It conjures images of something that is neither man nor beast, neither kith nor kin. Furthermore, the 'creature' speaks of attachments to a primitive nature that we cannot relinquish; one which might lack what Schopenhauer calls 'the natural omnipresence of compassion'.[206] Creatures carry a theological burden, echoing back to Genesis, giving the sense of something ever under the control of another, and when used with reference to human beings, raise doubts about where, as Jonathan Glover describes, 'one person ends and another perhaps begins'.[207] Metaphorically, then, creatures might help us understand something

---

[204] Booth, *Company*, 265.
[205] Ibid. 243, 245. Note his uncertainty about the term when he speaks of the formation of ' "character"—of self, of soul, of ethos, of personality, of identity', 229. He footnotes this sentence: 'Even after my brief definition in Chapter I, the word "character" may prove misleading as a general term covering all dimensions of whatever "self" exercises "characteristic" choices. But I trust that my use of it will be justified as we go along', 229 ff.
[206] Schopenhauer, *Basis*, 168.
[207] Jonathan Glover, *I: The Philosophy and Psychology of Personal Identity* (Harmondsworth: Penguin, 1988), 21.

about our own place in the theological and Darwinian framework. Meanwhile, the term's ambiguous 'moral overtones' make it a useful one with which to think about the protagonists created by my chosen authors.

'Anything created', 'a product of a creative action', can be a 'creature' (*OED* 1.a), and the word has a long standing in literary criticism. Henry James, for example, wrote of the way in which, for Turgenev, the fictive picture 'began . . . almost always with the vision of some persons who hovered before him soliciting him . . . he had . . . to imagine . . . the situations most useful and favourable to the sense of the creatures themselves', while Dickens, in both the 1850 and the 1869 prefaces to *David Copperfield*, confides that 'an Author feels as if he were dismissing some portion of himself into the shadowy world, when a crowd of the creatures of his brain are going from him for ever'.[208] It is also a term that critics lean upon when they are unsure as to how to refer to a fictional protagonist. This uncertainty often appears in Beckettian criticism—take the Scrutonian hesitation over Beckett's 'characters (if characters they can be called)', or John Pilling's admission that, in Beckett, character can become an 'impossibly complicated matter'.[209] Cohn is just one of many who refers to one of Beckett's narrators as a 'nameless, paradigmatic . . . creature', while Adam Piette writes of 'the creature fabricated by the textual potentialities of language' in *Malone Dies*.[210] P. J. Murphy also relies on the term when he criticizes those who simplify the 'problematic of the subject' in Beckett's work by identifying his characters as 'somehow real or human'. They should, he argues, recognize an author who 'has to find a means of accommodating the creature of the imagination'.[211] This uncertainty as to what to call fictional protagonists is related, in part, to what Stanley Cavell sees as 'a shift in emphasis' in criticism, in which post-Bradleyan critics 'shun

---

[208] Henry James, preface, *Portrait of A Lady* (Oxford: Oxford University Press, 1995), 5; Charles Dickens, preface to Charles Dickens edn. (1869) and preface to 1850 edn., *David Copperfield* (Harmondsworth: Penguin, 1985), 47, 45.

[209] Roger Scruton, *The Aesthetic Understanding* (London and New York: Methuen, 1983), 225; John Pilling (ed.), *The Cambridge Companion to Beckett* (Cambridge: Cambridge University Press, 1994), 8.

[210] Ruby Cohn, *Samuel Beckett: The Comic Gamut* (New Brunswick, NJ; Rutgers University Press, 1962), 180; Adam Piette, *Remembering and the Sound of Words* (Oxford: Clarendon Press, 1996), 205.

[211] P. J. Murphy, 'Beckett and the Philosophers', in Pilling (ed.), *Cambridge Companion to Beckett*, 224. In *Krapp's Last Tape: a Theatre Workbook* (London: Brutus Books, 1980), James Knowlson terms his edition of the drafts of the play 'living creatures . . . evolving during a final phase', p. viii.

direct contact with characters', favouring, it is presumed, a 'study of words'.[212] The shift in terms over the 'impossibly complicated matter' of who is speaking, bears witness to a certain discomfort as to whether one should be writing about a speaker at all. Advocates of the 'humanist revival' in reading suggest this is all a straightforward matter: '[a]lthough modes of characterisation differ, the psychology and morality of characters must be understood as if the characters were metaphors for real people.'[213] However, the repeated emphasis on the idea of the 'creature' in the texts of my chosen authors, and the criticism of those texts, suggests that such metaphors need more scrutiny.

For, as I have shown, even if our notion of a coherent protagonist seems to have been reduced from that of a character to a textually constructed creature, this may well have moral and theological implications. As Harold Bloom points out, if a textual character appears vulnerable, one will be disturbed by the notion that one's own self may be subject to the same unravelling: '[h]owever a reader seeks to reduce literary character to a question of marks on a page, she will come at last to the impasse constituted by the thought of death, her death.'[214] T. S. Eliot puts this feeling of dependence and creaturehood best when he declares that

What Shakespeare seems to ask me to do, and when I am in a sensitive enough mood makes me do, is to see *through* the ordinary classified emotions of our active life into a world of emotion and feeling beyond, of which I am not ordinarily aware. What he makes me feel is not so much that his characters are creatures like myself, but that I am a creature like his creatures, taking part, like them, in no common action, of which I am, for the most part, quite unaware.[215]

Eliot, here, seems to be suggesting (as Feagin and Nussbaum do) that our relationship with fiction works either by identification—or (as Carroll argues) by recognizing the logic of situations.[216] And in finding fictional 'creatures' part of our own narratives, there is always the sense that we may identify with their storied existence, rather than seeing the

212 Cavell, *Must We Mean*, 268, 267.
213 Schwarz, 'Humanistic Ethics', 4.
214 Bloom, *Caliban*, p. xiv.
215 T. S. Eliot, 'Shakespeare as a poet and dramatist', address, Edinburgh University, 1937 and Bristol University, 1941. The manuscript is kept in the Houghton Library, Harvard College Library, Harvard University. I owe my knowledge of this quotation to Eric Griffiths.
216 See Carroll, *Mass Art*, 350.

creatures as reflecting our reality. Through identification or recognition, then, we are given the sense that we might merely be living in a 'numinous' world, that we are merely symbols for a greater truth.

Gregory Currie considers the implications of this radically extended scepticism in *The Nature of Fiction*. 'How, then', he asks, 'do we know that *we* exist, since our epistemic situation is just like that of Holmes?' For Currie, this 'radically extended skepticism might make entertaining fiction in the style of Pirandello, but . . . is surely not a serious philosophical option'.[217] However, our responses to fiction—which range from a desire for fictional characters to escape their creatureliness (to be more than just 'made up' by an author) to the desire for a reliable, but not overly obstrusive, narrator—suggest that we do entertain aspects of this scepticism or solipsism in our reading life. As Anthony Nuttall notes, while 'the solipsistic fear', the 'fear that the external world of tables, bricks and mortar may not exist at all . . . is quite properly regarded as something absurd, or even comic . . . it sometimes happens that an idea which is in the strictest sense of the word incredible can prove a fertile source of disquiet', that we may endure '[*f*]eelings of unreality, *intuitions* of solipsism'.[218] In fact, then, such 'entertaining fictions' reflect real anxieties, anxieties that may have an effect on our sense of the possibilities for sympathy.

Even if one does entertain the sceptical/solipsistic point of view, arguing that we cannot identify, simulate, or clarify our experiences with relation to anyone (therefore precluding identification with fictional protagonists, or understanding the logic of their situations), my model of the fiction creature is still tenable. This is because we may still reflect their lack of understanding of other creatures' minds. Stanley Cavell's argument is helpful here: 'The difficulty lies in a refusal, a refusal expressed as a failure to acknowledge . . . in failing to see what the true position' of a creature is, 'in a given moment, we are exactly put in his condition, and thereby implicated in the tragedy'. As he puts it elsewhere: 'if I do nothing because there is nothing to do, where that means that I have given over the time and space in which action is mine and consequently that I am before the fact that I cannot do and suffer what it is another's to do and suffer, then I confirm the final fact of our

[217] Gregory Currie, *The Nature of Fiction* (Cambridge: Cambridge University Press, 1990), 132.
[218] A. D. Nuttall, 'Introduction', to *A Common Sky: Philosophy and the Literary Imagination* (London: Chatto and Windus for Sussex University Press, 1974).

separateness. And that is the unity of our condition.' 'It may', he notes 'seem perverse or superficial or plain false to insist that we *confront* the figures on a stage. It may seem perverse; because it is so obvious what is meant in saying we do *not* confront them, namely, that they are characters in a play. The trouble with this objection is its assumption that it is obvious what kind of existence characters . . . have, and obvious what our relation to them is, obvious why we are present.'[219]

The Tempest, then, and its 'creatures', could be seen as forming a metaphor for what I perceive as this dilemma of encounters with fiction and the problem of other minds. The play offers a world that demon-strates the contingency of our 'moral' language, and the story to which all these writers are drawn is one which is haunted by a creature that goes against ideas of normative morality and empathetic experience. It is a story set against a background which constantly inhibits and prob-lematizes our possibility of engaging or sympathizing with abnormality, and one that suggests that we may be under someone else's control. The dramatic monologues which it inspires show a constant concern about the extent to which the fictional creature may stand in relief, or gain relief from its textual existence, and how it may be understood and acknowledged. As they consider whether fictional characters may be '*reliev'd by prayer*', or by any other means, Browning, Beckett, and Auden, as I will show, are repeatedly drawn to *The Tempest* in order to question 'what kind of existence' a creature may have.

H. Porter Abbott notes that Beckett spoke of his characters in plays as his 'people'.[220] However, his prose protagonists, and those of other writers, were always 'creatures'. 'Yes, a little creature, I shall try and make a little creature, to hold in my arms a little creature in my image, no matter what I say.'[221] Malone goes on to think about eating his little friend—and Beckett's relationship with his creatures, like Malone's, is both sentimental and ambiguous. References are numerous, and varied. He writes in 1931 of 'Proust's creatures' as 'victims of . . . Time', Proust as a 'creature of habit', and muses on Proust's belief that 'Man is the creature that cannot come forth from himself'.[222] He turns, meanwhile, to his own fictional creatures in a letter to Donald McWhinnie about

---

[219] Cavell, *Must We Mean*, 276, 313, 339, 331.
[220] H. Porter Abbott, *Beckett Writing Beckett* (Ithaca, NY: Cornell University Press, 1996), 46.
[221] *The Beckett Trilogy: Molloy; Malone Dies; The Unnamable* (London: Calder, 1994), 226. Henceforth *T.*
[222] *Proust and Three Dialogues with Georges Duthuit* (London: Calder, 1965), 12, 22, 66.

How It Is: 'The work is in three parts, the first a solitary journey in the dark and mud terminating with discovery of a similar creature known as Pim', and notes, in relation to Winnie in *Happy Days* that while 'creatures are supposed to have no secrets for their author', his 'have little else.'[223] The word 'creature' means something special for an Irish writer. T. P. Dolan notes that in Hiberno-English, it has particularly fond connotations. 'Creature' or 'crétur' is used, mainly, as a term of endearment; he cites 'the poor creature, she's all alone'.[224] However, as Dolan's example suggests, it is also a word tinged with disdain; it has about it that 'strange paradox of compassion and contempt' which Nancy Cunard found in Beckett's work.[225] One thinks of the bountiful Lady Pedal's day-trip with 'the inmates of St John of God's' in *Malone Dies*: 'Come, Ernest, said Lady Pedal, let us find a place to picnic. And you Maurice, she added, stay by the dinghy . . . The thin one chafed to run about, but the youth had thrown himself down in the shade of a rock, like Sordello, but less noble . . . *The poor creatures*, said Lady Pedal, let them loose' (*T*, 289 (my emphasis)).

Beckett's concern with the idea of the creature is also partly theological. He is, as Declan Kiberd notes, 'a supremely religious artist', and his sense of protagonists as 'creatures' is deeply entwined with these theological anxieties.[226] As Mary Bryden argues, 'Beckett's creatures appear . . . to be tormented by the thorny theological question of the relationship between free will and God's will', and 'attitudes of indifference, blame or incomprehension are repeatedly struck'.[227] Kay Langdale rightly argues that Beckett's narrators suffer from an 'increasing sense of epistemological and ontological doubt', as they retaliate 'against a Godless universe'.[228] The texts that he chose to translate, such as Gutiérrez Nájera's neo-gnostic 'To Be', are preoccupied with 'the implacable | purveyor of suffering creatures', 'The creating God' who 'is the creature of another terrible God', while his own aesthetic and

---

[223] Knowlson, *Damned to Fame*, 461–2, 485.

[224] Terence Patrick Dolan (ed.), *A Dictionary of Hiberno-English* (Dublin: Gill & Macmillan, 1998), 79.

[225] Nancy Cunard, *These Were the Hours* (Carbondale: Southern Illinois University Press, 1969), 112.

[226] Declan Kiberd, *Inventing Ireland: The Literature of the Modern Nation* (London: Vintage, 1996), 454.

[227] Mary Bryden, *Samuel Beckett and the Idea of God* (Basingstoke: Macmillan, 1998), 71, 73.

[228] See Kay Langdale, 'God, the Narrator and the Quest for an Aesthetic in Samuel Beckett's Prose Fiction' (D.Phil. diss., Oxford University, 1987), 1, 266.

theological fable, *Company* (1980), is possessed by the similar overwhelming questions: 'Can the crawling creator crawling in the same
create dark as his creature create while crawling?'[229]

This pseudo-theological dynamic is highlighted by the way in which
Beckett's 'creatures' seem to feel anxious about their fictional status.
From the nods to the audience in *Godot* to the self-scrutinizing prose of
Ill Seen Ill Said, Beckett's fictions are consistently reflexive. The level of
self-consciousness that fictional creatures should be granted, preoccupied Beckett. His reputed dislike of Balzac derives from the fact that
his own character, Belacqua, claimed that the French novelist denied
his protagonists freedom, turning 'his creatures into clockwork cabbages'.[230] But as I will show in Chapter 4, Beckett is, in fact, deeply
attached to Balzac. His own creatures repeatedly express the anxiety that
they themselves have taken on Balzacian qualities, becoming automa-
tized or vegetative. Bim's admonition and warning to Murphy, that 'he
would never lose sight of the fact that he was a creature without
initiative', reflects, in part, on the Mercyseat where they both work,
but also on the 'chloroformed world' that both creatures inhabit—the
novel itself.[231]

Both Browning and Auden also probe the idea of the creature in their
poetry. Browning's interest is partly entymological. His liking for the
natural world was, Mrs Orr notes, 'conspicuous in his very earliest
days . . . one of his very juvenile projects was a collection of rare creatures'.[232] Meanwhile, many members of the insect world inhabit his
verse—from the famous snail on the thorn in *Pippa Passes*, to 'yon
worm . . . on yon happier world—its leaf!' (one of seventy-two worms
in his poetry) who is seen as 'man's fellow-creature' in *La Saisiaz*.[233]

---

[229] *Anthology of Mexican Poetry*, trans. Samuel Beckett (London: Calder and Boyars,
1970), 135–7; *Company* (London: Calder, 1996), 73.
[230] See *Dream of Fair to Middling Women*, ed. Eoin O' Brien and Edith Fournier
(London: Calder, 1993), 119–20. One of Beckett's pupils, Rachel Burrows, notes that in
1931 Beckett 'rejected the naturalistic writers like Balzac', claiming that 'there's no free
will at all because they're all puppets on a string', S. E. Gontarski, Martha Fehsenfeld,
and Dougald McMullan, 'Interview with Rachel Burrows', *Journal of Beckett Studies:
Special Double Issue*, 11–12 (1989), 6–15, at 8, 12.
[231] Samuel Beckett, *Murphy* (London: Calder, 1993), 91.
[232] Mrs Sutherland Orr, *The Life and Letters of Robert Browning*, new edn., ed. F. G.
Kenyon (London: Smith, Elder & Co., 1908), 26–7.
[233] 'The lark's on the wing; | The snail's on the thorn.' I quote from Robert Browning,
The Poems, ed. John Pettigrew, 2 vols. (Harmondsworth: Penguin, 1981). Henceforth
BCP i *and* ii. See *Pippa Passes, BCP* i. 311, ll. 225–6. See also *La Saisiaz, BCP* ii.
517, l. 357.

Browning's fondness encompasses the variety of eft-things, spiders, maggots, grigs, crabs with which Caliban plays, but he seems especially interested in those creatures that seemed to be slipping between states of existence. After admiring the 'strange butterfly! | Creature as dear as new' (*BCP* ii. 5, ll. 11–12) in the prologue to *Fifine at the Fair*, the speaker goes on to muse upon the ways in which evolution has allowed the 'creature which had the choice | Of the land once' to become airborne (*BCP* ii. 6, ll. 31–2). The butterfly leads him, in turn, to consider the ways in which man, too, tries to live in different realms—imitating flight through swimming, and substituting 'For heaven—poetry' (*BCP* ii. 7, l. 56). But though he admires a butterfly, the Prologue's subtitle compares man to a less glamorous member of the insect world—an 'Amphibian'—thus disenchanting Browning's readers, and alerting them to their slippery, frogged ancestry. Browning's repeated use of the word 'creature' to refer to human beings in his poetry hints at man's primitive roots. Like Babbage, Lyell, and Chambers, he was aware of '[t]he creature's new world-widened sense, | Dazzled to death at evidence | Of all the sounds and sights that broke | Innumerous at the chisel's stroke' (*BCP* i. 518, ll. 839–42).[234]

Browning did not find 'Geology' and other 'Greek endings' to be 'passing bell[s]' for his faith (*BCP* i. 634, ll. 680–1). He was, however, particularly conscious of the way in which the lack of evidence for God's existence in natural theology must be replaced by a reliance on a belief in a God of Love. As I show in Chapter 2, Browning's faith comes close to what the German theologian Friedrich Schleiermacher refers to as the 'feeling of dependence' which he saw as the basis for all religion—an idea which was to form the foundation of Rudolf Otto's theory of 'creature-feeling': a feeling of a relational existence.[235]

At times, the pressure of creaturehood in Browning's poetry can seem terrifying. In ' "Childe Roland to the Dark Tower Came" ', the terms of reference are so unclear that the speaker, surrounded by the hills 'like giants at a hunting', can be seen to be facing a hideous opponent as he cries to himself that he must 'Now stab and end the creature—to the

---

[234] See works such as Charles Babbage's *Ninth Bridgewater Treatise* (1837), Lyell's *Elements of Geology* (1838), and Chamber's *Vestiges of the Natural History of Creation* (1844).

[235] Friedrich Schleiermacher, 'Association in Religion', in *On Religion: Speeches to Its Cultured Despisers* (1799), trans. John Oman (London: Kegan Paul, 1893), 149. See Rudolf Otto's *The Idea of the Holy: An Inquiry into the Non-Rational Factor and its Relation to the Rational*, trans. John W. Harvey (London: H. Milford, 1925).

heft!' (*BCP* i. 591, l. 192). On the other hand, the voice could come from elsewhere, which would make the speaker himself the creature, facing his own demise. Browning often uses the word to convey the way in which man is hemmed in by his environment in such a way. Like some 'captured creature in a pound', a 'creature' that Nature 'dared' to 'frame' (*BCP* i. 160, l. 384; 134, l. 607), he is always struggling to assert himself. He also uses the term to describe those who seem beyond reach. Jules, in *Pippa Passes*, for example, finds himself surprised by the peculiar charms of Phene, 'distinguished from the herd of us by such a creature!', while *The Ring and the Book*'s Pompilia is a 'strange tall beautiful creature'.[236] Pompilia and Phene's near divine qualities lend a different edge to the sense of their creatureliness—they are alien to the self, incomprehensible and 'other'. This idea of creaturely difference is taken to an extreme in *Christmas-Eve* when the speaker craves the idea of self-transcendence in order to understand the 'supreme . . . spectral creature' of a moon-rainbow (*BCP* i. 472, l. 392). Browning also refers to works of art as 'creatures'—the narrator of *The Ring and the Book* speaks of a sculpture by Gianlorenzo Bernini, as 'Bernini's creature plated to the paps' (*TRB* i. 889; p. 47). Most importantly, however, for Browning, as for Beckett, the idea of creatureliness has implications for the artist. Browning's dramatic monologues show him to be deeply conscious of the way in which he was, himself, a creature of God, involved in acts of dependent imitation, or, as he puts it, in acts of 'Mimic creation' (*TRB* i. 741; p. 43).

Auden was also preoccupied with the idea of creatureliness. For him, too, it stands for a sort of solipsism: 'creature[s]' are 'so deeply in love with themselves | Their sin of accidie excludes all others' (*ACP*, 147). But this is a dark solipsism; in a perceptive article on his work during the thirties, Geoffrey Grigson notes that Auden inhabits a 'frightening border territory'—'the line between the known and the feared, the past and the future, and the conscious and everything beyond control, the region of society and the region of trolls and holders (and Goebbelses)'. Auden, Grigson concludes, 'is a monster'.[237] By this, Grigson means that Auden does not fit in with the expectations of his readers, but his comment also indicates the way in which Auden constantly uses

---

[236] See *Pippa Passes*, Part 1 (*BCP* i. 315, ll. 398–9); *The Ring and The Book*, iv. 322. I quote from *The Ring and the Book*, ed. Richard D. Altick (Harmondsworth: Penguin, 1971), 167. Henceforth *TRB*.

[237] Geoffrey Grigson, 'Auden as a Monster', *New Verse*, 26–7 (Nov. 1937), 13–14.

his verse to investigate the frontiers of the human. This seems to be the concern of his 1936 poem:

The Creatures

They are our past and our future: the poles between which our desire unceasingly is discharged.

A desire in which love and hatred so perfectly oppose themselves that we cannot voluntarily move; but await the extraordinary compulsion of the deluge and the earthquake.

Their affections and indifferences have been a guide to all reformers and tyrants.

Their appearances amid our dreams of machinery have brought a vision of nude and fabulous epochs.

O Pride so hostile to our Charity.

But what their pride has retained, we may by charity more generously recover.

(*EA*, 158)

It is not made clear who Auden's creatures are. The confusing use of the pronoun 'they' is designed, to borrow a phrase from Rostrever Hamilton, to give the impression that 'an entire stranger were claiming our acquaintance'.[238] The effect is derived in part from Edward Lear, who, as Auden put it, conjured 'legions of cruel inquisitive They' in his limericks (*ACP*, 183). The 'They' in 'The Creatures' are equally mysterious and menacing (echoing his poem entitled 'They' which asks 'Where do they come from? Those whom we so much dread'). The answer, for Auden, is that 'they' are part of ourselves: 'Terrible presences that the ponds reflect | back' (*ACP*, 253). Auden uses the word 'creature' to emphasize his perception that there are things about humanity that are both more, and less, than human. He is in a constant struggle to define' '[t]he place of all the creatures in the Scheme Divine' (*ACP*, 825). Indeed, his description of his encounter with the school matron in 'Letter to Lord Byron' makes him seem like a frisky zoologist. He likes, he declares 'to see the various types of boys' (*EA*, 192). Auden, like Browning, shows a special attraction to what he terms the 'wordless creatures' (*ACP*, 624) of the animal world. Auden, however, is less worried about this 'nineteenth-century evolutionary doctrine of man moving "upward, working out the beast"' than by what happens when

---

[238] Hamilton is referring to the use of the definite article. His book *The Tell-Tale Article* is quoted by Bernard Bergonzi in 'Auden and the Audenesque', in *Reading the Thirties: Texts and Contexts* (London: Macmillan, 1978), 43.

man has lost this relation with his animal past. As he writes in 'The Good Life', 'most of what we call evil is not primitive at all'.[239] In fact, for Auden, man's damaging self-consciousness or bad faith means that he consistently shies away from his animal urges, finding himself shocked when he is confronted by them in the shape of the 'large sad eyes' of the 'delectable creatures' of the Freudian night (*ACP*, 276), or the 'gibbering fist-clenched creature' that appears in *The Sea and the Mirror* (*ACP*, 433). As he writes in his 1953 poem, '"The Truest Poetry is the Most Feigning"', man is 'The self-made creature who himself unmakes, | The only creature ever made who fakes' (*ACP*, 621).

The word 'creature' for Auden, then, hovers between sadness for the loss of animal innocence, and contempt for the duplicitous fiction-maker that man has become. When Auden 'let[s] the living creature lie' in 'Lullaby', he says both these things at once (*ACP*, 157). '[C]reature' touches on the way in which the boy is still, in part, animal, worthy of innocent sleep, but it also speaks of his self-consciousness; his ability to 'lie' makes him a 'creature' of some moral ambiguity. This ethical uncertainty characterizes Auden as a creative artist—the delicacy with which he speaks of the sleeping 'creature' in 'Lullaby' is the result of a hard-won balancing act in which he struggles to master his urge to dominate others through fictions of his own making, and to admit to his own creatureliness, his vulnerability to the pressures of society which infects his speech. In this poem, as in so much of his work, there is the constant threat that the loved one may become merely 'a doll' (*EA*, 458). Meanwhile, the lyric voice itself attempts, as it negotiates through webs of allusion, to come to terms with its own powerlessness. Such anxieties about the responsibilities of creativity, and creatureliness haunt all three writers, but in different ways. In the final section of this chapter, I will suggest some of the ways in which these writers are in sympathy with one another, and consider some of the ethical implications of their differences.

MIRRORING TRAGEDY

As I have shown, Browning, Beckett, and Auden are all aware of the creaturely, Caliban-like elements within their own persons, as well of their desire to play at being Prospero. They have, as it were, a finely

---

[239] First published in *Christianity and the Social Revolution*, repr. in *EA*, 346. Also see his longing 'Address to the Beasts' (*ACP*, 889).

developed sense of the ways in which either an over-sophisticated sense
of self, or a primitive solipsism, could degenerate into radical scepticism,
or even acute pathology, as witnessed by Browning's 'Porphyria's Lover'
or 'Johannes Agricolae in Meditation', Auden's ANTONIO in *The Sea and
the Mirror*, and numerous creatures from Beckett's text—from the self-
sealing Murphy to the horrified and horrifying speaker in *How It Is*. But,
for the purposes of this book, the interest in their work is not in the
sceptical hypothesis per se—the claim or thought that knowledge of
others is impossible—but in the kind of stories that make the sceptic's
doubts intelligible. The problem, as Cavell puts it, 'is to discover the
specific plight of mind and circumstance within which a human being
gives voice to his condition'.[240]

If Browning, Beckett, and Auden are dealing with a 'specific' plight of
mind, and the problems of subjective limitations, this begs the question of
why they turn to *The Tempest*, when one might expect them to each write
a new story, which would express the specificity of their situation. The
answer lies in the relationship between allusion and their concerns about
sympathy. Sartre wrote in 1939 that a 'fictional technique always relates
back to the novelist's metaphysics' and the 'critic's task is to define the
latter before evaluating the former'.[241] But here, I argue, it is important to
look at these writers' fictional technique (specifically their allusive bent)
while trying to evaluate their metaphysics. For, the reason for Browning,
Beckett, and Auden's fondness for allusion is their concern with other
minds. As Cavell writes, what precedes certain discoveries, especially
discoveries concerning a realization that we have not acknowledged the
other, 'is a necessity to *return* to a work, in fact or in memory, as to
unfinished business'.[242] A viewer of tragedy can fail, perhaps initially must
fail, in the acknowledgement of the protagonists; and this failure can
mirror the failure in the dramatic events, thus serving, as Cavell sees it, to
implicate the viewer in the tragedy.[243] As he describes, 'in failing to see
what the true position of a character is...we are exactly put in his
position'.[244] Cavell is writing about *King Lear*, here, but his argument is
equally applicable to *The Tempest*. Each of these artists' practice of literary

[240] Cavell, *Must We Mean*, 240.
[241] Jean Paul Sartre, *On the Sound and the Fury: Time in the Work of Faulkner*, trans.
A. Michelson (New York: Collier Books, 1962), 84.
[242] Cavell, *Must We Mean*, 314.
[243] See Lamarque, *Fictional Points of View*, 153.
[244] Stanley Cavell, *Disowning Knowledge in Six Plays of Shakespeare* (Cambridge:
Cambridge University Press, 1987), 84–5.

allusion is deeply entwined with theories of acknowledgement and the philosophy of mind: they need to return to a work because they have failed to acknowledge it before. In many ways, therefore, their failure to perceive the 'true position of a character', or creature, derives from their sense of the peculiar ontology of fictional beings, and the difficulties of sympathizing with others, both of which I have discussed earlier. As I will show in the following chapters, all three writers wrestle with such difficulties by playing up, and playing with, their roles as author-as-god. But their interest in textual allusion always brings them down to earth. They are continually aware of the ways in which humans may catch or miss another's meanings in life, thus 'failing' to acknowledge the other. The way in which Caliban has been distorted, changed, and rewritten in readings and rewritings of the text is a concrete example of what it might be to suffer from a subjective identity. The methods by which Browning, Beckett, and Auden 'return to' and 'salvage' this 'deformed slave' show an awareness of the story of misacknowledgement and misunderstanding.[245]

There is a parallel in each of these authors turning towards *The Tempest*. Each had reached a crux in their career as authors—a crisis of confidence about ethics and writing and, in this sense, each variation of *The Tempest* could be seen as a version of Prospero's farewell, an apology for poetry. (Auden referred to *The Sea and the Mirror* as his 'Ars poetica', an attempt 'to show, in a work of art, the limitations of art'.[246]) Secondly, each poet found himself face to face with the possibility that there is no chance of moral improvement per se, that man's experience is essentially private, and that we are unable to sympathize with one another. This outbreak of moral scepticism, fuelled, perhaps, by an increasing religious uncertainty, suggests why the figure of Caliban haunted the imagination of writers at the turn of the century. As Wilde puts it in his 1891 'Preface' to *The Picture of Dorian Gray*, 'the nineteenth century dislike of Realism is the rage of Caliban seeing his own face in a glass. The nineteenth century dislike of Romanticism is the rage of Caliban not seeing his own face in a glass.'[247] The story which they all choose, then, is one which is possessed by a creature who

---

[245] I refer to the 'Names of Actors' in which Caliban is described as a 'salvage and deformed slave', Kermode, *Tempest*, 2.

[246] W. H. Auden, letter to Ursula Niebuhr, 2 June 1944, letter to Theodore Spencer, 24 Mar. 1944, quoted in Mendelson, *Later Auden*, 205.

[247] Oscar Wilde, 'Preface' to *The Picture of Dorian Gray*, ed. Donald Lawler (New York: W. W. Norton & Co., 1988), 3.

goes against ideas of normative morality and empathy, a story set against a background which constantly inhibits and problematizes our possibility of engaging or sympathizing with abnormality. *The Tempest* is a world that demonstrates the contingency of our 'moral' language. 'Shakespeare', as Auden puts it, 'really left it in a mess.'[248] Thirdly, the play offers a way in which these writers can explore their theological anxieties, through the figures of Caliban and Prospero. As Flannery O'Connor writes, it is 'writers who see by the light of their Christian faith' who 'have in these times the sharpest eyes for the grotesque, for the perverse and the unacceptable. Redemption is meaningless unless there is cause for it in the actual life we live.'[249]

The play itself engages and plays out questions concerning such radical scepticism about other minds, about the possibility of goodness and sympathy, and about the possibility for art to convey meaning. Spend too much time on the isle, and one tends to lose credibility. Scepticism aside, any possibility that an audience may put themselves in Prospero's place, or may sincerely understand his circumstance, is undercut by the play's epilogue, with which this chapter began. When Prospero speaks his final words there is 'a sea-change in special circumstances' as Austin would put it.[250] His stepping outside the play with an appeal for applause emphasizes the fact that his entire existence has been a performance. There is, then, perhaps, nothing to understand. If everything he has said has been an act, how are we to perceive, let alone sympathize with, his utterances, once disenchanted? Take, for example, his sympathetic owning up to Caliban: 'this thing of darkness I | Acknowledge mine' (V. i. 275–6), a comment which in 'ordinary language' terms, should be a performative utterance—a moment of recognition. However, his sympathetic acknowledgement in these words could now be seen to suffer from the affliction of all staged performative utterances, being '*in a peculiar way* hollow or void'.[251] But, in its peculiarity, this declaration retains its sense, whether the character of Prospero is pretending or not. Rather like the Cretan liar, the words are an acknowledgement of bad faith itself.

---

[248] Auden to Ansen, 30 Apr. 1947 in *The Table Talk of W. H. Auden*, ed. Nicholas Jenkins (London: Faber, 1990), 58.

[249] Flannery O'Connor, *Mystery and Manners* (London: Faber, 1984), 147.

[250] J. L. Austin, *How to Do Things with Words*, ed. J. O. Urmson and Marina Sbisà (Oxford: Oxford University Press, 1976), 22.

[251] Ibid.

This sense for the difficulties of fictional acknowledgement also sheds light on why each of these authors decides to express their problems with other minds through variations upon dramatic monologue form. Grouping 'Caliban upon Setebos', *The Sea and the Mirror*, and *How It Is* together as 'dramatic monologues' could be seen as overly sweeping, and genre criticism itself has its shortcomings, failing, at times, 'to keep in mind the strangeness of what it studies'.[252] However, as Shaw convincingly argues, '[u]nless we study poems as generic instances of some class or category larger than themselves, we are condemned to an extreme form of solipsism'.[253] Or, as Beckett dryly puts it, '[i]f we can't keep our genres more or less distinct, or extricate them from the confusion that has them where they are, we might as well go home and lie down'.[254] Throughout this book I will be working with the idea of the dramatic monologue as a slippery genre. Indeed, the very fluctuations in its generic definitions (like the fluctuating import of sympathy and indulgence) are itself part of the matter of discussion. However, I will be drawing on ideas of the dramatic monologue as defined by W. David Shaw, Eric Griffiths, Alan Sinfield, and Park Honan, and arguing against Langbaum's influential view that the dramatic monologue is a form whose 'end' is 'to establish the reader's sympathetic relation to the poem', and that we must 'adopt' the speaker's 'viewpoint' for 'entry into the poem'.[255] Shaw claims to 'trace the rise of the monologue to the dangerous legacy of agnostic theology' and to link it to 'nineteenth-

---

[252] Beckett called *Comment c'est* a 'roman' on its cover, but not on the title page, a title that he removed on its translation into English. As C. J. Ackerley and S. E. Gontarski note, the text resembles a dramatic monologue. See *The Grove Companion to Samuel Beckett* (New York: Grove Press, 1994), 105. Geoffrey Hartman, *Criticism in the Wilderness: The Study of Literature Today* (New Haven: Yale University Press, 1980), 184.

[253] Shaw, *Lucid Veil*, 183.

[254] In a letter to his publisher, Barney Rosset in 1957, quoted in Ruby Cohn, *Just Play: Beckett's Theatre* (Princeton: Princeton University Press, 1980), 207.

[255] Langbaum, *Poetry of Experience*, 78. W. David Shaw points out that 'In a recent article on Amy Levy', Cynthia Scheinberg has also revised Langbaum's 'theory of poetic sympathy by observing that the auditor in a dramatic monologue is often "unable to identify with the speaker"'. See Shaw, *Origins of the Monologue: The Hidden God* (Toronto: University of Toronto Press, 1999), 14; Cynthia Scheinberg, 'Recasting "Sympathy and Judgment": Amy Levy, Women Poets and the Victorian Dramatic Monologue', *Victorian Poetry*, 35 (Summer 1997), 173–91. Shaw also mentions John Maynard's 'Reading the Reader in Robert Browning's Dramatic Monologues', in Mary Ellen Gibson (ed.), *Critical Essays on Robert Browning* (New York: G. K. Hall, 1992), and Dorothy Mermin's *The Audience in the Poem* (New Brunswick: Rutgers University Press, 1983). Both Maynard and Mermin cast doubt on the possibility of sympathizing with the protagonist in a dramatic monologue.

century theories of . . . the unknown God'. For Griffiths, the monologue offers a way in which we may attempt, and fail, to imaginatively reconstruct the voice of another through print, thus questioning our 'presumptions of identity' and of sympathy.[256] Sinfield, meanwhile, argues for the broadest possible view in which a dramatic monologue is 'a poem in the first person spoken by, or almost entirely by, someone who is indicated not to be the poet'.[257] Relying on these specific qualities, or effects, such as the adoption of a persona or the tension between text and voice, may mean that much of my argument may be applicable to texts that are not dramatic monologues. But, I hope that as Park Honan notes, an analysis will not necessarily 'suffer if the isolated effect is one which is common to poetry not in the dramatic monologue form'.[258]

Through these definitions of the dramatic monologue, it is possible to consider the ways in which this form both engages with, and suggests an escape from, sceptical ideas through its conventional task of bringing three consciousnesses together—of bringing an imagined other to life. But, it is also a form that shows the way in which minds keep each other at a distance. The dramatic monologue is, formally, central to the ethical difficulties of reading, of the ways in which we deal with our voices, and those of others. Critics have pointed to the way in which a poem like Browning's 'My Last Duchess' creates a 'tension between sympathy and judgement' for both the reader and the writer. Ralph Rader argues that it asks for an 'imaginative act of conflation and compassion by which . . . we understand other people. We become them (sympathy) while remaining ourselves (judgement).' Surprisingly though, Rader claims that this 'double response is not a matter of ethical or psychological ambiguity'. Perhaps he overestimates the ease with which we 'understand other people'.[259] In the chapters that follow, I will demonstrate the ways in which the dramatic monologue is alert to the perils of

---

[256] Griffiths, *Printed Voice*, 189.

[257] See Shaw, *Origins of the Monologue*, 3. After discussing various generic definitions of the monologue, Shaw settles for the idea that a consideration of the form which involves 'apostrophic swerves', 'bad faith', 'double audiences', and 'hidden gods' would be the 'least distorting misfit', 12; Alan Sinfield, *The Dramatic Monologue* (London: Methuen, 1977), 8; Park Honan, *Browning's Characters: A Study in Poetic Technique* (New Haven: Yale University Press, 1961). See esp. Honan's fourth chapter, 'The Solitary Voice', where he discusses 'The Problem of the Dramatic Monologue', 104–25.

[258] Honan, *Browning's Characters*, 123.

[259] Ralph W. Rader, 'The Dramatic Monologue and Related Lyric Forms', *Critical Inquiry*, 3 (1976), 131–51, at 133.

this lack of acknowledgement; to the dangers of disowning the imagined voice as 'not I'. The way in which these authors use dramatic monologues, then, sheds light on their own handling of the sceptical dilemma. It also reveals something about their theological beliefs. While, at first glance, they seem to attempt to acknowledge the living voice of Caliban as 'other' to themselves, Browning, Auden, and Beckett are interested in the way in which they are unable to conceive, let alone sympathize with, another mind—the ways in which they attempt to, but cannot, be God. Here, my argument counters the work of Honan and Slinn. Browning, Beckett, and Auden, all too aware of their distance from divine truth, repeatedly play with the idea of themselves, and their fictional creations, as creatures of God, rather than (as Honan and Slinn emphasize) as 'characters'.[260]

In the end, in their failure to achieve perfect sympathy with others, Browning, Auden, and Beckett could be seen to be rehearsing the insincerity of Prospero's plight as he attempts to 'acknowledge' his 'thing of darkness'. Their partial responses, and their failed acknowledgement, mirror the magician, who in turn reflects his own pathologically sceptical creature. In this way, they are poets of tragedy as well as faith, for a 'tragic response', as Currie and Ravenscroft explain, is 'as much a response to our own responses as a response to the work itself'.[261] In the chapters that follow, I will consider the ways in which we, as readers, also respond to these failures, and the ways in which we fail to respond.

---

[260] See Slinn's Preface: 'my concern is with . . . the way characters are engaged in verbal acts which dramatize themselves, and with the way Browning considers the multiplicity and complexity of human personality', *Fictions of Identity*, p. ix. Honan argues that 'we have failed to inspect Browning's verse closely in the light of character', *Browning's Characters*, 3.

[261] Currie and Ravenscroft, *Recreative Minds*, 203.

2

Browning's Strangeness

APPREHENSIONS AND MISAPPREHENSIONS

Robert Browning's first letter to Elizabeth Barrett must have come as a bit of a shock. He had been reading her poetry for years and the effect, it seems, was profound. 'I do, as I say, love these books with all my heart—and I love you too.'[1] Her response was a little more measured. 'Sympathy', she wrote 'is dear—very dear to me: but the sympathy of a poet, & of such a poet, is the quintessence of sympathy to me!'[2] Barrett's response is neither a rejection nor an affirmation; it is an inference. She assumes his sympathetic understanding of her, and in doing this, claims hers of him. It also suggests something else—an understanding that, in the case of expressing one's feelings, sometimes less is more.

Reading the Brownings' correspondence, one is struck by the nuances of their understandings and misunderstandings, the call and response of words between them, the excitement and, at times, the frustration. Indeed, to a certain extent, their entire correspondence could be seen as a working-out of quite what each of them might mean, and how much they might mean to each other. Many of Robert Browning's ideas about sympathy revolve around the sympathetic gains and losses of the written word. As he would have learnt from Elizabeth Barrett, the 'physiology' of their 'intercourse' created a 'curious double feeling', confusing her about the disparity between her feelings about 'you personally, & you as the writer of these letters [. . .] "People say," I used to think, 'that women *always* know. . & certainly I do not know . . & therefore . . therefore'.[3] Reading the letters between the couple, one sees them exchanging their

[1] RB to EB, 10 Jan. 1845, *The Letters of Robert Browning and Elizabeth Barrett Browning 1845–1846*, ed. Elvan Kintner, 2 vols. (Cambridge, Mass.: Belnap Press of Harvard University Press, 1969), i. 3. Hereafter, Kintner, i and ii.
[2] EB to RB, 11 Jan. 1845, Kintner, i. 4.
[3] EB to RB, 4 Jan. 1846, ibid. 359–60.

own criticisms and judgements, and those of others. Feeling for each other seems to involve a balance of the demonstration and the justification of the self. A year after his initial protestation of love, Browning still has some explaining to do.

I suspect . . . you have found out by this time my odd liking for 'vermin'—you once wrote '*your* snails'—and certainly snails are old clients of mine . . . never try and catch a speckled gray lizard when we are in Italy . . . because the strange tail will snap off, drop from him and stay in your fingers . . . I always loved all those wild creatures God '*sets up for themselves*' so independently of us, so successfully, with their strange happy minute inch of candle, as it were, to light them; while we run about and against each other with our great cressets and fire pots.[4]

There is an oddity about this letter. While wooing Barrett, it seems, in some way, to wistfully long for a life away from her, from one that could be led as 'independently' as those 'wild creatures' he loves. This extract, in its richness, seems to capture so much of Browning's complexity both as a poet and as a man. In its choice of subject matter, it gives us Browning as theologian, as entymologist, as comedian, and as lover. Stylistically, this is characteristic Browning too. One sees the ways in which he edges towards intimacy with others—catching and quoting Barrett's own phrase '*your* snails'—and moves, gradually, from speaking of 'I', to 'we'. In its balance between sympathetic touch and distance, it seems to both run 'about' and 'against' its intended audience, but never quite reaches it. Such tensions are part of Browning's understanding of what it is to be a human creature. 'All this missing of instant understanding', he wrote elsewhere, '(for it does not amount to *mis*understanding)—comes of letters, and our being divided.'[5]

Browning's poems are full of strange, divided creatures. Awkward, apprehensive, and fearful, they appear constantly aware that they may need to request the indulgence of their audience. Browning's Cleon is a good example of such a divided man. First published in his 1855 collection *Men and Women*, this poem takes the form of a dictated letter from a Cretan bard to his ruler, Protus. One of the subjects that Cleon tackles is the question of how a man might end his life. Cleon, like Prospero, finds it a hard subject to apprehend. As he thinks about times to come, the poet speaks with terror of the way in which 'the heavy years increase—':

---

4 RB to EB, 1 Jan. 1846, ibid. 356.
5 RB to EB, 31 July 1846, ibid. ii. 919–20.

The horror quickening still from year to year,
The consummation coming past escape
When I shall know most, and yet least enjoy—
When all my works wherein I prove my worth,
Being present still to mock me in men's mouths,
Alive still, in the praise of such as thou,
I, I the feeling, thinking, acting man,
The man who loved his life so over-much,
Sleep in my urn.

(BCP i. 719–20, ll. 315–23)

The bard, usually so sure of the 'true proportions of a man' (*BCP* i. 713, l. 55), seems hesitant here, stammering as he wonders if he will always be quite himself. Being sage is central to Cleon's identity (his epistolary monologue consists of advice to the monarch Protus), but now his notion of 'I' appears to be crumbling. This is, perhaps, because thought itself is failing him. Indeed, the power of this monologue derives from the fact that this speaker knows so little; this poet is unable to see that he is, in fact, a creature of poetry. While we may imagine him reciting his verse, shaping his cadences' rise and fall, it is clear that larger beginnings and real conclusions are beyond him.

Cleon's relations with another nineteenth-century act of Attic imagining are an instance of one such unknown beginning. His musings on his own urn summon the memory of Keats's 'Ode', and with this allusive background in mind, Cleon's own songs start to seem like sad, degraded parodies, far from those of the 'happy melodist', 'For ever piping songs' of love '[f]or ever warm and still to be enjoy'd'.[6] For being 'still'—with its strangely opposing senses of continuance and paralysis—is a complex business. While Keats finds a world of 'wonder and delight' in the idea of the 'still unravished bride of quietness', the horror that Browning's Cleon feels at the idea of 'stillness' is highlighted by the ambiguities evident in the passage above: the series of near-oxymorons—'quickening still', 'present still', 'Alive still'—conjures some terrifying images of perpetual life and petrification, and makes for a poignant contrast with Keats's sublime thoughts on the relationship between the self, art, and time.

Cleon's lament is not simply about losing his voice and about the terror of parts of oneself continuing after death. As print is, by its nature, implicated in such matters of stillness, the poem also enacts this loss. The way in which the poem comes about on the page itself

---

[6] See Keats's 'Ode on a Grecian Urn' (1819), ll. 23, 24, 26. I quote from *The Poetical Works of John Keats*, ed. H. W. Garrod (Oxford: Clarendon Press, 1958), 260–1.

means that the reader is involved in questions about understanding voices and sympathizing with voices from afar; as we reimagine the speaker's accent, we become implicated in Browning's struggles with questions of how we may understand each other through distances of time and space. It is a struggle that showed itself in many different ways: in his critical reception, in his handling of the dramatic monologue form, in his thoughts on Higher Criticism, on natural theology, on love, and most of all, in his consideration of parody and mimicry. To look at his work in these ways is to show that throughout his poems, Browning concerns himself with how we can misunderstand each other, and how we try to get close to each other, always alive to the way in which our attempts might become a mockery.

In many ways, the narrative of Browning's ambivalent critical reception is strangely aligned with the subject matter of his verse. Indeed, with his concern about being 'mock[ed] in others' mouths', Cleon reflects his maker, for Browning was often parodied, complaining to Elizabeth Barrett Browning of 'the reviews & newspapers that laughed my "Paracelsus" to scorn'.[7] Browning's poetry and drama attracted numerous comic and critical jibes. After reading his work, Macready feared that Browning's 'intellect' was 'not clear', while Alfred Austin found it 'shockingly unintelligible, or at least painfully difficult to understand'.[8] After reading *Men and Women*, a writer in *Bentley's Miscellany* noted that 'the poet's *penchant* for elliptical diction, interjectional dark sayings, *multum in parvo* (and, sometimes, seemingly *minimum in molto*) "deliverances", flighty fancies, unkempt similitudes, quaintest conceits, slipshod familiarities, and grotesque exaggerations is unhealthily on the increase', while even a friendly letter from John Ruskin ridiculed Browning's 'abruptness . . . compression and elliptical syntax'.[9] Browning's reaction to Ruskin's letter seems resigned to misunderstanding: 'Do you think poetry was ever generally understood— or can be? Is the business of it to tell people what they know already, as they know it?', he retorts.[10] His tone echoes back to his poetic credo, as given in his 1852 'Essay on Shelley':

[7] RB to EB, 16 Sept. 1845, Kintner, i. 200.

[8] See his entry for 17 July 1840 in *The Journal of William Charles Macready*, ed. J. C. Trewin (London: Longmans, 1967), 158; Alfred Austin, *The Poetry of the Period* (London: Richard Bentley, 1870), 53.

[9] Unsigned review, 'Browning's *Men and Women*', *Bentley's Miscellany*, 39 (1856) 64–70, at 64; Daniel Karlin discusses Browning's correspondence with Ruskin in *Browning's Hatreds* (Oxford: Clarendon Press, 1993), 107.

[10] See W. G. Collingwood, *The Life and Work of John Ruskin*, 2 vols. (London: Methuen, 1893), i. 199–202.

the misapprehensiveness of his age is exactly what a poet is sent to remedy; and the interval between his operation and the generally perceptible effect of it, is no greater, less indeed, than in many other departments of great human effort. The 'E pur si muove' of the astronomer was as bitter a word as any uttered before or since by a poet over his rejected living work, in that depth of conviction which is so like despair.[11]

Among Victorian poets, Browning was second only to Tennyson in his number of appearances in William Hamilton's six-volume collection, produced at the end of the 1880s. He distinguished himself further. As Hamilton notes, it was the custom when including parodies of contemporary poets to include examples of the work that was being parodied, for 'some of the parodies may read rather flat and uninteresting to those who are unacquainted with the original poem'. 'Hitherto', he writes, 'the necessary authority has been gracefully accorded', but on receipt of 'a courteously worded letter... asking his permission to quote a few extracts from his shorter poems, with the assurance that no offensive parody of his works should be inserted', Browning put his foot down: 'Mr. Browning's reply was to the effect that as he disapproved of every kind of Parody he refused permission to quote any of his poems, adding in somewhat ungracious language, that his publishers would be instructed to see that his wishes were complied with.' The refusal, of course, gave Hamilton scope for further parody (and he sneaks an illicit copy of 'The Lost Leader' and 'The Patriot' into his sixth volume):

Perhaps the world does not greatly care whether Mr. Browning approves of Parody, or does not; neither can he very well expect that the completeness of this Collection should be sacrificed in deference to his distaste for a harmless branch of literature which has amused many of our greatest authors and the best of men. Byron and Scott could laugh at the *Rejected Addresses*, and enjoy a merry jest, even at their own expense, but let no dog bark when the great Sir Oracle opens his lips, and no daring humourist venture to travesty the poems of Mr. Robert Browning![12]

His popularity as a target does suggest that he was, to a certain extent, misapprehended by his age.[13] It also suggests a degree of respect.

[11] 'An Essay on Percy Bysshe Shelley' (1852), repr. in *BCP* i. 1001–13, at 1006.
[12] William Hamilton (ed.), *Parodies of the Works of English and American Authors*, 6 vols. (London: Reeves & Turner, 1884–9), vi. 46. 'The Lost Leader' and 'The Patriot' appear on 50–1.
[13] Hamilton continues to parody Browning, including examples of poems from 'The Weekly Dispatch' in 1883 and mocks the proliferation of 'Browning Societies', 54–5.

Relations between a parodist and the parodied are hard to define. But as Terry Caesar rightly argues, 'parody is by definition alert to the human presence in the work'.[14] It is, in part, a 'byway of tenderness', always feeling for the author, and their characteristic style.[15] C. S. Calverley's 1872 parody of Browning's *The Ring and The Book* is a good example of the difficulties of distinguishing between tenderness and mockery.

> You see this pebble-stone? It's a thing I bought
> Of a bit of a chit of a boy i' the mid of the day—
> I like to dock the smaller parts-o'-speech,
> As we curtail the already cur-tail'd cur
> (You catch the paronomasia, play' po' words?)
> Did, rather, i' the pre-Landseerian days.
> Well, to my muttons. I purchased the concern
> And clapt it i' my poke, having given for same
> By way o' chop, swop, barter or exchange—
> 'Chop' was my snickering dandiprat's own term—
> One-shilling and four pence, current coin o' the realm.
> O-n-e one and f-o-u-r four
> Pence, one and fourpence—you are with me, sir?—
> What hour it skills not: ten or eleven o' the clock,
> One day (and what a roaring day it was
> Go shop or sight-see—bar a spit o' rain!)
> In February, eighteen sixty-nine,
> Alexandrina Victoria, Fidei
> Hm—hm—how runs the jargon? Being on the throne.[16]

While ludicrously titled 'The Cock and the Bull', the accuracy of this parodic imitation of *The Ring and the Book* bears witness to Calverley's clear sense for the particularities of Browning's style and method—especially for the ways in which Browning tries to make himself closer to his audience. The parody replicates Browning's 'rugged abbreviations' of everyday conversation, while the teasing substitution of a 'pebble-stone' for Browning's ring, and the catching of Browning's reach for

---

[14] Terry Caesar, '"I Quite Forget What—Say a Daffodilly": Victorian Parody', *English Literary History*, 51/4 (Winter 1984), 795–818, at 796–7, 805.

[15] Gérard Genette notes that 'it is properly the irreducible ambiguity of teasing, in which mockery is a way of loving and irony (understand who must) only a byway of tenderness'. See his *Palimpsests: Literature in the Second Degree*, trans. Channa Newman and Claude Doubinsky (Lincoln: University of Nebraska Press, 1997), 120.

[16] C. S. Calverley, *Fly Leaves* (Cambridge: Deighton, Bell & Co., 1872), 113.

immediacy—'how runs the jargon'—is deftly done.[17] Calverley, in his own parodic way, appears to understand how much Browning wanted to be understood.

STRANGELY MODERN

Mr Browning unites within himself more of the elements of a true poet than perhaps any other of those whom we call 'modern' amongst us; yet there are few writers so little read, so partially understood.[18]

Despite his 'great ambition' to be 'familiar, modern and interlocutory', Browning was, the reviewers noted, 'not like unto any other poet!'[19] This is perhaps because modernity, as Matthew Arnold pointed out, the time in which Browning was writing, was making it harder for people to sustain such 'familiar' or 'interlocutory' relationships. As Arnold argued, the 'modern spirit' was not so much a feeling of being understood by one's time, but 'the awakening' of the sense that one is working in a system not of one's 'own creation'.[20]

For Browning, this was not just an awakening to the necessary self-alienation that accompanies the fact that we are required to use a common tongue, but also an awakening to the increasing new senses of self-estrangement in time and space that stem from the arrival of new technologies. As I will argue, Browning's formal choices are, in part, the result of a sensitivity to the way in which technical changes affect our ability to feel close to one another. Indeed, his favoured form, the dramatic monologue, began to emerge within a changing context of religious and philosophical uncertainty, in which, Eric Griffiths argues, there was a sense of lost community, 'a new philosophical articulation of self-consciousness . . . and, about the same time, "a decline of oratory along with a concomitant rise of writing as the primary mode of rhetoric . . . A major effect of this shift was an

---

[17] Bulwer Lytton comments on the 'rugged abbreviations' of everyday conversation in 'The Inarticulate English', *England and the English* (London: Richard Bentley, 1833), 143.

[18] Warburton, 'Review of "Poems *London 1833–4*. By Miss BARRETT," "Paracelsus, and other Poems. *London, 1835–45*. By ROBERT BROWNING", and "Poems. London, 1845. By COVENTRY PATMORE"', *English Review* (Dec. 1845). RB sent a copy of this journal to EB accompanying his letter of 6 Jan. 1846. See Kintner, i. 363, 368–9.

[19] See *Spectator* 66 (2584), 10 Mar. 1883, 320; unsigned review, *Athenaeum*, 1910, Saturday, 4 June 1864, 765–7, at 766.

[20] Matthew Arnold, 'Heinrich Heine', in *Lectures and Essays in Criticism*, iii. 109.

abstraction of audience".'[21] It is certainly true that advances in book production in the early 1800s, the development of stereotyping, and the increasing availability of cheap paper, meant that printed matter was available to a far wider audience. These changes (together with the invention of the gramophone and the telegraph later in the century) have led a number of critics to perceive that Victorian poets were working in an atmosphere in which it seemed as if people were working at increasing distances from each other, leading to what Steven Connor terms the 'formation of a phenomenology of disembodiment'.[22] Things, certainly, were never fully disembodied—reading aloud was still a favoured practice, and both Browning and Tennyson enjoyed reciting their poems. However, the desire among Victorian readers to see their authors (consider the popularity of Dickens's public readings, or the tourists stalking Tennyson 'up to the very windows of his house' on the Isle of Wight) bears witness to a growing fear of this mooted abstraction.[23] Browning was a poet who worked with these changing modes of reception and transaction; in spite of a wry view of the marketplace, he was determined to make his writing available to as many readers as possible. (He followed the suggestion of his publisher, Edward Moxon, in selling the first number of *Bells and Pomegranates—Pippa Passes—*for sixpence.)

Browning encountered some other aspects of modernity more hesitantly. When invited, in 1877, to speak into the newly developed wax cylinder, or phonograph, he only managed a brief passage of ' "How They Brought the Good News from Ghent to Aix" ', before forgetting the words, returning, and 'shout[ing] his signature, "Robert Browning", into the machine'.[24] In his 1890 letter to *The Times*, Haweis reported listening to this recording, and feeling a 'strange sympathetic significance . . . the voice of the dead man was heard speaking . . . from beyond the grave'.[25] Browning's behaviour during his recording indicates that

[21] Eric Griffiths, *The Printed Voice of Victorian Poetry* (Oxford: Clarendon Press, 1989), 68. Griffiths quotes M. Nystrand's 'Introduction' to *What Writers Know: The Language, Process, and Structure of Written Discourse* (New York: Academic Press, 1982), 4.

[22] Steven Connor, *Dumbstruck: A Cultural History of Ventriloquism* (Oxford: Oxford University Press, 2000), 363.

[23] See Blanche Warren-Cornish, 'Memories of Tennyson', *London Mercury* (1921–2), in Norman Page, *Tennyson: Interviews and Recollections* (Basingstoke: Macmillan, 1983), 117.

[24] H. R. Haweis, Letter, *The Times*, 13 Dec. 1830, 10, quoted in Michael Hancher and Jerrold Moore, ' "The Sound of a Voice that is Still": Browning's Edison Cylinder', *Browning Newsletter*, 4 (Spring 1970), 21–33, at 27.

[25] Haweis, Letter, 10, quoted in Ivan Kreilkamp, 'A Voice without a Body: The Phonographic Logic of *Heart of Darkness*', *Victorian Studies*, 40/2 (Winter 1997),

he found the idea of this posthumous intimacy less 'sympathetic'. As Kreilkamp argues, the development of the phonograph brought with it the 'dawning of an awareness that language might function with no clear connection to its human source'; it revealed the 'quotability' of an author's words:

When last words are recorded and re-played, they acquire the potential to be something altogether disconnected (even alienated) from the person who first spoke them...Edison lists as one of the essential features of the phonograph, '[t]he captivation of sounds, with or without the knowledge or consent of the source of their origin'; in the presence of a phonograph, a speaker's language becomes no longer only his or her own, and is subject to 'captivation' and possibly unwanted reproduction. It was as if speech were now, for the first time in history, subject to those same dangers and vagaries which we have known since Plato to be the lot of writing [it is the] authorial possession ('knowledge or consent') of final words, which the phonograph threatens by defining a speaker as no more than the 'source' or 'origin' of a voice.[26]

There is an ambiguity implicit in Edison's notion of the 'captivation of sounds', suggesting both that sound is captured and that this captured sound has the ability to enchant or enthral a listener. Browning, as a poet, was fully aware of the dangers of captivating voices. And, it is possible to argue that the potential for this new sort of literary stillness, caused by these technical advances, gave Browning the impetus to write in a form that was concerned with the preservation, and loss, of the individual voice: the dramatic monologue. Peter Porter is partly right, therefore, to take such technical matters as his starting point, when he claims Browning as a poet who was in tune with the new difficulties in recognizing the annunciating voice in texts.[27]

However, as I argued in my first chapter, the dramatic monologue is a slippery creature, prone to misunderstanding, both formally and generically, and it is difficult to isolate a series of events or contexts that might explain its popularity within the nineteenth century. For

211–44, at 221. See also John Picker's *Victorian Soundscapes* (New York: Oxford University Press, 2003), 122–3.

[26] Kreilkamp, 'A Voice without a Body', 217. Kreilkamp quotes from Edison's article, 'The Phonograph and Its Future', *North American Review* (Jan.–Feb. 1878), 527–36, at 530.

[27] Peter Porter, 'Recording Angels and Answering Machines', *1991 Lectures and Memoirs: Proceedings of the British Academy*, 80 (1991), 1–18, at 2.

Loehndorf, the monologue really does come out of nowhere or every-where; she argues that the shifting relations between auditor, speaker, and author that define the dramatic monologue can be seen as analo-gous to man's ongoing attempt to conceive himself in a relational existence, an attempt which became fraught with uncertainties by the middle of the nineteenth century.[28] Problems in locating a point at which this genre begins mirror, in some ways, the difficult attitude towards beginnings in Browning's poetry. For while Peter Porter might be right in terming Browning the 'Father of Us All' (where 'Us'—stands for those writing with a sense of uncertainty about their own begin-nings) the absence of literal fathers in Browning's monologues is oddly symbolic of the fact that the monologue itself is a form that appears to have no clear parentage.[29] A suggestion like Michael Mason's, then, that 'this genre might have deep roots in contemporary culture', must be weighed against the atmosphere of rootlessness that possesses 'a set of people living without God in the world'.[30]

Browning is much preoccupied by such rootlessness and loss of relations. This manifests itself, in part, in his poetic preoccupation with the presence or absence of the father or author (who may or may not be God), and his relationships with his possible creatures. In the end, what 'fascinated Browning', Oscar Wilde commented, 'was not thought itself but rather the processes by which thought moves'.[31] In fact, what also fascinated Browning was the way in which thought *fails to move*: the way in which thought cannot be articulated, or cannot appeal to others' sympathetic understanding. Throughout his writing career, he finds ways of coming to terms with these failed movements by thinking about the transcendental religious realm, and reconceiving his own role of a poet in relation to this realm. He writes, as I will show, of moving failures, and of creatures of God.

[28] Esther Loehndorf, *The Master's Voices: Robert Browning, the Dramatic Monologue and Modern Poetry* (Tubingen: Francke Verlag, 1997), 5.
[29] Porter, 'Recording Angels', 11.
[30] See Michael Mason, 'Browning and the Dramatic Monologue' in Isobel Armstrong (ed.), *Writers and their Background: Robert Browning* (London: G. Bell & Sons, 1974), 231–366, at 232. The observation that the Victorians were 'living without God in the world' is Thackeray's. See his *Letters and Private Papers*, ed. G. N. Ray, ii (London: Oxford University Press, 1945), 305.
[31] Oscar Wilde, 'The Critic as Artist', in *Selected Works*, ed. R. Aldington (London: W. Heinemann, 1947), 69.

PERFORMING ACTS OF MIMIC CREATION

J. Hillis Miller argues that Browning's 'decision to write dramatic monologues' came from such division: 'the direct way to God has failed'.[32] Ekbert Faas agrees, and claims that the dramatic monologue seemed like a solution for writers such as Browning who were suffering from religious doubt: 'authors of dramatic monologues were widely seen as embodying a new sort of empathetic relativism in their poetry. Thus "toleration for all men and things, consideration...of all sides in all cases"' was said to be ' "the most obvious characteristic of the manner in which (Browning) mirrors life to himself and us" ':

'In the tangle of possible motives,' he seems to say, 'who shall be hasty to give judgement for his brother's praise or blame?' Hence, Browning and others replaced traditional morality with a new 'empirical morality'—analyzing actions not so much in their relations to absolute right or wrong as in relation to the position and character of the actor.[33]

If true, this empathetic consciousness could be seen as eminently progressive. The philosopher Henry Sidgwick thought so. '[W]e suspend our judgement much more than our predecessors,' he wrote, 'and much more contentedly: we see that there are many sides to many questions: the opinions that we do hold we hold if not more loosely, at least more at arm's length: we can imagine how they appear to others, and can conceive ourselves as holding them.'[34] Like the early psychiatrists who tried to jettison all preconceptions about the human mind, so the poet, at least in Robert Buchanan's view, 'should free himself entirely from all arbitrary systems of ethics and codes of opinion' in this endeavour.[35]

There are a number of problems with this vision of an empathic consciousness, and Browning raises these in his dramatic monologues. The 'cultivation of the "relative" spirit in place of the "absolute"', in which, as Pater decided, 'nothing is or can be rightly known except

[32] J. Hillis Miller, *The Disappearance of God: Five Nineteenth Century Writers* (Cambridge, Mass.: Belknap Press of Harvard University Press, 1963), 151.
[33] Faas, *Retreat into the Mind*, 164. Faas cites C. Vaughan's review, *British Quarterly Review*, 80 (July–Oct. 1884), 17.
[34] H. Sidgwick, *Westminster Review* 85, NS 29 (Jan.–Apr. 1866), 106–32, at 107, quoted in Faas, *Retreat*, 164.
[35] R. W. Buchanan, *David Gray, and Other Essays, Chiefly on Poetry* (London: Sampson Low, Son & Marston, 1868).

relatively under conditions', teeters on the brink of amorality.[36] Browning certainly offers verse which suggests that he is able to empathize (and
encourages empathy) with those on the 'dangerous edge' of things—the
'honest thief, the tender murderer'—characters such as the speaker in
'Porphyria's Lover', or in 'Fifine at the Fair'.[37] But because these figures
offer a vision of alien psychology, as Douglas-Fairhurst notes, readers
could be 'disturbed by the prospect of sympathizing with the outpour-
ings of a mind which seemed incapable of responding in kind'.[38] This
double-edged problem was intentional. Browning showed both his
consciousness of the possibilities of sympathy, and the fear of an
ultimately solipsistic existence, by creating characters who appear to
be on the verge of a radical epistemological questioning about the sheer
existence of other minds. Woolford argues that it is scepticism, not
empathy, that is in evidence in *La Saisiaz*, which 'grounds . . . indifferentism in Lockeian principle': 'If my fellows are or are not, what may
please them and what pain,— | Mere surmise: my own experience—
that is knowledge, once again!' (*BCP* ii. 514, ll. 263–4). He notes the
same self-sealing concerns at work in *The Ring and the Book*: 'There is a
weird sense in which (. . . Guido's . . .) orgy of carnage, killing not just
his wife, but her parents too, represents the dark underside of the
subjective poet's will-to-power, just as Sludge's spiritualistic masquer-
ades attempt to control not only (in the first instance) his audience but
the larger reality which his spirit-world gathers into itself.'[39]

The possibility that Browning's emotionally closed characters could be
seen to be in some sense analogous to the poet who cannot extend
beyond himself, is to add an even more 'solipsistic' aspect to Browning's
verse, in which everything returns to the poetic subjectivity. As Everett
notes, to 'describe the poet's strongest creations as dark images of
the Artist is perhaps to give them some essentially modern colouring
of paradox—to make them sound like that critical version of Eliot's
Quartets which stresses their self-critique, their self-parody'.[40] E. Warwick Slinn argues that this is the case in Browning's poetry, pointing out

---

[36] Walter Pater, 'Coleridge's Writings', *Westminster Review* 85, NS 29 (Jan.–Apr.
1866), 106–32, at 107, quoted in Faas, *Retreat into the Mind*, 164.
[37] The phrase 'honest thief, the tender murder' comes from Browning's 'Bishop
Bloughram's Apology', *BCP* i. 627, l. 396.
[38] Douglas-Fairhurst, *Victorian Afterlives*, 203.
[39] John Woolford and Daniel Karlin, *Robert Browning* (Harlow: Longman, 1996),
215, 213.
[40] Barbara Everett, *Poets in their Time: Essays on English Poetry from Donne to Larkin*
(Oxford: Clarendon Press, 1991), 167.

that in these poems 'the power of sympathetic imagination' is always 'restricted by the power of an interfering ego' or 'reflexiveness of subjectivity'.[41] 'Browning's legacy... is not the authority of imagination', which, in Langbaum's terms, allows us an 'act of imaginative projection', but 'a scepticism' which 'anticipates the more modern view that perception and conceptualizing are barely separable'.[42] For Slinn, then, the idea of simulating the experience of others, of 'the bond of identification' discussed in Chapter 1, is impossible. Sympathy—it seems—is subsumed into a spiral of mimicry: '[s]ince all speakers engage in this means of reproducing others, they are alike in repeating various acts of mimicry; furthermore they reflect the poet whose own continuing mimicry animates the whole poem, and he in turn imitates God, who is the original creator of all heaven and earth.'[43] Slinn is partly right, but his account of *The Ring and the Book* overlooks the fact that the speakers in the poem are *imitations* of speakers, rather than real speakers.[44] Some, like Cleon and Karshish, are possibly even writers. Matthew Reynolds rightly points out that Bottinus, in Book IX, 'is not, as E. Warwick Slinn has assumed, improvising what "he *would* say if he could speak at the trial" but is reading out from a text, for written and performed, his words stand in relation to the utterances of other characters'.[45] Such questions about imitation are central to *The Ring and the Book*. Early in the poem, the narrator wonders about the truth or falsity of his tale—'which proves good yet seems untrue':

> This that I mixed with truth, motions of mine
> That quickened, made the inertness malleolable
> O' the gold was not mine,—what's your name for this?
> Are means to the end, themselves in part the end?
> Is fiction which makes fact alive, fact too?
>
> . . . .
>
> Man,—as befits the made, the inferior thing,—
> Purposed, since made, to grow, not make in turn,
> Yet forced to try and make, else fail to grow,—
> Formed to rise, reach at, if not grasp and gain
> The good beyond him,—which attempt is growth,—
> Repeats God's process in man's due degree,
> Attaining man's proportionate result,—

[41] E. Warwick Slinn, *Browning and the Fictions of Identity* (London: Macmillan, 1982), 112.
[42] Ibid. 7.   [43] Ibid. 113.   [44] Reynolds, 'Browning', 121.
[45] Ibid. Reynolds is quoting Slinn, *Fictions of Identity*, 113.

Creates, no, but resuscitates, perhaps,
Inalienable, the arch-prerogative
Which turns thought, act—conceives, expresses too!
No less, man, bounded, yearning to be free,
May so project his surplusage of soul
In search of body, so add self to self
By owning what lay ownerless before,—
So find, so fill full, so appropriate forms—
That, although nothing which had never life
Shall get life from him, be, not having been,
Yet, something dead may get to live again,
Something with too much life or not enough,
Which, either way imperfect, ended once:
An end whereat man's impulse intervenes,
Makes new beginning, starts the dead alive,
Completes the incomplete and saves the thing.
Man's breath were vain to light a virgin wick,—
Half-burned-out, all but quite-quenched wicks o' the lamp
Stationed for temple-service on this earth,
These indeed let him breathe on and relume!
For such man's feat is, in the due degree,
—Mimic creation, galvanism for life,
But still a glory portioned in the scale.

                    (*TRB* i. 700–5, 713–41; pp. 42–3)

This passage is '<u>still</u> a glory', and Browning, here, uses the verse to its fullest extent, playing off the tension between the spoken voice and the achieved pattern on the page. It is a pattern we have seen before; the syntax and diction owe much to an earlier poet. Milton, always fond of prolonging a phrase, finds an afterlife in this verse, which is, itself, about continuation. Each line ending offers a momentary conclusion, only to reach forward to the next. Meanwhile, the Latinate syntax suspends clause after clause. Lack of fulfilment seems to govern linguistic choice here too, as the narrator continually returns to words he has already used—'self to self', 'owning what lay ownerless', and 'fill full'. The linguistic repetitions here seem particularly strong when the speaker thinks about the idea of 'life', which repeats itself in clusters towards the end of this passage.[46] This repetition speaks of Browning's own

---

[46] For a discussion of such poetic repetitions, see Wordsworth's 'Note' to 'The Thorn'. See Wordsworth's *Poetical Works*, ed. Thomas Hutchinson, rev. Ernest de Selincourt (Oxford: Oxford University Press, 1936), 701.

consciousness of the inadequacy of language to create life, his consciousness that this poem is merely 'Mimic creation, galvanism for life'. The phrase is peculiarly poignant—summoning both the idea of the chemical production of electrical energy, and the idea that man is sentenced to this process of artificial quickening.

An 1864 review of *Dramatis Personae* attempts to touch on some of the difficulties of this process:

the poet comes upon the stage like a modern conjuror who dispenses with the old machinery for creating illusion. He has no external aid in sight, but relies on himself, - his own hand, voice, eyes, to work the miracle and represent any number of dramatic scenes and persons without change of dress for himself. Here, then, the work has to be chiefly done in the mind of the reader, which is the real world of action, rather than on the half-objective stage which belongs to other kinds of poetry. The appeal is to the inner eye. It requires that all the powers be awake, the apprehension quick, the mind alive and stirring with those sensitive *feelers* of thought and fancy which will lay hold of the least hint, and almost turn air into solid by the sureness of their grasp.[47]

Like so much writing of the period, this passage sets about questioning the readers' ideas of emotion. As Alison Winter points out, in their preoccupation with their own 'mental frame', one repeatedly finds Victorian writers monitoring 'their own sensibilities' and speculating 'about the sympathies that bound them'.[48] The reviewer seems clearly aware of the fact that, with this poetry 'dramatic in principle', Browning was attempting something of a new psychological depth. But as he looks back, allusively, to the Wordsworthian 'inner eye', the implication is that poet and reader must always remain confined within their own fields.[49] Browning, then, is figured, Prospero-like, as 'a great conjuror', working to 'turn air into solid'.

The implicit uncertainty that surrounds Browning's enterprise, as figured in this review, is the sense that mimicking, conjuring, performing, and understanding others, are curiously blurred.[50] Such a mixture of understanding and performance runs through Victorian culture.

---

[47] Unsigned, *Athenaeum* (1864), 765.
[48] Alison Winter, *Mesmerized: Powers of Mind in Victorian Britain* (Chicago and London: University of Chicago Press, 1998), 12.
[49] 'that inward eye | Which is the bliss of solitude', 'I wandered lonely' (1807), in Wordsworth, *Poetical Works*, 149.
[50] See Jane R. Goodall, *Performance and Evolution in the Age of Darwin* (London: Routledge, 2003) and Matthew Reynolds, 'Seriously Entertaining', rev. of Goodall, *Times Literary Supplement*, 20 June 2003, 37.

A look at an 1846 poster advertising the forthcoming performance by mesmerist William Davey, offers the academic lure of 'Three Experimental Lectures', together with 'the opportunity of witnessing the greatest wonder of the age':

The Lecturer will explain . . . the locality, use and abuse of the Organs. He will then undertake to produce Mesmeric Sleep, Rigidity of the Limbs, Power of Attraction and Repulsion, and the Transmission of Sympathetic Feelings . . . The Sleepers will perform Vocal and Instrumental Music, Dancing, Talking, Nursing, Eating, Drinking, and other feelings of mirth, imitation and independence, even up to the highest manifestations of benevolence . . . while in the Mesmeric Sleep.[51]

Contemporary accounts of ventriloquists and mimics offer the same ambiguous balance between ideas of psychological penetration and commercial entertainment. The famous mimic and theatre manager Charles Mathews ('Proteus for shape, and mocking bird for tongue') was a fierce defender of his art, claiming to know 'not why the exhibition of an imitator of manners should be classed with the mere grimaces of a buffoon'.[52] In this sense, he seems to follow the claims of philosopher Dugald Stewart that 'the propensity to imitation in human beings represents a principle of "*physico-moral* sympathy which, through the medium of the body, harmonizes different minds with one another"'.[53] Stewart concludes that 'there is often connected with a turn for mimickry a power of throwing one's self into the habitual train of another person's thinking and feeling, so as to be able, on a supposed or imaginary occasion, to support, in some measure, his *character*'.[54]

The philosophical and scientific registers used to describe the pseudo-sciences of mesmerism and ventriloquism bear witness to a more general anxiety relating to how minds might be understood during the period. In some senses, such performances may be seen as demonstrations of power (including powers of understanding). As Jane Goodall points out, 'enactment' may be seen as a way to test where nature set the boundaries between human types, where nature's boundaries 'could be cheated through techniques of mimicry'.[55] However, the tetchy super-

---

[51] See Winter, *Mesmerized*, 115.
[52] See Anne Mathews, *Memoirs of Charles Mathews, Comedian* (London: Richard Bentley, 1838–9), iii. 60.
[53] 'Observations on Ventriloquism', *Edinburgh Journal of Science* (1828), 241–52, quoted in Connor, *Dumbstruck*, 300.
[54] Ibid. 301.
[55] Goodall, *Performance*, 125.

iority of a performer such as Mathews bears witness to the fact that he could never fully reverse 'the hierarchical dynamics of aping'.[56] For while Goodall may perceive that '[i]mitation became a form of critical analysis demonstrating the superiority of the imitator over the imitated', mimicry still carried the shadow of primitivism.[57] A commentator on Mathews's work explicitly differentiates Mathews's approach to imitation from the 'very mean attainment' of savages who were given to copying the manners of strangers.[58] The need to make these distinguishing remarks suggests that mimicking, in the nineteenth century, is seen as a savage act—it is, after all, a cognate of 'aping', a last resort for those with no more sophisticated strategies for relating to other beings. The mesmerists, meanwhile, guarded the authenticity of their own performances, distinguishing themselves from the acts of mimicking and 'imitation' that their mesmeric power supposedly generated in their subjects.

Such ambiguities are important for an understanding of Browning's dramatic monologues, for, as Steven Connor points out, there is a close alliance between the idea of the ventriloquist, or mimic, and that of the dramatic poet:

> Ventriloquists . . . faced and enacted a version of the same aesthetic problem faced by many Romantic and post-Romantic writers: namely, how to balance the imperious claims of the individual, appetitive poetic self and the severalness of the many lives into which he longed to enter and vanish. The longing for what Coleridge liked to call 'multëity' . . . was at once the jeopardy and the cohering glue of the Romantic self.[59]

The monologues in Browning's *Men and Women* and *Dramatis Personae* could be seen as such acts of ventriloquism (A. S. Byatt refers to Browning as 'the great ventriloquist').[60] To a certain extent, these poems also force the reader to become involved in these ventriloquistic acts. For during the process of reading, one is forced to ask exactly *who* is throwing the voice into *whom*, and to ask what the boundary is between imagining the voice of another, and being possessed by them. Some of these discomforting questions find relief through comedy, and Browning makes it hard for us to gauge the level of satire that is directed

---

[56] Ibid. 119. [57] Ibid.

[58] Ibid.; see Mathews, *Memoirs*, 60, 181–2. In *The Voyage of the Beagle* (1839), Darwin commented that the Fuegians demonstrated that besides performing 'hideous grimaces', they would do an astute impersonation of any European, repeating words and gestures 'with perfect correctness', *Voyage*, ed. Kate Hyndley (Hove: Wayland, 1989), 173.

[59] Connor, *Dumbstruck*, 297.

[60] See Picker, *Victorian Soundscapes*, 126.

towards his various 'mediums', such as Abt Vogler, and the enthused speaker of *Christmas-Eve*. One thing is for sure: Browning's poetry is full of intimations that voice-throwing is a dubious experience. A key example may be taken from the Pope's speech in *The Ring and the Book*, when a deacon is asked to stand in and speak for the dead body of a former Pope who has been posthumously accused of corruption. Rewriting the infamous case of the 'Cadaver Synod', Browning describes the way in which the body of the dead Pope is 'exhumed', 'Clothed in pontific vesture now again, | Upright on Peter's chair as if alive':

> Then one, (a Deacon who, observing forms,
> Was placed by Stephen to repel the charge,
> Be advocate and mouthpiece of the corpse)
> Spoke as he dared, set stammeringly forth
> With white lips and dry tongue,—as but a youth,
> For frightful was the corpse-face to behold,—
> How nowise lacked there precedent for this.
>
> 					(*TRB* x. 50–6; p. 478)

This oddly tawdry act of ventriloquism appears to have a strange effect upon the Deacon. As he speaks through, and for, the dead man, his lips turn white, as if his own face is blurring with the 'corpse-face', turning the passage into a piece of neo-Gothic horror.

Any reader who takes on the task of reading *The Ring and the Book* has an analogical relationship with the Deacon, giving voice to the dead as they read, and the way in which both real or literary voice-throwing may be damaging or deathly seems even more clear in 'Mr Sludge, "The Medium"'. Like Childe Roland, Mr Sludge (who was based on the medium D. D. Home), never seems quite real; he 'is just not quite there'.[61] The division between the poet and his creature, the inability of the poetic self to 'vanish', is repeatedly in evidence in Browning's dramatic monologues. In 'Bishop Blougram's Apology', Browning's use of ventriloqual distance is notoriously out of key, as the poet's attempt to mimic Blougram becomes an arena for him to express his own religious doubts. Here, the very title—'Mr Sludge, "The Medium"'—draws attention to the poem's textual nature. By placing the spiritualist's title within quotation marks, Browning indicates a suspicion of his creature's language, a suspicion that gradually casts a shadow over the dramatic

---

[61] See Betty Miller, *Robert Browning: A Portrait* (London: John Murray, 1952), 191.

monologue or 'mediate word' as a whole.[62] On the level of the story, Sludge is forced to explain himself: is he the 'medium' that he purports to be, for his existence relies on the faked voices of others? This uncertainty continues on a meta-fictional level, as Browning gradually reminds the reader that Sludge himself is nothing more than a conjured voice. Browning, here, is touching on basic questions about the ethical responsibilities and necessities of dealing with one's own voice, and those of others. While '[t]ranscendence', as Eric Griffiths writes, may be the experience of finding one's way between worlds in this world, a poem like 'Mr Sludge, "The Medium"', helps us to guard against 'presumptions of identity'.[63]

Sludge has a theatrical ring about him; his 'But, for God? | Ay, that's a question!' (*BCP* i. 842, ll. 792–3), which picks up on Hamlet's 'To be, or not to be' is just one of the Shakespearean echoes that run through the poem.[64] This is a theatrical performance for poet as well as creature, for much of the monologue's interest revolves around some impressive handling of the poem's own 'dangerous edge': the line endings of the verse. Such playful poetic reflexiveness is evident in Sludge's question 'what projects the billiard balls?':

> 'A cue,' You answer: 'Yes, a cue,' said I;
> 'But what hand, off the cushion, moved the cue?
> What unseen agency, outside the world,
> Prompted its puppets to do this and that,
> Put cakes and shoes and slates into their mind,
> These mothers and aunts, nay even schoolmasters?'
>
> (*BCP* i. 844, ll. 895–901)

Sludge's reference to the billiard table derives from David Hume's 'Of the Idea of Necessary Connexion', from his 1748 treatise *An Enquiry Concerning Human Understanding*. Here, Hume notes that our notion of the way in which events unfold is due to a habitual imaginative trait:

The first time a man saw the communication of motion by impulse, as by the shock of two billiard balls, he could not pronounce that the one event was *connected*: but only that it was *conjoined* with the other. After he has observed several instances of this nature, he then pronounces them to be *connected*. What alteration has happened to give rise to this new idea of *connexion?* Nothing but

---

[62] 'Art may tell a truth | Obliquely, do the thing shall breed the thought, | Nor wrong the thought, missing the mediate word.' *TRB* xii. 855–7: p. 628.
[63] Griffiths, *Printed Voice*, 189.   [64] *Hamlet*, iii. i. 55.

that he now *feels* these events to be connected in his imagination, and can readily foretell the existence of one from the appearance of the other.

'No conclusions', Hume goes on, 'can be more agreeable to scepticism than such as make discoveries concerning the weakness and narrow limits of human reason and capacity.'[65] In the case of Browning's poem, the purported answer from the listener—'A cue'—is itself theatrically 'cued' by Sludge. Through the pun, Browning yokes together a scepticism about the connection of causal events with a readerly scepticism. The placing of the word 'cue' means that our belief in the 'silent interlocutor' can be upheld no longer. The notion of the listener is undermined as Browning intimates that he is merely a 'puppet' who acts upon Sludge's promptings. This, in turn, influences our perception of Sludge himself; it reminds us that he is 'cued' by Browning.

Sludge's self-conscious theatricality appears again in Browning's joking references to line endings:

> You'd fain distinguish between gift and gift,
> Washington's oracle and Sludge's itch
> O' the elbow when at whist he ought to trump?
> With Sludge it's too absurd? *Fine, draw the line*
> *Somewhere, but, sir, your somewhere is not mine!*
>
> Bless us, I'm turning poet! It's time to end.
> How you have drawn me out, sir! All I ask
> Is—am I heir or not heir?
>
> (*BCP* i. 851, ll. 1179–86)

For here, 'drawn me out' refers both to the interlocutor's designs on the speaker, and to the poet's designs on the page. As in *The Ring and the Book*, Browning here manages to 'push lines out to the limit', suggesting that the line endings (like those that caught the Duke of Ferrara) are weaving a spell around Sludge.[66] The 'medium' in which the poem was presented was crucial to Browning, the transition of the poem into a printed form enabling him to see, through 'alien charactery', the poem as something *other* than himself.[67] However, the 'printed voice' also

[65] David Hume, *An Enquiry Concerning Human Understanding* (1748), ed. Tom Beauchamp (Oxford: Clarendon Press, 2000), 59.

[66] 'I enter, spark-like, put old powers to play, | Push lines out to the limit', TRB i. 756–7; p. 43.

[67] See Robert Browning, 'To Julia Wedgwood', 1 Feb. 1868, *Robert Browning and Julia Wedgwood: A Broken Friendship as Revealed in Their Letters* (London: John Murray and Jonathan Cape, 1937), 175.

offered Browning an opportunity to keep his creatures to himself—to play with their reality, to show up their printed nature.[68] With this typographic elusiveness in mind, Sludge's question 'am I heir or not heir?' creates an aural pun on 'here', picking up, once more, on his alter ego, Hamlet. John Schad notes these tricks elsewhere in the poem, commenting that 'for Mr Browning, the monologist there is always the possibility that there is no *Horatio* to speak to, never mind ghosts. For Browning, the movement away from the question may lead not to apostrophe but, more terrifyingly, to an unaddressed cry.'[69]

For although the poem appears to offer the reader two figures, that of the speaker and that of the listener, appearances, Sludge points out, can be deceptive: 'Each thing may have two uses. What's a star? | A world, or a world's sun: doesn't it serve | As taper also, time-piece, weather-glass, | And almanac? Are stars not set for signs | When we should shear our sheep, sow corn, prune trees? | The Bible says so' (*BCP* i. 845, ll. 914–19). Sludge claims that the stars are also set as personal signs for him from the Gods. But as the monologue continues, the sense that there is 'no authentic intimation' (*BCP* i. 847, l. 1000) of grace increases. At one point Sludge describes natural phenomena as signs of doom or 'Providence | At work', signifying 'the dread traditional text | O' the "Great and Terrible Name"?' (*BCP* i. 849, ll. 1073–4). Then he notes the way in which 'Preachers and teachers try another tack': 'Thunderbolts fall for neither fright nor sport, | But do appreciable good, like tides, | Changes o' the wind, and other natural facts— | "Good" meaning good to man, his body or soul. | Mediate, immediate, all things minister | To man,— that's settled: be our future text | "We are His children!" ' (*BCP* i. 850, ll. 1130–6).

From a vision of a vengeful God who 'Stoop[s]' to 'child's play' (*BCP* i. 849, l. 1075) with symbols and signs, to that of the 'incessant play of love' (*BCP* i. 850, l. 1138) of the Christian God, Sludge seems to be hinting at a world that is difficult to read. In such an atmosphere it is hard for a reader to hold fast to Sludge's admission of sincerity that 'It's truth! I somehow vomit truth today' (*BCP* i. 842, l. 808). Sludge goes on to argue that he provides a contemporary version of biblical miracles: ' "What was before, may be today. | Since Samuel's Ghost appeared to Saul, of course | My brother's spirit may appear to me" ' (*BCP* i. 843,

---

[68] '(and since he only spoke in print | The printed voice of him lives now as then)', *TRB* i. 176–7; p. 27.
[69] Schad, *Victorians*, 109.

ll. 845.7). He is unconvincing at this point. This is not only because he
has proved himself to be a liar, but because he has pointed out that
language offers a vast arena for moral sliding. Sludge's entire argument
hangs on the possibility of reaching truth, through illusion, by 'analogic
likelihood'. He claims that he has cheated, but only as a movement
towards a greater good. As he puts it:

> If I should lay a six-inch plank from roof
> To roof, you would not cross the street, one step,
> Even at your mother's summons: but, being shrewd,
> If I paste paper on each side the plank
> And swear 'tis solid pavement, why, you'll cross
> Humming a tune the while, in ignorance
> Beacon Street stretches a hundred feet below:
> I walked thus, took the paper-cheat for stone.
>
> (*BCP* i. 854, ll. 1293–1300)

Words like 'truth', as Paul Valéry describes, work within our discourse
like 'thin planks that we throw over a mountain crevasse, only support-
ing a man who moves quickly'.[70] But, for a reader of Browning's
dramatic monologues, both Sludge and his language have been shown
to be so paper thin that one feels uncertain about moving in this way.
In the end, it is not just the truth of Sludge's claims that cannot be
sustained. Our fleeting suspension of disbelief in his existence as a real
figure collapses as the monologue ends. Such difficulties in keeping
literary faith have, as Browning knew, something in common with the
complexities of religious belief.

BROWNING'S CREATURELY BEGINNINGS

Many of Browning's poems show a particular concern with the difficulty
of imagining or sympathizing with what comes before us, with imagining the prime mover. As Herbert F. Tucker has argued, his poems return,
repeatedly, to the question of where a person begins, and to what might
have come before these beginnings. But while Tucker places an emphasis
on the way in which 'character analysis' can shed light on beginnings in
Browning, the model of the fictional creature which I discussed in

---

[70] My trans. See Paul Valéry, 'Poésie et Pensée abstraite', 'une de ces planches légères
que l'on jette . . . sur une crevasse de montagne, et qui supporter le passage de l'homme en
vif mouvement', *Œuvres*, i, ed. Jean Hytier (Paris: Gallimard, 1957), 1314–39, at 1317.

Chapter 1 tells us more about the difficulties of sympathy and distinguishing beginnings in his poems. As I showed there, Browning repeatedly refers to 'creatures' in his work. He was not alone; Nina Auerbach
notes that Victorian art 'specializes in creatures—slippery beings who
exist in some indeterminate stew of orthodox religion, myth, and
literary allusion'. Focusing on the mermaids and serpent women of
Edward Burne-Jones, she argues that 'the crisis of belief that characterized the nineteenth century brought with it unorthodox and sometimes
frightening new vehicles of transfiguration'.[71] She is right to draw
attention to the way in which many of these figures in art are slippery
'anomalies', full of 'hybrid energies', drawn from myth or legend.[72] The
interest in fairies, elves, goblins, and what Andrew Lang termed the
'creatures of mythology' is evident in all the arts.[73] Painters were
particularly drawn to the fairies and monsters from *A Midsummer
Night's Dream* and *The Tempest*, while Etins and dwarves had great
allure for writers, promising to provide an 'uncontaminated record of
our cultural infancy'.[74] Writers and artists of the period specialized in
more everyday creatures too.[75] Browning's poetry has been recognized
as 'packed with more references to animals than probably exist in any
city zoo'.[76] This imagery demonstrates his interest not simply in character (as Park Honan argues), but in what comes before character, in the
creatureliness of humanity. 'The Pied Piper of Hamelin' (included in his
1842 *Dramatic Lyrics*), which combines his sharp anatomical sense with
a touch of the supernatural, as the 'Brown rats, black rats, grey rats [and]
tawny rats' change places with children, captures something central
about Browning's work as a whole (*BCP* i. 386, l. 112). Of course,

[71] See Nina Auerbach's discussion of Victorian art on 'Nina Auerbach's Homepage',
University of Pennsylvania <http://www.english.upenn.edu/%7Enauerbac/>; Auerbach,
Women and the Demon, 7.

[72] Auerbach, *Women and the Demon*, 65.

[73] Andrew Lang, *Encyclopedia Brittanica* 11th edn., 1910–11, quoted in Carole Silver,
Strange and Secret Peoples: Fairies and Victorian Consciousness (Oxford: Oxford University
Press, 1999), 11.

[74] Michael Booth notes that 'throughout the period, the number of paintings of both
plays are extraordinary and the subjects are almost invariably the fairies and spirits (or
monster, in the case of Caliban) among the *dramatis personae*', *The Victorian Spectacular
Theatre* (Boston: Routledge & Kegan Paul, 1981), 35–6. I quote from Andrew Lang, *The
Blue Fairy Book* (London, 1889), p. xii.

[75] For attitudes towards animals in the 19th cent., see Harriet Ritvko, *The Animal
Estate: The English and Other Creatures in the Victorian Age* (Cambridge, Mass.: Harvard
University Press, 1987).

[76] Park Honan, *Browning's Characters: A Study in Poetic Technique* (New Haven: Yale
University Press, 1961), 171.

Browning's linguistic association of man, woman, animal, and creature was common in, but in no way exclusive to, nineteenth-century discourse. But, by an act of serendipitous imagination, he manages to work on this everyday use of 'creature', exposing a contemporary anxiety about beginnings, endings, and transformation.[77] As Dorothy Van Ghent noticed, many of Dickens's novels focus on the way in which characters seem to be on the brink of being translated, prey to 'grotesque transpositions'.[78] Consider a character such as Vholes, in *Bleak House*, who stands on the edge of vampirism as he sucks the life out of, and nearly transforms, Richard Carstone, or Quilp, in *The Old Curiosity Shop* whose borderline existence, part man, part demon, is matched by his strange way with walls, doorways, and thresholds breached.[79] Browning, like his Pied Piper, could be placed alongside the creator of these figures. He makes men and vermin dance to the same tune. Browning also repeatedly considers the religious implications of being a 'creature' in his poetry. For him, as for many of his contemporaries, reading the Higher Criticism revealed cracks in his idea of scriptural authority. As Strauss writes, 'the discourses of Jesus' were 'not seldom torn from their natural connexion, floated away from their original situation and deposited in places to which they did not properly belong'.[80] Browning shows his concern with being out of touch with the direct voice of God in his longer work, *Christmas-Eve and Easter-Day*, written after he had read Strauss in George Eliot's 1846 translation:

[77] Many 19th-cent. writers make use of the word 'creature' to establish social or racial hierarchies. A Texan Baptist church in the 1830s, for example, had two doors; one for white males and the other for 'women and other creatures'. See Joe. E. Trull, 'Women and Other Creatures: The Gender Debate', *Christian Ethics Today* (Apr. 2003), <http:// www.christianethicstoday.com/Issue/010/Women%20And%20Other%20Creatures%20% 20The%20Gender%20Debate%20By%20Joe%20E%20Trull_010_12_.htm>. Isobel Armstrong also notes the 'ambiguous status' of a woman described as a 'creature' in Tennyson's verse. See 'Tennyson in the 1850s: From Geology to Pathology—*In Memoriam* (1850) to *Maud* (1855)', in Philip Collins (ed.), *Tennyson: Seven Essays* (London: Macmillan, 1992), 102–40, at 120.

[78] Dorothy Van Ghent, 'The Dickens World: The View from Todger's', *Sewanee Review*, 58/3 (Summer 1950), 419–38, at 426.

[79] When Vholes in *Bleak House* informs Esther with that 'devouring look of his' that Richard is unwell, his mouth fills with blood as he sits in a corner of the courtroom, and is later to be found 'quite destitute of colour', *Bleak House* (1853), ch. lxv (London: Oxford University Press, 1948), 867–8. I am grateful to Bharat Tandon for pointing this out to me.

[80] David Friedrich Strauss, *The Life of Jesus Critically Examined*, trans. Mary Ann Evans, ed. Peter C. Hodgson (London: SCM, 1973), 342. Strauss discusses 'The Eclectic Christology of Schleiermacher' on pp. 768–73.

> How very hard it is to be
> A Christian! Hard for you and me,
> —Not the mere task of making real
> That duty up to its ideal,
> Effecting thus, complete and whole,
> A purpose of the human soul—
> For that is always hard to do;
> But hard, I mean, for me and you
> To realize it, more or less,
> With even the moderate success
> Which commonly repays our strife
> To carry out the aims of life.
>
> (*BCP* i. 496–7, ll. 1–12)

The ambiguities within this passage highlight the sense in which this speaker is having to construct, or work out, his religious position for himself—constantly aware that this may simply be a simulacrum, merely 'effecting' belief. A less secular version of Wallace Stevens's 'Old Philosopher in Rome', this speaker is an 'inquisitor of structures', unclear whether to 'realize' the presence of God, in the sense of acknowledging and recognizing his presence, or whether God himself must be conceived, and 'realized', through his own words.[81] Browning was reluctant to succumb to the sceptical position. Throughout *Christmas-Eve*, he considers the different ways of considering the central fact of the Christian faith, the Incarnation. The poem begins as the speaker hovers on the threshold of the dissenting 'Zion Chapel', waiting to enter. He has 'very soon had enough of it', appalled by the 'immense stupidity' of the preacher (*BCP* i. 466, ll. 139, 144), and the passive hunger of the congregation, and bursts out into the open air.

   The speaker resists being 'harsh on a single case' (*BCP* i. 469, l. 263), and considers the fact that people worship in different ways. At this point, he sees a rainbow, and then feels the presence of divinity with him. In the next, he finds himself in Rome, and thinks about faith obscured by the 'gross yoke' of tradition (*BCP* i. 478, l. 614). He then has the vision of listening to a lecture by a German Higher Critic, who sets out to prove that no such life as Jesus' 'was liveable' (*BCP* i. 484, l. 861). He finds this Critic's line hard to take: he 'leaves no air to poison | Pumps out with ruthless ingenuity | Atom by atom, and leaves

---

[81] See the final lines of 'To an Old Philosopher in Rome': 'He stops upon this threshold, | As if the design of all his words takes form | And frame from thinking and is realized', *The Collected Poems of Wallace Stevens* (London: Faber, 1984), 511.

you—vacuity' (*BCP* i. 485, ll. 911–13). The speaker then rejoins the
dissenters, realizing the entire experience has been a dream. In the end,
then, his opening sentiment about the dissenters, with their 'mingled
weft | Of good and ill' stands true: 'These people have really felt, no
doubt, | A something, the motion they style the Call of them; | And this
is their method of bringing about . . . | the mood itself' (*BCP* i. 468–9,
ll. 240–7).

This is a passage about a religion based on feeling, and 'A something',
is suitably vague. Browning's use of 'no doubt', here, ironically betrays
the speaker's own hesitation and longing in the face of these people's
conviction. In this sense, *Christmas-Eve* offers a message that demonstrates Browning's coming to terms with the dissenting Nonconformism
espoused by both his mother and by Elizabeth Barrett Browning.
Browning claimed to agree with Barrett Browning's fondness for 'the
simplicity of the dissenters . . . the unwritten prayer, . . . the sacraments
administered quietly & without charlatanism!'[82] But while his poem
shows that he was drawn to the idea of an Evangelical faith of feeling, it
also suggests that he felt more comfortable when unbounded by any
(even dissenting) walls, either literal, or metaphorical.[83] As Devane
argues, his 'lasting choice may be seen in the *Epilogue* to *Dramatis
Personae*, a poem akin to *Christmas-Eve*, where he prefers to worship
outside formal churches altogether'.[84] There, his speaker cries:

> XI
> Why, where's the need of Temple, when the walls
> O' the world are that? What use of swells and falls
> From Levites' choir, Priests' cries, and trumpet-calls?
>
> XII
> That one Face, far from vanish, rather grows,
> Or decomposes but to recompose,
> Become my universe that feels and knows.
>
> (*BCP* i. 865, ll. 96–101)

The speaker's metaphysical vision of the 'Face' that 'decomposes' yokes
together the notion of bodily transience with the idea of having one's
emotions translated into another substance. The sad fact of life's brevity
is supported by the belief in a religion of feeling, while the density of

---

[82] EB to RB, 15 Aug. 1846, Kintner, ii. 962.
[83] RB to EB, 16 Aug 1846, ibid. 969.
[84] William Clyde Devane, *A Browning Handbook* (New York: Appleton-Century-
Crofts, 1955), 199.

Browning's rhymes here, creating a chain of assonance on 'gro<u>ws</u>...
decomp<u>oses</u>...recomp<u>ose</u>...kn<u>ows</u>', provides the conclusion of the
poem with a sense of coherence and integrity, standing for the speaker's
efforts to compose himself. But 'composure' is, as Adam Phillips notes,
'the least innocent of virtues', and Browning was always wary of the
security that man-made compositions and visions might provide.[85] Like
the rock in a whirlpool which he describes as a 'mimic monarch' (*BCP* i.
865, l. 81), Browning continually shows an awareness that his efforts at
composure are just a parody of a larger compositional structure; his
triplets are patterned on the larger rhythm of the trinity.

Browning began to find a way of composing his religious ideas with
the help of the theologian Friedrich Schleiermacher, whose works have a
specific bearing on the ways in which Browning perceives human and
holy relations. W. David Shaw is the only critic to have drawn attention
to the relations between Browning and Schleiermacher. He notes that
'though W. C. DeVane and W. O. Raymond both acknowledge Strauss's
influence on Browning's poem *Christmas-Eve*, the specific influence of
Strauss's commentary on "The Eclectic Christology of Schleiermacher"
has not...been identified or explored'.[86] Schleiermacher, in his 1799
work *Über die Religion. Reden an die Gebilden unter ihren Verächtern*
(translated in 1893 as *On Religion: Speeches to Its Cultured Despisers*), has
been seen as having rediscovered the sense of the holy in the post-
Enlightenment age. He offered a new way of viewing faith as a feeling
or awareness, which was distinct from ethical and rational modes of
perception. He was later to speak of this as man's 'feeling of absolute
dependence' and his work had an enormous influence on later theologians, particularly Rudolf Otto (1869–1937), who took Schleiermacher's idea of 'absolute dependence' and developed the notion of
'creature-feeling' from it.[87] Rudolf Otto focuses on the strangeness
of being a creature in his book *The Idea of the Holy* (first published as

[85] Adam Phillips, *On Kissing, Tickling and Being Bored* (London: Faber, 1993), 40–1.
[86] Shaw, *Lucid Veil*, 209; see Devane, *Browning Handbook*, 201–2 and W. O.
Raymond, *The Infinite Moment and other Essays on Robert Browning* (Oxford: Oxford
University Press, 1950), 29–30. Browning kept a copy of Schleiermacher's *Introduction to
the Dialogues of Plato, translated from German* (London: W. Dobson, 1836) in his library,
inscribed, in his hand, 'EB and RB'. See *The Browning Collections: A Reconstruction with
Other Memorabilia*, comp. Philip Kelley and Betty Coley (Waco: Wedgestone Press,
1984), 172.
[87] See Clements, *Friedrich Schleiermacher*, 100; I quote from Friedrich Schleiermacher, 'Association in Religion', in *On Religion: Speeches to Its Cultured Despisers*
(1799), trans. John Oman (London: Kegan Paul, 1893), 149.

Das Heilige in 1917). For Otto, the mystical experience, or *mysterium tremens*, is described as a feeling of 'creature-consciousness' or 'creature-feeling'. In experiencing 'creature-consciousness', one is aware of a 'self-confessed "feeling of dependence"' which 'must be directly experienced in oneself to be understood'. It is, he notes, 'the emotion of a creature, abased and overwhelmed by its own nothingness in contrast to that which is supreme above all creatures'.[88] As Shaw notes, Browning would have encountered Schleiermacher through Strauss's critical engagement with *On Religion* in *Das Leben Jesu*. In this work, Strauss notes the advantages of what he saw as a 'simplification of the faith' in which Schleiermacher 'sets out from the consciousness of the Christian, from that internal experience resulting to the individual from his connexion with the Christian community, and he thus obtains a material which, as its basis is feeling, is more flexible, and to which it is easier to give dialectically a form that satisfies science':

> As a member of the Christian church—this is the point of departure in the Christology of Schleiermacher—I am conscious of the removal of my sinfulness, and the impartation of absolute perfection [...which...] must be the influence of one who possessed that sinlessness and perfection as personal qualities, and who moreover stands in such a relation to the Christian community that he can impart these qualities to its members...that which we experience [...is...] a strengthening of our consciousness of God.[89]

Strauss claimed that Schleiermacher was 'deceived' in his arguments, but from reading Browning's poetry, it seems that the poet was more convinced. As Shaw notes, 'the more radical side of Schleiermacher's thought...can be found in poems like "A Death in the Desert" and "Saul". Because all dogma must be based on the feeling of dependence, we must infer Christ's nature solely on that ground.'[90] The idea of religion based in feeling, connecting with God on a personal level, would also have appealed to Browning's desire to relocate himself within his firmly dissenting, Evangelical background. Meanwhile, the notion of the dependent 'creature' might shed light on Browning's sense of the ways we try, and fail, to get closer to each other (be that through identification, through sympathy, or through analogy) in literature and in life.

---

[88] Otto, *Idea of the Holy*, 10.   [89] Strauss, *Life of Jesus*, 769.
[90] Shaw, *Lucid Veil*, 209–10.

Much of this failure is linked to the inability of language to match up to feeling. To a certain extent, the words we use are always 'strange', both to us, and to what we wish to express. We are, to a certain extent, speaking with other's words—or *as others*. Browning, like Schleiermacher, was also aware of the way in which '[e]very human being is . . . in the power of the language she speaks; he and his whole thinking . . . are the offspring of it. He cannot . . . think anything that lies outside the limits of language.'[91] ' "Childe Roland to the Dark Tower Came" ' is peculiarly haunted by such a sense of personal and linguistic determination: the 'tempest's mocking elf', the hills 'like giants at a hunting', the echoes of previous 'lost adventurers', hold the speaker in thrall:

> There they stood, ranged along the hill-sides, met
> To view the last of me, a living frame
> For one more picture! in a sheet of flame
> I saw them and I knew them all. And yet
> Dauntless the slug-horn to my lips I set,
> And blew. *'Childe Roland to the Dark Tower came.'*
>
> (*BCP* i. 592, ll. 199–204)

His 'belated quester', Childe Roland, provides a model for those who know what it is to feel dependent.[92] Browning often keeps an ear out for such apparent failures and second chancers in his poetry, for those who seem to have lost their way, which is why, perhaps, both Auden and Beckett find their roots in his world. For with Browning, there came 'the hint of an entirely new and curious type of poetry, the poetry of the shabby and hungry aspect of the earth itself . . . the poetry of mean landscapes'. In answer to the question 'what does the poem of "Childe Roland" mean?', a Lear-like G. K. Chesterton asks: 'What does anything mean? Does the earth mean nothing? Do grey skies and wastes covered with thistles mean nothing? Does an old horse turned out to graze mean nothing? If it does, there is but one further truth to be added— that everything means nothing.'[93] Harold Bloom offers a phrase from Kierkegaard 'to serve as Roland's motto': 'the difference between a man

---

[91] Friedrich Schleiermacher, 'On the Different Methods of Translating' (1813), trans. Waltrud Barthscht, in Rainer Schulte and John Biguenet (eds.), *Theories of Translation: An Anthology of Essays from Dryden to Derrida* (Chicago: University of Chicago Press, 1992), 36–54, at 38.

[92] The phrase 'belated quester' is Harold Bloom's. See *A Map of Misreading* (Oxford: Oxford University Press, 1975), 106.

[93] G. K. Chesterton, *Robert Browning* (London: Macmillan, 1967), 159.

who faces death for the sake of an idea and an imitator who goes in search of martyrdom is that whilst the former expresses his idea most fully in death it is the strange feeling of bitterness which comes from failure that the latter really enjoys.' He comments that the 'great, broken music of the closing stanzas, which *seems* to rejoice in victory, may be only the apotheosis of a poet suffering as poet an apocalyptic conscious-ness of having failed to become himself'.[94] The possibility of Roland being an imitation is highlighted by the poem's allusive 'frame'. His announcement may be a triumphant completion—the heroic act of bringing the poem to its predestined full circle. However, there is a sense in which he might be merely lost for words. Like John Ashbery's dumbstruck narrator, who mounts 'the guillotine | Like Sydney Carton' but 'can't think of anything to say', this speaker clings, stage-struck, to a previous fictional prompt—a snatch from *Lear*, and his poem's own title.[95] The existential concern as to whether he is 'a hero . . . or merely an imitator' revolves, as Barbara Everett comments, around 'the point of the title's being a quotation':

a quotation, what is more, spoken by a character . . . disguised as a madman, and himself giving all the signs of quoting from some ballad or romance. The title acts as one of Browning's 'half-open doors' into long disappearing corridors of quotation upon quotation, the great tradition of poets interlinked one with another only by the high hopelessness of the enterprise they share.[96]

In this sense, 'Childe Roland' can be seen as a paradigm of Browning's interest in creatures. Meanwhile, Browning's quest as a poet has an analogical relationship with Childe Roland's mission. In different ways, both are conscious of being dependent creatures. Through Roland, then, we see the beginnings of Browning's anxiety about either find-ing, or creating, an authentic text which 'echo(es) back over Browning's career'.[97] Woolford takes the poem 'Development' from *Asolando* (1889) in order to examine Browning's own perception of his literary origins. 'We first see the child aimlessly playing. His Father (note the capital) sets about . . . contriving an enactment of *The Iliad* . . . Browning is both introduced to the mediate idiom of Pope, and prospectively

    [94] Bloom, *Map of Misreading*, 107–8.
    [95] John Ashbery, 'The Ongoing Story', in *Selected Poems* (Harmondsworth: Penguin, 1985), 307.
    [96] Everett, *Poets*, 180.
    [97] See John Woolford, 'Sources and Resources in Browning's Early Reading', in Isobel Armstrong (ed.), *Robert Browning: Writers and their Background* (London: G. Bell & Sons, 1974), 1–46, at 42.

seduced by the nicely-figured voluptuousness of the original . . . And he does learn Greek, and with it a mock-Gospel of "facts" about Homer.' But he soon finds there was

> No actual Homer, no authentic text,
> No warrant for the fiction I, as fact,
> Had treasured in my heart and soul so long—
> Ay, mark you! And as fact held still, still hold,
> Spite of new knowledge, in my heart of hearts
> And soul of souls
>
> (*BCP* ii. 920, ll. 71–6)

The memory of the discovery that he could not find an original Homeric text is accompanied by an interesting syntactical hover on the speaker's part, on the words 'fiction I', almost as if his sense of his own reality is faltering. The issue, Woolford argues, 'is grave enough . . . It would be fair, I think, to see the discrediting of Homer, and Renan's questioning of the existence of Christ, as reenactments of a formative dubiety, the polyseimic encroachment of "shades of the prison-house" to spoil an Edenic dream, whether of God, or Homer.'[98] This idea of finding, or creating, an authentic text has an influence on Browning's structural choices. Two critics have noticed Browning's fondness for his 'child-hood's pet book', Francis Quarles's 1632 *Book of Emblems*.[99] Another of his works, *Judgement and Mercy for Afflicted Souls*, shows equally strong ties to Browning's writing. The book of *Meditations, Soliloquies and Prayers* is divided into sections, each of which is governed by a different, degenerate personality, including 'The Sensual Man', 'The Vainglorious Man', and 'The Presumptious Man'. In his 1813 introduction, Reginald Wolfe notes that 'Quarles's plan will be found to be entirely novel, so is the execution of it equally happy. It may be difficult to discover, in the whole compass of English literature, the characteristics of vice or weak-ness more forcibly displayed, or the consolations of religion more efficaciously administered.'[100] In all these early 'dramatic monologues', Quarles attempts to take on the persona of his speaker. 'The Drunkard' in 'His Jubilee' is one such instance:

---

[98] Ibid. 41–3.

[99] See ibid. 39–40, and Victoria Hyde, 'Robert Browning's Inverted Optic Glass in *A Death in the Desert*', *Victorian Poetry*, 23/1 (Spring 1985), 93–6. For mentions of Quarles in Browning's letters see Kintner, i. 241 n., 404, 739, 739 n., and ii. 978, 739.

[100] Francis Quarles, *Judgement and Mercy for Afflicted Souls, or, Meditations, Soliloquies and Prayers*, new edn. (Philadelphia: W. W. Woodward, 1813), p. xxxviii.

What mean these strict reformers thus to spend their hour-glasses, and bawl against our harmless cups? To call our meetings riots, and brand our civil mirth with styles of loose intemperance? . . . My constitution is pot-proof, and strong enough to make a fierce encounter with the most stupendous vessel that ever sailed upon the tides of Bacchus. My reason shrinks not; my passion burns not.

Then the 'consolations of religion' arrive, in the form of passages from Scripture, appropriately chosen for the vice in question, and inserted after each character has spoken. Here, the drunkard's boast is stemmed by warnings:

O but, my soul! I hear a threatening voice that interrupts my language.
Woe be to them that are mighty to drink wine. Isaiah, v. 22.
Wine is a mocker; strong drink is raging, and whosoever is deceived thereby is not wise. Prov xx. 1
Woe be to them that rise up early in the morning to follow strong drink; that continue till night, until wine inflame them. Isaiah, v. 11.
Now I have written unto you, not to keep company, if any that is called a brother be a drunkard; with such a one, no, not to eat. 1 Cor v. 11[101]

This admonition has the effect of forcing the character into a more reflective 'soliloquy' and the section, like all the monologues, closes with the character in repentant prayer. Browning kept a copy of *Judgement and Mercy for Afflicted Souls* in his library, and there are evident similarities of form between his own dramatic monologues demonstrating 'the characteristics of vice or of weakness' and those of his Renaissance forebear.[102] (And Quarles's sensual man seems an exemplary ancestor for Browning's Fra Lippo Lippi.) However, while for Quarles, the biblical texts offered a firm line of both 'Judgement' and 'Mercy' for his fictional creatures, quotation, for Browning, offers a more precarious moral and textual framework.

As Browning has the Pope in *The Ring and the Book* put it, 'of the making books there is no end' (*TRB* x. 9; p. 477). He is citing Ecclesiastes 12: 12 here, and the effect is as if he is calling upon biblical authority and origin to confirm a declaration of the lack of such final authority and ultimate origin. The uncertainty is intensified because this is an allusion not only to the Bible, but also to his wife. The first line of

---

[101] Quarles, *Judgement*, 61–2.
[102] See Kelley and Coley, *Browning Collections*, 194.

Aurora Leigh—'Of writing many books there is no end'—picks up on the same snatch of Scripture. So here, an imagined Pope in seventeenth-century Florence alludes to a fictional poetess in nineteenth-century Britain.[103] Such 'half-open corridors' of quotation are typical of Browning's poetry; for many of Browning's speakers, the beginning is always in doubt. What is more, each speaker seems conscious, like Roland, that they may be an imitator, or a mimic, speaking in quotation marks themselves.

As I have argued, Browning's Cleon is such a one, fearful of being part of a framework larger than himself. This is demonstrated, in part, by his desire to envisage and explain the mysteries of life to King Protus. Cleon writes to Protus that there are, inevitably, things they cannot know about life—'Zeus has not yet revealed it; and alas, | He must have done so, were it possible!' (*BCP* i. 720, l. 335). The three books that Cleon has written on the soul seem to offer him little comfort. But Browning carefully creates the poem so that Cleon falls into patterns that his readers would find both familiar and comforting. Consider his speech about the beauties of civilized nature:

> The grapes which dye thy wine are richer far,
> Through culture, than the wild wealth of the rock;
> The suave plum than the savage-tasted drupe;
> The pastured honey-bee drops choicer sweet;
> The flowers turn double, and the leaves turn flowers;
> That young and tender crescent-moon, thy slave,
> Sleeping above her robe as buoyed by clouds,
> Refines upon the women of my youth.
>
> *BCP* i. 715, ll. 130–7)

Despite the fact that Cleon dismisses the teachings of 'Paulus' (who he presumes is the same as 'Christus') as those of a 'mere barbarian Jew' (*BCP* i. 720, l. 343), he finds himself speaking in Christian rhythms. His poetry, here, takes on the tones and textures of the Song of Solomon in the King James Version.[104] Karshish, who appeared a decade earlier in *Men and Women*'s 'An Epistle Containing the Strange Medical Experience of Karshish, the Arab Physician', finds himself involved in

---

[103] Elizabeth Barrett Browning, *Aurora Leigh* (1856), ed. Margaret Reynolds (New York: W. W. Norton & Co., 1996), 5.

[104] It echoes, for example, 'The flowers appear on the earth; the time of the singing of birds is come, and the voice of the turtle is heard in our land; The fig tree putteth forth her green figs, and the vines with the tender grape give a good smell' (Song Sol. 2: 12–13).

the same web of allusion. In this poem, we learn that the Arab medical researcher has encountered Lazarus, long after the latter was raised from the dead by Jesus, as recounted in John 11: 1–44. Despite writing *before* he could have read the gospels, Karshish alludes to Matthew 6: 28, as he speaks of Lazarus' love of 'old and young, | . . . | flowers of the field' (*BCP* i. 571, ll. 227–9). He also has a Shakespearean quality about him. His name (meaning 'the picker-up of learning's crumbs') echoes *The Winter's Tale*, while he perceives himself as 'not-incurious in God's handiwork'(*BCP* i. 565, ll. 1–2), chiming with *Richard III*.[105] In this sense, with Karshish, Browning gives us not the voice of an Arab physician, but 'an English notion of what an ancient Arab might be'.[106]

Browning's use of the epistolary form (which is comparatively rare in his work) puts even more emphasis on Cleon and Karshish as creatures. Writing is, according to Edward Said, 'a self-estrangement from speech'.[107] Both Cleon and Karshish seem aware of this, and continually attempt to touch their correspondents, bringing their writing closer to the spoken word. As Cleon considers the cup that Protus' 'lip hath bettered ere it blesses' his own mouth (*BCP* i. 712, l. 18), he compliments Protus' ideal letter which he 'read[s] and seem[s] as if I heard thee speak' (*BCP* i. 712, l. 6). Cleon craves the same immediacy. He replicates phrases from Protus' own letter: ' "For" (writest thou) | "Thou leavest much behind, while I leave naught" ' (*BCP* i. 716, ll. 168–70), and reimagines writing as conversation: ' "But," sayest thou—(and I marvel, I repeat | To find thee trip on such a mere word)' (*BCP* i. 719, ll. 301–2). Karshish's letter is also full of attempts to turn writing into speech, as he ends his letter then recommences with the gestural plea, 'Yet stay' (*BCP* i. 567, l. 62), punctuating his writing with asides to Abib, and parenthetical questions—'(dost thou mind?)', 'dost thou think?' (*BCP* i. 569, l. 169; 573, l. 304). Letters, as Janet Altman notes, may function as 'connector(s) between two distant points, as a bridge between sender and receiver', and the 'epistolary author can choose to emphasize either the distance or the bridge'.[108] Both of Browning's correspondents

---

[105] Reynolds notices the allusion to *The Winters Tale*, iv. iii. 26, 'Browning and Translationese', *Essays in Criticism*, 53/2 (Apr. 2003), 97–128, at 102. I refer to Margaret who speaks of Richard as a 'foul defacer of God's handiwork', iv. iv. 51.

[106] Reynolds, 'Browning', 102.

[107] The phrase is, in fact, a mistranslation of Gadamer's 'Selbstentfremdung der Sprache', which would, more correctly, be 'self-estrangement of speech'. See Hans-Georg Gadamer, *Warheit und Methode* (Tubingen: Mohr, 1965), 370–1 and *Beginnings: Intention and Method* (London: Granta, 1997), 205.

[108] Janet Gurkin Altman, *Epistolarity: Approaches to a Form* (Columbus: Ohio State University Press, 1982), 13.

choose the latter; continually attempting to make their text less estranged from the act of conversation, they try to make themselves, more clearly, the authors of their words, guarding against the distortions that may result from the fact that they will be 'still'.

Browning complicates the question of authorship even further. As Reynolds discusses, both of these letters are syntactically strained, as if they have been translated badly, bearing 'the marks of the foreign language which lies behind'.[109] But the question of exactly how many *times* they have been translated is also worth considering. His opening address—'Cleon the poet', 'To Protus in his Tyranny'—(*BCP* i. 712, ll. 1–3) gives the impression that Cleon is physically *writing* a letter (Reynolds refers to him as the 'imagined . . . scribe').[110] However, as the poem progresses, we become increasingly unsure about whether he might, in fact, be dictating his message. Furthermore, it is not clear how this letter will be received. Cleon writes that he will be 'Making this slave narrate thy fortunes' (*BCP* i. 713, l. 39), suggesting that the letter may well be recited back to Protus. Cleon's 'postscript' (in which he addresses Protus' anxieties about the writings of Paul on Christ) gives a strong hint that this document was never physically written by Cleon. The contempt that Cleon shows for 'one called Paulus' who 'writeth, doth he? well, and he may write' (*BCP* i. 720, l. 349) suggests that Cleon himself may be above such activities. Most records reveal that high-born Greeks dictated their missives to 'professional letter writers' or scribes.[111] We can be no more sure about the reception of Karshish's letter. He mentions that he is entrusting the letter to a 'Syrian runagate', whom he has treated for an 'ailing eye' (*BCP* i. 567, ll. 49, 51). The doctor frequently insults this 'ambiguous Syrian' (*BCP* i. 573, l. 299) (who, presumably, cannot understand the language which Karshish is speaking) and accuses him twice of theft. When Karshish 'writes' that the Syrian 'may lose, | Or steal, or give' the letter to Abib 'with equal good' (*BCP* i. 573, ll. 299–300), Browning hints to his readers that Abib may not ever read this letter. He also raises the possibility that we may not be reading the original, but a copy of a stolen text. While it might be simplest, then, to consider both 'Cleon' and 'Karshish' as poetic versions of 'Writing—to

---

109 Reynolds, 'Browning', 99.   110 Ibid. 101.
111 Stanley K. Stowers, *Letter Writing in Greco-Roman Antiquity* (Philadelphia: Westminster Press, 1987), 33.

the Moment', it is crucial to see that they could equally be transcriptions of such writing, traces of originals which have been endlessly recopied.[112]

Such possibilities involve the reader in complex acts of backwards imagining; Eric Griffiths's description of the reciprocity required in reading the letters that passed between Robert Browning and Elizabeth Barrett Browning, sheds some light on the ideal delicacy that such texts require. '[T]hey ask for the imagination and not the illusion of speech . . . the imagination of the writer reaches out both to present a self and to elicit a hearer for the self.'[113] But Browning makes sure that Victorian or modern readers of 'Karshish' and 'Cleon' will have difficulties in doing this. Furthermore, the possibility of truly imagining (or simulating) the situation of these writers, who remain convinced that the Incarnation is a peripheral occurrence, is complicated by our unavoidably ironic perspective. There is a conflict over what Culler refers to as the text's 'presuppositions'—'what a piece of writing assume(s) to take on significance', and the presuppositions of the characters.[114] This conflict is made evident in Browning's use of punctuation. As he ends his letter, firmly reassuring Protus that he should pay no attention to the writings of Paul, Cleon reveals his research methods: 'Oh, the Jew findeth scholars! certain slaves | Who touched on this same isle, preached him and Christ; | And (as I gathered from a bystander) | Their doctrine could be held by no sane man'(*BCP* i. 720, ll. 350–3). The parenthesis (an elocutionary device designed to make a statement seem less important) actually serves to highlight the words it contains: it points to the fact that Cleon's knowledge is founded on little more than a pile of gossip. Karshish is also a 'picker-up of learning's crumbs', and as he spreads them, he presupposes an audience of his own kind—one 'all-sagacious in our art' (*BCP* i. 566, ll. 1, 7), and familiar with medical cases. He goes on to write of the strange behaviour of Lazarus, who has 'a case of mania' which caused him to endure a 'trance prolonged unduly some three days' (*BCP* i. 567, ll. 81, 79). On recovery, he notes that this man is behaving strangely: 'Speak of some trifling fact,—he will gaze rapt | With stupor at its very littleness, | (Far as I see) as if in that indeed | He caught prodigious import' (*BCP* i. 569, ll. 150–3).

[112] Samuel Richardson described 'this new Manner of Writing—to the Moment' in relation to *Clarissa* in a 1756 letter to Lady Bradshaigh. See *Selected Letters of Samuel Richardson*, ed. John Carroll (Oxford: Clarendon Press, 1964), 329.

[113] Griffiths, *Printed Voice*, 204.

[114] Jonathan Culler, *The Pursuit of Signs: Semiotics, Literature, Deconstruction* (London: Routledge & Kegan Paul, 1981), 101–2.

Karshish's parenthesis has a double import. It is, in his terms, a rhetorical conversational gambit, a self-deprecatory turn. But the ironic possibilities of '(Far as I see)' are themselves far-reaching. The lunulae act as joking blinkers around Karshish, pointing to the fact that he cannot see far enough. This felicitous use of brackets, reappearing in his use of '(so to speak)' (*BCP* i. 567, l. 87), points to the fact that Karshish may well not be responsible for his own punctuation, an example of what Bharat Tandon terms a 'typographical "alienation-effect"'.[115] But by giving his fictional creature a turn towards thinking about 'the All-Loving' God (*BCP* i. 573, l. 305), Browning suggests that Karshish gathers more than Cleon, and allows us to gather something too. These dramatic epistles encourage us to think about how much, or how little, we know about other people through texts. Any possibility of unity, or unified sympathy, was, for Browning, always a simulacrum, a creaturely imitation of perfection. However, even creaturely imitation, and failed acts of sympathy, could be dedicated to God. It is to his dedicated mimicry that I now turn.

FAILURES OF READING

For John Ruskin, reading Browning's poems involved too much leaping. 'You are worse than the worst Alpine Glacier I ever crossed', he wrote; 'Bright, & deep enough truly, but so full of Clefts that half the journey has to be done with ladder and hatchet.' In this sense, Ruskin prefigures a deconstructive critic such as John Schad, who argues that the ways in which Browning's poems undercut themselves prove this, and lead to our loss of faith.[116] Schad argues that the arrival of the Higher Criticism brought Browning to a level of textual uncertainty that places him alongside the deconstructionists. Both Browning and Derrida, he notes, 'characteristically seek or describe a movement away from "the Greek origin", a movement away from the authority of reason, truth and, of course, origin'.[117] He goes on to note:

in 'A Death in the Desert'...St John's Gospel is...opened up to interrogation...of Higher Criticism; contradicting his Gospel, John admits, for instance,

[115] Tandon, *Jane Austen*, 101.
[116] See David J. DeLaura, 'Ruskin and the Brownings: Twenty-five Unpublished Letters', *Bulletin of the John Rylands Library*, 54 (1972), 324–7.
[117] Schad, *Victorians*, 79, 81, 80.

that he 'forsook' the arrested Christ . . . John fears that 'My book speaks on' (365); in the words of Roland Barthes 'the Text cannot stop'. This death in the desert is the death of not only *an* author but also *the* Author, the ending of (not only) his book but also *the* Book—as 'parchment', a writing on 'three skins glued together' (2–3), John's Gospel is a book that never was *one*.[118]

In line with the image of a disembodied text, full only of *différance*, John Schad offers a Derridean reading of ' "Childe Roland" ', noting that as 'Roland wanders towards that country he, like Derrida, mimics the detours of . . . writing: he fears that the cripple will "write my epitaph . . . in the dusty thoroughfare" (11–12), "turn(s) aside | Into that ominous *tract*" (13–14) and finally goes where other "strugglers (are) penned". "I had", he declares "been writ | So many times" (37–9)'. It is hard, in fact, to work out how a forever displaced textual play can be *like* anything and Schad's determination to keep Browning within his Derridean theoretical confines is obvious. It is surprising that he does not press on the fact that the 'slug-horn' itself derives from an instance of textual slippage; Browning's misreading of Chatterton's 'slogan', thereby offering the possibility of the idea of the slippage of a phrase.[119]

However, it is wrong to call Browning, in Derridean phrase, a 'poet caught within the error of language', forever destined to repetition, circularity, and meaninglessness. First, because it suggests that there may be some sort of bizarrely anachronistic 'telepathic contact' between the writers.[120] And second, because his dramatic monologues do promise some sort of transcendence. Elinor Shaffer notes that Browning was far from simply an opponent of 'the Higher Criticism'.[121] 'His own Christian apologetics follow lines laid down within the Higher Critical movement itself'.[122] In fact, as the final section of this chapter will show, Browning managed to absorb Higher Critical doubts and integrated them, with the help of Schleiermacher, into a form of faith.

---

[118] Schad, *Victorians*, 81.   [119] See *BCP* i. 1119.

[120] Schad refers to 'the poet caught within the error of language' citing Derrida's *Writing and Difference*, in *Victorians*, 66; Schad seems to be under the influence of J. Hillis Miller here, who 'rhapsodizes about the alleged telepathic contact between Hardy and Derrida'. See Valentine Cunningham, *Reading After Theory* (Oxford: Blackwell, 2002), 117.

[121] E. S. Shaffer, *'Kubla Khan' and the Fall of Jerusalem: The Mythological School in Biblical Criticism and Secular Literature 1770–1880* (Cambridge: Cambridge University Press, 1975), 192. Shaffer cites Drew's *Robert Browning: A Collection of Critical Essays* (London: Methuen, 1966).

[122] Shaffer, *'Kubla Khan'*, 192.

Such casuistical difficulties and solutions emerge in his 1864 dramatic monologue, 'A Death in the Desert', a poem based on St John's Gospel. The poem is set up with a complex frame; we learn that the poem is being recopied by the scribe, whose name contains the letters 'M' and 'E' ('*Mu* and *Epsilon* stand for my own name' (*BCP* i. 787, l. 9)). This scribe tells us that he was married to the niece of a figure called Xanthus, who had in turn tended the dying disciple John. Xanthus could not produce an account of John's death, as he was martyred in Rome ('Was burned, and could not write the chronicle' (*BCP* i. 789, l. 55)). The contents of the manuscript, however, are 'supposed' to be the words of Pamphylax, another of John's attendants, who later recounted John's dying words to his friend Phoebas. We may then guess that Phoebas passed the manuscript on to Xanthus' family. The poem, which takes the form of repeated and recopied texts is, then, a sort of fictional addition to the Gospel of John, and an ironic counterpoint to the Higher Critics, who had claimed that this gospel was entirely, or mostly, fabricated and that 'the literary constructions of the author of the Fourth Gospel are quite apparent and render his account useless as a historical source'.[123]

An unsigned review in 1864 in the *Athenaeum* commended the poem as 'massive and weighty thought, solemnly real and sagely fine': 'It embodies that death of St. John in the desert, and has the piquancy of making the beloved apostle reply with last words, in far-off ghostly tones, which come, weirdly impressive, from that cave in the wilderness, to the Frenchman's "Life of Jesus". It is done simply and naturally but could any sensation-novelist contrive anything half so striking?'[124] The reviewer rightly notes the way in which the poem resembles a sensation novel—the conflicting witnesses, and high body count, require the reader to turn detective in order to locate the truth. But 'truth', as Browning reveals, is hard to find. The Gospel of John ends, as Daniel Karlin notes, with 'an assertion of historical accuracy: "This is the disciple which testifieth of these things, and wrote these things: and we know that his testimony is true" (John 21: 24).'[125] John, as Elinor Shaffer comments, was meant to be 'the direct witness to salvation' for man, according to his gospel. However, according to the Gospel of

---

[123] Peter Hodgson, introd., *Life of Jesus*, p. xxx.
[124] Unsigned, *Atheneaum* (1864), 767.
[125] See Robert Browning, *Selected Poetry*, ed. Daniel Karlin (Harmondsworth: Penguin, 1989), 319.

Mark, John forsook Christ and fled, in the garden of Gethsemane, and Renan picks up John's lie about being at the Crucifixion. For Shaffer the crux of Browning's poem is John's confession of this lie: 'John's confession that he was not, as the Fourth Gospel claims, present at the Crucifixion after all, thereby points to Browning's use of Renan in his conception of the poem.'[126]

> 'Look at me who was present from the first!
> Ye know what things I saw; then came a test,
> My first, befitting me who so had seen:
> "Forsake the Christ thou sawest transfigured, Him
> Who trod the sea and brought the dead to life?
> What should wring this from thee!"—ye laugh and ask.
> What wrung it? Even a torchlight and a noise,
> The sudden Roman faces, violent hands,
> And fear of what the Jews might do! Just that,
> And it is written, "I forsook and fled":
> There was my trial and it ended thus.'
>
> (*BCP* i. 795, ll. 301–11)

Browning, as Shaffer notes, 'adopts Renan's emphasis on this singular particular'. His John, like Renan's, is revealed as a dissimulator: '[b]ut Browning's John is not yet done with his aggrandizement. He makes a claim to have performed a miracle himself.' Here, Shaffer refers to John's claim in Browning's poem that he gave a blind man sight (l. 460), a parody of Jesus' miracle in John 9. Browning was obviously interested in the possibility of John's fiction making. He had read Renan's description in which

not only does the author wish to pass for the apostle John, but we see clearly that he writes in the interest of this apostle. On each page he betrays the desire to fortify his authority, to shew that he has been the favourite of Jesus; that in all the solemn circumstances (at the Lord's supper, at Calvary, at the tomb) he held the first place . . . We are tempted to believe that John, in his old age, having read the Gospel narratives . . . was hurt at seeing that there was not accorded to him a sufficiently high place in the history of Christ.[127]

This newly conceived vision of John as a liar meant that for some, the direct witness to the Crucifixion was lost. The fear was, as Matthew

---

[126] Shaffer, '*Kubla Khan*', 193.

[127] Joseph Ernest Renan, *The Life of Jesus* (London: Trübner, 1864), 288–9. Browning had read Renan. See his letter to Isa Blagden on 19 Nov. 1863, in Edward C. McAleer (ed.), *Dearest Isa: Robert Browning's Letters to Isabella Blagden* (Austin: University of Texas Press, 1951), 180.

Arnold wrote, great. 'Our religion has materialised itself in the fact, in the supposed fact; it has attached its emotion to the fact, and now the fact is failing it.'[128] The result, for Browning, was a poem founded upon doubt. Like many of Browning's epistolary dramatic monologues, 'A Death in the Desert' revolves around the concern to establish 'truth' through the medium of text, constantly blocking a sense that we are reading words that were actually spoken. John 'speaks' of doubt:

> Yet now I wake in such decrepitude
> As I had slidden down and fallen afar,
> Past even the presence of my former self,
> Grasping the while for stay at facts which snap,
> Till I am found away from my own world,
> Feeling for foot-hold through a blank profound,
> Along with unborn people in strange lands,
> Who say—I hear said or conceive they say—
> 'Was John at all, and did he say he saw?
> Assure us, ere we ask what he might see!'
>
> (*BCP* i. 792, ll. 188–97)

As John contemplates his own demise, feeling himself 'away from' his 'own world', he is, ironically, being read by 'unborn people'. Doubt and uncertainty are created for readers in a number of ways. Once again, Browning plays with the potential of the verse paragraph, resisting fulfilment, as if the poetry itself is '[f]eeling for foot-hold' on the page's blankness. It is unclear quite who is writing these words, as they move to the beat of a ghostly iambic pentameter. The phrase 'blank profound' appears, in some ways, to suggest that this poem is a Miltonic creature, just as the reversal of conventional word order, placing the adjective ('profound') after the noun ('blank'), echoes Milton's Latinate inversions. But the grammatical functions of the words could equally be reversed. The tonal blankness of the page allows both possibilities to coexist. And as the poem progresses, Browning offers a series of John's prophetic hypothesizings. John imagines Christian disciples of the future, questioning his word:

> 'Why must I hit of this and miss of that,
> Distinguish just as I be weak or strong,
> And not ask of thee and have answer prompt,

---

[128] Matthew Arnold, 'The Study of Poetry', in *Essays in Criticism*, 2nd ser. (London: Macmillan, 1888), 1.

> Was this once, was it not once?—then and now
> And evermore, plain truth from man to man.
> Is John's procedure just the heathen bard's?'
>
> (*BCP* i. 800, ll. 525–30)

Elinor Shaffer goes on to note that 'Perceptual skepticism . . . was closely bound up with higher critical apologetics. The inaccessibility, the uncertainty of what really happened . . . characterize all historical events because we cannot perceive in any other way.'[129] The parallel between poetry and prophesy, here, suggests a degradation of the word of God. John's answer, however, revolves around the necessity for man's word to be indirect: 'God's gift was that man should conceive of truth | And yearn to gain it, catching at mistake, | As midway help till he reach fact indeed' (*BCP* i. 802, ll. 605–7). 'God only makes the live shape at a jet. | Will ye renounce this pact of creatureship? | The pattern on the Mount subsists no more, | Seemed awhile, then returned to nothingness; | But copies, Moses strove to make thereby, | Serve still and are replaced as time requires: | By these, make newest vessels, reach the type!' (*BCP* i. 803, ll. 623–9).

The 'pact of creatureship' is crucial to Browning—and it is crucial that he describes the pact in terms of the reception and transmission of texts (punning on printed 'type' and biblical typology and playing once again on the idea of literary 'stillness', with 'Serve still'). To be a creature, it seems, is to be destined to read things only second-hand, never to hear the direct voice. Nor, it seems, is one able to speak directly to others. The original 'pattern on the Mount'—the design for the tabernacle—no longer exists, but copies suffice. As the scribe ('M' 'E') transcribes:

> many look again to find that face,
> Beloved John's to whom I ministered,
> Somewhere in life about the world; they err:
> Either mistaking what was darkly spoke
> At ending of his book, as he relates,
> Or misconceiving somewhat of this speech
> Scattered from mouth to mouth, as I suppose.
>
> (*BCP* i. 803–4, ll. 654–60)

The poem, here, picks up on the hope of the New Testament from St Paul's letter to the Corinthians: 'For now we see through a glass darkly; but then face to face' (1 Corinthians 13: 11). However, it is overshadowed

---

[129] Shaffer, *'Kubla Khan'*, 210.

by the sense of things 'darkly spoke'—a reference to the 'dark speech' of the fourth chapter of Numbers, in which Miriam and Aaron complain about God's exclusive conversations with Moses when he appears from a pillar of cloud. God replies: 'My servant Moses is not so, who is faithful in all mine house. With him will I speak mouth to mouth even apparently, and not in dark speeches, and the similitude of the Lord shall he behold: wherefore then were ye not afraid to speak against my servant Moses?' Frank Kermode notes that 'the Greek for "dark speeches" means parables'—a narrative form which 'is, first, a similitude'.[130] And there is a sense in which 'A Death in the Desert' revolves around the difficulties of interpretation through such darkness and similitudes—asking a key question about whether it is possible to reach God through indirection. The vision of the direct voice, of being 'incorporate with all', is, for Browning, certainly God's alone. But the 'pact of creatureship' invoked in 'A Death in the Desert' necessarily entails some element of contractual *understanding*. For Browning, despite the failures of meaning of the dramatic monologue, be they the failures of Sludge or of John, there is the possibility of understanding the pact of creatureship itself, which is that fact that man is dependent, reliant on parables, similitudes, and analogies—and that he feels this fact.

Browning was, like his Pompilia, ever conscious that things 'on earth' are 'counterfeit, | Mere imitation of the inimitable' (*TRB* vii. 374–5; p. 375). He reveals this in 'A Death in the Desert' through slyly undercutting our belief in the scribe, whose initials 'Mu' and 'Epsilon' reveal that Browning himself is the author, a preoccupation with forgery that, as John Woolford notes, ran throughout his career.[131] This 'pact of creatureship' drove Browning to create texts that explicitly demonstrated failures of sympathy. Their 'feeling of dependence' is the fact that they are counterfeit, acts of mimicry, not incarnation.

BROWNING AND SHAKESPEARE

This pact of creatureship is, perhaps, most clearly shown in the 1864 dramatic monologue 'Caliban upon Setebos; or, Natural Theology in the Island' which has been said to contain 'an expression of Browning's

---

[130] Frank Kermode, *The Genesis of Secrecy: On the Interpretation of Narrative* (Cambridge, Mass.: Harvard University Press, 1979), 25, 23.
[131] Woolford, 'Sources', 89.

own opinion on certain religious questions of considerable importance'.[132] Like many of Browning's poems, 'Caliban upon Setebos'
encourages readers to consider how we theorize about, or simulate,
the experience of others. When considering any nineteenth-century
writer's thoughts on questions of beginnings, origins, and imitation,
their relations with Shakespeare prove interesting. As Nina Auerbach
argues, Shakespeare was, to many Victorians, 'the supreme instance of
the artist as magus, revered as his own Prospero creating flights of
imperishable characters'. For readers of the nineteenth century, this
had profound implications. It suggested that despite the religious uncertainties of the time, there was the possibility of 'immortal life'
through transfiguration into fictional character.[133]

Browning was repeatedly styled by the Victorian literary community
as the Shakespeare of his day (a title he did not attempt to shirk). 'For at
least twenty years', Robert Sawyer notes, 'Robert Browning had carefully manipulated his public image in order to borrow Shakespeare's
cultural authority.'[134] For some contemporary reviewers, it seemed that
Browning had succeeded in 'Shakespeareanizing' himself. As Oscar
Wilde noted, 'Browning is the most Shakespearian creature since
Shakespeare', and an anonymous reviewer in the *Athenaeum* seemed
to agree, claiming that the 'revelation of what "Caliban" "thinketh"
would have delighted Shakspeare himself, who would have been the first
to have acknowledged that it faithfully represented the inner man of his
original creation'.[135] It is also notable that 'Caliban upon Setebos'
appeared in the year of the tercentenary of Shakespeare's birth (although
the poem was possibly composed earlier, in 1859).[136] This comment,
which recalls Prospero's acknowledging his thing of darkness, emphasizes the feeling that there was a poetic sympathy between Browning and
Shakespeare. However, what Browning's poem provides is a complex

[132] C. R. Tracey, 'Caliban upon Setebos', *Studies in Philology*, 35 (July 1938), 487–99,
at 487–8.
[133] Auerbach, *Women and the Demon*, 190.
[134] Robert Sawyer, 'The Shakespeareanization of Robert Browning', in Christy Desmet and Robert Sawyer (eds.), *Shakespeare and Appropriation* (London: Routledge,
1999), 142.
[135] Unsigned, *Athenaeum* (1864), 767. See Devane, *Browning Handbook*, 299. For
details of the Shakespeare Tercentenary, see Adrian Poole, *Shakespeare and the Victorians*
(London: Thomson, 2004) and Richard Foulkes (ed.), *Shakespeare and the Victorian
Stage* (Cambridge: Cambridge University Press, 1986).
[136] See Devane, *Browning Handbook*, 299. For details of the Shakespeare Tercentenary, see Poole, *Shakespeare and the Victorians*, and Foulkes (ed.), *Shakespeare and the
Victorian Stage*.

exploration of these relationships with Shakespeare and the possibilities of sympathy between the two authors. Indeed, Caliban's natural theology has an implicit parallel in Browning's use of Shakespeare. Browning had a number of works debating Shakespeare's texts in his library, and in this poem he is attempting to reach back to find the voice of the bard, in a similar way to the manner in which Caliban is groping to find the presence of Setebos.[137] But there is, meanwhile, a parodic aspect to Browning's attempt to 'be' Shakespeare. As John Woolford comments, Browning made a number of changes to the manuscript of the poem before it was printed, which included 'the introduction into the first edition of a series of *graphic signs* to the punctuation and layout of the poem', in which 'capitals and apostrophes are decisively emphasised' while the 'italics and square brackets—are unique to the first edition'.[138] These changes are notable because, as Woolford argues, they are 'unequivocally graphic signs, superimposed upon a sequence of speech which remains, so to speak, unaware of them . . . their effect is to play off the convention that the poem is *spoken* against the fact that it is *printed*'.[139] In this sense, as with 'Cleon' and 'Karshish', Browning produces a poem about a highly *textual* creature—a mere imitation of Shakespeare's transcendent, immortal creatures. Like Sludge, he is reliant on his medium. The poem's epigraph, 'Thou thoughtest I was altogether such a one as thyself', is, then, among other things Browning's self-reproach. It draws attention to the fact that Browning cannot incarnate Shakespeare—this is, to a certain extent, another burlesque. In producing a figure who utters 'pithy, cramped, and sybilline insights in Shakespearean pentameters', Browning shows himself to be a mimic, or—rather like his own Caliban—an ape.[140]

The original scene in *The Tempest* finds a disgruntled Caliban lugging wood, and cursing his master's powers:

> All the infections that the sun sucks up
> From bogs, fens, flats, on Prosper fall, and make him
> By inch-meal a disease! his spirits hear me,
> And yet I needs must curse. But they'll nor pinch,

---

[137] See Kelley and Coley, *Browning Collections*, 176, 206, 25, 54, 63, 84, 134.

[138] John Woolford, 'Self-Consciousness and Self-Expression in Caliban and Browning', in id. (ed.), *Robert Browning in Contexts* (Winfield, Kan.: Wedgestone Press, 1998), 86–100, at 96.

[139] Ibid. 97.

[140] Gillian Beer, *Open Fields: Science in Cultural Encounter* (Oxford: Oxford University Press, 1996), 32.

> Fright me with urchin-shows, pitch me i'th'mire,
> Nor lead me, like a firebrand, in the dark
> Out of my way, unless he bid 'em

(II. ii. 1–7)

Browning's Caliban echoes this lexicon of fearful cursing. The poem consists of his speculation about his origins, his existence, and Setebos, the god worshipped by his 'dam', the witch Sycorax, as he sprawls 'Flat on his belly in the pit's much mire, | With elbows wide, fists clenched to prop his chin' (*BCP* i. 805, ll. 2–3). Critics of the poem cannot make up their mind quite what sort of creature Browning's Caliban is meant to be, and whether he demands our compassion or our contempt. Park Honan describes him as 'probably not a human being... he seems to be an anthropoid animal, capable of speech'.[141] In this case he figures as man's ancestor, and the poem should be read in the light of Darwin. William Devane also argues that 'the starting point of *Caliban* was Darwin's *Origin of Species*, which set Browning thinking of primitive man, perhaps of the "missing link", a popular phrase of the 1860s'.[142] Michael Howard agrees, arguing that 'Caliban upon Setebos' is a poem of sympathy for this missing link, as this metaphysician's 'struggle for knowledge is limited by his own sensibility'. Howard proposes that Caliban's ability 'to see only parallel relationships' reflects Browning's feelings for man's own defective understanding of God.[143] For Devane, the poem is less sympathetic:

> Fired by the conception of half-man, half-beast, Browning's mind leapt to the literary anticipation of such a creature—the figure of Caliban in Shakespeare's late play, *The Tempest*. Being Browning, he gave Caliban an interest in theology... and... made the poem a timely satire upon all those people who, having no revelation of God save that afforded by reason, insist upon creating Him in their own human image without admitting the limitations of their conception.[144]

Here, Devane also joins a number of critics who argue that the poem was a satire upon works of natural theology, such as Paley's *Natural Theology; or, Evidence of the Existence and Attributes of the Deity* (1802) and *The Bridgewater Treatises* (1833–40), which attempted to prove the existence of God through his presence in the visible world. Devane also

---

[141] Honan, *Browning's Characters*, 120.
[142] Devane, *Browning Handbook*, 299–300.
[143] 'the reader eventually tends to sympathise [with Caliban]', Michael Howard, 'Caliban's Mind', *Victorian Poetry*, 1 (1963), 249–57, at 257, 256, 254.
[144] Devane, *Browning Handbook*, 299–300.

notes that the poem may have been inspired by Browning's friend Theodore Parker, whose satirical tract on 'A Bumblebee's Thoughts on the Plan and Purpose of the Universe' aimed to expose the weaknesses of natural theology, and overly anthropomorphic approaches to natural history. Gillian Beer joins them, claiming that the poem is written against the same 'arrogant' anthropomorphism that Darwin had mocked in his *Notebooks*.[145] Caliban's own attempts at natural theology do seem to demonstrate Parker's warning thesis that 'a man rude in spirit must have a rude conception of God. He thinks the deity like himself. If a buffalo had a religion, his conception of a deity would probably be a buffalo.'[146] Take the way he metes out justice to the sea-life, assuming that Setebos must have the same brutal approach to his creatures as Caliban himself:

> 'Thinketh, such shows nor right nor wrong in Him,
> Nor kind, nor cruel: He is strong and Lord.
> 'Am strong myself compared to yonder crabs
> That march now from the mountain to the sea,
> 'Let twenty pass, and stone the twenty-first,
> Loving not, hating not, just choosing so.
> 'Say, the first straggler that boasts purple spots
> Shall join the file, one pincer twisted off;
> 'Say, this bruised fellow shall receive a worm,
> And two worms he whose nippers end in red;
> As it likes me each time, I do: so He.
>
> (*BCP* i. 807, ll. 98–108)

The inability of critics to decide whether the poem intends us to satirize or sympathize with Caliban (and their determination that it must be one or the other) results from certain misunderstandings about the poem itself. Just as, on a small scale, Browning creates an ambiguity over Caliban's use of 'just' ('just choosing so'), which could mean 'simply', or 'merely', but could also be an indication of his sense of the almost divine, objective fairness of his actions, he allows the poem to sustain the possibility that he may be satirizing or sympathizing with Caliban (or perhaps both). The reader cannot be certain, for the poem centres on the notion of frustrated understanding and distance given in its epigraph: 'Thou thoughtest I was altogether such a one as thyself.'

---

[145] Gillian Beer, 'Darwin's Reading' in David Kohn (ed.), *The Darwinian Heritage* (Princeton: Princeton University Press, 1985), 543–88, at 579.
[146] *BCP* i. 1158.

Browning's Caliban survives by the making of 'new world[s]' (*BCP* i. 811, l. 245) to understand his own predicament, lording it over 'his Ariel a tall pouch-bill crane' and reasoning that if he himself 'Taketh his mirth with make-believes: so He' (*BCP* i. 809, ll. 161, 169). Analogy works on another level as well, as the question of whether 'He' (Setebos, Caliban's god), is cruel or kind finds its analogy in the critical debate as to whether Browning is satirizing or sympathizing with his creature—or whether, as the 'creator', he is *able* to sympathize with his creature. Caliban's difficulties in finding God's design in the natural world are mirrored by the way in which he is woven into the pattern of Browning's verse. It is, as John Killham puts it, 'the old parallel between an artist and God: both are creators and lawgivers in their created worlds'.[147] The parallel between the artist and the God is heightened by Browning's poetic apparatus. The epigraph to 'Caliban upon Setebos' is from Psalm 50, in which an unsympathetic and unsympathizing God warns mankind to praise him in a correct manner:

14 Offer unto God thanksgiving; and pay thy vows unto the Most High:
15 And call upon me in the day of trouble: I will deliver thee, and thou shalt glorify me.
16 But unto the wicked God saith, What hast thou to do to declare my statutes, or that thou shouldest take my covenant in thy mouth?

.   .   .   .

21 These things hast thou done, and I kept silence; thou thoughtest that I was altogether such a one as thyself: but I will reprove thee, and set them in order before thine eyes.
22 Now consider this, ye forget God, lest I tear you in pieces, and there be none to deliver.
23 Whoso offereth praise glorifieth me: and to him that ordereth his conversation aright will I shew the salvation of God.

As I have shown, critics obviously find the level of satire and sympathy in the poem hard to gauge. One of Browning's contemporaries, J. Cotter Morrison, notes that the poem is a 'scathing satire of a rather painful class of reasoners who, while beginning with the admission that the nature of the Godhead is an inscrutable mystery, proceed to write long books to prove their special and minute knowledge of its character'.[148]

---

[147] John Killham, 'Browning's "Modernity": *The Ring and the Book* and Relativism', in Isobel Armstrong (ed.), *The Major Victorian Poets: Reconsiderations* (London: Routledge, 1969), 153–70.
[148] J. Cotter Morrison, '"Caliban upon Setebos" with some Notes on Browning's Subtlety and Humour', *Browning Society Papers*, l (1881–4), 489–98, at 494.

Meanwhile, C. R. Tracey warns that one 'must beware of seeing a satirical warning against anthropomorphism' in the poem.[149]

There are a number of problems with perceiving the poem either as a satire on natural theologians and anthropomorphists, or as a poem of sympathy for the 'missing link'. The latter reading is tempting, attracting both contemporary critics (most famously Daniel Wilson, in his 1872 work, *Caliban: The Missing Link*, as well as more recent critics, such as Gillian Beer and Alden and Virginia Vaughan).[150] However, there is no evidence that Browning actually intended this poem to be read in relation to the idea of the 'missing link'.[151] Therefore, Wilson's claim that Browning recognized that Shakespeare had pre-empted scientific naturalists by some two and a half centuries, is unfounded.[152] Browning's copy of Daniel Wilson's *The Missing Link* that he kept in his library is notably inscribed 'still unread!'.[153] On the other hand, as De Graef notes, 'to interpret Caliban' as Michael Timko does, 'as a satirical version or a monstrous antetype of Butler or Paley, is equally problematic . . . For . . . was Caliban ever a natural theologian, let alone . . . a human being in the first place?'[154] De Graef is not alone in locating the point of the poem in relations between the reader and the text. Joseph A. Dupras comments that '[t]he process of reading the poem, like the process of writing it, involves boldly resisting dominance and anxiously daring authority to assert itself in order to compose a text that is never fully composed'.[155] That is to say, the poem encourages us both to read it and fit it into familiar frameworks, or make analogical comparisons, and to resist such readerly actions. 'Caliban upon Setebos' demonstrates the Cavellian dilemma discussed in Chapter 1; we cannot 'simulate' the experiences of the creatures we read about—we can only parody such simulations, and theorize about the texts.

---

[149] Tracey, 'Caliban upon Setebos', 492.

[150] See Daniel Wilson, *Caliban: The Missing Link* (London, 1872); G. Beer, 'Darwin's Reading'; Alden T. Vaughan and Virginia Mason Vaughan, *Shakespeare's Caliban: A Cultural History* (Cambridge: Cambridge University Press, 1991).

[151] As G. Beer admits, 'we do not know for certain whether Browning was reading Darwin between 1859 and 1864', 'Darwin's Reading', 550.

[152] D. Wilson, *Caliban*, 26.

[153] Kelley and Coley, *Browning Collections*, 208.

[154] Ortwin De Graef, 'Browning Born to Wordsworth: Intimations of Relatability from Recollections of Early Monstrosity' in N. Lie and T. D'haen (eds.), *Constellation Caliban* (Amsterdam: Rodopi, 1997), 113–43, at 134.

[155] Joseph A. Dupras, 'The Tempest of Intertext in "Caliban upon Setebos"', *Concerning Poetry*, 19 (1986), 75–88, at 75.

In the end, Browning's strongest link with Shakespeare was their similar understanding of what it might be to be 'strange'. With its resonances of foreignness or liminality, the word 'strange' haunts *The Tempest*, appearing more times in this play than in any of his others. It is also a word that characterizes Browning's religious dramatic monologues, in particular, 'An Epistle Containing the Strange Medical Experiences of Karshish, the Arab Physician', as Karshish mulls over the story of Lazarus:

> The very God! think, Abib; dost thou think?
> So, the All-Great, were the All-Loving too—
> So, through the thunder comes a human voice
> Saying, 'O heart I made, a heart beats here!
> Face, my hands fashioned, see it in myself!
> Thou hast no power nor mayst conceive of mine,
> But love I gave thee, with myself to love,
> And thou must love me who have died for thee!'
> The madman saith He said so: it is strange.
>
> (*BCP* i. 573, ll. 304–12)

The confusion of this final line is typical of Browning's monologues; we are left uncertain as to whether the final words—'it is strange'—are those of Karshish, appearing in a dictated letter and referring to the oddity of the Christian faith, or those of Lazarus quoting Jesus, who has declared that the Christian life itself 'is strange'.

Things, as always, are not easy for us to understand, and Browning's twin attempts to seek similarity and resist easy understanding, are entwined in both his religious and his everyday existence. He had, he admitted, an 'odd liking' for 'strange' creatures. And within the dramatic monologue 'Caliban upon Setebos', we see Browning attempting to set him up for himself, to confuse a reader who tries to familiarize or draw analogies. Browning wants to make him strange, and to keep him strange. Strangeness in Browning's poetry also functions on a textual level. The 'difficulty' that incited so much criticism makes his poetry the stuff of a perplexing borderland, a perplexity that affects both his subject matter and the quality of his language. Such perplexity bears witness to his heroic struggle with epistemological uncertainty—his sceptical attempt to make one realize that one is unable to be certain about what someone else is experiencing, that one cannot transcend the self.

It was not a struggle that Browning always won. As Browning's friend Eliza Flower noted, transcending the self to create another life, and allowing that life a life of its own, was always, ultimately, beyond Browning's grasp. It is, she writes, that 'egoism of the man, and the pity of it'. Teasingly parodying Browning's own disclaimer to *Dramatis Personae* (in which he refers to the poems as 'so many voices' in tones both nonchalant and preening), she notes that 'He cannot metempsychose with his creatures, they are so many Robert Brownings'.[156] This is not a failure that was peculiar to Browning, but he was peculiarly sensitive to his failings. He wrote to Elizabeth Barrett Browning that he had been 'all my life asking what connection there is between the satisfaction at the display of power, and the sympathy with—ever increasing sympathy with—all imaginable weakness?'[157] The connection, it seems, is the fact that, however much sympathy a human attempts to feel, this sympathy inevitably turns into thinking that the other is, in the words of the epigraph to the poem, 'such a one as thyself'. Sympathy, in human terms, is more akin to mimicry, a display of power, and such powers are evidence of human weakness. In considering 'Caliban upon Setebos', Devane notes that 'one must be careful in ascribing . . . satire of such anthropomorphism to Browning, since he saw the human need for such thinking'.[158] It is this 'human need' which explains why one can defend 'Caliban upon Setebos' as a sympathetic poem, and Browning as a poet who believes in the possibility for sympathy of a specifically 'creaturely' sort, while understanding that this is imbued with doubt. A poem such as 'Cleon' was written in response to Matthew Arnold's fear in 'Empedocles upon Etna' that 'the gods mock us'.[159] But mocking can be kind as well as cruel. Sometimes, when in difficulties, it is the only way we can attempt understanding. Mrs Sutherland Orr writes that Browning once said that he knew 'the difficulty of believing'. He knew

'all that may be said against it, on the ground of history, of reason, of even moral sense. I grant even that it may be a fiction. But I am none the less convinced that the life and death of Christ, as Christians apprehend them, supply something which their humanity requires, and that it is true for them'. He then proceeded to say why, in his judgment, humanity required Christ. 'The evidence of Divine

---

[156] Quoted in *The Poems of Robert Browning*, ed. John Woolford and Daniel Karlin, ii (London: Longman, 1991), 17.

[157] RB to EB, 16 Nov. 1845, Kintner, i. 271.

[158] Devane, *Browning Handbook*, 300.

[159] 'Mind is a light which the Gods mock us with', *Empedocles on Etna: A Dramatic Poem*, I. ii. 32, in *The Poems of Matthew Arnold*, ed. Kenneth Allott (London: Longman, Green & Co., 1965), 157.

power is everywhere about us; not so the evidence of Divine love. That love could only reveal itself to the human heart by some supreme act of *human* tenderness and devotion; the fact, or fancy, of Christ's cross and passion could alone supply such a revelation.'[160]

For Browning, the perfection of the incarnation was the idea that God 'mocks' us in an entirely different way. Condescending to work on human terms, he takes on the idea of mimicking (as man can only understand through likeness) but manages to become 'such a one as thyself'.

---

[160] Mrs Sutherland Orr, 'The Religious Opinions of Robert Browning', *Contemporary Review*, 60 (Dec. 1891), 876–91, at 879.

3

W. H. Auden: 'as mirrors are lonely'

KNOWING YOURSELF:
BIG BABIES AND THE FAIRY TALE

In late 1941 Donald Pearce attended a series of W. H. Auden's lectures entitled 'Fate and the Individual in European Literature'. Auden asked his students not to take notes. Pearce kept a few on the sly, recording the final lecture on *The Tempest*:

'All literature is allegory', he was saying, 'You only know yourself, your own reactions . . . When you read, what you see is yourself in different situations . . . yourself as different persons . . . Your knowledge of the world is wholly within yourself . . . Poems, fictions, merely tap it and let it out. One's knowledge of Shakespeare is strictly commensurate with one's experience of life.'[1]

Writing nearly a century after Robert Browning, and during a world war, Auden found himself facing new theological and political concerns. His return to the Anglican faith in 1940, together with the death of his mother in 1941, meant that he spent a good deal of time reading theology. He was particularly drawn to works by Kierkegaard, Niebuhr, Tillich, and Otto. Barbara Everett notes that, by 1940, his 'attempts to secure a new certainty of belief and tone' took him into 'a new decade, a new continent, and—theologically speaking—a new world'.[2] Everett's nod towards Miranda suggests some of the ways in which Auden was listening to tones from the past, as well as new voices. While struggling with uncertainties about the relations between art and religion, he found solace and sympathy in the old 'new world' of *The Tempest*, a work which raises questions about the ethical responsibilities of the artist,

---

[1] Donald Pearce, 'A Fortunate Fall: W. H. Auden at Michigan', in Alan Bold (ed.), *W. H. Auden: The Far Interior* (London: Vision, 1985), 129–57, at 129, 148–9.
[2] Barbara Everett, *Auden* (Edinburgh: Oliver & Boyd, 1964), 65.

and, with its island setting, the difficulties of understanding others. As Mendelson notes, whenever Auden 'needed an emblem for his separation from responsibility, audience, love, history, all that is real outside the mind's chamber, he invoked the solitary island. This was both the image of isolation and its etymological source, the *isola*.'[3]

Auden's most succinct expression of his concerns is found in his 1962 essay 'Postscript: Christianity and Art': 'No artist... can feel comfortable as a Christian... No artist, *qua* artist, can understand what is meant by *God is Love* or *Thou shalt love thy neighbor*.'[4] But these anxieties emerged far earlier. His 1941 'New Year Letter' has the formal pedigree of religious uncertainty, being based on the 'sparkling octosyllabics' of Browning's *Christmas-Eve*.[5] Here, as Mendelson points out, 'its syntax and meter struggled to restrain the anarchic whirlwind of its ideas'.[6] It was not a metre that Auden felt happy with, and the next five years mark a period of intense formal experimentation leading to *For the Time Being*, *The Sea and the Mirror*, and *The Age of Anxiety*. Postscripts of a different kind, each draws on a pre-existing literary source; the first is a *Christmas Oratorio* based on the nativity, the second *A Commentary on Shakespeare's The Tempest*, the third a variation upon the *Baroque Eclogue*. These long poems of the forties are also variations upon the dramatic monologue. They rely on the discrepancies between print and voice, and in each, characters take turns to speak, unwittingly finding their conversational rhythms absorbed into metrical form. Sometimes Auden's cast appear to be in dialogue, but they often end up talking to themselves. HEROD in *For the Time Being* complains 'I've tried to be good. I brush my teeth every night... I'm a liberal', PROSPERO the 'late and lonely master' in *The Sea and the Mirror* is ignored by his sidekick ARIEL, and the loners in *The Age of Anxiety* rarely seem to converse, merely catching each others' 'unrelated | Groans' (*ACP*, 394, 405, 512). For any poet struggling with concerns about responsibility, theology, and solipsism, the dramatic monologue form would hold an attraction. Its focus on individual rather than abstract experience forces a reader to interpret life with an awareness of the self's subjectivity. Auden was thinking deeply about the difficulties of such interpretative transitions, arguing that 'you cannot tell people what to do, you can only tell them parables... particular stories of particular people and experiences, from

[3] Edward Mendelson, *Early Auden*, 335.   [4] *DH*, 456.
[5] Everett, 'Auden Askew', *Poets*, 167.   [6] Edward Mendelson, *Later Auden*, 100.

which each according to his immediate and peculiar needs may draw his own conclusions' (*EA*, 341).[7]

By November 1942 he wrote that as 'a writer, who is also a would-be Christian, I cannot help feeling that a satisfactory theory of Art from the standpoint of the Christian faith has yet to be worked out'.[8] For Auden, as for many other writers, *The Tempest* offered the opportunity to ask questions about other selves and other minds, including the mind of God. As John Fuller argues, *The Sea and the Mirror* provides 'a semi-dramatized discussion of the relationship between life and art in the context of spiritual possibility', beginning with Prospero's 'Epilogue':

> Prospero's words are, of course, a kind of pun, an actor's appeal for applause, but for Auden their suggestion that the artist as a maker of illusions is in need of supernatural grace when his belief in these illusions has shattered, is a powerful one. It is one which is heavily reinforced by the allegorical interpretations of *The Tempest* which circulated in the nineteenth century, that Prospero is the artist, Ariel his imagination, Caliban his animal nature . . . If we accept a crude identification of Prospero with Shakespeare, then it is possible to see the familiar Kierkegaardian categories lurking in Auden's interpretation of Prospero's course of action: his enchantment belongs to the aesthetic, his forgiveness to the ethical, and his abdication to the religious sphere, and the whole action of the poem . . . symbolises a similar process of self-awareness, in a vocational context, going on in Auden's own consciousness.[9]

Fuller seems wary about the idea of 'crude identification'; Auden was also suspicious of easy elisions and assumptions of sameness. His writings in the 1930s and 1940s discuss the ways in which we find 'identity' too easily, repeatedly questioning the way in which we may succumb to what he terms the 'sterility of this substitution of identity for analogy'.[10] Nevertheless, Auden still found it necessary to make links between what he was doing in his art, and the created figures of other artists. Prospero, Ariel, and Caliban were particularly useful in this regard. As he noted in his 1957 lecture on 'Robert Frost', 'every poem shows some sign of rivalry between Ariel and Prospero; in every good poem their relation is more or less happy, but it is never without its tensions'.[11] He goes on to

---

[7] As C. F. Evans notes, the 'language of parable is analogical and suggests; the language of theology is substantial and states'. See his *Parable and Dogma* (London: Athlone Press, 1977), 9.

[8] *Prose*, ii. 163.

[9] John Fuller, *W. H. Auden: A Commentary* (London: Faber, 1998), 357.

[10] *DH*, 61–71, at 70.

[11] *DH*, 337–53, at 337–8.

note that 'the role of each varies in importance from one poet to another: it is usually possible to say of a poem, and sometimes of the whole output of a poet, that it is Ariel-dominated or Prospero-dominated'. The 'Ariel' poem, he claims, is one without moral force: 'Ariel, as Shakespeare has told us, has no passions. That is his glory and his limitation . . . An anthology selected by Ariel, including only poems like the *Eclogues* of Vergil, *Las Soledades* of Góngora and poets like Campion, Herrick, Mallarmé, would, in the long run, repel us by its narrowness and monotony of feeling.' The Prospero poet, Auden writes, sets out to 'provide us with some kind of revelation about our life which will show us what life is really like and free us from self-enchantment and deception'.[12] Like *The Sea and the Mirror*, this lecture betrays some of Auden's uncertainties and anxieties about the ethical role and motivation of the artist. Should an artist be writing with an ethical imperative, or simply aim to provide a beautiful artefact? Is beauty necessarily linked to pure ethical motivations? Can a beautiful poem stand alone? As Allen Tate asked in 1955, to '*whom* is the poet responsible?'[13] Ten years later, even this seemed to be too great a task. After *The Sea and the Mirror*, McDiarmid notes, he was never again to 'attempt any poem that could be mistaken for parable-art'.[14] *The Sea and the Mirror* has its own peculiar relation with parable. Beginning as it does with PROSPERO's rejection of ARIEL, it suggests to the reader the need for a poet to consider the ethical implications of creativity, and, possibly, to reject the narcissistic artistic enterprise. However, to equate Auden's desires and concerns with those of his fictional creature is to ignore the very message that Auden finds in *The Tempest* itself. Prospero, for Auden, read himself into the world too much; he has erred 'through an egotistical determination . . . to enter . . . the fairyland of the subjective life'.[15]

For Auden, the 'fairyland of the subjective life' connects with his interest in the psychoanalytic narrative of human development. Auden's interest in Freud had its origins in his father's medical profession, while his meeting with John Layard, in 1928, introduced him to the ideas of Groddeck and Lane, which combined psychology and anthropology. Although, as Rod Mengham notes, 'he was later to refer rather cruelly to

---

[12] *DH*, 340, 338.

[13] Allen Tate, 'The Man of Letters and the Modern World', in *Essays of Four Decades* (London: Oxford University Press, 1970), 27.

[14] Lucy McDiarmid, *Auden's Apologies for Poetry* (Princeton: Princeton University Press, 1990), 38.

[15] 'Balaam and his Ass', in *DH*, 129.

"loony Layard", this name-calling owed less to Auden's opinion of Layard's ideas than to his shock at being asked to finish the job when Layard bungled a suicide attempt'.[16] Man, for Auden, as for Freud, would always be 'his majesty', the '*Big Baby*' (*ACP*, 427).[17] However, the Freudian developmental schema was, for Auden, an insufficient guide to how we should read ourselves, and others. Shakespeare's late plays offered a suggestive arena in which to consider these complexities:[18]

'Pardon's the word to all' is the note of all the late plays, the note to which everything is made to lead up. The characters are not separate individuals in their own right, you are not fond of them as you are of Beatrice and Rosalind, and they are not terrifying as they are in the tragedies where they are isolated in their own self-love. But like a fairy tale story, this is the world as you want it to be, and nothing makes one more inclined to cry.[19]

And it is the balance between the satisfaction of infantile desire, and theological aspiration, that drew him to late Shakespeare. For Auden, these plays offer 'the world as you want it to be' in a double sense. You may have everything that you desire, but it is so constructed that you desire nothing. Like a world of happy infancy, all personal demands are met. For some, this notion of sympathy as an extension of eudaimonism would suffice, but Auden found himself looking elsewhere.

DOUBLE 'O'S: SOLIPSISM AND DUPLICITY

'Pardon' may well be the 'word to all' in the late plays, but Auden's writing senses how an encompassing phrase may conceal overwhelming divisions. *The Tempest*, then, provided Auden with a basis for exploring his anxieties about two forms that seem similar, but which are in fact quite distinct. On the one hand, he saw how sympathy could be seen as

---

[16] Rod Mengham, 'Auden, Psychology and Society' in Stan Smith (ed.), *The Cambridge Companion to W. H. Auden* (Cambridge: Cambridge University Press, 2005), Cambridge Collections Online. <http://cco.cambridge.org/extract?id=ccol0521829623_CCOL0521829623A014>.

[17] Sigmund Freud, 'On Narcissism', *Collected Papers*, iv, ed. Joan Riviere and James Strachey (New York: Basic Books, 1959), 48.

[18] Pearce remembers that before the lecture he shouted to his departing class, '"Read lots of fairy stories over the weekend . . . as you study *The Tempest*!"', Pearce, 'Fortunate Fall', 144.

[19] *LOS*, 283.

the satisfaction of personal desire. On the other, he perceived the ideal of compassion or wonder. Such questions of separation are raised in the very first stanza:

> (*The* STAGE MANAGER *to the Critics*)
>
> The aged catch their breath,
> For the nonchalant couple go
> Waltzing across the tightrope
> As if there were no death
> Or hope of falling down;
> The wounded cry as the clown
> Doubles his meaning, and O
> How the dear little children laugh
> When the drums roll and the lovely
> Lady is sawn in half.
>
> (*ACP*, 403)

For Wittgenstein, an honest religious thinker is 'like a tightrope walker. He almost looks as though he were walking on nothing but air. His support is the slenderest imaginable. And yet it really is possible to walk on it.'[20] Auden's poem is similarly precarious, and equally tricksy. The world that the STAGE MANAGER describes is visually and verbally hollow. The clown's physical play is matched by Auden's ambiguities (we are left unsure as to whether 'cry' is verb or noun), while 'drums roll' as preface to illusion. Like Joyce's 'Circe', a three-dimensional performance is flattened before our eyes; the visibility of textual apparatus, such as the capitalized dramatis personae, give the game away. But the poem is also hollowed out by its own fallen nature. It is attempting to discuss matters of faith, something that, as Auden repeatedly states, can only be done through analogy. The images of separation that appear in this first stanza (the 'nonchalant couple' are balanced by the isolation of the 'clown', 'the wounded cry', and the divided lady) echo the sense in which this verbal world will always be separate from its desired signified.

The poem includes these images of separation and imperfect identity because Auden, like Browning before him, was aware of ways in which *Imitatio Christi* could easily shade into playing God. Auden had been preoccupied with the figure of Faust since 1931, and 'New Year Letter' echoes the same fable.[21] 'Genius and Apostle', meanwhile, focuses on

---

[20] Ludwig Wittgenstein, *Culture and Value* (Oxford: Blackwell, 1980), 73.
[21] See his discussion of Faust in 'Balaam and his Ass', *DH*, 115; See Mendelson, *Later Auden*, 101.

Ibsen's Brand, a figure who disregards the idea that 'God is God and man can never | be like him'.[22] Auden's isolation from the miraculous is encapsulated by the poem's 'apparent grace note of "O"'. This, as Peter McDonald rightly notes, provides a crux of sorts to the poem, as it occurs again at the beginning of the next stanza, and throughout the poem:

The character of Antonio, resistant to all that Prospero intends, provides codas to the individual poems in Chapter Two, all of them rhyming on -o and -own, the last of which makes 'O' into a symbol:

> One link is missing, Prospero,
> My magic is my own;
> Happy Miranda does not know
> The figure that Antonio
> The Only One, Creation's O
> Dances for Death alone.

Death is what Antonio calls 'Creation's O', but the phrase itself is heavy with Shakespearean association: in one draft, it is 'the Royal O', and here the presence of *Henry V*'s 'wooden O' is unmistakable. The figure for the stage itself is part of Antonio's Dance of Death; and Auden seems to have sense for the resonance between the Chorus in *Henry V* and Prospero's Epilogue to *The Tempest*—both asking forgiveness for illusion, and appealing for an audience's help in making the imagined seem true.[23]

An 'O' also has a special resonance on the printed page as it presents so many problems for reading aloud: in 'emotional reference and in grammatical function it seems locked unconstruably into the interiority of the uttering subject'. In this sense, it suggests the 'peculiar and private' self that is beyond articulation, the Bradleyan 'circle closed on the outside'. However, it also stands as a 'form of appeal or invocation', a 'vocative calling to another in the form of outward facing apostrophe'.[24] In its most extended sense, an 'O' is a symbol of 'apparent grace'— summoning the ouroboros, a sign of psychic continuity, eternal process, and divinity—as well, of course, as symbolizing nothing. The tonal

[22] Auden's essay appears in *DH*, 433–55. I quote from Geoffrey Hill's translation of *Brand* (Harmondsworth: Penguin, 1996), 154.

[23] Peter McDonald, 'The Dreadful Choice', rev. of *The Sea and the Mirror* by W. H. Auden, ed. Arthur Kirsch, *Times Literary Supplement*, 2 Jan. 2004, 3–6, at 6.

[24] J. H. Prynne, 'English Poetry and Emphatical Language', *Proceedings of the British Academy*, 74 (Oxford: Oxford University Press, 1989), 135–69, at 140–1. Bradley's note that 'my experience falls within my own circle, a circle closed on the outside' is given in Eliot's 'Notes on *The Waste Land*', *Complete Poems*, 80.

ambivalence of Auden's printed drama at this point is crucial, echoing back to Miranda's exchange with Prospero ('O brave new world'). These unspeakable 'O's, then, stand for the difficulties of making the imagined real, the difficulties of finding identity in the tones of another, and the difficulties of finding a way of speaking of eternity; acts of imagination that elude the merely human.

Being human, for Auden, meant being unsure of oneself. Like ANTONIO, who invokes these peculiar, private 'O's, Auden repeatedly returned to the difficulties and comedies of the peculiar and private self, and was allusively drawn to texts that referred to crises of identity. In his essay on 'Writing', he looks back on Alice: ' *"Let me think: was I the same when I got up this morning?... But if I'm not the same, the next question is "Who in the world am I?" At the next peg the Queen turned again and this time she said: "Speak in French when you can't think of the English for a thing—turn your toes out as you walk—and remember who you are."* '[25] While in an American lecture, he mused 'on the idea of the Ego in St Augustine and Franz Kafka': '"I think" Descartes says, "therefore I am"... How very comfortable... How very simple... But who, in fact, is this "I" who "thinks"?... Which of my several self interested egos... is the one who can arrogate to itself... the authority to say that it... rather than any of my other "I"s is the "I" that does the thinking?'[26] Auden was attracted to the idea that one should stand forward as an individual, an act that is only possible if others define such individuality. He notes in *The Enchafèd Flood* (1950) that such self-definition can be dangerous:

A cartoon by Charles Addams which appeared some years ago in *The New Yorker* illustrates admirably the urban situation in which individuality is lost. It shows a residential street in New York. Along the pavement a motionless line of spectators is staring at a little man with an umbrella engaged in a life-and-death struggle with a large octopus which has emerged from a manhole in the middle of the street. Behind the crowd two men with brief cases are walking along without bothering to turn their heads and one is saying to the other 'It doesn't take much to collect a crowd in New York'. The cartoon contains three groups: 'The majority crowd', 'The minority crowd', 'The single man struggling with the octopus'. He is a real individual, yet even with him, the question arises, 'Would he be standing out there in the street by himself if the octopus had not attacked him?' i.e. If he had not been compelled by a fate outside his personal control to become the exceptional individual. There is even a suggestion about his bourgeois umbrella of a magician's wand. Could it be possible that, desiring

<hr/>

[25] 'Writing', *DH*, 20.   [26] Pearce, 'Fortunate Fall', 135.

to become an individual yet unable to do so by himself, he has conjured up a monster from the depths of the sea to break his spell of reflection and free him from just being a member of the crowd?[27]

Here, the 'single man' appears, Prospero-like, with his wand of an umbrella. The suggestion is that instead of recognizing the reality of others he 'conjured up a monster'. Perhaps, however, this monster is, itself, a Calibanesque sign of his own solipsism. The fact that he is drawn to the graphic equivalent of a parable—a cartoon—in order to express these problems is telling. It indicates his awareness of the need for analogy. Just as the umbrella is only *like* a magician's wand, the picture resembles only, analogically, man's existential problems. 'Poetry', as Auden wrote in *The Dyer's Hand*, 'is not magic.'[28]

Auden's concern about the relation between the man and the crowd continues in 'Brothers and Others'. Here, he raises the possibility that we can never truly understand others, that we merely see them as tokens. Despite the need 'that we accept all other human beings on earth as brothers, not only in law, but also in our hearts', our 'temptation . . . is to do just the opposite . . . to regard everybody else on earth not even as an enemy, but as a faceless algebraical cipher'.[29] Auden was familiar with A. N. Whitehead's notion that '[a]lgebra reverses the relative importance of the factors in ordinary language', reducing 'accident to the ghost-like character of the real variable'.[30] But for the poet, algebraic language was simply a code of communication. In truly personal speech, terms and subjects of speech should never be reduced to ciphers. 'Whenever we use the pronouns "you" and "I" not as a mere convention, but meaning what we say, uttering them is accompanied by a characteristic feeling-tone . . . Common to both the I- and the You- feeling is the feeling of being in the middle of a story with a personal past to remember and a personal future to make.'[31]

Auden's existential questionings were, evidently, entwined with the time in which he was living. During the 1940s, writers and philosophers were emphasizing the way in which people were responsible for his own self-creation. As Sartre put it, 'we remind man that there is no legislator but himself; that he himself, thus abandoned, must decide for himself . . . that it is not by turning back upon himself, but always by seeking, beyond himself, an aim which is one of liberation . . . that

[27] W. H. Auden, *The Enchafèd Flood, or, the Romantic Iconography of the Sea* (London: Faber, 1951), 37.

[28] *DH*, 27.   [29] *DH*, 235.   [30] Quoted in *SW*, 116.   [31] *SW*, 108.

man can realise himself as truly human'.[32] The growing feeling that philosophy could no longer be something abstract or theoretical, but had to be personal and subjective, put particular pressure upon the artist, with poetry being seen as 'far more powerful and truer than traditional philosophy'.[33] Such a need was driven, in part, by the pressure of 'war-time', when, as the NARRATOR of *The Age of Anxiety* comments, 'everybody is reduced to the anxious status of a shady character or a displaced person' (*ACP,* 449). However, the existential attitude does not, in itself, encompass Auden's concerns. Richard Davenport-Hines notes that, at this point, Auden was seeking a 'Christian-Freudian synthesis that would preserve his integrity'—a way in which 'that which hitherto we could only passively fear as the incomprehensible I AM, henceforth we may actively love with comprehension that THOU ART' (*ACP,* 388).[34] Davenport-Hines's 'integrity' has a threefold resonance. It points to the rhetorical sense of 'sincerity' or personal authenticity and originality, to the moral sense of 'innocence, sinlessness', and to the formal notion of completion or independence. The ambiguity of the word itself explains why such a triangulation was difficult to achieve.[35] When Auden declares that the 'gift of being an artist is being shameless', the duplicity of language could be seen as a 'manifestation of empirical guilt'.[36]

Along with his consciousness of self-appraisal, a feeling of being confusingly lost in corridors of quotation and repetition captured Auden's imagination during and after the Second World War. The 'everlasting Not Yet' described by his CALIBAN, in which the 'grey horizon of the bleaker vision' (*ACP,* 441) offers only 'Cones of extinct volcanoes' and 'tautological repetitions' (*ACP,* 438), and the fearful quest that his SIMEON ponders, where 'Every invalid is Roland defending the narrow pass against hopeless odds' (*ACP,* 389), both have affinities with Browning's fictional worlds. Auden was reading Browning during the 1940s, the period in which he drew most on the dramatic monologue form; the 'magnificence is in the psychology…the great

---

[32] Jean-Paul Sartre, *Existentialism and Humanism*, trans. Philip Mairet (London: Methuen, 1948), 55–6.

[33] Eric Weil, 'The Strengths and Weaknesses of Existentialism,' *Listener* 47 (8 May 1952), 743–4, at 744; Clare Morgan, 'Existentialism in England 1945–1960: The Growth of its Influence on Literature and Art' (D.Phil. diss., University of Oxford, 1995), 5.

[34] Richard Davenport-Hines, *Auden* (London: Vintage, 2003), 271.

[35] *OED* 3b., *OED* 3a.

[36] *LOS*, 184; I quote Geoffrey Hill, *Lords of Limit* (London: Deutsch, 1984), 7.

ingeniousness of the work is undeniable', he told Ansen.[37] For any poet facing existential difficulties, the example of Browning's Caliban 'coming to terms with the awful situation of living humanly as artist without...any ethical or magical equipment for it' would provide a welcome model.[38] It is in using techniques he had learnt from Browning—the dignifying, individualizing, and satirizing of small-time characters—that Auden celebrates the philosophy that was seen by some, like Lévi-Strauss, as illegitimate due to its 'over-indulgent attitude towards the illusions of subjectivity'. Auden's ROSETTA, 'a buyer for a big department store', who muses on such 'philosophical problems' as 'why were the men one liked not the sort who proposed marriage and the men who proposed marriage not the sort one liked?' (*ACP*, 450), provides a sharp answer to Strauss's snotty observation that '[t]he raising of personal preoccupations to the dignity of philosophical problems is far too likely to lead to a sort of shop-girl metaphysics'.[39]

T. S. Eliot was also drawn towards the dramatic form during the late thirties and forties, and his concerned attempt 'to be living on several planes at once | Though one cannot speak with several voices at once' is picked up by Auden.[40] His movement towards poems inhabited, as the narrator of *The Age of Anxiety* puts it, by 'several voices' (*ACP*, 509), each forging its own narrative, shows Auden's leanings towards the idea that making ourselves and other people up is central to, yet in some senses circumvents the possibility of, understanding ourselves and others. The delicate balance between judging and sympathizing with others (in cognitive terms, the difference between theorizing about others, and simulating their experience) permeates Auden's sense of what it is to write, and to read. Such a quest also suggests why Auden looked to *The Tempest*, a structure which itself revolves around the conflicting senses of preordained patterns, and personal autonomy. His attraction to *The Tempest* is that it just slips out of this fairy-tale world: 'it is concerned with a wrong done, repentance, penance and reconciliation'; but whereas the other late plays 'all end in a blaze of forgiveness and love...in *The Tempest* both the repentance of the guilty and the pardon of the injured seem more formal than real'.[41] It is significant

---

[37] Ansen, *Table Talk*, 38.
[38] Hillis-Miller, *Disappearance*, 155.
[39] Claude Lévi-Strauss, *Tristes Tropiques* (Harmondsworth: Penguin, 1976), 71.
[40] *The Family Reunion*, in *Complete Poems*, 324.
[41] 'Balaam and his Ass', *DH*, 128.

that *The Sea and the Mirror* begins, then, with an uncertainty about forgiveness. As Auden saw it:

Alonso is the only one who seems genuinely sorry; the repentance of the rest, both the courtly characters, Antonio and Sebastian, and the low, Trinculo and Stephano, is more the prudent promise of the punished and frightened, 'I won't do it again. It doesn't pay,' than any change of heart: and Prospero's forgiving is more the contemptuous pardon of a man who knows that he has his enemies completely at his mercy than a heartfelt reconciliation. His attitude to all of them is expressed in his final words to Caliban: 'as you look | To have my pardon trim it handsomely'.[42]

PROSPERO's ambivalent attitude is evident in his opening speech. He tells ARIEL that

> The extravagant children, who lately swaggered
> Out of the sea like gods, have, I think, been soundly hunted
>   By their own devils into their human selves:
> To all, then, but me, their pardons. Alonso's heaviness
>   Is lost; and weak Sebastian will be patient
> In future with his slothful conscience—after all, it pays;
>   Stephano is contracted to his belly, a minor
> But a prosperous kingdom; stale Trinculo receives,
>   Gratis, a whole fresh repertoire of stories, and
> Our younger generation its independent joy
>
> (*ACP,* 407)

Auden crafts the speech in order to show the way in which there is nothing free about PROSPERO's pardon. He thinks of himself ('To all, then, but me, their pardons'), and makes a light satire of each of the characters. His criticism of SEBASTIAN picks up on the mercenary nature of conscience pointed out in 'Balaam and his Ass'—'it pays'; the future of STEPHANO and TRINCULO, too, are seen in terms of pecuniary loss and gain (STEPHANO is contracted to 'a prosperous kingdom', TRINCULO receives his stories 'Gratis').

The Kantian requirement to regard people as ends in themselves rather than means governs Auden's relations with *The Tempest* and his resistance to PROSPERO. It is also integral to his wariness about the way in which both writing and reading experiences may be manipulative and unsympathetic. Real possibilities of forgiveness, and a promise of reform, rely, as Auden realizes, on recognizing the validity of others. He cites Hannah Arendt on this issue:

---

[42] *DH*, 128–9.

The possible redemption from the predicament of irreversibility—of being unable to undo what one has done—is the faculty of forgiving. The remedy for unpredictability, for the chaotic uncertainty of the future, is contained in the faculty to make and keep promises. Both faculties depend on plurality, on the presence and action of others, for no man can forgive himself and no one can be bound by a promise made only to himself.[43]

Crucially, then, the characters in *The Sea and the Mirror* are created in a way that precludes them from recognizing the presence and action of others. Each speaks in a different poetic form (PROSPERO in sprung rhythm, ANTONIO in terza rima, MIRANDA in a sort of villanelle).[44] None converse. As such, they are denied what CALIBAN, in the poem's close, craves; an 'authentic molar pardon' (*ACP*, 444).

What is at work in the poem could be read as an analogy for Auden's sense of the life of writers, and readers. His claim to his American students that '[y]ou only know yourself, your own reactions' repeatedly manifests itself in his reading and writing life. Auden claimed that Shakespeare in the sonnets 'desperately tries to do that which is forbidden: to create a human being'.[45] Through his relations with Shakespeare's creatures, Auden attempts to come to terms with the dangers of the creative gift. In 'The Globe', he claims that 'we can notice' Shakespeare's 'ambivalence in his feelings towards his characters which is perhaps characteristic of all great dramatists . . . the tension of this ambivalent attitude, torn between reverence and contempt, of the maker towards the doer'. While Auden argues that a 'character for which his creator felt absolute contempt would not, I think, be actable', he recognizes this peculiar ambivalence of creator to creature—the difficulty of acknowledging the otherness of the fictional creation. One of Auden's most devoted critics, John Bayley, discusses these difficulties in his book *The Characters of Love*: '[t]aking other people's reality for granted is, as I have persistently implied, the first requirement of love. And it is also the first requirement for character creation.' However, Bayley notes, authors are rarely able to treat their characters with such a 'vision of love': 'more often he is in love with his own vision and with his characters as projections of it and the novel, Narcissus-like, comes to love only itself.'[46]

[43] *DH*, 218.
[44] See Malcolm Cowley, 'Virtue and Virtuosity: Notes on W. H. Auden', *Poetry*, 65 (1945), 202–9.
[45] Howard Griffin, *Conversations with Auden* (San Francisco: Grey Fox Press, 1981), 98.
[46] John Bayley, *The Characters of Love: A Study in the Literature of Personality* (London: Chatto & Windus, 1968), 106.

Auden shares this concern. Mirrors recur in his work—like the island, these are an emblem for the difficulty of moving out of the self, and of seeing other people, through texts. The epigraph to his essay on 'Reading', taken from Lichtenberg, is a good example—'A book is a mirror: if an ass peers into it you can't expect an apostle to look out', while in 'The Joker in the Pack', he claims that 'a play, as Shakespeare said, is a mirror held up to nature . . . when we look into it the face that confronts us is our own'.[47] Meanwhile, he chooses Malcolm de Chezal's idea that a mirror 'has no heart but plenty of ideas' as epigraph to his essay 'Hic et Ille'. Perhaps the clearest example of his complex thoughts on the idea of mirroring appears in MIRANDA's speech in *The Sea and the Mirror*. William Empson thought that Auden 'wiped the eye of everybody who tries to revive a villanelle': 'Miranda comes out panting, completely astonished by the world—she has never seen a man before, except a monster and her father—and what she talks is a perfect villanelle, and this is an astounding piece of technical skill.' He recalls pointing this out to Louis MacNeice when it first appeared, who was 'rather cross and said "Of course it isn't a villanelle; it may remind you of one but it isn't" '.[48] This disagreement over matters of form is mirrored by the variety of critical reactions to MIRANDA's poetic 'panting'. Lucy McDiarmid and Edward Mendelson note that the poem 'begins where the ego ends, in compassionate love', pointing towards 'a divine love that lovingly desires fulfilment for its human counterpart.[49] Stan Smith is less enchanted by the pair, commenting that MIRANDA and FERDINAND 'run the risk of the kind of narcissism represented by Tristan and Isolde', in Auden's description: 'so indifferent to each other as persons with unique bodies and characters that they might just as well . . . have drawn each other's names out of a hat.'[50] For Auden, such conflicting responses to the couple's new found world of love would have come as no surprise. Art, as he writes, 'is a mirror in which each person sees his face reflected'.[51]

MIRANDA's villanelle centres on problems of self-transcendence, and it reflects the search to make art more than a mere reflection of the artist's or the reader's face. It is a poem in which Auden returns, once more, to

---

[47] 'The Joker in the Pack,' *DH*, 269. See also his discussion of mirrors in 'Lecture Notes' (1942), *Prose*, ii. 215.

[48] *Morris Gray Poetry Reading*, quoted in *The Complete Poems of William Empson*, ed. John Haffenden (Harmondsworth: Penguin Press, 2000), 346.

[49] McDiarmid, *Auden's Apologies*, 107; Mendelson, *Later Auden*, 226.

[50] S. Smith, *Auden*, 160; *DH*, 121.

[51] *New York Times*, 22 Jan. 1956, quoted in Mendelson, *Later Auden*, 392.

the sense in which the 'conceits' of linguistic expression are helpless in the quest for a place where there might be, as he writes in 'The Prophets', 'no such thing as a vain look' (*ACP*, 256). The sense of 'vain' here, which reflects an image of the conceited sideways glance in the glass blocking the recognition of the outward gaze, is picked up in MIRANDA's opening line:

> My Dear One is mine as mirrors are lonely,
> As the poor and sad are real to the good king,
> And the high green hill sits always by the sea.
>
> (*ACP*, 421).

PROSPERO's reflections on his daughter's business—'The hours of fuss and fury, the conceit, the expense'—direct the reader to the spiritual perils of love mediated by aesthetics. John Fuller argues that these lines indicate that FERDINAND is MIRANDA's 'as mirrors are lonely' in the sense 'that since a mirror doesn't fulfil its function unless someone is looking into it, and yet cannot see its own reflection, it is inevitably lonely'.[52] However, MIRANDA's opening words are an admission, as well as a demonstration, of conceit. The sense in which her Dear One is hers *because* mirrors are lonely, hints at the fact that she has, in the past, spent many hours making herself up, in keeping her 'admirable' nature. More clearly, though, 'as' also signifies *in the same way in which*. This gives the line the sense that FERDINAND belongs to MIRANDA in the same way in which a mirror possesses its loneliness. The latter reading is difficult enough as a grammatical construction. As a declaration of union it suggests that something is amiss. The analogous yoking of 'mine' and 'lonely' indicates that, perhaps, FERDINAND is only present to her in the way that a pseudo-person is reflected in a mirror. One half of the analogy, then, seems to undo the logic of the other. Not least, it makes FERDINAND appear to be part of an equation—she is treating him, merely, as one of those 'algebraic ciphers' that Auden warned against in 'Brothers and Others'. While, for Auden 'the only serious thing is loving God and your neighbour', he found the practicalities of Jesus' commandment to the disciples 'Thou shalt love thy neighbour as thyself' (Mark 12: 31) difficult. He would agree with William James who asks:

What, then, is our neighbour? Thou hast regarded his thought, his feeling as somehow different from thine. Thou hast said, 'A pain in him is not like a pain in

52 Fuller, *W. H. Auden: A Commentary*, 363.

me, but something far easier to bear.' He seems to thee a little less living than thou; his life is dim, it is cold, it is a pale fire beside thy own burning desires ... So, dimly and by instinct hast thou lived with thy neighbour, and hast known him not, being blind. Thou hast made [of him] a thing, no Self at all.[53]

Auden's neighbourly difficulties manifest themselves in the painful nursery-rhyme cadences of 'As I Walked Out One Evening', where 'You shall love your crooked neighbour | With your crooked heart' (*ACP*, 135), or in the repetitious struggles of his 1948 essay 'Squares and Oblongs': ' "Why doesn't my neighbour love me for myself?", but ... "I do not love my neighbour as myself and may God have mercy on my soul" .'[54] These sorts of questions chime with Simone Weil's concern that 'what we love in other human beings is the hoped-for satisfaction of our desire. We do not love their desire. If what we loved in them was their desire, then we should love them as ourself.'[55] Like MIRANDA, Auden's narcissistic wrestling revolved around the complexity of reading, and writing, of another, and loving them 'as much as' oneself, rather than 'as if they were the same'.

FORMAL FAILURES AND EXTEMPORIZING LIVES

The Sea and the Mirror begins and concludes with disappointment. Auden's ANTONIO notes the fact that the harmony at the end of the play is more 'formal than real': 'Yes, Brother Prospero, your grouping could | Not be more effective':[56]

> given a few
> Incomplete objects and a nice warm day,
> What a lot a little music can do.
>
> (*ACP*, 411)

Auden uses ANTONIO ironically here, to highlight one of his own concerns; he points to the way in which aesthetics can give a false impression of transcendence or completion in the face of psychic pain. As McDiarmid notes, Auden had confessed his own confusion

[53] William James, 'On A Certain Blindness in Human Beings', in *Selected Papers on Philosophy* (London: Dent, 1917), 8–9.
[54] Auden, *Prose*, ii. 342.
[55] Simone Weil, *First and Last Notebooks*, trans. Richard Rees (London: Oxford University Press, 1970), 284.
[56] *DH*, 128.

of 'aesthetic effect with spiritual transformation' in *New Year Letter*.[57] CALIBAN admits, in fact, that

> Our performance . . . which we were obliged, all of us, to go on with and sit through right to the final dissonant chord, has been . . . indescribably inexcusably awful . . . Now it is over. No, we have not dreamt it. Here we really stand, down stage with red faces and no applause; no effect, however simple, no piece of business, however unimportant, came off; there was not a single aspect of our whole production, not even the huge stuffed bird of happiness, for which a kind word could, however patronisingly, be said.   (*ACP*, 443–4)

In both endings, artistic form has failed to sustain the speaker; in both, disbelief is bluntly unsuspended by the declaration of an ending— 'Well, so that is that', 'Now it is over'.

Throughout his life, Auden was interested in persuasive forms— those of religious dogma, politics, and psychoanalytic theory—and the ways in which these might help him to find a tone with which to speak. The sense of the existential pressure, and longing for new forms, shows itself in a poem such as 'Christmas 1940': 'What properties define our person since | The massive vagueness moved in on our lives, | What laws require our substance to exist?' (*EA*, 259). A world of formal security, it seems, has been lost:

> The universe of pure extension where
> Nothing except the universe was lonely,
> For Promise was occluded in its womb
> Where the immortal families had only
> To fall to pieces and accept repair,
> Their nursery, their commonplace, their tomb,
> All acts accessory to their position,
> Died when the first plant made its apparition.
>
> (*EA*, 259)

This poem, as it follows the human spirit through 'a long adolescence', then a final metamorphosis towards 'Fate by Faith', shows the speaker moving from a belief in Layard's psychoanalytic theory to an embrace of Christianity. Both were important to Auden, for as Davenport-Hines notes, 'Christianity and Freudianism were ways of coping with or re-imagining pain; they mirrored one another in such metaphors as the yearning for Eden or the womb'.[58] Both of these 'metaphors' provide, in this sense, an integrated shape around which to define one's life. In *New*

---

[57] McDiarmid, *Auden's Apologies*, 17.   [58] Davenport-Hines, *Auden*, 271.

Year Letter, however, Auden is suspicious about the way in which the Freudian model allows one to 'cope', as the 'Devil' takes on the words of Rilke:

> ' "You know the *Elegies*, I'm sure
> — *O Seligkeit der Kreatur*
> *Die immer bleibt im Schosse*—womb,
> In English, is a rhyme to tomb" '

(ACP, 213)

The passage refers to the eighth 'Duino Elegy', in which Rilke offers the image of the gnat, who is conceived, born and lives in the internal world, and is therefore forever in the womb: 'Oh bliss of the *tiny* creature which remains | Forever inside the womb that was its shelter | Joy of the gnat which, still *within*, leaps up | Even at its marriage | . . . | And bewildered is any womb-born creature | That has to fly.'[59] The passage echoes Rilke's *Notebooks*, in which he reveals his envy for that 'multitude of creatures which come from externally exposed seeds' and 'have that as their maternal body. . . how much at home they must feel in it all their lives . . . for this same space has both conceived them and brought them forth, and they never leave its security . . . (Rivalry between mother and world—)'.[60]

The Freudian notion of the womb as a mythical paradise was popularized by Otto Rank in his *Trauma of Birth*, published in English in 1929.[61] Admirers, such as Salvador Dalí, identified the 'intra-uterine period with . . . paradise, and . . . the traumatism of birth—with the myth, so decisive in human life, of the "Lost Paradise" ', while Orwell spoke of the human desire for 'a womb big enough for an adult. There you are, in the dark, cushioned space that exactly fits you.'[62] Such images would attract poets interested in challenging theoretical forms of thought. T. S. Eliot, for example, mocks those who rely on 'the horoscope', 'the womb, the tomb, or dreams' in *The Dry Salvages* (1941), while Beckett parodies Belacqua's 'wombtomb' in his 1932 work *Dream of Fair to Middling Women*.[63] Auden was thinking along

---

[59] *The Selected Poetry of Rainer Maria Rilke*, ed. and trans. Stephen Mitchell (London: Picador, 1997), 195.

[60] Notebook Entry, 20 Feb. 1914, quoted ibid. 330.

[61] See Sigmund Freud, *Civilisation and Its Discontents* (1929), trans. James Strachey (Harmondsworth: Penguin, 1984), 254.

[62] Salvador Dalí, *The Secret Life of Salvator Dalí* (New York: Dial, 1942), 26–7; George Orwell, *Inside the Whale and Other Essays* (Harmondsworth: Penguin, 1976), 43.

[63] Beckett, *Dream of Fair to Middling Women*, 133, 123.

the same lines with his lightly satirical note to *New Year Letter* (taken from 'Shorts'): 'Do we really want to return to the womb? Not at all | No one really desires the impossible: | That is only the image out of the past | We practical people use when we cast | Our eyes on the future.'[64] Auden's suspicion of the Freudian developmental model is reflected in his use of poetic form. His wariness about forms of theoretical escape resonates in the nursery-rhyme patterns of poems like 'Miss Gee' and 'Victor'. Here, a parodic style demonstrates the simultaneous attraction and perils of a Freudian schema. The pat physio-psychological explanation for Miss Gee's cancer is matched by the bouncing insistence of the comforting rhyme scheme, as if believing in Layard's Freudian theory of predetermination is itself a way of escaping the necessary act of choosing. As Nabokov later puts it, 'to fulfil the fish wish of the womb | A school of Freudians headed for the tomb', playing on the same sing-song rhyme.[65] Robert Douglas-Fairhurst has pointed out how rhymes can often function as 'clues to some of the most basic ways in which a culture has come to think about itself'. A rhyming couplet, he argues, may provide 'a sort of "grammar of assent" in its revelation of the channels of sympathy—the social agreements—which have been gradually carved out in a language by repeated use, so that in English verse "breath" invariably ends with "death", "womb" leads to "tomb", and so on'. In this sense the 'rhyme-words of a language' become a sort of 'audible residue of cultural development, the "mutual understandings" which can be heard joining speakers across divisions of space and time'. So, just as rhymes 'imply meetings they cannot make', they are also a form of meeting place, or mutual ground.[66]Auden, as has been shown, is wary of easy conceptions of mutuality, and this suspicion is demonstrated through his use of rhyme. 'Rhymes', as Auden noted in his lecture on 'A Comedy of Errors', 'can have a . . . comic effect if the rhymed words . . . look as if they have taken charge of the situation: as if, instead of an event requiring words to describe it, words have power to create an event.'[67] There is, it seems, something too secure about the neatness of Layard's theories as worked out in poetry—the ease of their masterly formal 'integrity' shaping the matter of human life into a predetermined pattern, could be seen to cast doubt on the 'integrity'

[64] W. H. Auden, *New Year Letter* (London: Faber, 1941), 108. See 'Shorts', *ACP,* 296–7.
[65] Vladimir Nabokov, *Pale Fire* (London: Weidenfeld & Nicolson, 1962), 57.
[66] Douglas-Fairhurst, *Victorian Afterlives*, 177–8.
[67] *LOS,* 24.

of their content. Geoffrey Hill cautions against such ease in an essay on Henry Vaughan's 'The Night':

> One is impelled, or drawn, to enquire whether that metaphysical rapport felt to exist between certain English rhyme-pairings is the effect of commonplace rumination or the cause of it. Auden, in *New Year Letter*, makes 'womb: tomb' a trick in his Devil's sophistry, implying that the easy availability of the rhyme is complicit with our trite melancholy and angst.[68]

Hill himself invoked many of these 'easy' rhymes in his first translation of Ibsen's *Brand*, in order to summon the voice of the mystic who attacked 'the inane | clap-trap of our Age': 'The brave panache each fool | wears now to conceal | his threadbare courage.'[69] Later, however, he removed these five lines—perhaps realizing that his own condemnation of Brand's inanity itself had an unpleasant facility.[70] Auden prefigures Hill in his awareness that, as Ricks puts it, 'the dignity and indignity of death, and of life, ask for more than trite melancholy and angst', and in his ability to show this through poetic form.[71] Hence the ease with which Auden's dramatis personae in *The Sea and the Mirror* fall into metrical and rhyming patterns should be looked upon with suspicion. He courts an easy effect (what he refers to, elsewhere, as the 'wrong kind of facility') in order to show the weakness of such effects.[72] This use of formal patness is a criticism of the ways in which we imagine all things fitting together into patterns we know well, and, in particular, a criticism of how we see the patterns of our own lives in those belonging to other people. We may, as Auden writes, 'love, not friends or wives, | But certain patterns in our lives' (*ACP*, 210). Such criticism of easy mappings is evident when Auden plays on the 'womb: tomb' rhyme again in *For The Time Being*. The rhyme indicates how the Freudian story of the death-wish and Oedipal longings provides these characters with refuge:

---

[68] Geoffrey Hill, 'A Pharisee to Pharisees: Reflections on Vaughan's "The Night"', *English*, 38 (1989), 97–113, at 103. Hill claims that rhyme may be 'troublesomely binding as much because it is easy as it is because it is hard', ibid. 104.

[69] Henrik Ibsen, *Brand*, trans. Geoffrey Hill, 2nd edn., rev. with introd. by Inga-Stina Ewbank (Minneapolis: National Theatre Plays Series, 1981), 83.

[70] See the rev. 1996 edn. of *Brand* (Harmondsworth: Penguin), 75.

[71] Christopher Ricks, *Beckett's Dying Words* (Oxford: Oxford University Press, 1993), 41.

[72] He notes that 'On the whole ... the paucity of rhymes in English has not proved a disadvantage, for it has discouraged or at least instantaneously revealed the wrong kind of facility'. See *Langland to Spenser*, p. xvi.

CHORUS

.   .   .   .

How can he wait without idols to worship, without
Their overwhelming persuasion that somewhere, over the high hill,
    Under the roots of the oak, in the depths of the sea,
Is a womb or a tomb wherein he may halt to express some attainment?
How can he hope and not dream that his solitude
Shall disclose a vibrating flame at last and entrust him forever
    With its magic secret of how to extemporise life?

(ACP, 355)

THE THREE SHEPHERDS
O here and now our endless journey starts.

WISE MEN
Our arrogant longing to attain the tomb,

SHEPHERDS
Our sullen wish to go back to the womb,

WISE MEN
To have no past,

SHEPHERDS
No future,

TUTTI
Is refused.

(<i>ACP</i>, 382)

Both aurally and structurally, 'womb: tomb' provides a sense of closure, an escape from the demands of choice, and of never knowing when things will end, or where they begin, offering in exchange a predetermined pattern.

The desire to act and to understand life without relying upon previous models of action and understanding—to see it as strange—resonates in Auden's work. It is a quest that is in line with existential philosophy. Sartre notes that the 'most mysterious aspect of the mystery of time is the present...the infinitesimal instant, the nothingness between the future which is not yet and the past which is no more'.[73] Auden, therefore, has the CHORUS suggest the need to resist this security, to develop the ability to 'extemporise life'. The notion evokes the sense of making things up, or improvising, which would offer an alternative to

---

[73] See F. Temple Kingston, *French Existentialism* (Toronto: University of Toronto Press, 1961), 39.

leaning upon past patterns. Indeed, etymologically, 'extempore' breaks down to 'ex tempore'—'out of the time'—thus leading to its meaning, to act 'on the spur of the moment'.[74] In this way, extemporizing could also offer a new slant on questions of sympathy. If a poet, or a reader, were to 'extemporize' the life of a fictional character, then they could offer a level of sympathetic engagement that did not rely on previous theories, or patterns, of how other minds work. It would be new, specific, and non-judgemental—entirely in contrast with the eudaimonistic theory of the emotions.

As can be seen, Auden's poetry of the forties was imbued with a sense of the need to frustrate images of perfection. His use of allusion, and of rhyme (which is, in itself, a form of imperfect allusion), is integral to this. Allusion can be seen as an active dialogue with the past—a 'lifeline', connecting past and present minds by analogical means, a way of understanding other minds. However, Auden was aware that drawing upon forms of the past by rhyming or alluding might also be a form of retreat. Indeed, allusion, as Cyril Connolly notes, can be uterine: '[t]he mind has its own womb to which, baffled by speculation, it longs to return; the womb of Homer and Herodotus, of the pastoral world.'[75] Through his creatures, Auden offers the possibility that allusions and rhymes are a crutch of sorts, for they confirm the similarity of the past to the present, rather than embracing its difference. An allusion may offer an illusion of community, rather than an ideal sympathy. Like Ricks's notion of a poem, an allusion 'cannot but be company', but it may also 'be too easily, too built-in, an assuaging of loneliness'.[76] Auden, through his creatures, expresses a desire to 'extemporise life' through metrical means, and through their voices he demonstrates the impossibility of realizing this desire.

Auden's consciousness of the urge to embrace each moment for itself, without regard for past or future, is evident in his attention to poetic boundaries and line endings, the smallest instances of beginnings and endings. As Ricks writes, 'the use of line-endings can be a type or symbol or emblem of what the poet values, as well as the instrument by which his values are expressed'.[77] The value of such endings is expressed in Auden's 1968 poem 'Ode to Terminus', in which he presents the

---

[74] *OED* B.1.
[75] Cyril Connolly, *The Unquiet Grave* (London: Hamish Hamilton, 1945), 43.
[76] Christopher Ricks, *Allusion to the Poets* (Oxford: Oxford University Press, 2002), 263.
[77] Christopher Ricks, *The Force of Poetry* (Oxford: Clarendon Press, 1984), 91.

dilemma of how, 'discarding rhythm, punctuation, metaphor', an 'eru-
dite | mind behaves in the dark without a | surround it is called on to
interpret' (*ACP*, 809). The formal isolation of 'without a', pushed up
against empty space, gives the impression of formlessness. It provides
the sense of what it might be to 'experience an existence which is
authentic and genuine to the facts, and which is legitimized not by
external standards but from within'.[78] In this sense, the poem seems
analogous to the difficulty of being literally 'without'—in the sense of
both being outside, and lacking, a 'surround'. Mendelson notes that this
poem refers to the same 'principle of coherence and particularity' that
Auden had prayed to in 1932 when he addressed a poem to the twin
'Lords of Limit', without whom man is 'Lunging, insensible to injury, |
Dangerous in a room or out wild- | -ly spinning like a top in the
field, | Mopping and mowing through the sleepless day' (*ACP*, 64).
Here, the enjambed hyphenation represents a sense of a gulf, a lack of
coherence, without the surrounding comforts of Terminus's 'games and
grammar and metres'.

Such lonely line breaks appear again in *The Age of Anxiety*, as the
characters are described: 'Blindly, playfully, | Bridging death's | Eternal
gap | With quotidian joy' (*ACP*, 502). As the 'gap' of death is partially
enacted by the reading process, the eye moves from line ending to
beginning. Monroe Spears argues that in *New Year Letter*, Auden
'hesitates on the edge of belief in Christianity', and his poetry could
be seen as repeatedly providing a structural analogy, for the reader, to
this being on the edge of things.[79] Consider, for instance, 'The Dark
Years', in which the speaker asks that 'the shabby structure of indolent
flesh | give a resonant echo to the Word which was | from the beginning,
and the shining | Light be comprehended by the darkness' (*ACP*, 285).
The effect is similar to Milton's trick of 'sense variously drawn out from
one verse into another' in *Paradise Lost*: 'now conscience wakes despair |
That slumber'd, wakes the bitter memory | Of what he was, what is, and
what must be | Worse; of worse deeds worse sufferings must ensue'.[80]
Here, 'the reader arrives at the line-end and makes a prediction about
how the next line will complete the phrase—only to have that expect-
ation thwarted. The momentary shock of our *error*, we may believe, is the

---

[78] C. F. Evans, *Explorations*, 156.
[79] Monroe K. Spears, *The Poetry of W. H. Auden: the Disenchanted Island* (New York:
Oxford University Press, 1963), 134.
[80] Milton's note on 'The Verse' of *Paradise Lost*. See *Paradise Lost*, ed. Scott Elledge
(New York: W.W. Norton and Co., 1975), p. 6; *Paradise Lost*, iv. 23–6, pp. 85–6.

Miltonic exhibition of our post-lapsarian nature.'[81] Milton, then, seems able to surprise his readers, making them feel secure about beginnings and endings, then unsettling their 'certain patterns'. It is unsurprising, therefore to see Auden acknowledge the poet who rejected the 'bondage of rhyming', in the epigraph to the Epilogue of *The Age of Anxiety*: '*Some natural tears they drop'd, but wip'd them soon;* | *The world was all before them, where to choose . . .* JOHN MILTON *Paradise Lost*' (*ACP*, 531). In 'The Dark Years', by placing the line ending after 'the Word which was', Auden leaves the phrase bereft—as if to suggest that the 'Word', in the sense of the Logos, is eternally in the past tense. But in the enjambment the phrase is given, as it were, new life.

Only 'as it were', because the eternal irony of artistic expression is, as Auden puts it in 'In Memory of W. B. Yeats', that 'poetry makes nothing happen' (*ACP*, 248). This is partly because, however extemporized Auden's verse may appear, it always demands an element of thinking ahead, of prescription. As MALIN describes, the traveller 'in quest of his own | Absconded self' has to get ahead of himself—to be 'at once | Outside and inside his own demand | For personal pattern.' (*ACP*, 463). Auden's special effects are only 'resonant echoes' of religious experience. And there is something terrifyingly casual about those who would make equivalence between the leaps on the page and leaps in life, like the 'nonchalant couple' who go 'Waltzing across the tightrope | As if there were no death' (*ACP*, 403). Edward Callan points that 'one reason for choosing the end of *The Tempest* as a point of departure was the implication in Prospero's dialogue that the artistic life could be incompatible with spiritual values'.[82]

AUDEN AND HENRY JAMES: 'IT'S A SORT OF KINDERGARTEN!'

'The real "life-wish"' as, Auden wrote in 1929, is not the retreat into art, but 'the desire for separation'. That said, Auden was well aware of the allure of the familiar aesthetic environment. As CALIBAN admits in his description of the time spent before beginning the 'Journey of Life':[83]

---

[81] T. V. F. Brogan (ed.), *The New Princeton Handbook of Poetic Terms* (Princeton: Princeton University Press, 1999), 71.

[82] Edward Callan, *W. H. Auden: A Carnival of the Intellect* (New York: Oxford University Press, 1983), 191.

[83] Mendelson, *Early Auden*, 40.

You will never, after all, feel better than in your present shaved and breakfasted state which there are restaurants and barber shops here indefinitely to preserve; you will never feel more secure than you do now in your knowledge that you *have* your ticket, your passport *is* in order, you have *not* forgotten to pack your pyjamas and an extra clean shirt; you will never have the same opportunity of learning about *all* the holy delectable spots of current or historic interest—an insistence on reaching *one* will necessarily exclude the others—than you have in these beposterd halls...But once you leave, no matter in which direction, your next stop will be far outside this land of habit that so democratically stands up for your right to stagestruck hope, and well inside one of those, all equally foreign, uncomfortable and despotic certainties of failure or success.   (*ACP,* 436–7)

The 'you' in CALIBAN's speech has something in common with Huysman's Des Esseintes, who takes refuge from the pressure of travel by spending his time in a Parisian English bar rather than going to London, and, in this way, always leaves the question of travelling abroad as an imagined possibility.[84] Superficially, CALIBAN's speech appears to be a warning *against* this longing to remain in this womb-like life.[85] Indeed, if one sees the image of the formally bounded poem or play as itself a refuge from the reality in aesthetics, then the breaking in of his long, prose monologue effectively ruptures its security. However, through his use of Henry James, Auden consciously sets out to show that CALIBAN's monologue is also escapist, as fixed in the aesthetic realm as the rest of the poem.

Auden's reading of James in the 1940s is reflected in all aspects of his work. Numerous critics, for instance, have noticed that his CALIBAN speaks in the Master's late style.[86] As McDiarmid rightly observes, one reason for this is because James's is the most obviously 'written' style possible—and, at this time, Auden was courting the page. He was purposely flattening his dramatic monologues, much as Browning does, in order to demonstrate the ways in which he fails to live up to Bayley's 'first requirement of love', and 'of character creation'—the

<hr>

[84] See ch. xi of J. K. Huysmans, *A rebours* (1884), ed. Marc Fumaroli (Paris: Gallimard, 1977), 231–48.

[85] Des Esseintes has 'une immense aversion pour la voyage, un impérieux besoin de rester tranquille', ibid. 247.

[86] Auden alludes to the novelist in *New Year Letter*, draws on him in *A Rake's Progress*, and writes a homage to him in 1941. Critics who notice CALIBAN's Jamesian quality include McDiarmid, *Apologies*, 32; J. Fuller, *W. H. Auden: A Commentary*, 363; Callan, *Carnival*, 199.

belief in another's reality.[87] However, Auden's use of James also allowed him a further disquisition into the value of the aesthetic.

James famously guarded his own genius. As he writes in his *Notebooks*: '[t]hus just these first little wavings of the oh so tremulously passionate little old wand (now!) make for me, I feel a sort of promise of richness and beauty and variety; a sort of portent of the happy presence of the elements . . . my poor blest old Genius pats me so admirably and lovingly on the back that I turn, I screw round, and bend my lips to passionately, in my gratitude, kiss its hand'.[88] A further example of James's delicate aesthetic sense is evident in his account of the end of *The Tempest*. He asks in his 1907 'Introduction', '[w]hat manner of human being was it who *could* so, at the given moment, announce his intention of capping his divine flame with a twopenny extinguisher, and who then, the announcement made, could serenely succeed in carrying it out?'[89] Auden's CALIBAN has obvious echoes of James's camp, stagy indignation. His impersonation of the audience as they supposedly converse with 'our so good, so great, so dead author' is one such instance:

How *could* you, you who are one of the oldest habitués at these delightful functions, one, possibly the closest, of her trusted inner circle, how could you be guilty of the incredible unpardonable treachery of bringing along the one creature, as you above all men must have known, whom she cannot and will not under any circumstances stand, the solitary exception she is not at any hour of the day or night at home to, the unique case that her attendant spirits have absolute instructions never, neither at the front door nor at the back, to admit?   (*ACP*, 424)

This is, of course, an elaborate analogy. While the audience is apparently talking about their distress at Shakespeare bringing CALIBAN upon the stage, an offence to 'Our Native Muse', it is impossible not to read their reproach on a number of other levels. They note that 'At Him and at Him only does she draw the line . . . she cannot conceivably tolerate in her presence the represented principle of *not* sympathising, *not* associating, *not amusing*, the only child of her Awful Enemy . . . "that envious witch" is sign sufficient—who does not rule but defiantly is the unrectored chaos'

[87] Bayley, *Characters of Love*, 106.
[88] Entry for 4 Jan. 1910, *The Complete Notebooks of Henry James*, ed. Leon Edel (New York; Oxford: Oxford University Press, 1987), 268.
[89] Henry James, 'Introduction to *The Tempest*', in Peter Rawlings (ed.), *Americans on Shakespeare 1776–1914* (Aldershot: Ashgate, 1999), 449–62, at 457–8.

(*ACP*, 424). Here, then, CALIBAN stands not only for himself, but also for the disruption of art. And, in this sense, their objections spread to Prospero, in the guise of the author, too—who has, after all, been the one to break the play's spell. This leads us to the next analogy. The use of the capitalized 'Him' implies that their objections are also to the way in which the religious has made its way into the realm of the aesthetic: 'she foresaw what He would do to the arrangements, breaking, by a refusal to keep in step, the excellent order of the dancing ring, and ruining supper by knocking over the loaded appetising tray'. The theme of the audience's complaints is emphasized by its Jamesian tones. The audience, like James in his essay on *The Tempest*, have had their sacred feelings hurt over the breaking of the magic circle, the crossing of the 'prohibitive boundaries' of art.

Auden, however, recognized how this image of a stagy and melodramatic James is itself a caricature. He was alert to the fact that James could, and had been, misread, noting in 1944 that he, like other readers of James, 'had been using him as a refuge... very understandably turning to the clean, clear, calm, blessed sanctities of art as the one *defense* against the unimaginable, unmanageable public honours of life'. Regretting this, he emphasized that James 'was not... an esthete', but an artist who displayed 'consistent integrity'.[90] This is why, in 1948, Auden praised a late short story by Henry James, 'The Great Good Place', as 'a religious parable'.[91] The parallels between *The Sea and the Mirror* and 'The Great Good Place' have not been fully explored by critics, but much can be revealed about Auden's own concerns by examining his allusions to James's work. The story, which first appeared in *Scribner's Magazine* in 1900, is a strange one. It tells of a famous author, George Dane, who, like many of James's heroes, carries a burden—his is the social responsibility of celebrity. One morning an aspiring author visits Dane, and Dane complains about his load. Like the protagonist of 'A Round of Visits' in James's early notes, Dane looks 'vainly for the ideal sympathy, the waiting, expectant, responsive recipient'.[92] He falls asleep, and the story then enters the realm of fantasy: Dane enters a paradise, 'an abyss of negatives, such an absence of positives and of everything', while the aspiring author steps into his body and takes over

---

[90] See 'Henry James and the Dedicated' and 'Address on Henry James', in *Prose*, ii. 242, 297.

[91] *Prose*, ii. 281.

[92] *The Notebooks of Henry James*, ed. F. O. Matthiessen and Kenneth B. Murdock (New York: G. Braziller, 1947), 159.

his responsibilities.[93] Refreshed after this experience, Dane returns to his body, which has been conveniently inhabited by the aspiring author in his own absence.

The meaning of this story has been debated. James himself claimed that 'any gloss or comment would be a tactless challenge' to the tale.[94] Meanwhile, Silverstein writes that the 'general aspect of Dane's world of enchantment is as much religious as it is secular, though there hovers over it a faint aura of uncertainty in keeping with a land of dreams'.[95] That is—it offers multiple images of incarnation and the beatific vision— as the story has it, 'moments in which every apprehension counted double and every act of the mind was a lover's embrace'.[96] One thing, however, is clear; James handles the religious aspects of the tale very strangely. Dane's dream world suggests unity, where, as he feels at the story's close, '[e]very one was a little some one else'; people speak with the 'effect of a single voice', but there is the implication that there is something escapist or infantile about this utopia.[97] As the 'good Brother' who leads him round this new world tells Dane, ' "It's a sort of kindergarten!" "The next thing you'll be saying that we're babes at the breast!" "Of some great mild invisible mother who stretches away into space and whose lap's the whole valley—?" "And her bosom"—Dane completed the figure—'the noble eminence of our hill?" '[98]

Shroeder notes that 'the burden of life...has exhausted Dane. He returns, symbolically, to the maternal depths...by relapsing into a condition of what we might describe as foetal dependency.'[99] There is nothing accidental about this. As Howard Pearce argues, James's use of this ' "pastoral fallacy" is ironic'; for James, the 'Arcadian metaphor... became a recurrent motif in his dramatizing the basic human need to deny death or an insufferable actuality'.[100] In producing a tale in which

---

[93] Unless otherwise stated, I quote from the 'The Great Good Place' in the 1909 New York text, repr. in *The Author of Beltraffio, The Middle Years, Greville Fane and Other Tales* (London: Macmillan, 1922), 205.

[94] As James says himself, the story 'embodies a calculated effect', preface, 'The Great Good Place', p. x.

[95] Henry Silverstein, 'The Utopia of Henry James,' *New England Quarterly*, 35/4 (Dec. 1962), 458–68, at 461.

[96] 'The Great Good Place', 222.

[97] Ibid. 231.

[98] Ibid. 227.

[99] John E. Shroeder, 'The Mothers of Henry James', *American Literature*, 22/4 (Jan. 1951), 424–31, at 427.

[100] Howard Pearce, 'Henry James's Pastoral Fallacy', *PMLA* 90/5 (Oct. 1975), 834–47, at 834, 845.

a land of ultimate sympathy is seen as a 'hyperbolized' infantile escape, James parodies our desire *for* such identification, and such escape. Writing of the tale, Auden pointed out that in reality the 'Great Good Place' is nearer 'than James himself, perhaps, suspected' to the mundanity of everyday life—nearer to 'the implacable juke-boxes, the horrible Rockettes and the insane salads, nearer to the anonymous countryside littered with heterogeneous *dreck* and the synonymous cities besotted with electric signs, nearer to radio commentators...nearer to all the "democratic lusts and licences"'.[101]

These relations between Auden and Henry James shed light on CALIBAN's speech. Because Auden's CALIBAN is an ersatz Henry James, he provides the reader with another religious analogy: CALIBAN is as inferior to James, as—Auden believes—man is to God. He is placed there to allow us to question both the pseudo-Jamesian desire to escape in the aesthetic realm, and the belief that one may gain moral profit from such an escape. As Auden wrote, 'by its very nature art is an act of making experience conscious which means that it cannot and must not try to deal with any experience which is "existential" that is, falsified by reflection'.[102] Specific parallels between CALIBAN's monologue and James's short story are also significant. The 'gay apprentice in the magical art', searching for 'the Good Right Subject that would never cease to bristle with importance' (*ACP*, 430, 434) finds a counterpart in the young man who comes to visit George Dane, heedless of the dangers of the 'conjurer's profession' that he enters (*ACP*, 431). Meanwhile, CALIBAN's vision of the purely aesthetic world—'that Heaven of the Really General Case...tortured no longer by three dimensions and immune from temporal vertigo' (*ACP*, 440)—is none other than a version of George Dane's utopia, with its 'masterly general care', 'general charm', and 'general refuge'.[103] Dane only leaves his dream when he is woken up by his manservant; 'his eyes slowly opened; it was not his good Brother, it was verily Brown who possessed his hand. If his eyes had to open it was because they had been closed and because Brown appeared to think he had better wake up.'[104] But in Auden's world 'there is probably no one whose real name is Brown' (*ACP*, 441) to wake the audience up. This takes the matter of James's story even further. In James's story, Brown awakes the sleeper from the false utopia of the aesthetic world, where every desire is met. In CALIBAN's speech, it is a

---

[101] *Prose*, ii. 281.   [102] Ibid. 321.
[103] 'The Great Good Place', 223, 205, 219.   [104] Ibid. 229.

world from which one may not escape. We may imagine, then, that 'The Great Good Place' is the perfect 'religious parable' for Auden's purposes as the story suggests that sadly, we cannot help but think in terms of identity. James tells of a false paradise in which everything is just like us, and in which everything fits into our own pattern. It is, in this sense, a parable of sadness, reminding us that we can only ever see things in our own likeness.

A CATECHISM OF CLICHÉ: WANTING TO BE YOUR OWN CAUSE

Auden's attraction to the story is tonal as well as thematic. 'The Great Good Place' is a story full of quotations, as the characters cite snatches of *Hamlet*. 'There was the rub', the Brother says to Dane. 'Ah, a hit!', Dane muses to the Brother.[105] Even the hero's own name suggests a despairing Hamlet. Auden shares this propensity to create characters that suffer from 'incorrigible staginess' (*ACP*, 444). In many ways, Auden's own predicament as a poet echoes that of his creatures. As he told Howard Griffin, 'out of their monstrous vanity human creatures want to be their own cause'.[106] The comedy of Auden's speakers comes from the fact that, despite their attempt to speak their own selves, they utter forms of previous poetry. Apart from the extended pastiche of Henry James, the pastiches in *The Sea and the Mirror* include a Petrarchan sonnet from FERDINAND, a Horatian epistle by ALONSO, and a villanelle by MIRANDA. Even ANTONIO speaks the 'conventional braggadocio' of the villain, falling into the pattern of a 'refrain' to the other characters.[107] The effect is the same when the protagonists of *The Age of Anxiety*, with their 'Seven Ages' (*ACP*, 465), emulate the world of *As You Like It*, where 'All the world's a stage, | And all the men and women merely players'.[108] In *Secondary Worlds*, Auden explains how personal speech *should* always be extemporary. 'When we genuinely speak, we do not have the words ready to do our bidding; we have to find them.'[109] However, within *The Sea and the Mirror*, the urge for identity is constantly blocked by repetition. As the STAGE MANAGER describes:

---

[105] 'The Great Good Place', 215, 209. James added this second Shakespearean emphasis in the 1909 revision. The 1900 text gives 'There was the hitch!' See *The Complete Tales of Henry James*, xi (London: Rupert Hart-Davis, 1964), 19.
[106] Davenport-Hines, *Auden*, 225.   [107] *LOS*, 70.
[108] *As You Like It*, ii. vii. 139–40.   [109] *SW*, 105.

Well, who in his own backyard
Has not opened his heart to the smiling
Secret he cannot quote?
Which goes to show that the Bard
Was sober when he wrote
That this world of fact we love
Is unsubstantial stuff:
All the rest is silence
On the other side of the wall;
And the silence ripeness,
And the ripeness all.

(*ACP*, 403–4)

John Fuller points out that these last lines blend 'Shakespeare quotations . . . with the garden quest of Eliot's "Burnt Norton" '.[110] Aptly, for a poet concerned with existential matters, there is also a hint of Al Jonson's 'Back in your own Backyard'.[111] Set against this, though, is the image of 'the smiling | Secret he cannot quote'. As Lucy McDiarmid observes, Auden's poetry 'revolves around' this 'border between the quotable and the unquotable, between literary textuality and extraliterary value': '[t]he notion of private release of emotion to an unknown, mysterious being suggests that God is referred to, but no such simple appellation is given this deity. He or she can only be described as extraliterary, unquotable. Shakespeare, by contrast, is eminently quotable. Allusion', she notes, 'is one way to show the difference between literary and metaphysical gods.'[112]

Allusive difficulties haunt Auden. As Peter Porter writes, it was perhaps not the words 'we must love one another or die', in 'September I, 1939', but the declaration that 'all I have is a voice', that stuck in Auden's throat.[113] As he wrote to Isherwood, with reference to the Second World War, '[i]t is terrible to realize that even great and real suffering can be turned into a theatre and so be no help'—a concern which is picked up again by Edward Mendelson, who observes that when Theodore Spencer read the typescript of *The Age of Anxiety* he commented on the 'made-up' quality of some of the verse. Auden replied that he had set out precisely

---

[110] J. Fuller, *W. H. Auden: A Commentary*, 358.
[111] 'But someday you'll come | Weary at heart | Back where you started from | You'll find your happiness lies | Right under your eye | Back in your own backyard.'
[112] McDiarmid, *Auden's Apologies*, 18.
[113] Porter, 'Recording Angels', 7.

to devise a rhetoric which would reveal the great vice of our age which is that we are all not only 'actors' but know that we are [reduplicated Hamlets] and that it is only at moments, in spite of ourselves, and when we least expect it, that our real feelings break through. The Elizabethans and even the Victorians could be rhetorical without realizing it. We have lost that naiveté, at the same time we have to go on being rhetorical, so that for us sincerity is almost a matter of luck.[114]

And Clive James rightly points out that Auden's retraction of early works, such as 'September I, 1939' was driven by an inability to realize 'the pluralism of his own personality'.[115]

Such pluralism and linguistic relativism runs through *The Sea and the Mirror*. As PROSPERO gives up his 'heavy books' he claims that 'words carry no weight', playing on the cliché here, to give himself a curious meta-fictional awareness. After all, nearly every word he speaks carries with it the weight of allusion, which in turn means that each is threatened with the loss of authenticity. Like MALIN's mentioning of 'the *Schadenfreude* | Of cooks at keyholes' which looks to Sartre, or ROSETTA's sense of the 'homesick little obstinate sobs | Of things thrown into being' that echoes Heidegger's concept of 'Geworfenheit', PROSPERO's image of 'Sailing alone, out over seventy thousand fathoms' is not as lonely as he thinks—being a direct quotation from Kierkegaard's journals, which Auden himself had quoted in his 1941 review of 'Christianity and Power Politics' in the *Nation* (*ACP*, 452, 500, 409). The sense of language losing its resonance is touched on again in *The Age of Anxiety*, in the epigraph to 'The Masque': ' "*Oh, Heaven help me,*" *she prayed, "to be decorative and to do right."* RONALD FIRBANK *The Flower beneath the Foot*' (*ACP*, 517). This is a light-hearted take on the source of the Logos, seen again in CALIBAN's speech with 'heaven knows and heaven be praised' (*ACP*, 423). The epigraph to *For the Time Being*, taken from Paul's letter to the Romans, also points to the way in which we have fallen into an age of secular cliché: '*What shall we say then? Shall we continue in sin, that grace may abound? God forbid.* ROMANS VI' (*ACP*, 347). For in the poem's context, the sense of 'God Forbid' itself, seems to have lost its command. There is, as Lucy McDiarmid describes, a 'gulf between human words' and what Auden's CALIBAN calls the 'real Word which is our only *raison d'être*' (*ACP*, 444); 'Instead of trying to

[114] Mendelson, *Later Auden*, 243.
[115] 'A Testament to Self Control', rev. of *Epistle to a Godson* by W. H. Auden, *Times Literary Supplement*, 12 Jan. 1973, 25–6, at 25.

cross the border between poetry and some kind of spiritual value, Auden in his later poems plays fanfares around the barrier, trumpeting and flaunting his inability to cross over. He revels in art's inability to be anything but itself, at most a rite of praise, at least, frivolity, amusement, play.'[116] And these very borders, the line endings themselves, although gesturing towards religious transcendence, tie the text to the page. As McDiarmid argues, 'poetry that flaunts its typographical features implicitly acknowledges its status as play...a game played with marks on the page'.[117] Auden concludes his series of long poems with his *Baroque Eclogue*. While punning on the setting of the poem itself (a bar), the title also indicates the repetitive mode in which Auden has found himself. As Borges notes, baroque is a 'style that deliberately exhausts (or tries to exhaust) its own possibilities, and that borders on self-caricature', it 'is the final stage in all art, when art flaunts and squanders its resources'. Borges seems a little ashamed of his own baroque tendencies, commenting that he resorted to this mode of writing when he 'was a pitiable sort of creature...who could not bring himself to write short stories, and so amused himself by changing and distorting (sometimes without aesthetic justification) the stories of other men'.[118]

Auden might have been all too aware of his capacity for baroque repetition, and careful about easy notions of authenticity, he never ignores the ethical repercussions of his situation. As he noted, 'Scepticism, said Santayana, is the chastity of the intellect...But a chastity which is not founded upon a deep reverence for sex is nothing but tight-arsed old maidery.'[119] Auden felt the same about the question of inauthenticity, and his poetic technique was deeply entwined with his theological beliefs. Mendelson writes that in the early 1940s, Auden found his doctrines and beliefs in the works of German theologians such as Paul Tillich, whose ideas were based on the acknowledgement of 'a clear separation between divine judgment and human inadequacy'.[120] Tillich was a disciple of Rudolf Otto, and he was, he wrote, in agreement 'with Rudolf Otto's analysis of "the idea of the holy"':

Otto expresses the relation of our mind to the Ultimate and its mystery in two terms: '*tremendum*'—that which produces trembling, fear, and awe; and '*fascinosum*'—that which produces fascination, attraction, and desire. Man's

---

[116] McDiarmid, *Auden's Apologies*, 39.   [117] Ibid. 41.
[118] Jorge Luis Borges, preface to 1954 edn., *Collected Fictions*, trans. Andrew Hurley (London: Allen Lane, 1998), 4–5.
[119] *SW*, 110.   [120] Mendelson, *Later Auden*, 148–9.

unconditional awe of and unconditional attraction to the holy are what he means in these two terms, and they imply the threat of missing one's possible fulfilment. The dread of missing one's fulfilment—this is the awe. The desire to reach one's fulfilment—this is the attraction.[121]

Auden's familiarity with, and attraction to, Tillich's work makes him, by proxy, a disciple of Rudolf Otto, and, therefore, a disciple of Robert Browning.[122] For Otto's mentor was the theologian who had so attracted Browning—Schleiermacher. Otto was deeply impressed by Schleiermacher's description of the 'feeling of absolute dependence' of the creature upon the creator, drawing on his ideas and substituting the notion of 'creature-feeling' for 'feeling of dependence'.[123] It could be argued that the reason why Auden's poetry is persistently possessed by quotation and pastiche is because he was possessed by the dilemma of the human 'creature'. As Niebuhr, another figure who influenced Auden, writes: 'Man is insecure and involved in natural contingency; he seeks to overcome his insecurity by a will-to-power which overreaches the limits of human creatureliness. Man is ignorant and involved in the limitations of a finite mind; but he pretends he is not limited.'[124] In fact, an examination of Auden's use of quotation and self-quotation reveals something about his own particular selfhood and about the specifically religious qualities of his verse. In this way he is clearly Browning's heir, and while his long poems do not strictly fall into the genre of the dramatic monologue, they nevertheless derive from the Victorian poet. Meanwhile, his use of the 'mode' of dramatic imitation—learnt from Browning—is crucial to an understanding of the ethics of his verse. Repetition and quotation are for Auden as for Browning, 'radically undermining'—but with a reason. As he writes in *The Dyer's Hand*: '[s]ome writers confuse authenticity, which they ought always to aim at, with originality, which they should never bother about.'[125] While Barthes sees our predicament as language-users lacking an absolute truth as a sign of our post-theological condition, Auden

---

[121] Paul Tillich, 'My Search for Absolutes', *Religion Online*, ed. Ruth Nanda Anshen, <http://www.religion-online.org/showchapter.asp?title=1628&C=1619>.

[122] Mendelson, *Later Auden*, 152.

[123] 'Desiring to give it a name of its own, I propose to call it "creature-consciousness or creature-feeling". It is the emotion of a creature submerged and overwhelmed by its own nothingness in contrast to that which is supreme above all creatures', Otto, *Idea of the Holy*, 9–10.

[124] Reinhold Niebuhr, *The Nature and Destiny of Man: A Christian Interpretation*, i (London: Nisbet & Co. Ltd, 1941).

[125] *DH*, 19.

views this as a vital part of theological experience. For him, we find kin in our inauthenticity and iterability, working towards another version of what Flann O'Brien terms a 'catechism of cliché'.[126]

CALIBAN wrestles with the problem of art and religious truth in his final speech: 'what else exactly is the artistic gift which he is forbidden to hide, if not to make you unforgettably conscious of the ungarnished unoffended gap between what you so questionably are and what you are commanded without any questions to become.' For the artist is, CALI-BAN points out, 'doomed to fail the more he succeeds', 'the more sharply he defines the estrangement itself... the more he must strengthen your delusion that an awareness of the gap is in itself a bridge' (*ACP*, 442). In its own way a 'repentant felicitous' form (*ACP*, 449), *The Sea and the Mirror* is an attempt to demonstrate an 'awareness of the gap' that does not attempt to be a bridge.

As Everett argues, Auden's literary resurrections, parodies, and pas-tiches present 'peculiar problems' when one is criticizing his work for 'there is a wholeheartedness about Auden's acceptance of the situation at this point that differentiates his method from that of other poets'.[127] His poetry realizes that for the time being, our 'extempore' inauthenticity, both 'makeshift' and 'contrived for the occasion', may have its virtues.[128] As CALIBAN has it, there comes a point when 'for the first time in our lives we hear, not the sounds which, as born actors, we have hitherto con-descended to use as an excellent vehicle for displaying our personalities and looks, but the real Word which is our only *raison d'être*' (*ACP*, 444).

'Condescended' is another word that, in Auden's world, seems to have lost its resonance. In this context, it signifies CALIBAN's archness as he turns, with his pseudo-Jamesian weakness for French nouns, the strength of the 'real Word' into the cliché—'*raison d'être*'. But Auden is fully aware that 'condescended' once gestured towards the incarnation of Christ on earth who speaking 'our creaturely cry': 'Condescended to exist and to suffer death | And, scorned on a scaffold, ensconced in His life | The human household' (*ACP*, 535). As CALIBAN describes, it is due to *this* condescension that 'even sin is valid as a sign'. It is not 'in spite of' our sins 'but with them that we are blessed by that Wholly Other Life from which we are separated by an essential emphatic gulf of which our

---

[126] Flann O'Brien (Brian O'Nolan), *The Best of Myles*, ed. K. O'Nolan (London: Grafton, 1987), 202.
[127] Everett, *Auden*, 76–7.   [128] See *OED* sense B.1, 2, 3.

contrived fissures of mirror and proscenium arch—we understand them at last—are feebly figurative signs' (*ACP*, 444).

Auden differs from T. S. Eliot here in his sense of the relation to the Logos. Eliot, too, had difficulties reconciling his poetry to the realm of the spiritual—the 'hint half guessed, the gift half understood, is Incarnation', he writes in *Four Quartets*, and his consciousness of a separation from the Word is evident in *Ash-Wednesday*'s final cry: 'Suffer me not to be separated | And let my cry come unto Thee.'[129] For Eliot, it seems, the only way to bridge the gulf is to cling to the words of the liturgy— there is even a comfort in the integration of his single poetic voice into the unity of the Anglo-Catholic tradition. However, Eliot's world was decidedly that of traditional, not of extemporized, prayer. For Auden, it is the lack of integration of the Logos into his poetry, and the beauty that he makes of it, which makes him, as Marianne Moore writes, 'exceptional, if not alone, in imparting propriety to words *separated* from the words to which they belong' (my emphasis).[130] Auden's use of the secular sense of 'condescended'—a mere echo of the divine condescension—is one example of this. Moore takes the separated rhyming echo of the postscript to *The Sea and the Mirror* as another:

> (ARIEL *to Caliban. Echo by the* PROMPTER)
>
> Never hope to say farewell,
> For our lethargy is such
> Heaven's kindness cannot touch
> Nor earth's frankly brutal drum;
> This was long ago decided,
>
>   Both of us know why,
>   Can, alas, foretell,
> When our falsehoods are divided,
>   What we shall become,
> One evaporating sigh
>   . . . *I*
>
>   (*ACP*, 445)

That the poem ends with a 'Postscript' which includes a PROMPTER's echo seems a poignant conclusion to a poem revolving around the difficulty of establishing an unscripted self. This ARIEL will never be free—his words will always be written for him. John Hollander's historical account of

---

129 See T. S. Eliot, *Complete Poems*, 105, 190.
130 Marianne Moore, 'W. H. Auden', in Monroe K. Spears (ed.), *Auden: A Collection of Critical Essays*, 39–53, at 49.

the 'figure of echo', and its ability to undercut authenticity, may be usefully thought about in relation to this aspect of Auden's poetry. 'No writer before the twentieth century', Hollander claims, 'has so keenly perceived the relation between the ironic voice of echoing and the mockeries of poetic derivativeness as Kierkegaard.' Hollander notes the angst of one of that philosopher's diary entries, as he claims that 'each time I wish to say something... it is as though I thought double'.[131] But Hollander's isolation of Kierkegaard is, perhaps, not quite right. As Auden well knew, Shakespeare, too, keenly perceived such echoing relations. The Shakespearean pastiche of the 'Postscript' takes the reader back to the existential despair of the doubled-up ANTONIO—'*I am I, Antonio, | By choice myself alone*' (*ACP*, 412 and *passim*). And ANTONIO is, perhaps, the 'kind of person' that Auden described in *The Dyer's Hand*: 'so dominated by the desire to be loved for himself alone that he has constantly to test those around him by tiresome behaviour; what he says and does must be admired, not because it is intrinsically admirable, but because it is *his* remark, *his* act.'[132] Ironically, ANTONIO's declaration of solitude is itself an echo, recalling his brother PROSPERO's claim: 'Now, Ariel, I am that I am, your late and lonely master' (*ACP*, 405). Both brothers are quoting snatches from Shakespeare, and Auden focused on a number of these in his Michigan lectures on Shakespeare. In one lecture he quotes Richard, from *Henry VI* Part III: 'I have no brother, I am like no brother; | And this word "love" which greybeards call divine, | Be resident in men like one another | And not in me: I am myself alone' (*3 Henry VI*, v. vi. 80–3).

Another echo appears in the exam paper that Auden set for the students at the end of the year—'No, I am that I am; and they that level | All my abuses reckon up their own' (Sonnet 121, ll. 9–10)—a passage that Auden recycled in his 'Letter to Lord Byron'.[133] This Shakespearean assertion of self carries, as he notes in his lecture on *Othello*, wistfully godlike overtones, echoing Exodus' 'I AM THAT I AM'.[134] Auden's continual return to this quotation confirms that for him, the self can only ever be 'an inverted saint, a saint manqué', repeating snatches of 'Holy Writ'.[135] It is, as will be seen, a cliché of a religious predicament.

[131] John Hollander, *The Figure of Echo: A Mode of Allusion in Milton and After* (Berkeley and Los Angeles: University of California Press, 1981), 57.
[132] *DH*, 19.   [133] *LOS*, 11, 342; *EA*, 190.   [134] *LOS*, 205.
[135] *LOS*, 205.

KIN IN ITERABILITY

McDiarmid is, like Hollander, also keen to single people out. For her, Auden is 'the *only* poet for whom italics and quotation marks leap up and bar the way between poetry and forgiveness or love' (my emphasis).[136] But, in the end, it is a very <u>lack</u> of exceptionality that Auden attempts to achieve through his quotations. Marianne Moore gets nearer when she notes that Auden is '*not alone*, in imparting propriety to words separated from the words to which they belong' (again my emphasis); Auden, then, joins a long line of writers who set out to redeem the echo. Moore makes brief mention of the fact that the 'Postscript' to *The Sea and the Mirror* rivals Herbert's 'Heaven':

> O who will show me those delights on high?
> *Echo.*   I
> Thou Echo, thou art mortall, all men know
> *Echo.*   No[137]

Herbert's poem is itself a 'sacred parody'—in this case a reworking of the conventional echo, 'a commonplace of the sixteenth century song-books', used, for example, in his brother Lord Edward of Cherbury's 'Echo to A Rock'. As Mary Rickey comments, 'it is especially curious that several of the devices which strike one as being particularly characteristic of the highly wrought lyrics of the holy Mr. Herbert should have been suggested to him by the more flippant verses' of his brother. Both poets were interested in the use of echo for devotional purposes, 'the nature of the echo-answers serving to set them off from the human speech of the piece'.[138] Herbert's parody works against poems whose 'purpose [is] to deceive the eare and also the mind, drawing it from plainnesse and simplicitie into a certaine doubleness, whereby our talke is the more guilefull & abusing'.[139] It manages to use this doubleness against itself, as the poet giving God's voice as an 'echo' signifies the act

---

[136] McDiarmid, *Auden's Apologies*, 18, 11, 45.

[137] *The English Poems of George Herbert*, ed. C. A. Patrides (London: J. M. Dent & Sons, 1974), 191.

[138] See Mary E. Rickey, 'Rhymecraft in Edward and George Herbert', *JEGP*, 58 (1958), 502–11, at 511. She notes George Herbert may have borrowed the echoing religious lyric from Edward, whose 'Echo in a Church' is 'the first example of the use of the echo form for devotional purposes': ibid. 506–7.

[139] George Puttenham, *The Arte of English Poesie*, ed. G. D. Willock and A. Walker (Cambridge: Cambridge University Press, 1936), 154.

of God 'condescending' to man. Herbert's sanctifying of pastiche and echo would appeal to Auden. The importance of such double-thinking to him is evidenced by the title of his 1940 book *The Double Man*. Mendelson explains the significance of this:

The dialectic between self-betrayal and recall was already so important to 'New Year Letter' that Auden almost immediately chose a phrase from Williams for the title of the book that would include the poem. Williams, who seems to have forgotten his source, quoted 'a certain brother': 'It is right for a man to take up the burden for them who are near him . . . to put his own soul in the place of that of his neighbor, and to become, if it were possible, a double man.'

But Auden used the word 'double' in a different sense, which he found elsewhere in *The Descent of the Dove*, in a passage that quoted Montaigne's 'De la gloire': 'We are, I know not how, double in ourselves, so that what we believe we disbelieve, and cannot rid ourselves of what we condemn.'[140]

John Fuller notes that Charles Williams 'also quotes Athanasius on becoming "a double man" through Christian neighbourly empathy . . . though whether this sense was intended to be operative in the title is doubtful'.[141] In fact, it seems almost certain that Auden was referring to this double sense. While it is possible, then, to see the act of being double as a 'feebly figurative sign' of what we cannot 'rid ourselves of' it is also a sign of what it is to be most godlike and most human. The divine voice is an echoing one; as Evans describes it, 'almost all the main constituents of the passion story . . . either have attached to them explicit Old Testament citations or have Old Testament vocabulary woven into the narrative':

In this way it was precluded that the events, and hence the total event which they made up, were either haphazard or accidental . . . This result was achieved all the more forcibly when the chief protagonist in the story, Jesus himself, not only is made to use scripture to express the character of the events, and the participation of his own will in what is decreed, but also to use it alongside and in support of what he independently initiates and predicts.[142]

God, then, is not—as McDiarmid argues—'extraliterary, unquotable'. As Jesus, he speaks in quotation marks, quoting (according to Mark and Matthew) Psalm 22 at the moment of his Crucifixion.[143] The doctrine

---

[140] Mendelson, *Later Auden*, 124.   [141] Ibid. 319.
[142] C. F. Evans, *Explorations*, 13–14.
[143] See Evans who discusses the fact that the opening words of Psalm 22 'My God, my God, why hast thou forsaken me?' are according to Mark and Matthew (though not according to Luke and John) the last words of Jesus, ibid. 7; 'this original matrix of

that God incarnates himself as man, as an acknowledgement that we can only understand things that are like us, was crucial to Browning. 'Only a loving God, a God who wishes the world and himself to remain bound together, would condescend to incarnate himself as a man, and to suffer and die as a man', as Hillis Miller writes.[144] For Auden, too, it was important that the divine came down to a human scale. The incarnation in Auden's verse, therefore, could be seen, literally, as a sacred parody. As MALIN puts it, 'It is where we are wounded that is when He speaks | Our creaturely cry' (ACP, 545). The virtues of duplicity are played out repeatedly in The Age of Anxiety: as the characters 'plunge into the labyrinthine forest and vanish down solitary paths, with no guide but their sorrows, no companion but their own voices', they too hear echoes: 'Their ways cross and recross yet never once do they meet though now and then one catches somewhere not far off a brief snatch of another's song' (ACP, 507). Thus 'Quant's voice' echoes As You Like It ('Sans youth or use, sans uniform' (ACP, 507)) recalling the 'Last scene of all | That ends this strange eventful history, | Is second childishness, and mere oblivion, | Sans teeth, sans eyes, sans taste, sans everything'.[145] Or ROSETTA's version of Rosalind. Running '[t]hrough forests far from father's eye/ To look for a true love' she puts it well: 'Faintly our sounds | Echo each other, unrelated | Groans of grief at a great distance' (ACP, 512).

For there is a way in which this 'irony' need not be seen solely as weakness. As Mendelson notes, in 'romantic thought, repetition is the enemy of freedom, and the greatest form of repression both in the mind and in the state', but 'outside romanticism, repetition has a very different import: it is the sustaining and renewing power of nature, the basis for all art and understanding'.[146] QUANT's snatch from Robert Browning—'God's in his greenhouse, his geese in the world' (ACP, 514)—indicates quite how repetitive things are in this quest. QUANT is echoing a line from Pippa Passes, 'God's in his heaven, all's right with the world', which itself has ironic overtones (BCP i. 311, ll. 225–6). While this sequence of misquotations and echoing signifies some sort of distancing from authenticity, it could also be seen as the sin which

---

Christian interpretative thought' means that 'thought is permanently bound to the Old Testament', and religion 'may, perhaps, be said to consist basically in a sense of awe before a power that is other and holy, Rudolf Otto's mysterium tremendum et fascinans' Explorations, 16.

[144] Hillis Miller, Disappearance, 155.   [145] II. vii. 164–6.
[146] Mendelson, Early Auden, 172.

leads to grace—as EMBLE puts it 'We err what we are as if we were not' (*ACP*, 514). Auden, then, recognizes a possibility for human community in the medium of quotation—a deliberate courting of inauthenticity. Mendelson confirms that this change of mind began as early as the 1930s, when 'repetition in nature, history and poetry' changed, in his mind, from being 'a mortifying compulsion' to 'the ground of memory, the medium of love'.[147] This explains, in part, his attraction towards phrases that are seen as banal, or clichéd. Banality and cliché are traps, as he notes in *The Dyer's Hand*:

The human person is a unique singular, analogous to all other persons, but identical with none. Banality is an illusion of identity for, when people describe their experiences in clichés, it is impossible to distinguish the experience of one from the experience of another. The cliché user is comic because the illusion of being identical with others is created by his own choice. He is the megalo-maniac in reverse. Both have fantastic conceptions of themselves but whereas the megalomaniac thinks of himself as being somebody else—God, Napoleon, Shakespeare—the banal man thinks of himself as being everybody else, that is to say, nobody in particular.[148]

So it is to court failure deliberately, then, that he creates CALIBAN's speech, made up of 'fugitives from some Book of Clichés', in order to reach towards that mode that Barthes condemned as 'discourse without a body': 'banality'.[149] And, in this way, Auden has provided a model for a poet like John Ashbery who celebrates 'the everyday speech rhythms which are very much a part of our life' as a form of communion.[150] Ashbery might agree with Scruton's assessment that cliché is 'the ultim-ate universal, the ultimate negation of the particular. It involves an escape from the suffering of solitude into a comforting association with the commonplace and the normal—with the condition the exist-entialists have described as "otherness".'[151] But Auden uses these tones with an implicit, tacit knowledge that he is creating a false utopia—a place where people's 'nursery, their commonplace, their tomb' are all

---

[147] Ibid.   [148] *DH*, 379.

[149] Richard Boly, *Reading Auden: The Returns of Caliban* (Ithaca, NY: Cornell University Press, 1991), 205; Roland Barthes, *Roland Barthes*, trans. Richard Howard (London: Papermac, 1995), 137.

[150] Ashbery argues that clichés have 'beauty because of being hallowed somehow by so much use', Richard Jackson, *Acts of Mind: Conversations with Contemporary Poets* (Tuscaloosa: University of Alabama Press, 1983), 106.

[151] Roger Scruton, *The Aesthetic Understanding* (London and New York: Methuen, 1983), 222.

one. 'Art is born of humiliation', he told the young Spender, and it is this poetic sense of, and for, not being exceptional, for being human, and subject to irony, that defines his relation to his poetic and religious tradition.[152] Throughout the writing of *The Sea and the Mirror*, Auden seems conscious of the temptation to play God that self-definition may involve.

In his lecture on *The Tempest*, Auden draws a vision of a Prospero who comes near to the figure of Faust; and for Auden, the transcendental claims of Faust who claimed 'all things that move between the quiet poles | Shall be at my command' had to be balanced by a more existential sense of one's command being defined by one's own 'creatureliness'.[153] Irony, as Thomas Mann notes, is both 'diabolical and divine'.[154] While, for Faust, the attraction was to wield a godlike irony over creatures, for Auden, it is necessary to recognize that one is a creature, and, therefore, to recognize the possibility of being ironized. 'What Faust is totally lacking in is a sacramental sense, a sense that the finite can be a sign for the infinite, that the secular can be sanctified', he writes in 'Balaam and His Ass'.[155] Auden's insistence on cutting poetry down to size, his assertion that 'poetry makes nothing happen' (*ACP*, 248), is related to his habit of pastiche, parody, and allusion. Through all these means, he shows the text to be 'a way of happening', a point of (sometimes condescending) relation. Sometimes this is directed towards others; Mendelson picks up on a slight parody of Robert Frost in 'Their Lonely Betters' (1950): 'Let them leave language to their lonely betters | Who count some days and long for certain letters; | We, too, make noises when we laugh or weep: | Words are for those with promises to keep' (*ACP*, 583).

The final line is an allusion to Robert Frost's 'Stopping by Woods on a Snowy Evening': 'The woods are lovely, dark and deep, | But I have promises to keep.'[156] It is, Mendelson notes, 'a tribute to another poet's verbal mastery and a claim to moral understanding deeper than his'.[157] It is hard to square the idea of Auden paying 'tribute' *to* Frost with the

---

[152] See James Fenton, 'Auden at Home', *New York Review of Books*, 27 Apr. 2000, 8–14, 8.

[153] Christopher Marlowe, *Dr Faustus* (1604), i. 56–7, 2nd edn., ed. Roma Gill (London: A & C Black, 1989), 9.

[154] Quoted in D. C. Muecke, *Irony and the Ironic* (London and New York: Methuen, 1982), 50.

[155] *DH*, 118.

[156] Robert Frost, *Collected Poems, Prose, and Plays*, ed. Richard Poirier and Mark Richardson (New York: Library of America, 1995), 207.

[157] Mendelson, *Later Auden*, 364.

possibility that he is simultaneously claiming 'moral superiority' *over* him. However, this line touches on the modes of humble parody and parodic humility that are central to the ethics of Auden's verse.

It also raises questions about his relationship with language. With the line 'Words are for those with promises to keep', Auden acknowledges that it is language that offers the opportunity of acknowledging the other, but that language simultaneously blocks the notion of a pure promise; what Auden saw as 'the aura of suggestion round every word' allows for a multiplicity of meanings in every exchange (*EA*, 327). In this sense, Auden is evidently a disciple of Schleiermacher, as he thinks through the way in which he is 'in the power of the language' he speaks, while also 'taking his part in forming it'.[158] Only through recognizing the 'presence and action of others' implicit within language itself can one speak truly—but the 'presence and action of others' within one's language preclude authentic speech. Auden's language, like his nature, is 'subdu'd/ To what it works in, like the dyer's hand'.[159]

The 'impulse to realize the jarring double-takes in words of common usage', as Geoffrey Hill puts it, pervades Auden's later works—often as a partial atonement for his earlier poetry, in which he confidently enjoyed, he admitted, the 'manipulation of the common abstract word' (*EA*, 327).[160] Auden's poem 'At the Grave of Henry James' is an example of this atoning work:

> Shall I not especially bless you as, vexed with
> My little inferior questions, I stand
>   Above the bed where you rest,
> Who opened such passionate arms to your *Bon* when It ran
> Towards you with Its overwhelming reasons pleading
>   All beautifully in Its breast?
>
> (*ACP*, 311)

'It' is James's term for the 'Guardian angel of his inspiration' and the final lines of this first verse, Fuller points out, are a 'direct quotation from James's *Complete Notebooks*, appearing again in chapter 14 of *The Awkward Age*'. Fuller adds that 'At the Grave of Henry James' is 'not a little foretaste of Caliban' in *The Sea and the Mirror*: 'allusions and mild

[158] Schleiermacher, 'On the Different Methods of Translation', 36–54, at 38.
[159] See Sonnet 111, *Riverside Shakespeare*, 1769.
[160] See Hill's letter to Kenneth Allott, in Allott (ed.), *The Penguin Book of Contemporary Verse* (Harmondsworth: Penguin, 1950), 391.

Jamesian pastiche aside: it comes out in the feeling that there is something unmanageable about life, and that therefore the writer should
avoid any attempt to manage it.'[161] In fact, the use of pastiche in this
poem is a key factor in the creation of the 'foretaste' of Auden's CALIBAN.
The devices of pastiche and parody are set against the idea of authority,
and against the notion that an artist might speak with a single voice. The
diction here acknowledges in every word the users that have come before
it. This becomes even clearer in the final stanza:

> All will be judged. Master of nuance and scruple,
> Pray for me and for all writers, living or dead:
>   Because there are many whose works
> Are in better taste than their lives, because there is no end
> To the vanity of our calling, make intercession
>   For the treason of all clerks.

(ACP, 312)

The 'treason of the clerks' is a reference to Julien Benda's 1927 work, *La
Trahison des clercs* which was translated by Richard Aldington as *The
Treason of the Intellectuals* in 1928. There, Benda claimed that the
modern poet (or 'clerk' as he termed him), was betraying his aesthetic
vocation: 'determined to have the soul of a citizen and to make vigorous
use of it; he is proud of that soul; his literature is filled with his contempt
for the man who shuts himself up with art or science and takes no
interest in the passions of the State...Today the "clerk" has made
himself Minister of War.'[162] The book—which claims that poets should
have nothing whatsoever to do with politics—is an important one to
Auden. He used it as a title for a 1942 review written on the day that
America entered the war, noting that 'to be spending the day of
America's entry into the War in literary criticism must seem preposter-
ous'. However, he adds that 'the external conflict of classes and nations
and political systems is paralleled by an equally intense internal conflict
in every individual'.[163] Such an 'intense internal conflict' can be seen at
work in the poem. For while it attempts a pastiche of Henry James,
Auden's poem also refers back to another pastiche—Empson's 1937
poem 'Just a Smack at Auden':

[161] See J. Fuller, *W. H. Auden: A Commentary*, 399.
[162] Jules Benda, *The Treason of the Intellectuals*, trans. Richard Aldington (New York: Norton, 1928), 53.
[163] 'La Trahison d'un Clerc', *Perspectives* (Jan. 1942), repr. in *Prose*, ii. 148.

What was said by Marx, boys, what did he perpend?
No good being sparks, boys, waiting for the end.
Treason of the clerks, boys, curtains that descend,
Lights becoming darks, boys, waiting for the end.[164]

Haffenden claims that this is a fond pastiche; Empson was a great admirer of Auden in the 1930s. He admits, however, that Auden 'had initially felt the force of Empson's baying at the "boys"'.[165] In picking up the diction of a boy's boarding-school master, used by Auden in *The Orators*, Empson is slyly knocking the superior clubbinness, or cosiness, of Auden and the other 'pylon poets' of the 1930s, with their verse that simultaneously appeared to foresee, and crave, disaster.[166] In the final lines of 'At the Grave of Henry James', Auden alludes to Empson's pastiche twice: 'because there is no end | To the vanity of our calling, make intercession | For the treason of all clerks.' With the reference to the 'treason of the clerks' he performs, in a way, a critique of his own attempts to play God with words. The 'absolutely banal', Auden noted, is 'my sense of my own uniqueness'. Realizing Empson's parody, he jokes about his own banality.[167] The turning of Empson's phrase 'waiting for the end' into 'because there is no end', once again hanging on a line's end, points, truly, to the 'unmanageable' nature of life. There is 'no end | To the vanity of our calling'. The phrase hints at the impossibility of escaping personal vanity (a nod to the fact that he has integrated a pastiche of himself into the poem), while simultaneously gesturing towards the gravity of language, and the loss of authentic voice, meaning that all attempts to 'call', to issue parables, or to preach, are in vain.

Auden's later poetry certainly became less instructive. He writes in 'Words and the Word' that the 'political and social history of Europe would be what it has been if Dante, Shakespeare, Goethe, Titian . . . had never existed'.[168] In many ways, it also becomes less clearly voiced— more orientated towards a poetics of failure, or creaturehood. Auden's recognition of Empson's pastiche is as close to creaturehood as one can

---

[164] *Complete Poems of William Empson*, ed. John Haffenden (London: Allen Lane, 2000), 82.

[165] Ibid., 355.

[166] The phrase 'pylon poets' is used by Empson: 'It is very hard . . . to write what years later people called pylon poetry—to write about how you ought to have the socialist state . . . without sounding phoney.' See his essay 'Early Auden', in *Argufying: Essays on Literature and Culture* (London: Hogarth, 1987), 375–6.

[167] *DH*, 95.

[168] *SW*, 123.

get. As he writes in 'Notes on the Comic', the fact of literary parody presupposes that every authentic writer has 'a unique perspective of life' and 'that his literary style accurately expresses that perspective':

> The trick of the parodist is to take the unique style of the author, *how* he expresses his unique vision, and make it express utter banalities; *what* the parody expresses could be said by anyone. The effect is of a reversal in the relation between the author and his style. Instead of the style being the creation of the man, the man becomes the puppet of the style.[169]

In noting the way in which he could, himself, become a 'puppet' of his own style, Auden captures the feeling that he explores in Rilke's poem 'The Spirit Ariel'. He gives himself up to the idea that one might ask mercy of one's own poem:

> Now he terrifies me,
> This man who's once more duke.—The way he draws
> the wire into his head, and hangs himself
> beside the other puppet, and henceforth
> asks mercy of the play! . . . what epilogue
> of achieved mastery! Putting off, standing there
> with only one's own strength: 'which is most faint'[170]

If we are to take Auden's dramatic monologues as parabolic, then they are parables about failing to individuate the voices of others. Already, he fulfils what he desired in a lecture a decade later—that artists might become 'both more modest and more self-assured, that they may develop both a sense of humour about their vocation and a respect for that most admirable of Roman deities, the god Terminus'.[171] Through the limits of 'games and grammar and metres' (*ACP*, 811), Auden finds a way to recognize and mirror his own limits. If mirrors are lonely, he manages, at least, to reflect the dilemma.

---

[169] *DH*, 382.
[170] Auden quotes this poem in his lecture on *The Tempest*; see *LOS*, 307.
[171] *SW*, 126.

4

Samuel Beckett: 'humanity in ruins'

Writing just after the Second World War, in a broadcast originally intended for transmission on Radio Éireann, Beckett makes some observations about sympathy and understanding. He had joined the Irish Red Cross in 1945, assisting the French in bringing aid to the civilians of Saint-Lô, a town that had been blitzed by Allied forces. His role had been that of a driver, interpreter, and storekeeper for what became known as the Irish Hospital there, but he had obviously been a keen observer too. The piece is a subtle but biting attack on the 'unregarding munificence of the French Ministry of Reconstruction', which begins with an account of the equipment and conditions of the hospital in which he worked:

The buildings consist of some 25 prefabricated wooden huts. They are superior, generally speaking, to those so scantily available for the wealthier, the better-connected, the astuter or the more flagrantly deserving of the bombed-out. Their finish, as well without as within, is the best that priority can command. They are lined with glass-wool and panelled in isorel, a strange substance of which only very limited supplies are available. There is real glass in the windows. The consequent atmosphere is that of brightness and airiness so comforting to sick people, and to weary staffs.[1]

With its diplomatic evasions (one might ask, after all, what their 'priority' is, and whether 'unregarding' means disinterested, or uncaring), Beckett's poker-faced prose plays on the rhetoric of institutionalized compassion. '[I]t is a regular thing', he notes, 'for as many as 200 to be seen in the out-patients department in a day. Among such ambulant cases a large number are suffering from scabies and other diseases of the skin, the result no doubt of malnutrition or an ill-advised diet.'[2] The yoking together of starvation and bad-eating habits is deftly done,

---

[1] 'The Capital of the Ruins', repr. in Samuel Beckett, *The Complete Short Prose 1929–1989*, ed. S. E. Gontarski (New York: Grove Press, 1995), 275–8, at 275.
[2] Ibid. 276.

as if the invalids had a choice. Throughout the piece, Beckett also catches and satirizes utilitarian statistical analysis in a Swiftian manner, where quantity is a necessary good, and human beings are reduced to case histories. As he draws to a close, he writes of the relationship between the Irish and French workers:

the whole enterprise turned from the beginning on the establishing of a relation in the light of which the therapeutic relation faded to the merest of pretexts. What was important was ... the occasional glimpse obtained, by us in them and, who knows, by them in us (for they are an imaginative people), of that smile at the human condition as little to be extinguished by bombs as to be broadened by the elixirs of Burroughes and Welcome [*sic*],—the smile deriding, among other things, the having and not having, the giving and the taking, sickness and health.[3]

Eoin O'Brien argues that the broadcast 'is of interest in that it gives not only an account of the Irish Hospital but describes also the emotional consequences of the experiences, or, at least, what the emotional consequences were for one of Beckett's sensitivity'.[4] If true, then it is clear that 'emotional consequences' were, for Beckett, a complex matter. The level of irony surrounding human feeling is hard to gauge. On the one hand, 'the smile deriding', which Beckett sees as the relation between 'us' and 'them', could be an expression of tenderness. It is a sign that it is in the nature of 'the human condition' to remain hopeful in spite of 'having and not having ... sickness and health'. But it also sounds a little like a sneer, chiming with 'the mirthless laugh ... the laugh that laughs ... at that which is unhappy' encountered in his 1953 novel *Watt*.[5] Beckett's parenthesis—'(for they are an imaginative people)'—is also telling. Modestly undermining the generosity of the Irish, it figures the notion of psychic unity, the thought of 'them in us', as an ideal that can only ever exist through, or perhaps in, our imagination.

The difficulties of Beckett's tone become even more evident if his sense of post-war spirit is set against the account of Dr James Gaffney, the pathologist and acting director of the hospital. Gaffney also writes of the 'wholesale destruction' in Saint-Lô. He catalogues the recovery of about one thousand five hundred bodies, of twenty-nine prisoners burnt to death in the local jail, of the remaining survivors, some five thousand,

---

[3] 'Captial' Beckett, 276–7.
[4] Eoin O'Brien, *The Beckett Country: An Exhibition for Samuel Beckett's Eightieth Birthday* (Dublin: Black Cat, 1986), 337.
[5] Samuel Beckett, *Watt* (London: John Calder, 1998), 47. Henceforth *W*.

'mostly in boarded up cellars, on mattresses'. 'Yet', he adds, 'with all their sufferings, they are tackling the problems of reconstruction cheerfully.'[6] Gaffney does not analyse his descriptions of others' pains, and Beckett might have felt uneasy about such a breezy embrace of 'all their sufferings'. The phrase is summoned, perhaps, a little too easily. Beckett's writing makes us think again about such easy phrases, especially those that seem to concern feeling. Cliché, for Beckett, in its very texture, is a presumption of commonality, an assumption of easy understanding.

Beckett notes at the close of his broadcast that 'some of those who were in Saint-Lô will come home realising that they got at least as good as they gave, that they got indeed what they could hardly give, a vision and a sense of a time-honoured conception of humanity in ruins'.[7] At a time when the notion of 'giving as good as you get' was the patriotic and the moral norm, Beckett remakes the cliché to give a little more. Cutting through our habitual ways of speaking about pain, Beckett's writing continually touches on the fragility of human compassion, and the possibility for human heartlessness.

Beckett's art has been held up for ethical scrutiny by a number of critics. '[S]educed and disturbed by the attitudes of Beckett's characters', Stephen Rosen 'wonder[s] about the mentality that motivated their creation', while less sympathetic readers have attacked 'the seamier side of Mr. Beckett's nasty unconscious'.[8] Even biographical accounts suggest that Beckett had a strained relationship with sentiment. His lover, Peggy Guggenheim, recalls him saying that 'he was dead and had no feelings that were human'—a phrase which peculiarly recalls Ariel's description of his own lack of humanity.[9] Martha Nussbaum has particular reservations about Beckett's ethical and emotional stance, which she raises in her 1990 essay 'Narrative Emotions: Beckett's Genealogy of Love'.[10] Nussbaum criticizes Beckett's writing for its

---

[6] James Gaffney, letter to his sister Maureen, 31 Aug. 1945, quoted in E. O'Brien, *Beckett Country*, 322.

[7] E. O'Brien, *Beckett Country*, 337.

[8] Stephen Rosen, *Samuel Beckett and the Pessimistic Tradition* (New Brunswick, NJ: Rutgers University Press, 1976), 5; Roy Walker, 'Samuel Beckett's Double Bill: Love, Chess, and Death', *Twentieth Century*, 166 (Dec. 1958), 533–44, at 533.

[9] Peggy Guggenheim, *Out of this Century: Confessions of an Art Addict* (London: Andrew Deutsch, 1979), 175. Prospero asks Ariel if his 'affections | Would become tender' if he saw the reformed visitors to the island. His reply is 'Mine would, sir, were I human,' v. i. 18–19.

[10] Martha C. Nussbaum, 'Narrative Emotions: Beckett's Genealogy of Love', in *Love's Knowledge*, 286–313.

lack of feeling, its emotional heartlessness, and, what she terms, its 'monologism'. Why, she asks, are his 'voices so intolerant of society and of shared forms of thought and feeling?'[11] She is, however, perhaps, not listening to Beckett's voices carefully enough; the nature of his allusions, and his variations on the dramatic monologue form, demonstrate the more complex aspects of his views on 'shared forms of thought and feeling'. The highly allusive *How It Is*, which repeatedly echoes *The Tempest*, is, perhaps, his most extreme variation on the dramatic monologue. It provides a useful case-study, as it shows Beckett's continual preoccupation with the difficulty of conveying and hearing the voice of another, and his thoughts on the relationship between a powerful godlike figure and his possible creatures. In considering these aspects of Beckett's writing, it can be seen that Beckett is far less certain than Nussbaum about the positive role that narratives play.

Gaffney noted that the Beckett he met was of 'no religious persuasion; I should say he was a free thinker'.[12] For Nussbaum, however, Beckett's piety is a matter of concern. She writes that 'mortality in Beckett's world is seen not as our neutral and natural condition but as our punishment for original sin'; his voices have 'not been able to go far enough outside the Christian picture to see how to pose the problem of self-expression in a way that is not shaped by that picture'.[13] Nussbaum differs in her view from a critic such as Shira Wolosky who comments that 'Beckett's work frequently invokes religious materials, but it resides within none of them.'[14] Perhaps Mary Bryden comes closest to understanding when she comments that if he was 'in exile from heaven, he was also in exile from earth . . . His home was in the border country.'[15] Here, Beckett finds company with both Browning and Auden. All three spent their religious life 'living on the dangerous edge of things', avoiding religious complacency.[16] Auden, Geoffrey Grigson noted, also inhabited a 'frightening border territory'.[17] As Bryden argues, Beckett mistrusted the 'easy and

[11] Nussbaum, *Love's Knowledge*, 310.

[12] James Gaffney, letter to his sister Nora, 22 Oct. 1945, quoted in E. O'Brien, *Beckett Country*, 327.

[13] Nussbaum, *Love's Knowledge*, 309–10.

[14] Shira Wolosky, *Language, Mysticism: The Negative Way of Language in Eliot, Beckett and Celan* (Stanford, Calif.: Stanford University Press, 1995), 2.

[15] Bryden, *Samuel Beckett and the Idea of God*, 4.

[16] The phrase is from Browning's 'Bishop Bloughram's Apology' (*BCP* i. 627, l. 396). See my discussion of this in Ch. 2.

[17] Geoffrey Grigson, 'Auden as a Monster', *New Verse*, 26–7 (Nov. 1937), 13–14. See my discussion of this in Ch. 3.

warm intercourse which appears to operate between the poetic ' "Ich" of Rilke, and God'. For Beckett, '[s]uch a turmoil of self-deception and naïf discontent gains nothing in dignity from that prime article of the Rilkean faith, which provides for the interchangeability of Rilke and God'.[18] Beckett then, unlike Nussbaum, found 'mortality' neither a 'neutral', nor a 'natural condition'.

Beckett's main worry about Christian dogma was, in part, a problem of understanding God's actions. In this sense, it was a problem of sympathy; he had trouble conceiving God's mind, or imagining God's intentions, particularly in the matter of suffering. As Bryden notes, Beckett 'rejects any posited linkage between suffering and salvation', asking Thomas McGreevy whether one was 'to insist on a crucifixion for which there is no demand?' Bryden continues:

The image of God the Father [in Beckett], then, tends to be one of implacability, unresponsiveness and even cruelty. Indeed, the voice in *L'Innommable* thinks of himself as a squirming fish being baited by God the fisherman: 'L'essential est de gigoter jusqu'au bout au bout de son catgut, tant qu'il y aura des eaux, des rives et déchaîné au ciel un Dieu sportif, pour taquiner la créature.' There is an interesting parallel here with the figure of Jesus, who, on the whole, is not seen as part of a Trinity of conspirators. On the contrary, in his crucified manifestation, Jesus can evoke a feeling of empathy within the Beckettian consciousness. Far from representing the incarnation, or human face, of God, as Christian theologians would maintain, the Jesus who emerges from Beckett's work is often one who is also a helpless victim of God.[19]

If Beckett had so little sympathy with the Christian God, one might ask why he repeatedly puts his characters into positions that resemble that of crucifixion. Take the Unnamable, who speaks of the 'thorns they'll have to come and stick in me, as into their unfortunate Jesus' (*T*, 321), or the terrified voice in *How It Is*, the 'arms spread yes like a cross'.[20] Or, of the petrified figure in his 1967 work *Ping*:

Hands hanging palms front legs joined like sewn. Head haught eyes holes light blue almost white fixed front silence within ... Given rose only just nails fallen white over. Long hair fallen white invisible over. White scars invisible same white as flesh torn of old given rose only just. Ping image only just almost never one second light time blue and white.[21]

---

[18] Bryden, *Samuel Beckett and the Idea of God*, 22. Bryden quotes from Beckett's 1934 review of Rilke's *Poems*, first published in *Criterion*, repr. in *Disjecta*, 67.
[19] Bryden, *Samuel Beckett and the Idea of God*, 86, 83.
[20] Samuel Beckett, *How It Is* (London: Calder, 1964), 159. Henceforth *HII*.
[21] Samuel Beckett, *Ping*, in *No's Knife* (London: Calder & Boyars, 1967), 165–8, at 166–7.

One could argue that Beckett's narrators are created in order to satirize the notion of a cruel God. As with 'Caliban upon Setebos', a double meaning allows the tentative leitmotif—'only just'—to airily indicate that this scene meets the conditions of divine justice. The ambiguity is also present in his drama, reappearing in the 1964 *Play*, where a figure trapped in an urn asks, 'when will all this have been . . . just play?' (*CDW*, 313).

However, the notion of satire alone does not encompass Beckett's religious understanding, or his religious sympathies. In order to satirize, as T. S. Eliot notes, one has to have a clear position from which to start: 'the existence of a pose implies the possibility of a reality to which the pose pretends'.[22] While Browning and Auden managed to make leaps of faith in order to comprehend divine mystery, things, for Beckett, were even more uncertain. His prose and drama show him (like Auden and Browning before him) continually longing for divine understanding, while recognizing the dangers of playing God. It is these concerns—those of sympathy, authorial control, and religious uncertainty—which drew him to the world of *The Tempest*.

THE INSUFFERABLE MIRANDA AND THE DRAMA OF SYMPATHY

Samuel Taylor Coleridge had endless admiration for the compassionate nature of Shakespeare's women. Everyone wishes them 'for a wife', he writes, 'creatures who, though they may not understand you, do always feel you, and feel with you'.[23] Beckett's long engagement with one of the most famously feeling characters in fiction was rather more precarious. William Hutchings writes that his 'earliest allusion' to *The Tempest* occurs in *Waiting for Godot*, when Lucky thinks highly of Miranda: [24]

Given the existence as uttered forth in the public works of Puncher and Wattmann of a personal God quaquaquaqua with white beard quaquaquaqua outside time without extension who from the heights of divine apathia divine athambia divine aphasia loves us dearly with some exceptions for reasons

[22] T. S. Eliot, *The Varieties of Metaphysical Poetry*, ed. Ronald Schuchard (London: Faber, 1993), 209.

[23] Samuel Taylor Coleridge, *The Table Talk and Omniana* (Oxford, 1917), 131–2.

[24] William Hutchings, ' "As Strange a Maze as E'er Man trod": Samuel Beckett's Allusions to Shakespeare's Last Plays', in Anne-Marie Drew (ed.), *Past Crimson: Past Woe: The Shakespeare–Beckett Connection* (New York: Garland, 1993), 3–15, at 11.

unknown but time will tell and suffers like the divine Miranda with those who for reasons unknown but time will tell are plunged into torment . . . (*CDW,* 42)

In fact, he wrote of 'Mumps and an orchid for Fraulein Miranda' some twenty-one years earlier, in his 1931 poem 'Return to the Vestry'.[25] Such sterile gifts show little promise for a fruitful relationship, but Beckett was enchanted, in spite of himself, by Shakespeare's heroine. His lingering aversions and attractions show themselves in the way in which her play allusively inhabits a number of his other texts, indicating something about the complex nature of sympathy in his work.

A number of critics have dwelt on Miranda's appearances in Beckett's texts.[26] Katherine Worth comments that Lucky's ' "divine" plays with Shakespeare's word "admired" ("Admired Miranda! . . . ") taking even further the Latinate sense the word had then, "to be wondered at". Miranda's capacity to feel so keenly the sufferings of strangers, seems to place her in another dimension than that inhabited by the unpitied carrier.' In this way, *The Tempest*, Worth writes, 'sends out . . . echoes into Beckett's world through the name Miranda, she who was able to suffer "with those that I saw suffer": the authentic Beckettian note'.[27] Lucky is alluding to the moment in *The Tempest* when Miranda watches the shipwreck, and cries out in pain: 'O, I have suffered | With those that I saw suffer!' (I. ii. 5–6). Worth is moved by Miranda's feelings, and her admiration informs her impassioned assurance that Beckett 'did care', that he 'touches the springs of our sympathy' and shows us 'the high road to human feeling'.[28] However, in her belief that Beckett offers the 'camaraderie' of Miranda's 'shared words', Worth misses the tone in which, and the place from which, he quotes. At the moment in *The Tempest* when Miranda's lament reaches its peak, her suffering is misplaced:

MIRANDA   O, woe the day!
PROSPERO   No harm.
   I have done nothing but in care of thee,
Of thee, my dear one; thee, my daughter, who
Art ignorant of what thou art; nought knowing
Of whence I am . . .

(I. ii. 15–19)

---

[25] See Laurence E. Harvey, *Samuel Beckett: Poet and Critic* (Princeton: Princeton University Press, 1970), 311.
[26] See Ruby Cohn's 'Tempest in an Endgame', *Symposium,* 19 (1965), 328–34.
[27] Katherine Worth, *Samuel Beckett's Theatre: Life Journeys* (Oxford: Oxford University Press, 1999), 12.
[28] Ibid. 1, 13, 1.

In telling Miranda that she, 'ignorant of what thou *art*' (my emphasis), is the daughter of a magician (and has been, therefore, caring for a figment), Prospero also hints that her reaction is a touch contrived. T. S. Eliot found in Shakespeare a sense in which characters find escape from the reality of suffering through 'dramatizing' themselves, 'adopting an aesthetic rather than a moral attitude'.[29] It seems that Beckett, too, like Auden before him, had a feeling for the choreographed Shakespearean emotion. Lucky's 'divine Miranda' has a thespian ring to it—it gestures towards staged hyperbole.

Such melodramatic sympathizing echoes back to an earlier reference to Miranda in Beckett's work—she has a cameo role as a day-nurse in 'Yellow', the penultimate story in his 1934 work, *More Pricks than Kicks*. 'Yellow' tells of Belacqua Shuah's ill-fated stay in hospital, and Beckett recalls Miranda from *The Tempest* to disinfect the hero's hammer toes and tumour before his minor, but fatal, operation. Like her dramatic namesake who 'suffered | With those' she 'saw suffer', this woman's pity knows no bounds: 'She lashed into the part with picric and ether... When his entire nape was as a bride's adorned (bating the obscene stain of the picric) and so tightly bandaged that he felt his eyes bulging, she transferred her compassion to the toes. She scoured the whole phalanx, top and bottom. Suddenly she began to titter.'[30] There are biblical echoes here, as Miranda's ministerings comically recall those of the Magdalene, anointing the feet of Jesus (John 12: 3), giving her laughter a blasphemous air. It is Belacqua's 'lang tootsy', one of the pediatric deformities which he has 'suffered with... almost continuously' (at least since 'Dante and the Lobster'), that causes Miranda's 'forgetting herself' (*MPTK*, 14–15). Belacqua reflects throughout the tale about the appropriate reactions to misery. 'Was it to be laughter or tears?' he asks himself (*MPTK*, 175). However, faced with Miranda's mirth, an indignant Belacqua—'There were limits, he felt, to Democritus'—stands on ceremony: ' "I say" he roared "that that toe you like so much will soon be only a memory". He could not put it plainer than that' (*MPTK*, 182). Belacqua has held back the tears until this pathetic moment, for fear of being thought unmanly: 'All the staff, from matron to lift-boy, would make the mistake of ascribing his tears, or, perhaps better, his tragic demeanour, not to the follies of humanity at

---

[29] T.S. Eliot, 'Shakespeare and the Stoicism of Seneca', in *Selected Essays*, 167.
[30] *More Pricks than Kicks* (London: Calder, 1993), 181–2.

large...but rather to the tumour the size of a brick that he had on the back of his neck' (*MPTK*, 176).

Belacqua's concern with the way in which generous displays of emotion may be misinterpreted is characteristically Beckettian. John Pilling and James Knowlson note that Beckett's early work showed him 'striving to avoid all sentimentality'. In a letter to Tom McGreevy, Beckett wrote of the artistic difficulties of handling Murphy's death, which was 'to consist with...the mixture of compassion, patience, mockery and "tat twam asi"...with the sympathy going so far and no further'.[31] As this comment suggests, the question of how much emotion or sympathy should be evoked by a work of art, and how far it should go, was at the centre of Beckett's practice, from early in his writing life.

PAIN AT A DISTANCE: HEARING ALLUSIONS

These sensitive matters, central to the art of 'Yellow', are foregrounded by its title. Nicholas Zurbrugg argues that it refers to the 'yallar wall' of the nursing home in which Belacqua is treated, and makes reference to Proust's dying writer, Bergotte, who 'drags himself from his deathbed in order to ponder...the "petit pan de mur jaune"...in Vermeer's "View of Delft"'. Contemplating Vermeer's painting, Bergotte thinks '"I should have written like that...My last books are too arid. I should have used several layers of colour".' Zurbrugg is right to notice that 'Yellow' is concerned with the technicalities of artistic expression. However, he is hesitant about this 'somewhat oblique parodic allusion', and, perhaps, his argument is hampered by this exclusive emphasis on Proustian echoes.[32] The story's title might also refer to the way in which feeling can manifest itself as a 'property', setting the coloured 'stain of the picric' against the figurative sense of craven or cowardly emotional behaviour. Beckett's handling of suffering in *More Pricks than Kicks* caused one reviewer to write that his 'language is as fluid as [his] morals'.[33] In fact, 'Yellow' shows an acute sense for the ways in which

---

[31] John Pilling and James Knowlson, *Frescoes of the Skull: The Later Prose and Drama of Samuel Beckett* (New York: Random House, 1980), 5; Samuel Beckett, 'To Tom MacGreevy', 17 July 1936, *Disjecta*, 102.

[32] Nicholas Zurbrugg, *Beckett and Proust* (Gerrards Cross: Colin Smythe, 1998), 221–2.

[33] Arthur Calder Marshall, 'Dubliners', *Spectator*, 1 June 1934, quoted in Lance St John Butler (ed.), *Critical Essays on Samuel Beckett* (Aldershot: Scolar, 1993), 9.

the linguistic and moral realms might meet. The word 'yellow' also has an established history in moral philosophy. G. E. Moore uses the colour in his attempts to put ethical and emotional qualities into words. 'My point', he writes in *Principia Ethica*, 'is that "good" is a simple notion just as "yellow" is a simple notion; that, just as you cannot, by any manner of means, explain to anyone who does not already know it, what yellow is, so you cannot explain what good is'.[34] Moore, here, is pointing out the way in which an ethical quality is beyond words. Such philosophical and verbal difficulties inhabit this story, for Beckett knew from Joyce that 'moral effect' and 'aesthetic integrity' were profoundly linked.[35]

Beckett's prose style continually plays on the ways in which emotion both can and should be made concrete in art—and the ways in which one can understand the emotions of another. The title could be seen as making reference to a particular literary style. 'Yellow' was originally an Americanism, applied in 1855 to newspapers, or journalists, of 'a recklessly or unscrupulously sensational character'. By the turn of the century, the term was applied to any literature that was seen as cheap or vulgar, 'sensational books and magazines issued in inexpensive form, as in yellow covers'.[36] *More Pricks than Kicks* has a title worthy of the bodice-ripping author Paul de Kock, and within the stories, Beckett pokes fun at the clichés of emotive, sensational writing—sex, suicide attempts, and billets-doux abound as he mocks and plays on versions of 'yellow' texts. Take what follows Belacqua's plain speech:

'I say' he roared 'that that toe you like so much will soon be only a memory.'
He could not put it plainer than that.
Her voice after his was scarcely audible. It went as follows:
'Yes'—the word died away and was repeated—'yes, his troubles are nearly over.'
Belacqua broke down completely, he could not help it. This distant voice, like a cor anglais coming through the evening, and then the his, the his was the last straw. He buried his face in his hands, he did not care who saw him.
'I would like' he sobbed 'the cat to have it, if I might.'   (*MPTK*, 182)

[34] G. E. Moore, *Principia Ethica*, ed. Thomas Baldwin (Cambridge: Cambridge University Press, 1999), 59.
[35] Beckett said that 'Joyce had a moral effect on me: he made me realise aesthetic integrity', quoted in Ruby Cohn, *Back to Beckett* (Princeton: Princeton University Press, 1973), 14.
[36] See W. Craigie and J. Hulbert (eds.), *A Dictionary of American English on Historical Principles* (London: Oxford University Press, 1936–44), sense 2 (1855), and *OED* sense 3.

It is hard to work out quite why the 'his', is for Belacqua, the 'last straw'. Perhaps it seems to him that Miranda is suggesting that the physical ailment in some way *belongs* to the toe in question, rather than being the result of an arbitrary force from without. In this sense, Belacqua (rather like Susan Sontag) is appalled at the way in which physical suffering can be used to create and manipulate moral frameworks.[37] On a simpler level, he may simply have been moved by the intensity of her emotional pitch. For while Miranda is meant to be sympathizing, and Belacqua suffering, both are in fact performing. The sense in which the characters are luxuriating in their feelings is mirrored by the narrator's overwritten prose style. Miranda's rendition 'like a cor anglais coming through the evening' is lauded and matched by the mixing of cliché. In exaggerating the 'yellow' writing style, Beckett is manufacturing a 'hitch in the lyrical loinstring', as he puts it in an early poem, highlighting the comic, stagy nature of their emotions.[38] While, conventionally, a narrator might sympathize with his characters, here, they are seen as aesthetic objects, as phrases to be mulled over: 'the his, the his was the last straw.' Such parody hints at the falsities of human feeling, as played out in this institution 'calculated . . . to promote . . . the relief of suffering in the long run'. As Miranda accompanies him 'down to the theatre', Belacqua cannot resist making a scene. With perfect timing, 'just when the silence was becoming awkward', he hands her his glasses in a parting shot worthy of the most heart-rending pulp:

'Can I trust you with these?' he said.
She put them into her bosom. The divine creature!   (*MPTK*, 186)

Lucky's 'divine Miranda', it seems, echoes back to the ironic tones of this drama of sympathy. Though, at first glance, her gesture may be as generous as her chest, the comic exchange points to the manner in which Miranda's admirers get carried away by the romance of it all.

'Yellow' fictions were noted for the way in which they could manipulate their protagonists, as well as their readers, for emotional effect. In the opening lines of the story, Belacqua broods on a text which critics disliked for such a reason—'Hardy's Tess' (*MPTK*, 171)—which ends with the 'nasty fancy' of the President of the Immortals'

---

[37] See Susan Sontag, *Illness as Metaphor and AIDS and its Metaphors* (London: Penguin, 1991).
[38] See 'A Casket of pralinen for a daughter of a dissipated mandarin', quoted in John Pilling (ed.), *The Cambridge Companion to Beckett* (Cambridge: Cambridge University Press, 1994), 21.

'sport' with humanity.[39] Beckett's story also sports with such playfulness. Belacqua's sudden death on the operating table is a surprise ending in the style of American sensation writer O. Henry: 'By Christ! He did die! They had clean forgotten to auscultate him!' (*MPTK*, 186). O. Henry became notorious for his 'cheap and tawdry effects' and his appeal to the mass market: 'He knew precisely how much of the sugar of sentimentality, the great average reading public must have, and how much of the pepper of sensation, and the salt of facts and the salad dressing of romance.'[40] In using the O. Henry formula, however, Beckett takes care to build up several layers of emotional colour. Belacqua's demise, here, recalls the first episode of the book 'Dante and the Lobster'. On realizing that the seafood he has carried around all day, in preparation for dinner, is alive, Beckett's hero has a flicker of feeling, akin to the 'rare movements of compassion' (*MPTK*, 18) that he has previously noted in Dante: 'Suddenly he saw the creature move, this neuter creature. Definitely it changed its position. His hand flew to his mouth. "Christ!" he said "it's alive"' (*MPTK*, 20).

However, this feeling for suffering is soon dampened by his Aunt's reprimands, and his own appetite:

'You make a fuss' she said angrily 'and upset me and then lash into it for your dinner.'
She lifted the lobster clear of the table. It had about thirty seconds to live.
Well, thought Belacqua, it's a quick death, God help us all.
It is not.   (*MPTK*, 21)

'Yellow', then, is the other half of a story about death and mercy; the sudden boiling of the lobster for dinner chimes with the playful demise of Belacqua. Such parallels indicate the way in which an author might sport with his creatures, in a recipe for readerly satisfaction. They also intimate that the reader's compassion for Belacqua might be as short-lived as Belacqua's feelings for his dinner. The relishing of grief continues in the next story, 'Draff', as Mrs Shuah thinks of her 'friends, their unassumed grief giving zest to their bacon and eggs, the first phrases of sympathy with her in this great loss modulating from porridge to marmalade' as they read Belacqua's obituary (*MPTK*, 189).

One way in which Beckett holds his characters at arm's length emotionally, is by drawing attention to the text's printed nature. *More*

---

[39] William Empson compares Cordelia's death in *King Lear* to Thomas Hardy's 'nasty fancy, in *The Dynasts*, of the Spirit Ironical' in *Structure of Complex Words*, 154.
[40] Eugene Current-Garcia, *O. Henry (William Sydney Porter)* (New York: Twayne Publishers, 1965), 135.

Pricks than Kicks seems oddly aware of its typography and punctuation. Seized with inhibitions about asking for the toilet, Belacqua speaks 'all in a rush, without any punctuation' to Miranda (*MPTK*, 178). Earlier, he removes his glasses '(a precautionary measure that he never neglected when there was the least danger of his *appearing* embarrassed, appearing in italics because he was always embarrassed)' (*MPTK*, 82).[41]

On the one hand, this textual self-consciousness has the effect of 'flattening' the protagonists, drawing attention to their printed nature. However, there is an alternative reading. The narrator may be implying that Belacqua is thinking of the way in which he speaks 'without any punctuation'. If so, this gives him a curious meta-fictional autonomy, as if he is showing himself to be sentient, aware of the mechanics of the creative medium that he inhabits. Either way, as Farrow puts it, such ambiguities about punctuation call into question the assumption that the 'man who writes is separable from the matter about which he writes'.[42] They also demonstrate Beckett's consciousness of the way in which questions of sympathy, and the replication of the tones of another's voice, are deeply interwoven.

It is hard to decide quite how distant Beckett's various Mirandas are from Shakespeare, or how attached Beckett's Belacqua is to his Dantescan original. Such acts of revisiting a fictional character, like acts of allusion more generally, are at the heart of sympathy. The way, perhaps, in which these two fictional worlds relate, might be compared to the manner in which a phrase might inhabit two different tonal registers. The Shakespearean notes in Beckett sound like Prospero's ''Tis new to thee': a repetition and a revoicing by a parent to a child who never quite knew them, and never will. The moment before Miranda embraces her 'brave new world' she has her mind on things apart from her father—a game of chess:

> *Here Prospero discovers Ferdinand and Miranda playing at chess.*
>
> MIRANDA Sweet lord, you play me false.
>
> FERDINAND   No, my dearest love,
>   I would not for the world.
>
> MIRANDA Yes, and for a score of kingdoms you should wrangle,
>   And I would call it fair play.
>
>   (v. i. 171–4)

---

[41] Part of this phrase first appears in *Dream of Fair to Middling Women*, 233.

[42] Anthony Farrow, *Early Beckett: Art and Allusion in 'More Pricks than Kicks' and 'Murphy'* (New York: Whitston, 1991), 116.

Among the critics who have noticed Beckett's allusions to *The Tempest*, few have considered the echoes of this game of chess in the cell.[43] In an article about *Endgame*, James Acheson considers the many allusions in the text, from Genesis to Dante's *Inferno* to *David Copperfield*. He begins by recounting that Beckett told friends who translated *Fin de Partie* as 'End of the game' that it was '*Endgame*, as in chess' and his thesis depends on the claim that Beckett is playing a form of theatrical chess *against* his audience, or his reader. Acheson does not dwell on any one textual link. His aim, in collecting a selection of the possible 'interpretations' of *Endgame*, based on its allusive texture, is to dismiss them all: 'checkmate occurs when we recognise that the play is deliberately designed to resist even the most ingenious of explanations.'[44] In this sense, Acheson reads *Endgame* as a text that is so 'open' that it resists interpretation—he closes the possibility for a reader to follow any allusion in order to conjecture authorial intention, or make a connection to another text. Like Hugh Kenner, then, he offers us a Beckett in which 'all is a game within the realm of "art as a closed field"'.[45] So, although Acheson is careful to emphasize that the play 'is clearly too complex to yield to either a straightforward naturalistic, expressionistic or symbolic interpretation', he goes on to make such an interpretation based on the allusion to chess in the play's title.

Critics like comparing Beckett's texts to chess games because it seems to support the theory that his works are, as far as possible, a 'closed field'.[46] That is to say that they present us with a complete world in miniature, a world in which the 'separation from exteriority' precedes all other relations.[47] Farrow, for example, writes that 'the notion of the game' in Beckett is hermetic: 'any additional assumptions of intentions are superfluous'.[48] However, Beckett's use of the chess game in his first

---

[43] Brief mentions are made in Walker, 'Samuel Beckett's Double Bill', 532–40 and Ruby Cohn, *Modern Shakespearean Offshoots* (Princeton: Princeton University Press, 1976), 376.

[44] James Acheson, 'Chess with the Audience: Samuel Beckett's "Endgame"', *Critical Quarterly*, 22/2 (1980), 33–45, at 39.

[45] Quoted in Murphy, *Critique of Beckett Criticism*, 19.

[46] See Hugh Kenner, 'we have begun to encounter much theory concerning language as a closed field', *The Stoic Comedians* (London: W. H. Allen, 1964), p. xiv.

[47] The phrase 'separation *from* exteriority' comes from Thomas Trezise, who sees a Beckettian universe 'in which . . . the separation *from* exteriority precedes, founds, and conditions any and every relation *to* exteriority', *Into the Breach: Samuel Beckett and the Ends of Literature* (Princeton: Princeton University Press, 1990), p. ix.

[48] Farrow, *Early Beckett*, 46.

play, *Eleuthéria* (1947) suggests that the conventional imagery of the game as a counterpart for fiction in his work is missing something. In a Pirandello-like moment, the 'Spectator' steps onto the stage, unable to stand the drama any more, and unable to leave. He compares his experience to 'watching a game of chess between two fifth-rate players':

> *Spect*: For three quarters of an hour neither of them has made a move, they're sitting there like a couple of morons, yawning over the chess board, and you're...rooted to the spot, disgusted, bored, tired, marvelling at so much stupidity. Until the moment when you can't stand it any longer. So you tell them, but do this, do this, what are you waiting for?...It's unforgivable, it's against all the most elementary rules of polite behaviour...but you can't help yourself...Do you follow me?
> *Glaz*: No. We aren't playing chess.[49]

The Glazier and the Spectator do not seem to be getting on very well here. However, their inability to touch each other is not due to the fact that their individual worlds are *entirely* 'closed systems'. The Glazier is unable to 'follow' the Spectator's point of view because, as he puts it, 'all that stuff about chess...doesn't make sense'; the failed transmission of meaning comes from an inability to catch an intentional tone—one is speaking of an imaginary game of chess, the other, of a real one.

  This extract from *Eleuthéria* suggests another way of thinking about how readers might feel, confronted by the allusive and elusive sense of Beckett's dramatic game-playing. There are subtle nuances to the spirit and intentions of literary chess games, from Miranda and Ferdinand, who play by the rules of love, not logic, to Murphy and Mr Endon, who play according to an incomprehensible theory, each of his own.[50] To leap into a text, or into a chess game, like the injudicious Spectator, might be misdirected, but, as he puts it, 'you can't help yourself'. Acheson, like Worth, makes the wrangle of linguistic allusion too simple. While Worth believes that a direct line can be drawn between the Shakespearean and the Beckettian Miranda, Acheson believes that no connections can be made at all. The truth, perhaps, is somewhere in between. An understanding of a writer's allusive language games relies on attempting to catch the tone and context of play. Such tones are often lost in print. As Michael Dummett puts it, 'the notions of sense and

---

[49] *Eleuthéria*, trans. Barbara Wright (London: Faber, 1996), 133–4.
[50] See the chess game in *Murphy*, 135–8.

reference do not suffice for a complete account of the language', just as 'a "theory" of chess as an activity. . . is not enough to tell anyone what it is to play chess'.[51]

The complex tonal nature of Beckett's allusions is evident in his 1931 study on Proust:

The narrator recalls an incident that took place during his first stay at Balbec, in the light of which he considered his grandmother a frivolous and vain old woman. She had insisted on having her photograph taken . . . And she had been very particular about her pose and the inclination of her hat, wishing the photograph to be one of a grandmother and not of a disease. All of which precautions the narrator had translated as the futilities of coquetry. So, unlike Miranda, he suffers with her whom he had not seen suffer, as though, for him as for Françoise, whom Giotto's charitable scullion in childbirth and the violent translation of what is fit to live into what is fit to eat leave indifferent, but who cannot restrain her tears when informed that there has been an earthquake in China, pain could only be focussed at a distance.[52]

At first glance, it appears that Beckett is setting Françoise, the cook, in *A la recherche du temps perdu* (who happily slaughters the chickens for supper and weeps over the newspaper, while ignoring the hideous labour pains suffered by the maid), against the tenderness of Miranda.[53] Coleridge writes of the way in which such a feeling for imaginary creatures may hamper more pressing sympathy for those closer to home:

True Benevolence is a rare Quality among us. Sensibility indeed we have to spare—what novel-reading Lady does not overflow with it to the great annoyance of her friends and family—her own sorrows like the Princes of Hell in Milton's Pandemonium sit bulky and vast—while the miseries of our fellow creatures dwindle into pigmy forms, and are crowded, an unnumbered multitude, into some dark corner of the heart where the eye of sensibility gleams faintly on them at long intervals.[54]

---

[51] Michael Dummett, *Frege: Philosophy of Language* (London: Duckworth, 1973), 295. My argument here, and my later discussion about tone in *How It Is*, is indebted to Eric Griffiths.

[52] Beckett, *Proust*, 45.

[53] Beckett refers to an episode from *A la recherche du temps perdu*: 'la Charité de Giotto, très malade de son accouchement recent, ne pouvoir se lever; Françoise, n'etant plus aidée, était en retard. Quand je fus en bas, elle était en train, dans l'arrière-cusine qui donnait sur la basse-cour, de tuer un poulet qui, par sa résistance désespérée et bien naturelle, mais accompagnée par Françoise hors d'elle, tandis qu'elle cherchait à lui fender le cou sous l'oreille, des cris de <<sale bête!>> <<sale bête!>>' *A la recherche du temps perdu*, i ed. Jean-Yves Tadié (Paris: Gallimard, 1987), 120.

[54] Samuel Taylor Coleridge, *Lectures 1795 on Politics and Religion*, ed. Lewis Patton and Peter Mann (Princeton: Princeton University Press, 1971), 249.

But while Coleridge saw Miranda as truly benevolent, a figure who 'errs . . . in the exaggerations of love alone', Miranda's suffering is seen by Beckett in an ironic light.[55] After all, her 'piteous heart' *is* moved, like Françoise, and the 'novel-reading Lady', by art. The distant 'direful spectacle of the wrack, which touch'd | The very virtue of compassion' in her, is prelude to the prenuptial 'majestic vision' that Prospero arranges (I. ii. 26–7). Meanwhile, feeling for the sufferings of Caliban, closer to home, is beyond her. Perhaps this is not surprising, considering Caliban's attempt to violate her. However, it is Miranda's ambivalence towards the 'real' world, coupled with her innocent faith in her own emotional capacity, which is carried through into Beckett's work. The 'authentic Beckettian note' that Worth attempts to hear, chimes with the ethical difficulties that feeling for pain, and our emotional reactions to art, involve.

HUMANIST READERS

Nussbaum is more disturbed by Beckett than Worth because he un-settles her core belief that 'fictional narratives play a . . . positive role in self-understanding'. There is, however, something suspect about her attack on Beckett. Her dislike of the 'stoicism', 'solipsism', 'disgust and loathing' in his work is not unusual.[56] Critics such as Toynbee have repeatedly condemned 'the excrement, the blasphemy, the reiterated indifferentism', and 'the emotional aridity' of his work.[57] What is particular to Nussbaum is her concern with Beckett's 'unwriting of stories', which she sees, specifically, as a 'criticism of emotion'.[58] She opens her essay with a passage from near the end of *The Unnamable*:

They love each other, marry, in order to love each other better, more conveni-ently, he goes to the wars, he dies at the wars, she weeps, with emotion, at having loved him, at having lost him, yep, marries again, in order to love again, more conveniently again, they love each other, you love as many times as necessary, as necessary in order to be happy, he comes back, the other comes back, from the wars, he didn't die at the wars after all, she goes to the station, to meet him, he dies in the train, of emotion, at the thought of seeing her again,

---

[55] *Coleridge's Shakespearian Criticism*, 134.
[56] Nussbaum, *Love's Knowledge*, 308.
[57] Philip Toynbee, 'Going Nowhere', *Observer*, 18 Dec. 1958, repr. in L. Butler (ed.), *Critical Essays*, 26.
[58] Nussbaum, *Love's Knowledge*, 308.

having her again, she weeps, weeps again, with emotion again, at having lost him again, yep, goes back to the house, he's dead, the other is dead, the mother-in-law takes him down, he hanged himself, with emotion, at the thought of losing her, she weeps, weeps louder, at having loved him, at having lost him, there's a story for you, that was to teach me the nature of emotion, that's called emotion, what emotion can do, given favourable conditions, what love can do, well well, so that's emotion, that's love, and trains, the nature of trains, and the meaning of your back to the engine, and guards, stations, platforms, wars, love, heart-rending cries.   (*T*, 410)

Stories, Nussbaum writes, 'contain . . . and teach forms of feeling, forms of life', and Beckett's voices 'invite us to consider critically these contingent structures and the narratives that are their vehicle'. However, Beckett's writing is reduced for the sake of her argument when she claims that his increasingly radical attempts to put an end to the entire project of storytelling are a 'criticism of emotion', that 'if stories are learned they can be unlearned. If emotions are constructs, they can be dismantled.'[59] Simon Critchley engages with Nussbaum, commenting that although she 'justifiably . . . assert[s] that Beckett's undermining of traditional patterns of narrative details a critique of the emotions correlated to storytelling . . . she is wrong . . . to infer from this that Beckett is attempting to divest readers of their emotionality'. Critchley suggests that Beckett is working 'not towards an elimination of the emotions, but rather towards a less communally authorised and ritualised sense of pathos, that of the self in its separation from the other and its ever-failing desire for union, for love'.[60] However, in this lyrical argument, styling a wistfully romantic Beckett, Critchley himself is falling into that 'ritualised sense of pathos' which Beckett resists. Both Critchley and Nussbaum would be helped by noting that the 'story for you' is a highly allusive one, echoing, and parodying, a famously heart-wrenching 'yellow' text, Balzac's 'admirable histoire de revenant', *Le Colonel Chabert*.[61] 'De fortes emotions attendent celui qui tient ce livre entre ses mains', Stéphane Vachon writes of this painful narrative in which the elderly Colonel, left for dead in the Napoleonic Wars, returns to Paris to find his wife remarried.[62] Beckett's story, then, may be

    [59] Nussbaum, *Love's Knowledge*, 287.
    [60] Simon Critchley, *Very Little . . . Almost Nothing: Essays on Philosophy and Literature* (London: Routledge, 1997), 201.
    [61] Paul Morand, *Monplaisir . . . en littérature* (Paris: Gallimard, 1967), 89.
    [62] Stéphane Vauchon, 'Introduction' to Honoré de Balzac, *Le Colonel Chabert* (Paris: Librairie Générale Française, 1994), 5.

seen not as 'criticism of emotion' but as a criticism of Balzacian 'forms of feeling', a parody of the ways in which many texts incite formulaic, and possibly complacent, emotional reaction in both their nineteenth- and their twentieth-century readers. The intention behind such parodic allusion is, of course, hard to confirm. But while, as Bryden comments, considerations about 'writerly empathy...can often be tentative, they are not irrelevant'.[63] Beckett's relations with Balzac, which I touched on in Chapter 1, are a case in point. James Knowlson comments that Beckett 'disliked the "chloroformed world" of Balzac's novels, where characters are turned into "clockwork cabbages"'.[64] He bases this insight on the authority of a dense passage in *Dream of Fair to Middling Women*:

To read Balzac is to receive the impression of a chloroformed world. He is absolute master of his material... he can write the end of his book before he has finished the first paragraph, because he has turned all his creatures into clockwork cabbages and can rely on their staying put wherever needed or staying going at whatever speed in whatever direction he chooses. The whole thing, from beginning to end, takes place in a spellbound backwash. We all love and lick up Balzac... but why call a distillation of Euclid and Perrault *Scenes from Life*? Why *human* comedy?[65]

However, it is not Balzac's 'characters', as Knowlson puts it, but his 'creatures' that are thought about here. Beckett's relation to Balzac was not as simple as Knowlson, in his conflation of his fictional and real narrators, describes. For the snatches from the world of Balzac that drift into Beckett's writing, from the parody of *Le Colonel Chabert* to the echoes of *Louis Lambert* in *Malone Dies* (*T*, 199), may also be seen as tender remembrances. As Christopher Logue remembers it, 'Beckett rated Balzac'. He recalls a conversation:

'You know his house in the rue Visconti?'
'Yes.'
'He worked on the first floor. On either side of his table there was a hole in the floor. On the floor below, his printers. When he finished a page, he dropped it through the hole on his right and began the next. Later, his pages came through

[63] Mary Bryden, 'Balzac to Beckett via God (Eau/Ot)', *Samuel Beckett Today /Aujourd'hui* 3, ed. Marius Buning (Amsterdam: Rodopi, 1994), 47–56, at 51.
[64] James Knowlson, *Damned to Fame: The Life of Samuel Beckett* (London: Blooms-bury, 1996), 146.
[65] Beckett, *Dream of Fair to Middling Women*, 119–20.

the hole on his left to be corrected, dropped back down, then printed and published.' . . .
Then Beckett would look straight at you for an instant, saying nothing. Then 'Balzac died at 51. Alone. His wife left him to die.'[66]

Logue was one of Beckett's publishers, and Beckett, perhaps, had sympathy as well as contempt for the self-styled secretary of contemporary society that they discuss here. Balzac, in this anecdote, seems to have grown to resemble one of the 'creatures' of his own fictions, Lucien de Rubempré, who writes, lamenting, to his sister of being under the control of the villainous Vautrin: 'Je ne m'appartiens plus, je suis plus que le secrétaire d'un diplomate espagnol, je suis sa créature.'[67] While noticing that Balzac turned his 'creatures into clockwork cabbages', Beckett also felt for the way in which an author might be turned into a 'creature' driven by the mechanics, and the conventions, of the printed text. In this sense, Beckett's parodies of Balzac are also an attempt at understanding, a 'byway of tenderness'.[68] The stories of his Molloys and Malones, his Unnamables and Pims, are attempting, not as Nussbaum sees it, to criticize emotion, but to reflect upon the way in which narrative, 'abstracted to death', may be disconnected and distant from emotions. In 'Dante . . . Bruno . Vico .. Joyce', Beckett wrote of his ambitions for an alternative 'desophisticated language':

We hear the ooze squelching all through Dickens's description of the Thames in *Great Expectations*. This writing that you find so obscure is a quintessential extraction of language and painting and gesture, with all the inevitable clarity of the old inarticulation. Here is the savage economy of hieroglyphics. Here words are not the polite contortions of 20th century printer's ink. They are alive.[69]

And in his later prose, Beckett makes a return, to salvage and play upon these 'polite contortions of . . . printer's ink'—and attempts to make them live. The texture of his work may be very different from Nussbaum's, but that does not, necessarily, make it less humane. As P. J. Murphy writes, the 'most important development in the post-trilogy prose involves somehow giving voice to the "somethings" or creatures trapped in the timeless world of the literary artefact'.[70]

---

66 Christopher Logue, 'A Man of his Words', *Guardian*, 1 Sept. 1999. Quoted with the permission of Christopher Logue.
67 Honoré de Balzac, *Illusions perdues* (Paris: Gallimard, 1974), 655.
68 See Genette, *Palimpsests*, 120.
69 *Disjecta*, 28.
70 See Pilling (ed.), *Cambridge Companion*, 235.

Writing to Thomas MacGreevy in 1937, Beckett reflected on his mother. 'I am', he said, 'what her savage loving has made me.'[71] It is a paradoxical phrase, but one which reflects both his notions of writing and of attachment. As Susan Sontag has pointed out, to 'name a sensibility... to draw its history, requires a deep sympathy modified by revulsion'.[72] The idea of 'deep sympathy modified by revulsion' is an apt description for the relationship Beckett's writing has to the idea of sympathy itself. Beckett's parodic allusions—in fact a feeling for the way in which he uses parody tentatively, in order to own up to, and stand back from, sympathetic attitudes—may shed light on the ethical understanding of his work. Much of Beckett's sympathy and his revulsion takes the form of 'savage loving'.[73] It is in *How It Is*, through Beckett's experimentation with the dramatic monologue, that his concerns with savage loving find their most 'extorted voice' (*HII*, 101).

SAVAGE LOVING: UNDERSTANDING CALIBAN

As *The Tempest* draws to a close, Prospero sets all his creatures free, but one:

> This mis-shapen knave,
> His mother was a witch; and one so strong
> That could control the moon, make flows and ebbs,
> And deal in her command, without her power.
> These three have robb'd me; and this demi-devil—
> For he's a bastard one—had plotted with them
> To take my life. Two of these fellows you
> Must know and own; this thing of darkness I
> Acknowledge mine.
>
>   (v. i. 268–76)

His owning of 'this thing of darkness', in a phrase both grudging and fond, is full of possessive guilt—grateful, at least, for the company. The 'thing' in question is Caliban—the character described in the Folio's

---

[71] To Thomas McGreevy, 10 Dec. 1937, Trinity College Dublin Library, quoted in Knowlson, *Damned to Fame*, 273.

[72] Susan Sontag, 'Notes on "Camp"', in *A Susan Sontag Reader* (Harmondsworth: Penguin, 1982), 105.

[73] To Thomas McGreevy, 10 Dec. 1937, Trinity College Dublin Library, quoted in Knowlson, *Damned to Fame*, 273.

'Names of Actors' as 'a salvage and deformed slave'. As I noted in my first chapter, the meaning of 'salvage' here is restricted; it is a variant of savage, indicating the primitive nature that Prospero and Miranda despise.[74] However, there is a sense in which Caliban is also seen as 'salvage', the property of a verbal rescue operation:

> MIRANDA   I pitied thee,
> Took pains to make thee speak, taught thee each hour
> One thing or other: when thou didst not, savage,
> Know thine own meaning, but wouldst gabble like
> A thing most brutish, I endow'd thy purposes
> With words that made them known.
>
>   (I. ii. 355–60)

Throughout the play, however, Prospero and Miranda attempt to distance themselves from this creature, regretting both the compassion and the language with which they have 'endow'd' him. Caliban, for his part, cannot relinquish his attachment to them. Unburdening himself, he shifts blame for his actions upon his controlling creator, in terms that he has humanity to thank for—'You taught me language; and my profit on't | Is, I know how to curse' (I. ii. 365–6). Such retributive, symbiotic relations recur in Beckett's writings. Some have noted echoes of Prospero and Caliban in *Waiting for Godot*, others in the verbal entanglements of *Endgame*:[75]

HAMM: Go and get the oilcan.
CLOV: What for?
HAMM: To oil the castors.
CLOV: I oiled them yesterday.
HAMM: Yesterday! What does that mean? Yesterday!
CLOV: (*Violently.*) That means that bloody awful day, long ago, before this
      bloody awful day. I use the words you taught me. If they don't mean anything
      any more, teach me others. Or let me be silent.

(*CDW*, 113)

---

[74] See Kermode, *Tempest*, p. xxxix.

[75] John Northam mentions the 'suggestive evidence that Caliban's character may be reflected in Gogo's coarse physicality, his greed, his flashes of poetry, his reluctant waking from a dream', 'Waiting for Prospero' in M. Axton and R. Williams (eds.), *English Drama: Forms and Development: Essays in Honour of Muriel Clara Bradbrook* (Cambridge: Cambridge University Press, 1977), 186–202; Ruby Cohn argues that Hamm's contrition in *Endgame*, ' "Forgive me. I said, Forgive me" . . . inverts a pardoning Prospero', Cohn, *Modern Shakespearean Offshoots*, 380.

Iain Wright notices something familiar about the tones of verbal disgust in *The Unnamable*: 'Does this voice sound familiar?' he asks:

It is Caliban's of course . . . Language for Caliban, for the Unnamable, for so many of Beckett's characters, is not only no aid to knowing 'thine own meaning', it is precisely that which prevents and blocks access to authentic selfhood . . . 'Do they believe I believe it is I who am speaking? That's theirs too. To make me believe I have an ego all my own, and can speak of it, as they of theirs. Another trap' . . . There we have it then. A problematic of stories, in which all our fictionalisings about ourselves are relentlessly deconstructed, revealed as arbitrary, counter to our own purposes.[76]

By the end of *The Unnamable*, it seems that Beckett felt he had reached some sort of impasse over this 'problematic of stories'. *Texts for Nothing* was, he commented in 1956, a failed 'attempt to get out of the attitude of disintegration'.[77] It is in *How It Is*, however, that Beckett's struggle with concepts of verbal ownership and dispossession is given its fullest 'inarticulation'. Alfred Simon writes of the original French text that 'c'est dans *Comment c'est* que l'univers de la perception, la réalité du monde objectif sont le plus radicalement mis en question. Il n'y a plus que les mots. Il n'y a plus que l'écriture, la voix, dans l'écriture, faite écriture, transcrite.'[78] Describing the work in progress to Donald McWhinnie, Beckett emphasized that the theme of the work would be the difficult relations between a creator and his 'creature known as Pim', in a manner that echoes, distantly, the relation between Prospero and Caliban:

A 'man' lying panting in the mud and dark, murmuring his 'life' as he hears it obscurely uttered by a voice inside him. This utterance is described throughout the work as the fragmentary recollection of an extraneous voice once heard 'quaqua on all sides'. In the last pages he is obliged to take the onus of it on himself and of the lamentable tale of the thing it tells.[79]

This resistance to authorial obligation begins in the first five words: 'how it was I quote before Pim with Pim after Pim how it is three parts I

---

[76] Iain Wright, ' "What Matter who's speaking?": Beckett, the Authorial Subject and Contemporary Critical Theory', *Southern Review*, 16/1 (Mar. 1983), 5–29, at 27.

[77] Quoted in Victor Sage, '*Innovation and Continuity* in *How It Is*', in Katherine Worth (ed.), *Beckett the Shape Changer* (London: Routledge & Kegan Paul, 1975), 87–103, at 88.

[78] Alfred Simon, *Beckett* (Paris: P. Belford, 1983), 143.

[79] Samuel Beckett, letter to Donald McWhinnie, 6 Apr. 1960, Trinity College Dublin Library, quoted in Knowlson, *Damned to Fame*, 461–2.

say it as I hear it' (*HII*, 7). The words 'I quote' are a crucial indication of just how much it mattered to Beckett who is speaking here. In speech, the quotation mark is usually indicated by an adjustment in vocal tone, such as the shift, which implicitly takes place at the beginning of a dramatic monologue, as one moves from the title to the poem, to the voice of the speaker. However, it is hard to decide how a reader should inflect this text with regard to these vestigial inverted commas. Should the rest be read as if between speech marks? If so, should another vocal shift take place at every point within the text at which 'I quote' (there are four more instances in the first twenty-nine strophes), occurs?

here then part one how it was before Pim we follow I quote the natural order more or less my life state last version what remains bits and scraps I hear it my life natural order more or less I learn it I quote a given moment long past vast stretch of time on from there that moment and following not all a selection natural order vast tracts of time   (*HII*, 7)

For are the 'I quote's here outside, or inside, the first 'I quote'? Would a speaker be required to perform a regress of reported speech, or to give the sense of one speaker who is reminding their audience that he is speaking the words of another? H. Porter Abbott comments that the opening of *How It Is*, like the last words of *Texts for Nothing*—'all said, it said, it murmurs'—is suggestive of 'a quotational hall of mirrors':

by 'quoting'—that is by implying that the voice that transmits the text is somehow separate from the voice that originates it—these opening lines connect directly with a central theme of the Trilogy and *Texts for Nothing*: the bewildering multiplicity of the speaking subject . . . a riddle that moves like a ghost through almost everything Beckett wrote in the forties.[80]

Post-structuralist critics see the 'multiplicity of the speaking subject' in Beckett's work, in which 'sources and recipients of speech are not distinguishable', as evidence that Beckett was working towards a textual world made up of untethered utterances; in Blanchot's words, 'images vides tournant mécaniquement autour d'un centre vide qu'occupe un *Je* sans nom'.[81] Judith Dearlove, for example, sees the whole of Beckett's work as a movement towards 'the incoercible absence of relation

---

[80] H. Porter Abbott, 'Beginning Again: The Post Narrative Art of *Texts for Nothing and How It Is*', in Pilling (ed.), *Cambridge Companion*, 106–23, at 112.
[81] Victor Sage writes that 'In *How It Is* the sources and recipients of speech are not distinguishable', Sage, 'Innovation and Continuity', 94; Maurice Blanchot, 'Où maintenant? Qui maintenant?', *Nouvelle Revue française*, 10 (1953), 678–86, at 681.

between the artist and his occasion', while Thomas Trezise perceives a
Beckettian universe 'in which...the separation *from* exteriority precedes, founds, and conditions any and every relation *to* exteriority'.[82]
Steven Connor, meanwhile, writes of Beckett's attempts to show 'how
every utterance can be taken up or enveloped by some other occasion,
some other context of understanding', describing how Beckett's works
become 'a web of mutually enveloping, self-quoting moments, each
endlessly displaced from its originating context, and regrafted elsewhere'.[83] Such readings of Beckett's 'problematic iterability' stem from
the belief that he works within a Derridean tradition, where 'every
sign...can be *cited*, put between quotation marks', indicating 'the
possibility of its functioning being cut off, at a certain point, from its
"original" desire-to-say-what-one-means (*vouloir-dire*) and from its participation in a saturable and constraining context'.[84] This image of
Beckett, creating 'an art cut off from all...points of relation between
the subject and the object' has been supported by Derrida's recent
thoughts on their affiliation: 'This is an author to whom I feel very
close or to whom I would like to feel myself very close.'[85] Derrida's
hesitation about the possibility of feeling close to another is characteristic of his philosophy's placing of disinterested play over contextualized
attachments. However, there is something particular to the Beckettian
action of 'quoting' that distances him from the Derridean school. In a
general criticism of Derrida's theories, Eric Griffiths argues that the
philosopher has an inadequate definition of 'intentionality', grounded
on a belief that the authorial intention lurks, in some mysterious way,
behind the work. He argues that textual intention lies rather between
utterances, in the tones of voices in which we catch or miss each other's
meanings. He adds that 'the features of context dependency and intention within a context which Derrida believes citation destroys, provide
the criteria which distinguish a citation from a repetition'.[86] In *How It*

---

[82] *Into the Breach: Samuel Beckett and the Ends of Literature* (Princeton: Princeton
University Press, 1990), p. ix.

[83] See J. E. Dearlove, *Beckett's Nonrelational Art*, quoted in Steven Connor, *Samuel
Beckett: Repetition, Theory and Text* (Oxford: Basil Blackwell, 1988), 205; Connor,
Samuel Beckett: Repetition, Theory, Text, 130.

[84] Jacques Derrida, 'Signature Event Context' (1971), trans. Samuel Weber and
Jeffrey Mehlman, *Glyph*, i (Baltimore: Johns Hopkins University Press, 1977), 185.

[85] Quoted in Uhlmann, *Beckett and Poststructuralism* (Cambridge: Cambridge University Press, 1999), 14.

[86] Griffiths, *Printed Voice*, 54.

Is, then, one might argue that the words 'I quote' speak to the reader. They reveal something of the voice's illocutionary concerns, to disown the voice of which, and with which, it speaks.

For, to 'quote' is not, as Abbott claims, the same as 'to say it as one hears it'.[87] It suggests a particular tone of voice. Inverted commas may indicate 'some kind of doubt...over the "truthfulness"...or..."validity" of a word or phrase', visually separating it from the rest of the text.[88] However, such markings are not simple separations; they might lead one to doubt the deviser as much as the material. In his essay 'Poetry as "Menace" and "Atonement"', Geoffrey Hill claims that his punctuation may seem at once 'assertive and non-committal. The quotation marks around "menace" and "atonement" look a bit like raised eyebrows' around this 'conflation of...cliché.' Hill goes on to admit that '[b]ehind the façade' is the 'attraction of terminology itself, a power at once supportive and coercive.'[89]

Derrida accuses critics such as Gilbert Ryle, J. L. Austin, and J. R. Searle, who believe in the importance of illocutionary redescription, and context-based understanding of speech acts, of being too 'confident in the law of quotation marks'.[90] However, some Derridean readers of Beckett, convinced of the 'incoercible absence of relation' between text, reader, and originator, overlook the nuances of these junctural features and the 'coercive power' of that which they frame. Hill's anxiety over his quotation marks may seem, as he admits, 'obsessively neurotic'. However, the apostrophizing fussiness of this writer 'possessed by a sense of language itself as a manifestation of empirical guilt' touches Beckett's concerns in a way that Dearlove and Trezise cannot.

How It Is attempts to resist, through the words 'I quote', possessing the 'thing it tells'—and the 'quote' in Beckett indicates, not a clear separation between the voice that speaks and the voice it speaks of, nor a spiral of fictional groundlessness, but something between the two. It marks the delicate passage from one voice to another, and the feelings one might have about such connections and differences.

---

[87] 'to say it as one hears it is to quote', Abbott, 'Beginning Again', 112.

[88] John Lennard, *The Poetry Handbook* (Oxford: Oxford University Press, 1996), 67.

[89] Geoffrey Hill, *The Lords of Limit* (London: Deutsch, 1984), 6.

[90] Jacques Derrida: 'This is the problem of " 'Fido'—Fido" (you know, Ryle, Russell, etc.)...they will always be confident in the law of quotation marks', *The Post Card from Socrates to Freud and Beyond*, trans. Alan Bass (Chicago: University of Chicago Press, 1987), 98.

BROWNING AVERSIONS: *HOW IT IS* AND THE DRAMATIC MONOLOGUE

It is through the act of quotation in *How It Is* that Beckett reveals his particular associations with a writer who continually dwelt on his attachments to and detachment from the words of others: Robert Browning. Stephan Chambers notes the snatch of Browning in the fourth strophe: 'in me that were without when the panting stops scraps of an ancient voice in me not mine' (*HII*, 7).[91] The words, he notes, recall the 1842 'advertisment' to *Dramatic Lyrics*: 'Such Poems as the majority in this volume might also come properly enough, I suppose, under the head of "Dramatic Pieces"; being, though often Lyric in expression, always Dramatic in principle, and so many utterances of so many imaginary persons, not mine.—R. B.' (*BCP* i. 347). The echo is light, admittedly—and James Knowlson has warned against 'unduly explicit' and 'over-referential' readings of Beckett's allusions.[92] However, the allusions to Browning in Beckett's work deserve explication precisely because they shed light on the manner in which the quotational snatches from 'without' should be read, and on what the act of quoting, or speaking the words of another, may involve. A sense for Browning's poetic practice may be imaginatively enlarging, rather than 'restrictive', shedding light on the workings of the Beckettian text.

Like Browning, Beckett was concerned to keep his distance from his quoted words. In answer to Knowlson's enquiry about the choice of allusions in *Happy Days*, he wrote:

I simply know next to nothing about my work in this way, as little as a plumber of the history of hydraulics. There is nothing/nobody with me when I am writing, only the hellish job in hand. The 'eye of the mind' in *Happy Days* does not refer to Yeats any more than the 'revels' in *Endgame* to *The Tempest*. They are just bits of pipe I happen to have with me. I suppose it's all reminiscence from womb to tomb. All I can say is I have scant information concerning mine—alas.[93]

---

[91] Stephan Chambers, 'The Later Prose of Samuel Beckett' (diss., Oxford University, 1985), 40.

[92] James Knowlson, 'Beckett's Bits of Pipe' in Morris Béja (ed.), *Samuel Beckett: Humanistic Perspectives* (Ohio: Ohio State University Press, 1983), 18.

[93] Ibid. 16.

He showed a similar ambivalence towards his sources when writing of the 'hint of Browning' in *Happy Days*.[94] When Alan Schneider asked for the references to Winnie's misquotations, including the line 'Ever uppermost—like Browning', Beckett wrote that 'No one will get this reference, *tant pis*. It is to a line of Browning—"I'll say confusedly what comes uppermost".' After more perplexity on Schneider's part, he added that 'The revolver is called "Browning—Brownie" not because there is a weapon of that name—but because it is always uppermost. If the line was by another poet the revolver wd. be called by the name of that other poet.'[95] It is, however, hard to credit this dismissal of the importance of the 'hint of Browning'. The way in which Beckett both wishes for his readers to 'get' the reference, while simultaneously holding it at arm's length, shows his affinities with that Victorian poet of dramatic monologues who was so concerned to claim his utterances 'not mine'.

When Beckett published the first part of *How It Is*, he gave it a title suggestive of both salvage and ownership: 'From an Unabandoned Work.'[96] And it is towards a recognition of this owning, towards correcting 'improper attributions' that *How It Is* works its way:

and the mud yes the dark yes the mud and the dark are true yes nothing to regret there no

but all this business of voices yes quaqua yes of other worlds yes of someone in another world yes whose kind of dream I am yes said to be yes that he dreams all the time yes tells all the time yes his only dream yes his only story yes   (*HII*, 158)

But still, in the final lines, the voice attempts to resist the savage nature of 'this thing of darkness' as 'the lamentable tale of the thing it tells' rests between its inverted commas: 'good good end at last of part three and last that's how it was end of quotation after Pim how it is' (*HII*, 160).

For a poet such as Auden, it was hard to conceive of a sense of self without acknowledging the presence of others. Beckett takes this further. His speaker's use of quotation is also a poignant attempt to disown the self. In this sense the speaker of *How It Is* shares much with one of the text's allusive sources, Browning's 'Caliban upon Setebos'. Both

[94] Beckett's refers to the 'hint of Browning' in *Happy Days: The Production Notebook of Samuel Beckett*, ed. James Knowlson (London: Grove Press, 1985), 99.
[95] Samuel Beckett, 'To Alan Schneider', 17 Aug. 1961, *No Author Better Served*, ed. Maurice Harmon (Cambridge, Mass.: Harvard University Press, 1998), 13.
[96] Published in the *Evergreen Review*, 4 (Sept.–Oct. 1960): 58–65.

speakers figure themselves in third person—either too primitive, or too fearful of an imagined God, to speak up for themselves.

ANCIENT VOICES: CALIBAN IN BROWNING AND BECKETT

Some readers of *How It Is* have heard it all before. Victor Sage comments that the text 'exploits a reductive myth—that of the paradigmatic "nothing new"', while John Updike describes Beckett as a 'proud priest perfecting his forlorn ritual'.[97] Among the ancient voices of the text are the 'noises' of *The Tempest*'s isle—and a sense for these allusions reveals the ways in which the text makes a new world and feels for an old one, with a distinctive voice, a voice struggling to make itself distinct.[98]

When Hugh Kenner mentions that *How It Is* 'contains no ingredient (unless perhaps mud) which we have not encountered before' he is forgetting its piscine flavour.[99] There is something fishy about the text, as the speaker imagines:

sea beneath the moon harbour-mouth after the sun the moon always light day and night little heap in the stern it's me all those I see are me all ages the current carries me out the awaited ebb I'm looking for an isle home at last drop never move again a little turn at evening to the sea-shore seawards then back drop sleep wake in the silence eyes that dare open stay open live old dream on crabs kelp (*HII*, 94)

There is also a touch of *The Tempest* about the slapstick-style intimacies and anatomical confusions in Part II. The finding 'Pim's right buttock then first contact' (*HII*, 59) and ensuing ambiguities—'cries tell me which end the head' (*HII*, 60)—might bring to mind the Trinculo-cum-Caliban pairing which Stephano feels for. '[M]isery acquaints a man with strange bed-fellows', as Trinculo puts it, climbing under the 'gaberdine'.[100]

---

[97] Sage, 'Innovation and Continuity', 102; John Updike, 'How How It Is Was', *New Yorker*, 19 Dec. 1964, 164–6, at 164.

[98] 'Be not afeard; the isle is full of noises, | Sounds and sweet airs ... and sometimes voices', *The Tempest*, III. ii. 133–4, 136.

[99] Hugh Kenner, *Samuel Beckett* (London: Calder, 1965), 199.

[100] Trinculo, on finding Caliban: 'What have we here? a man or fish? dead or alive? A fish: he smells like a fish; a very ancient and fish like smell ... my best way is to creep under his gaberdine ... misery acquaints a man with strange bedfellows', *The Tempest*, II. ii. 24–6, 40–1.

The most distinctive 'ancient voice' within the text, though, is the creature with 'the ancient and fish-like smell'—Caliban. Times have changed, however. Though he is related to Shakespeare's creation, Beckett's mud-crawling connoisseur of tinned sardines and canned cod's liver has gone through some sort of evolutionary process. The missing link is Browning. The 1864 poem 'Caliban upon Setebos; or, Natural Theology in the Island' bears a family resemblance to Beckett's text. It is of the same species—like the quote-ridden *How It Is*, a sort of double dramatic monologue. Browning's Caliban repeatedly speaks in the third person, in what is possibly 'a curious attempt to mislead his hearer'.[101] Meanwhile, a fear of Setebos, at the close of the poem, prompts Caliban in an almost Beckettian idiom to 'disown all he has said as "fools-play, this prattling"'.[102]

The 'monster of solitude' of *How It Is* shares much with Browning's Caliban. There are explicit verbal echoes. His physical position recalls his Victorian counterpart as he describes himself as 'flat on my belly in the mud' (*HII*, 159), 'in the warm mire' (*HII*, 43), 'in a daze on my belly' (*HII*, 47). Browning's Caliban is discovered 'Flat on his belly in the pit's much mire, | With elbows wide, fists clenched to prop his chin' (*BCP* i. 805, ll. 2–3), a posture which echoes Shakespeare's monster. Beckett's creature is, like Browning's Caliban, 'monstrous but sensitive' to his predicament, especially in his 'close observation of the natural world'.[103] Browning's Caliban has a delicate habit of plucking the legs off grubs ('I might hear his cry, | And give the mankin three sound legs for one, | Or pluck the other off, leave him like an egg' (*BCP* i. 807, ll. 91–4) which is picked up in the lepidopterous torture of *How It Is*: 'I scissored into slender strips the wings of butterflies first one wing then the other sometimes for a change two abreast never so good since' (*HII*, 10).

Crucially, what the two characters share is the fact that they are both natural theologians. They both have an urge for metaphysical speculation, somewhat hampered by their unusually restricted, recumbent view of the world. It is such a view that inspires a type of ontological angst on the part of both creatures—the sense that although there may be some other world, they are unable to see it. This ontological confusion is

[101] E. M. Naish, *Browning and Dogma* (London: George Bell & Sons, 1906), 16.
[102] E. K. Brown, 'The First Person in "Caliban upon Setebos"', *Modern Language Notes*, 66 (June 1951), 392–5, at 393.
[103] The characterization of Browning's Caliban as 'monstrous but sensitive' is from Robert Browning, *Selected Poetry*, ed. Daniel Karlin (Harmondsworth: Penguin, 1989), 322.

echoed by the reader's knowledge of the 'intertextual' nature of each poem—as each of these 'creatures' is unaware that they have been 'authored' by a previous fiction.

As has been seen, Browning's Caliban finds himself in difficulties because he can only envisage the minds of others, including the mind of God, in his own image. Like de Montesquieu's triangles, of whom it 'has been well said that if [they] had a god, they would give him three sides', Caliban can only conceive of a God who is as cruel and vindictive in his handling of himself as Caliban is to the isle's creatures.[104] Furthermore, Caliban's difficulties in finding God's design in the natural world are echoed by the way in which he is part of the pattern of Browning's verse. *How It Is* echoes 'Caliban upon Setebos' in these ways. The speaker is also haunted by the question 'how I got here' (*HII*, 8), and 'knowing nothing of my beginnings' (*HII*, 13), conceiving of himself in a sort of purgatory. The only explanation for his situation is that he is being tortured in the same way as he is torturing Pim, 'each one of us is at the same time . . . tormentor and tormented' (*HII*, 153). The greatest tormentor, meanwhile, is the 'ear above somewhere above' (*HII*, 146), 'an ear above in the light' (*HII*, 147). While Auden dreamt of man being blessed with 'the gift of ears' in which one would have a sensitivity to the ways in which each individual spoke, in this hellish world, the divine listener is conceived as a tormentor.[105]

Like 'Caliban upon Setebos', *How It Is* plays on the parallel between the artist and God. Take the way in which 'Pim' is animated by the speaker in the same way as the speaker is brought to typographical life by Beckett: 'my part who but for me he would never Pim we're talking of Pim never be but for me anything but a dumb limp lump flat for ever in the mud but I'll quicken him you wait and see and how I can efface myself behind my creature when the fit takes me now my nails' (*HII*, 58). Levy comments that the relationship between the speaker and Pim is 'never one between two human beings', but 'that between frail man . . . and a deity', and that the 'hint is rather strong with its use of the Christian word "creature" '.[106] The hint is there, too, in Beckett's use of 'quicken', which echoes the 'so-called Apostles' Creed' (*HII*, 17): 'And he shall come again in glory to judge both the quick and the dead.' To 'quicken' something is to animate it, touch its 'quick', the seat or

104 Montesquieu, *Persian Letters*, trans. C. Betts (Harmondsworth: Penguin, 1993), 124.
105 *SW*, 122.
106 Eric Levy, *Beckett and the Voice of Species* (Dublin: Gill & Macmillan, 1980), 57.

feeling of emotion (*OED* v. 1a). Writers often attempt such divine quickening. Browning again:

> 'You're wounded!' 'Nay', the soldier's pride
> Touched to the quick, he said:
> 'I'm killed, Sire!' And his chief beside,
> Smiling the boy fell dead.
>
> (*BCP* i. 37–40)

Browning is doing something typographically in this passage from the 1842 dramatic lyric 'Incident of the French Camp'. While the narrative pulls at the heart-strings, the line breaks flatten the emotion, giving the narrator's voice prominence, rhyming 'he said' against 'fell dead'. Browning thus draws the reader's attention to the mechanics of the emotive process, refusing to become invisible, to 'efface' himself behind his literary creations. How a writer should handle the mechanical or routine aspects of his medium is a vexing question. Henry James disliked the way his scaffolding showed through his work, feeling himself to be 'condemned to deal with a form of speech consisting . . . as to the one part, of "that" and "which", as to a second part, of the blest "it" '.[107] Browning, in contrast, was a writer who was keen to make his presence felt. He was, as John Lennard notes, 'consistently interested in the typography of fictional transcription', using spacing and punctuation 'to combine the subtlest graphic exploitations with the clearest functional uses'.[108] In *How It Is*, Beckett develops this interest in the ways in which an artist can make himself appear or disappear within his work. The phrase 'how I can efface myself behind my creature when the fit takes me now my nails' recalls Stephen Dedalus' classic statement of the modernist ideal of impersonality: 'The artist, like the God of the creation, remains within or behind or beyond or above his handiwork, invisible, refined out of existence, indifferent, paring his fingernails.'[109] Lynch's riposte, '[t]rying to refine them also out of existence', brings Stephen's vision back to earth. Lynch (and Joyce) are poking fun at Stephen's vanity; the way in which he is making himself over, manicuring himself to a level of Flaubertian invisibility. For Joyce, as for Beckett, the author's hand would always get in the way.

---

[107] Henry James, *Notes on Novelists* (London: J. M. Dent, 1914), 83–4.
[108] John Lennard, *But I Digress* (Oxford: Oxford University Press, 1991), 147.
[109] James Joyce, *A Portrait of The Artist as a Young Man* (Harmondsworth: Penguin, 1992), 223.

THE MERE STOPS

Typographical arrangement is one of the ways in which an author may demonstrate his attachment to or his presence within a written text; it is a means not only of connecting syntactical parts, but of hinting at the intended authorial tone, thus connecting with one's audience. Browning was a writer who attached great importance 'to the mere stops', as he told his editor, Edward Chapman.[110] As the strange punctuation of 'Caliban upon Setebos' shows, his sensitivity to the way in which it could be used not only sympathetically, as it were, 'to aid in the delineation of his characters', but satirically, to frame and control them, means that he will 'occupy an interesting place in the position of English poetic punctuation'.[111] As I have shown in Chapter 3, Auden was also greatly aware of the way in which his fictional creatures could be satirized, their tones of voice flattened, through obvious use of punctuation, line breaks, and typography. Beckett has inherited this interest. Critics cannot but mention the apparent absence of those elocutionary, signalling pauses that usually aid one's sense of a vocal intonation in a text, thus bringing *How It Is* 'perilously close to the unreadable'.[112] Beckett was planning for Patrick Magee to read this 'translation of opening of French Work in Progress' aloud at a *Music Today* concert in April 1960. Indeed, Cohn notes that the text has a 'strong oral quality'.[113] However, this quality comes in part, perhaps, from its total lack of the conventional features of a written text— punctuation marks: 'how it was I quote before Pim with Pim after Pim how it is three parts I say it as I hear it' (*HII*, 7). Such a lack of tonal instruction could be seen, in part, as a demonstration of the text's 'openness'. You can say it as *you* hear it. Wright argues that 'in a key-text for the development of the anti-authorial polemic, "What is an Author?" (Foucault) cites the opening of the third section of *Textes pour rien*—"Qu'importe qui parle, quelqu'un a dit qu'importe qui

---

[110] Robert Browning, 'To Edward Chapman', 31 Oct. 1855, quoted in Honan, *Browning's Characters*, 284.
[111] Ibid.
[112] A. Alvarez, *Beckett* (London: Woburn, 1973), 189.
[113] 'I am trying to translate opening of new work for Magee to read at some Literary-musical do in the Festival Hall Recital Room in April, I think? Poor man', Samuel Beckett, 'To Alan Schneider', 25 Feb. 1960, in *No Author*, ed. Harmon, 67; Cohn, *Back to Beckett*, 227.

parle" | "What matter who's speaking, someone said what matter who's speaking"—as the very embodiment of "one of the fundamental ethical principles of contemporary writing" '. If Foucualt's work has become 'key' for the development of such an 'anti-authorial polemic', this is mainly due to misreadings of the text itself. However, Wright's location of the preoccupation with the relationship between authorial presence and 'ethical principle' in Beckett's work is worth dwelling on. The 'ethical principle' in mind here, is the neo-Derridean image of the death of the work tyrannically centred on the author and its replacement with a freeplay of signifiers. However, one could argue that the assurance that such textual openness is, in some sense, 'contemporary' or progressive, belongs to the Beckettian theorists, and not to the author himself.[114]

There is, after all, a sign of the author's hand, 'clawing for the take' (*HII*, 54) in the textual breaks of *How It Is*. The strophic structure of the work has left critics wondering if it is prose or verse:

my life last state last version ill-said ill-heard ill-recaptured ill-murmured in the mud brief movements of the lower face losses everywhere

recorded none the less it's preferable somehow somewhere as it stands as it comes my life my moments not the millionth part all lost nearly all someone listening another noting or the same   (*HII*, 7)

Marjorie Perloff sees the 'successive blocks of type made up of abrupt phrasal groupings' as an example of what Frye calls a 'kind of thought-breath or phrase'.[115] However, in a text allegedly spoken 'when the panting stops' (*HII*, 7) it seems clear that there is a struggle between the sense of each strophe and the break which follows it, which makes this 'thought-breath' seem uncomfortable. The breaks are at odds with the creature's will, as it were—it often seems as if the text has been cut off in mid-speech, or has been forced to begin too soon.

In a review in which he writes about the difference between prose and verse, Christopher Ricks claims that 'in prose the line-endings are without significance, and are the creation not of the writer but of the compositor; in poetry the line-endings are significant, and they effect their significance . . . by using the white space, by using a pause which is not necessarily a pause of punctuation and so only equivocally a

---

114   Wright, 'What Matter', 13.
115   Marjorie Perloff, 'Between Verse and Prose', *Critical Inquiry*, 9 (Dec. 1982), 415–33, at 425.

pause at all'.[116] Ricks admits that some writers make 'poetic' use of paragraphs, but there is a confidence about his dismissal of the compositor's line endings which will not square with *How It Is*. Peopled, as it is, by hierarchies of scribes that are imagined to note the text, *How It Is* is preoccupied by the relation of spoken voice to recorded voice, and the relations between compositor, author, and editor. His inclusion of a reference to Browning's *The Ring and the Book*, the 'rich testimony I agree questionable into the bargain especially the yellow book' (*HII*, 91), augments the sense that it is difficult to reach understanding, through layers of convoluted reinscriptions.[117] The very fact that there might be a line ending in texts 'without significance' is significant to Beckett. The speaker mentions textual breaks in relation to Pim:

the gaps are the holes otherwise it flows more or less more or less profound the holes we're talking of the holes not specified not possible no point I feel them and wait till he can out and on again or I don't and opener or I do and opener just the same that helps him out as I hear it as it comes word for word to continue to conclude to be able part two leaving only three and last   (*HII*, 93)

Pim's 'extorted voice' (*HII*, 101) is gained, by the speaker's operations with the tin-opener, or his nails. It might be natural to assume that the 'gaps' mentioned here are the pauses in Pim's narrative. One might guess that they refer to a gap either for panting, or for pain, as the speaker attends to Pim's anus ('holes not specified'). However, their significance is, in fact, 'more or less profound'. Any confidence that 'the gaps' in the speaker's narrative are represented by the blanks between strophes in the text is misplaced, for 'the holes not specified not possible no point'. There is a question as to how one is to react emotionally to a narrative in which there is, literally, no mark of punctuation except the apparently arbitrary blank—is there literally 'no point'? As Lennard observes, punctuation 'is to the written word as cartilage is to bone, permitting articulation and bearing the stress of movement . . . in poetry it may be the opportunity to delicately shade a meaning'.[118] However, as T. S. Eliot remarks, punctuation of a text may also 'include the absence of the usual marks of punctuation where the reader would expect them'.[119]

---

[116] Christopher Ricks, 'Distinctions', rev. of *Visible Words: A Study of Inscriptions as Books and Works of Art* by John Sparrow, *Essays in Criticism*, 20/2 (1970), 259–64, at 262.
[117] See *TRB* i. 138–40; p. 26 'interfilleted with Italian streaks | When testimony stooped to mother-tongue,— | That, was this old square yellow book about'.
[118] Lennard, *Poetry Handbook*, 58.
[119] Quoted in Ricks, *Force of Poetry*, 342.

There are moments, in the text, of pointed poignancy about this lack of shading:

the blue there was then the white dust impressions of more recent date pleasant unpleasant and those finally unruffled by emotion things not easy

unbroken no paragraphs no commas not a second for reflection with the nail of the index until it falls and the worn back bleeding passim it was near the end like yesterday vast stretch of time

but quick an example from among the simple   (*HII*, 78)

The proximity of 'unruffled by emotion' and 'unbroken no paragraphs', here, suggests the way in which the text on Pim's 'worn back' might provide an insight into the ethical ambiguity of textual pointings. A text with 'no paragraphs no commas not a second for reflection' is suggestive of a lack of feeling both for his reader (Pim) and on his own part. However, though Levy argues that this is not the relation of 'two human beings', there is always a hint that the speaker has some tender points.[120] The command 'but quick' intensifies as Part II draws to a close, 'murmur to the mud quick quick soon' (*HII*, 108) forcing the unreflecting narrative forward. However, 'quick' also touches on the soft flesh beneath the nails he writes with, a premonition of the tenderness that he shall soon feel at the hands of his tormentor. The speaker, perhaps, is not as 'unbroken' as he thinks. At the beginning of Part III, he looks back with, it seems, a degree of nostalgia: 'before Pim long before with Pim vast tracts of time kinds of thoughts same family divers doubts emotions too yes emotions some with tears yes tears motions too and movements' (*HII*, 111). However, the 'tract' of *How It Is* keeps slipping, comically, over modes of feeling, even while it resists them. Take the moment when the sack falls apart: 'no emotion all is lost the bottom burst the wet the dragging the rubbing the hugging' (*HII*, 51).

The voice, here, hints that there is 'no emotion', for 'all is lost', but in the very cadence of the phrase 'all is lost' it summons up the emotion that is denied, recalling Byronic tones:

> It is not in the storm nor in the strife
> We feel benumb'd, and wish no more,
> But in the after-silence on the shore
> When all is lost, except a little life.[121]

120 Levy, *Voice of the Species*, 87.
121 'Lines on Hearing that Lady Byron was Ill', in Byron, *Complete Poetical Works*, ed. Page, rev edn. ed. John Jump (Oxford: Oxford University Press, 1970), 94.

Here, the text, in spite of itself, loses hold of, and finds, its own tones of voice. Punctuation, as *How It Is* shows, is intimately connected with pain; it is 'a gap or a wound that rips the fabric of the text at irregular intervals'.[122] The relation of the speaker to Pim's 'little blurts midget grammar' (*HII*, 76) seems, at times, to be that of a vicious compositor:

training continued no point skip

table of basic stimuli one sing nails in armpit two speak blade in arse three stop thump on skull four louder pestle on kidney

five softer index in anus six bravo clap athwart arse seven lousy same as three eight encore same as one or two as may be   (*HII*, 76)

While the lack of pointing in these lines leaves it unclear whether the phrase means 'training continued, do not skip any point', or 'training continued, there is no point in reading this, skip', it seems that this 'table' is an attempt to avoid such ambiguity, to gain complete tonal control of Pim's voice, through his mathematical system of 'apposite stab[s]' (*HII*, 79). Voices are difficult to systematize though, as one Victorian grammarian noted: 'forms of thought are infinite in number, so are modes of expression: and punctuation, adapting itself to these, is an instrument capable of manipulation in a thousand ways.'[123] Though Allardyce is, here, praising the flexibility of modern punctuation, there is evidently a breach between the 'thousand' ways of typographical manipulation and the 'infinite' modes of expression—a breach which is felt for in *How It Is*: 'that for the likes of us and no matter how we are recounted there is more nourishment in a cry nay a sigh torn from one whose only good is silence or in speech extorted from one at last delivered from its use than sardines can ever offer' (*HII*, 157).

There is a tacit pun, here, on 'recounted', referring both to how they are 'told this time', and to how many there turn out to be by the speaker's mathematical reckonings. Such frustrated recountings show themselves earlier in the text: 'I must bear how long no more figures there's another little difference compared to what precedes not the

122 Maud Ellmann writes that 'the subject...erupts...as punctuation, as a gap or a wound that rips the fabric of the text', 'Disremembering Dedalus', in Robert Young (ed.), *Untying the Text: A Post-Structuralist Reader* (London: Routledge & Kegan Paul, 1981), 189–206, at 192.

123 Paul Allardyce (pseud.), *'Stops' or How To Punctuate* (1864), quoted in Park Honan, 'Eighteenth and Nineteenth Century Punctuation Theory', *English Studies*, 41 (1960), 92–102, at 101.

slightest figure henceforth all measures vague yes vague impressions of length' (*HII*, 57). And the speaker's vagaries of counting—'I bring up finally what seems to me a testicle or two' (*HII*, 60) can be comically acute, if physically alarming. However, throughout the text the speaker shows himself to be continually counting and re-counting—and this attachment to the language of mathematics might be seen as a reflection of his attempts to see his world as a closed system, lacking in those equivocal tones that words allow: 'how it was I quote before Pim with Pim after Pim how it is three parts I say it as I hear it' (*HII*, 7). For to 'quote' is also to number off, to 'mark (a book) with numbers (as of chapters etc.)' (*OED* I.1a). On the largest typographical scale, 'Pim' could be seen as punctuating the speaker's life, enabling him to divide it, typographically, into 'three parts'. This mechanical reduction of fellow creature to a punctuation mark is a painful symptom of the stoicism of Beckett's typographical world.

In *Beckett's Dying Words*, Ricks describes the way in which Beckett torments his creatures through his equivocal lack of punctuation, creating a 'modern vision of ancient eternal torment, where Dante's sufferers are newly scored with tin-openers, *How It Is* longs to put a stop and has no stops or punctuation at all other than white line spacing'.[124] Punctuation is unspeakable; and its absence, for these characters in unspeakable torment, is spelt out: 'question am I happy in the present still such ancient things a little happy on and off part one before Pim brief void and barely audible no no I would feel it and brief apostil barely audible not made for happiness unhappiness peace of mind' (*HII*, 20).

The voice here is denied the refuge of the 'apostil' or marginal note in this format. Another feature of typographical tact which *How It Is* misses is the parenthesis: 'clasped but how clasped as in the handshake no but his flat mine on top the crooked fingers slipped between his the nails against his palm it's the position they have finally adopted clear picture of that good and parenthesis the vision suddenly too late a little late of how my injunctions by other means more humane' (*HII*, 99). A parenthesis may be used for many things, but, as Ricks notes in an essay on Geoffrey Hill, it may handle what 'one cannot speak of . . . any more than you can speak . . . brackets'.[125] Here, this sudden moment of belated, Belacqua-like repentance beseeches the humanity of such textual recalcitrance, a humanity that its own 'injunctions', 'no paragraphs

[124] Ricks, *Beckett's Dying Words*, 4.   [125] Ricks, *Force of Poetry*, 300.

no commas', have denied. However, there is, perhaps, human emotion in the humour of this stream of words:

I withdraw it thump on skull the cries cease it's mechanical end of first lesson second series rest and here parenthesis

this opener where put it when not needed put it back in the sack with the tins certainly not hold it in the hand in the mouth certainly not the muscles relax the mud engulfs where then

between the cheeks of his arse not very elastic but still sufficiently there it's in safety saying to myself I say it as I hear it that with someone to keep me company I have been a different man more universal   (*HII*, 74)

By this point in the text, one has become so immured to the lack of narrative subtlety, in both form and matter, that an appeal to the 'parenthesis', while the speaker wedges his tool in place, seems comically coy. Its absence, typographically, is symptomatic of the physical and verbal modesty that is denied to these creatures. This lack of distinguishing tones is, however, a black comedy:

having already appeared with Pim in my quality of tormentor part two I have not to take cognizance of a part four in which I would appear with Bom in my quality of victim it is sufficient for this episode to be announced Bom comes right leg right arm push pull ten yards fifteen yards

or emotions sensations take a sudden interest in them and even then what the fuck I quote does it matter who suffers faint waver here faint tremor   (*HII*, 143–4)

There is a question here, though no question mark, for 'does it matter who suffers' in this text? Beckett's placing of 'I quote', here, is a partial answer. It attempts to perform, vocally, a tonal difference—a sudden embarrassed distancing from 'what the fuck'. Though this tonal variation is unimaginable for this creature, the very impossibility of these varied tones, and its longing for them, make his voice matter.

LOOKING BEFORE AND AFTER PIM:
WHAT *HOW IT IS* ASKS OF THE READER

Perhaps the feature of punctuation that *How It Is* misses most is the question mark. While Browning's Caliban plays at Hamlet, bemoaning his discomfort—'But wherefore rough, why cold and ill at ease? | Aha, that is a question!' (*BCP* i. 808, ll. 127–8)—Beckett's speaker thinks back on the reason of that noble mind, struggling to see a shape to his life. As the Dane puts it:

> Sure He that made us with such large discourse,
> Looking before and after, gave us not
> That capability and godlike reason
> To fust in us unus'd.[126]

Initially, though, *How It Is* seems to resist, and remake, Hamlet's query. The prepositional assurance of 'before Pim with Pim after Pim' suggests that the speaker can see both ends of his narrative. As the text continues, it holds out against open-ended discourse:

part one before Pim how I got here no question not known not said and the sack whence the sack and me if it's me no question impossible too weak no importance

life life the other above in the light said to have been mine on and off no going back up there no question no one asking that of me   (*HII*, 8)

There is a refuge, perhaps, in the 'certainties the mud the dark'. The stoical acceptance of 'no question of thirst either no question of dying of thirst either' (*HII*, 9) is mirrored in the 'mouth resigned to an olive and given a cherry but no preference no searching not even for a language': 'the sack when it's empty my sack a possession this word faintly hissing brief void and finally apposition anomaly anomaly a sack here my sack when it's empty bah I've lashings of time centuries of time' (*HII*, 19). The string of verbal assonance, here, from 'a possession' to 'apposition' to 'anomaly' to 'a sack', is suggestive of a text stuck in a typographical groove. The rhetorical device of 'apposition'—'the addition of a parallel word by way of explanation' (*OED* 2.5 *Rhet*)—has degenerated here to its cognate meaning of the mere 'placing of things in contact, side by side' (*OED* 2.3), resulting in syntactical breakdown. The sense in which the voice in *How It Is* is out of control, possessed by the mechanics of its typography, increases in the next passage: 'that's the speech I've been given part one before Pim question do I use it freely it's not said or I don't hear it's one or the other all I hear is that a witness I'd need a witness' (*HII*, 19).

There is something coercive about this 'speech I've been given'; any possibility of alternative modes of expression is flattened by the tonal

[126] *Hamlet*, IV. iv. 36–9. I am indebted, here, to Adrian Poole's discussion of questions and answers in *Hamlet* in *Tragedy: Shakespeare and the Greek Example* (Oxford: Oxford University Press, 1987), 124.

ambivalence of the phrase 'question do I use it freely'. The violent possibilities of Beckett's punctuation come into full force in Part II, as the text beseeches its absent question mark:

silence more and more longer and longer silences vast tracts of time we at a loss more and more he for answers I for questions sick of life in the light one question how often no more figures no more time vast figure vast stretch of time on his life in the dark the mud before me mainly curiosity was he still alive YOUR LIFE HERE BEFORE ME   (*HII*, 81)

Being, as it is, 'at a loss for questions', the capitalized engraving terrifies. With the intonation restored, it might refer to the nature of Pim's life before the torture began. However, in its unpunctuated state, 'YOUR LIFE HERE BEFORE ME' could be seen to enclose a textual death threat. The horror, and the fear of the end, cry out in the next scrap: 'God on God desperation utter confusion did he believe he believed then not couldn't any more his reasons both cases my God' (*HII*, 81). The phrases here, echo back to the voice of Christ in St Mark's Gospel, abandoned in his questioning—'My God, my God, why hast thou forsaken me?' (Mark 15: 34). Though, at times, there is a touch of nonchalance about the speaker's contact with Pim—'purely curiosity was he still alive thump thump in the mud vile tears of unbutcherable brother' (*HII*, 82)—there is also a godforsaken desperation for response as the 'question old question if yes or no' (*HII*, 44) accumulates at the text's end:

only me yes alone yes with my voice yes my murmur yes when the panting stops yes all that holds yes panting yes worse and worse no answer WORSE AND WORSE yes flat on my belly yes in the mud yes the dark yes nothing to emend there no the arms spread like a cross no answer LIKE A CROSS no answer YES OR NO yes   (*HII*, 159)

Questions are also important to this text because its title is, in part, an answer. Like 'Caliban upon Setebos', *How It Is* is attempting a type of explanation, it 'serves to remove or avert a misunderstanding'.[127] Both texts make an appeal to the possibility of comprehension. The speakers aspire to comprehend their predicament, to see 'before and after'. Wayne Booth notes that the title *How It Is* 'trumpet[s] such claims' for a godlike breadth of vision, a claim strengthened by the pun on 'beginning' in the French title, *Comment c'est*. However, as I have shown, comprehension in

---

[127] Ludwig Wittgenstein: 'an explanation serves to remove or avert a misunderstanding—one, that is, that would occur but for the explanation; not every one that I can imagine', in *Philosophical Investigations* (Oxford: Blackwell, 1958), no. 87.

Beckett's world is repeatedly seen as difficult, flawed, and complex. He carefully unpicks the conventions of understanding in order to make us think more carefully about them. In the next section, I will show how he presses on grammatical constructions in order to do this.

THE GIFT OF UNDERSTANDING: ETHICAL AND GRAMMATICAL LAWS

Like Browning's Caliban, the speaker of *How It Is* also craves a different sort of comprehension; he desires to make his situation comprehensible to another. The desire for responsiveness and solidarity haunts this text, as Beckett plays on the nuances of what it is to 'understand' someone (especially someone who seems very different to us) both in the sense of comprehending their language—'we use the same idiom what a blessing'—(*HII*, 70) and of apprehending and feeling for their pain. In this sense, *How It Is* has an intriguing relationship with the questions of theory-theory and simulation theory discussed in my first chapter. Beckett's speakers seem to be suggesting, once again, that our knowledge of others can only ever be theoretical:

all that among other things so many others ill-spoken ill-heard ill-remembered to the sole end that may be white on white trace of so many and so many words ill-given ill-received ill-rendered to the mud and whose ear in these conditions the gift of understanding the care for us the means of noting what does it matter   (*HII*, 147)

The 'gift of understanding' in Browning, Auden, and Beckett's texts is hampered by their 'ill-spoken' nature. In Beckett and Browning, readers must encounter a syntactical obscurity and lack of 'explanatory' features of punctuation. In Auden, they must negotiate the winding sentences of Jamesian pastiche, or complex syllabic ordering. Laurence Harvey argues that the 'fragmentation of form' in Beckett's poetry is a resolution of 'no confidence in the logical order of grammar'.[128] Meanwhile, Susan Brienza notes the manuscript evidence that shows Beckett working towards 'creating his own language . . . devising his own paradigms for phrasal construction'.[129] Beckett's syntactic experiments stem, in part,

---

[128] Harvey, *Samuel Beckett*, 134.
[129] Susan Brienza, *Samuel Beckett's New Worlds* (Norman: University of Oklahoma Press, 1987), 8.

from Jolas's modernist arguments that the artist is 'free to disintegrate the primeval matter of words imposed on him by text books and dictionaries . . . to disregard existing grammatical and syntactic laws'.[130] Some of Beckett's greatest admirers have admitted to finding such syntactical disintegration alarming. Ricks notes that 'in destroying the sentence, Beckett seems to me to have destroyed the extraordinary rhythms and cadences of his style, and it is possible to find his lifelong and total consistency impressive but also blood-chilling.'[131] The consistency of *How It Is*, means, Knowlson notes, that it will find 'fit audience though few.[132] Indeed, the instinct that chills Ricks's blood, here, is perhaps the same instinct that drove Dr Johnson to condemn Milton: '[o]f him at last, may be said what Johnson said of Spenser, that *he wrote no language*, but has formed what Butler called a *Babylonish dialect*, in itself harsh and barbarous.'[133] Johnson, like Ricks, here, is making a connection between linguistic and moral qualities. The fact that Milton is difficult to understand implies that he is savage, beyond the realms of human comprehension.

Browning was such another who stood in linguistic isolation. 'It appears', G. H. Lewes wrote, 'as if he consulted his own ease more than the reader's; and if by any arbitrary distribution of accents he could make the verse satisfy his own ear, it must necessarily satisfy the ear of another.'[134] He was, Oliver Elton comments, 'one of the few English poets since Milton who may be said to have a grammar of his own'.[135] Indeed, the biblical text that he uses for his epigraph to 'Caliban upon Setebos', contains a phrase which explicitly addresses the moralities of grammar: 'to him that ordereth his conversation aright will I shew the salvation of God' (Psalm 50: 23). In its salvaging of a creature who inclines towards 'a grammar of his own', Browning's dramatic monologue poses questions about the justice of such grammatical rectitude. Caliban's inability to 'ordereth his conversation' demands that the reader considers how they might understand a voice which stands outside the laws of syntax, and of morality, that they take for granted. Beckett, too,

---

[130] *Transition* 3 (June 1929), 17, quoted in Brienza, *Samuel Beckett's New Worlds*, 10.
[131] Christopher Ricks, 'Beckett and the Lobster', *New Statesman*, 14 Feb. 1964, 254–5, repr. in L. Butler, *Critical Essays*, 134.
[132] Pilling and Knowlson, *Frescoes*, 61.
[133] Samuel Johnson, *Lives of the English Poets* (New York: Everyman, 1906), 112.
[134] G. H. Lewes, *British Quarterly Review*, 66 (Apr. 1848), 357–400, in Litzinger and Smalley (eds.), *Critical Heritage*, 122.
[135] Quoted in Honan, *Browning's Characters*, 271.

plays on the idea of what it is to 'ordereth . . . conversation aright'. His 'midget grammar' (*HII*, 76), so different from conventional intelligible structures that are skimmed with ease, makes the reader question the ways in which we may understand, and misunderstand, others. Parsing, Lanham argues, is usually an activity that the reader performs intuitively.[136] But Beckett's prose has, as Knowlson puts it, the effect of unsettling our intuitive activities, 'reminding us that the mechanism of syntax, when it becomes the object of scrutiny, is as miraculous and as complicated as the phenomenon of walking'.[137] The fact that syntax is a 'mechanism' is crucial to *How It Is*, as it dwells, repeatedly, upon what is innate, and what is constructed in its textual world. Thoughts of nature pervade its phrasing—'I hear it my life natural order', 'following not a selection natural order' (*HII*, 7), 'I learn it natural order'—and while the speaker is proud of his general knowledge—'always understood everything except for example history and geography' (*HII*, 46), he has special feelings for the rarer species of the natural world: 'Or failing kindred meat a llama emergency dream an alpaca llama the history I knew my God the natural' (*HII*, 15). The line break after 'natural' here, cutting off the sentence, points to the artificial construction of this text. For as *How It Is* goes on, it hints at the possibility that its entire narrative is an unnatural, arbitrary arrangement: 'nothing to prevent one mix up change the natural order play about with that' (*HII*, 115).

Wittgenstein comments that 'the *facts* of our natural history which throw light on our problems are hard to detect, for our way of speaking *passes them by*, it is occupied by other things. (In the same way that we tell someone: "Go into the shop and buy . . . "—not: "Put your left foot in front of your right foot etc. etc. . . . . ").'[138] The moral philosopher Colin McGinn displays such conversational avoidance when he argues that 'our ethical "intuitions" are . . . like our "intuitions" that certain strings of words are grammatical'.[139] For McGinn, perhaps, is too confident of his prose, too certain that his grammatical intuitions are correct and natural, and this is reflected in his ethical philosophy. Though he worries that 'our ethical knowledge is aesthetically mediated', McGinn grounds and relieves his fears with 'common-sense'

---

[136] Richard A. Lanham, *Analyzing Prose*, 2nd edn. (New York: Scribner, 1983), 3.

[137] Pilling and Knowlson, *Frescoes*, 65.

[138] Ludwig Wittgenstein, *Remarks on the Philosophy of Psychology*, i, ed. G. E. M. Anscombe and G. H. von Wright, trans. G. E. M. Anscombe (Oxford: Basil Blackwell, 1980), no. 78.

[139] McGinn, *Ethics*, 59.

statements like '[s]uffering and death are what they are, *prosaically* and horribly, and no amount of aesthetics can change their nature' (my emphasis).[140] The relation that McGinn makes between literature and morality has, at heart, a confidence in stable conventions of reading and understanding linguistic structures. It could be argued that there is something wrong with this; where would McGinn's ethical intuitions be in a world of prose like *How It Is*, in which the rules of grammar are revealed to be arbitrary, contingent, and subject to sudden rearrangement?

THERE'S SOMETHING WRONG: INDIVIDUAL GRAMMATICAL SPECIES

Aesthetics may not be able to change the nature of 'suffering and death', but, through aesthetic means, these painful considerations may be understood in a different light. One way of understanding differently is to consider the relationship between ethical and grammatical comprehension, raised in my previous section. In his book *Contingency, Irony, Solidarity*, Richard Rorty discusses the arbitrary nature of 'the paradigm of coherent, meaningful, literal speech' and considers the merits of Donald Davidson's views:

Davidson tries to undermine the notion of languages as entities by developing the notion of what he calls 'a passing theory' about the noises and inscriptions presently being produced by a fellow human. Think of such a theory as part of a larger 'passing theory' about this person's total behaviour—a set of guesses about what she will do under what conditions. Such a theory is 'passing' because it must constantly be corrected to allow for mumbles, stumbles, malapropisms, tics, seizures, psychotic symptoms, egregious stupidity, strokes of genius and the like.[141]

There is, Davidson writes, 'no . . . chance of regularising, or teaching, this process . . . we should give up the attempt to illuminate how we communicate by appeal to conventions'.[142] Without such an appeal, though, things can get lonely. In *How It Is*, the speaker is making some

---

[140] Ibid. 141, 175.
[141] Rorty, *Contingency*, 14.
[142] Rorty refers to Davidson's 'A Nice Derangement of Epitaphs', in Ernest Lepore (ed.), *Truth and Interpretation: Perspectives on the Philosophy of Donald Davidson* (Oxford: Blackwell, 1984), 446; Rorty, *Contingency*, 15.

sort of attempt to 'regularize' Pim's utterances, by devising his own conventions: 'thump on skull he stops and stop it likewise the thump on skull signifying stop at all times and that come to think of it almost mechanically at least where words involved' (*HII*, 71).

And this attempt has, he believes, some degree of success: 'arduous beginnings then less he is no fool merely slow in the end he understands all almost all' (*HII*, 77). However, if one applies Davidson's theory, Pim does not 'understand' the speaker so much as develop some sort of 'passing theory' (or theory-theory), from the pattern of his inscriptions and insertions. While the speaker is trying to communicate emotion, Pim receives a message of torture. In this exchange, at least, 'suffering' is not necessarily what it appears to be. The way in which ethical certainties may be lost in translation finds a parallel in a moment from Edward Albee's *The Zoo Story* in which a man named Jerry tells of his unsuccessful attempt to feed a stray dog: 'Was trying to feed the dog an act of love? And perhaps, was the dog's attempt to bite me *not* an act of love? If we can so misunderstand, well then, why have we invented the word love in the first place?'[143]

One might compare the way in which Pim cannot 'understand' the speaker's text, and the way in which the reader cannot comprehend *How It Is*. While the typographical format offers the convention of closure, there is incoherence behind their printed words:

fleeting impression I quote that in trying to present in three parts or episodes an affair which all things considered involves four one is in danger of being incomplete

that to this third part now ending at last a fourth should normally be appended in which would be seen among a thousand and one other things scarcely or not at all to be seen in the present formulation this thing   (*HII*, 142)

And one of the 'things scarcely or not at all to be seen' is the speaker's own torture at the hands of another: 'of the four three quarters of our total life only three lend themselves to communication' (*HII*, 143).

Ethically speaking, Deleuze and Guattari write of a mode of thought that 'might overthrow a system of judgement'. 'All one needs', they comment, 'in order to moralize is to fail to understand.'[144] Such links between judging and understanding become grammatically alive in

[143] Edward Albee, *The Zoo Story* (1959), in *The Zoo Story and Other Plays* (Harmondsworth: Penguin, 1995), 20. My thanks to Shane Weller for providing this example.
[144] Quoted in Uhlmann, *Beckett and Poststructuralism*, 107.

Beckett's texts, as the reader is presented with a barrier to conventional modes of 'understanding' a narrative. Our theories about understanding a textual voice are unsettled. Deleuze and Guattari propose an alternative. They argue for a way of relating 'ethics' to 'ethology', of considering an ethical approach which takes account of a body's particularity, its 'haecceity... the assemblage that is defined by longitude and latitude, by speeds and affects'.[145] In the case of *How It Is*, this would mean an understanding of the text's affectlessness, and an attempt, perhaps, at a different way of reading. It is difficult, however, to determine how this alternative mode of understanding could take place. In an essay on stylistics and reader-response, Stanley Fish offers one positive way forward, urging critics to recognize not just the ' "tears, prickles" and "other psychological symptoms" of reading, but all the precise mental operations involved in reading, including the formulation of complete thoughts, the performing (and regretting) of acts of judgement, the following and making of logical sequences'.[146] That is to say, we all have our individual ways of reading, and theories about other minds— theories that are difficult to change, and it is important that we think about these. This is why Fish makes an attack on the idea of 'linguistic competence', which is the idea that 'it is possible to characterise a linguistic system that every speaker shares'.[147] '[U]nderstanding', he writes, 'is more than a linear processing.'[148]It is a sentiment that the speaker of *How It Is* would understand well, and, what is more, one which he asks us to share. When he declares, 'do I use it freely it's not said or I don't hear it's one or the other all I hear is that a witness I'd need a witness' (*HII*, 19), there is a clear sense in which he puts the burden of 'understanding', and of witnessing, upon his readers, and the nuances of their perception. In a similar sense to the way in which Auden asks his readers to think carefully, regarding fictional others as analogous rather than identical to us, Beckett's speaker makes us reassess our ways and motives of reading.

'Linear processing' has already provided some distorted readings of *How It Is*. Judith Dearlove notes that the phrase 'something wrong

---

145 Ibid. 121.
146 Stanley E. Fish, 'Literature in the Reader: Affective Stylistics', *New Literary History*, 2/1 (Autumn 1970), 123–62, at 140. Fish is quoting Wimsatt and Beardsley, *The Verbal Icon*, 34.
147 Fish, 'Literature in the Reader', 141. Fish quotes Ronald Wardhaugh, *Reading: A Linguistic Perspective* (New York, 1969), 60.
148 Fish, 'Literature in the Reader', 143.

there', which punctuates the text, must be an authorial interruption: it 'abruptly destroys any suspension of disbelief we may have willed' in relation to this text in which 'everything is self-consciously fictive'. However, here she misses something about the text itself.[149] For there is, perhaps, another sense of this refrain. '[S]omething wrong there' (*HII*, 15 and *passim*) implies that, as the speaker tells his tale, he is suffering torture—another figure claws at his back, forcing him to speak—and that this torture has either caused him to speak his words out of sequence, or his words have been moved about when his story has been copied. This view is, certainly, wishful thinking, as it considers the 'life of afterlife' of these creatures in the missing fourth part. But this non-linear reading does keep a sense for the 'real richness of ontology' of this work.[150] It feels for how these fictional creatures have got lost in translation, or suffered in rearrangement, how one man's arse may be another one's armpit, and that 'something wrong there' might, if read another way, be a cry for help, a painful admission by 'an extorted voice' that there is something wrong.[151]

INDULGENCE: HUMANITY REGAINED

Coming to a conclusion about Beckett's work isn't easy. It is common-place to note that he was drawn to prolonging the final moments. It would also be helpful to consider how this ascetic 'writer of the greatest reticence' was tempted, on occasion, to the textual equivalent of a binge.[152]

It has been argued that by the end of *How It Is* Beckett found a way 'to escape fiction'.[153] It represents, Knowlson and Pilling write, 'humanity regained':

[149] J. E. Dearlove, 'The Voice and its Words: How It Is in Beckett's Canon', *Journal of Beckett Studies*, 3 (summer 1978), 56–75, at 73.

[150] Nuttall, *Openings*, 123.

[151] 'what a cunt this Pim damn it all confuse arse and armpit', *HII*, 74.

[152] Coleridge speaks of the 'moved and sympathetic imagination' in relation to *The Tempest, Coleridge's Shakespearian Criticism*, 133. See Ricks, *Beckett's Dying Words*, 208 and Eric Griffiths: 'his writing eloquently often seems to long for absolute cessation . . . The four monosyllables "Oh all to end" express both a hope and a regret', *Independent*, 27 Dec. 1989, quoted in *Beckett's Dying Words*, 8.

[153] Dieter Wellershoff, 'Failure of an Attempt at De-Mythologisation: Samuel Beckett's Novels', in Martin Esslin (ed.), *Samuel Beckett: A Collection of Critical Essays* (Englewood Cliffs, NJ: Prentice-Hall, 1965), 92–107, at 105–6.

There is an immense relief in reaching the 'end of quotation' that marks the termination of fictional life and the inception of 'how it is' . . . The inscriptions with which *How It Is* concludes signify not so much the arrival of another tormentor as the resolution of the dichotomies and trichotomies that have prevailed up to this point. Despite its overtones of crucifixion (and in a sense because of them) the end of *How It Is* is a kind of birth, with its own distinctive labour pains. In acknowledging the voice as 'mine yes not another's' whereas at the start it was 'in me not mine' the speaker finds his own voice at last.[154]

There is something questionable and possibly sentimental about this argument. The relief that 'at last' Beckett has stepped out of the fictional frame with the 'implicit acknowledgement that Pim is nothing but a wish fulfilment' is, in fact, unsettled by a lack of 'resolution' in the closing words of the text: 'good good end at last of part three and last that's how it was end of quotation after Pim how it is' (*HII*, 160).[155] For there is a difficulty in *How It Is* about final moments, and to dismiss Pim 'at last' is to miss the verbal attachment that the speaker shows towards his creature: 'a formulation that would eliminate him completely. . . while rendering me in the same breath sole responsible for this un-qualifiable murmur of which consequently here the last scraps very last' (*HII*, 157). Throughout the text, the speaker is sustained by images 'that must have lasted a good moment with that I have lasted a moment' (*HII*, 34), and despite his craving for elimination, there is a desperation, here, for the text *to* last, as the word functions both as a final closure and imperative plea for continuance.[156]

The end of a text, for Beckett, did not signify the end of the imagined creature. His writing, with its constant allusions to past texts, has a sense for their ability to persist. Beckett has, as Abbott notes, 'if not a conviction, then a fascination regarding what might lurk in the *hors texte*'.[157] While many writers speak of the fictional world extending beyond the textual boundaries. Beckett's accounts of his own writing have an intense sense of fictional obligations—an awareness of begin-nings and endings, beyond the world of his text. Take the publishing history of his short story 'The End', his earliest piece of prose fiction in French. Knowlson describes the way in which Beckett sent the first half of the story—then called 'Suite'—to Sartre's *Les Temps modernes* in

---

154 Pilling and Knowlson, *Frescoes*, 77.
155 Ibid. 71.
156 My comments on the words 'last' and 'still' are indebted to Ricks, *Beckett's Dying Words*, 144.
157 Abbott, *Author in the Autograph*, 3.

1946, and 'was led to believe that the second part of his story would appear in the autumn issue'. Due to a misunderstanding, Simone de Beauvoir failed to print the second part of the story. Beckett's protest shows, once again, his difficulty in letting go. 'It is', he wrote, 'quite impossible for me to escape from the duty I have towards one of my creatures . . . You halt an existence before it can have the least achievement . . . I find it difficult to believe that concerns of presentation could justify in your eyes such a mutilation.'[158] De Beauvoir's version would have cut out the story's, arguably crucial, final lines: 'The sea, the sky, the mountains and the islands closed in and crushed me in a mighty systole, then scattered to the uttermost confines of space. The memory came faint and cold of the story I might have told, a story in the likeness of my life, I mean without the courage to end or the strength to go on.'[159] Crucial, because they give a sense of the way in which Beckett attempted to make his last things last.[160]

Beckett shared this resistance to cutting things short, to convenient endings, with one of his most important literary forebears, Samuel Johnson. 'They can', he wrote, 'put me wherever they want but it's Johnson, always Johnson who is with me. And if I follow any tradition, it is his.'[161] Johnson's lack of conviction in endings is demonstrated in his only work of fiction, *Rasselas*, with its famous 'conclusion, in which nothing is concluded'.[162] Some of Johnson's public were surprised by the shape of this 'ill-contrived, unfinished, unnatural and uninstructive tale'.[163] Indeed, his novel, with its let-down of an ending, was, in part, an attempt to sate and correct the excesses of such a fictional appetite of his age, 'that hunger of the imagination that preys incessantly on life'.[164] Nevertheless, the shape of Johnson's inconclusive novel reveals a sense of this author's own hungry imagination, hinting at his own strong attachments to fictional characters. It was Johnson's lack

---

[158] Quoted in Knowlson, *Damned to Fame*, 360.

[159] 'The End', in *The Expelled and Other Novellas* (Harmondsworth: Penguin, 1980), 93.

[160] Charles Dickens, preface (1869), *David Copperfield* (Harmondsworth: Penguin, 1985), 47.

[161] Quoted in Deidre Bair, *Samuel Beckett: A Biography* (London: Simon and Schuster, 1990), 23.

[162] See Samuel Johnson, *Rasselas,* in *Rasselas and Other Tales*, ed. Gwin J. Kolb (New Haven: Yale University Press, 1990), ch. xlix, p. 175.

[163] Mrs Chapone asked in a letter of 28 Apr. 1759 'whether you do not think [Johnson] ought to be ashamed of publishing such an ill-contrived, unnatural and uninstructive tale'. See ibid., p. lvi.

[164] Imlac's words to Rasselas, ibid., 78.

of 'courage to end' that Beckett felt for, the tender inability to close the book on his creatures, to turn them into fictional contrivances 'to point a moral and adorn a tale'.[165] The manner in which things 'ill-seen' and 'ill-said' bear on his early fictions and persist to his last provides an example of Beckett's difficulties with finding his way to an ending. Marjorie Perloff notes that the 'germ' of a late text, *Ill Seen Ill Said*, is found among the opening fragments of *How It Is*: 'my life last state last version ill-said ill-heard ill-recaptured ill-murmured in the mud' (*HII*, 7). In fact, this 'germ' had been evolving for far longer. It echoes back to Watt's meeting with the Galls, father and son, who come to tune the piano. This incident makes a strange impression on Watt, for it 'was not ended, when it was past, but continued to unfold, in Watt's head, from beginning to end, over and over again'. The scene, for Watt, 'ceased so rapidly to have even the paltry significance of two men, come to tune a piano, and tuning it, and exchanging a few words, as men will do, and going, that this seemed rather to belong to some story heard long before, an instant in the life of another, ill-told, ill-heard, and more than half forgotten' (*W*, 71). The Messrs Gall lose 'all meaning', becoming part of an elaborate pattern in Watt's mind. He is struck by 'the complex connections of its light and shadows, the passing from silence to sound and from sound to silence, the stillness before the movement and the stillness after, the quickenings and retardings, the approaches and separations, all the shifting detail of its march and ordinance, according to the irrevocable caprice of its taking place' (*W*, 69). Such dimensionless patterning, 'abstracted to death', hints at the shape that Beckett's prose was to take. The progress of this 'ill-told ill-heard' tale, as 'it developed a purely plastic content, and gradually lost, in the nice processes of its light, its sound, its impacts and its rhythms, all meaning, even the most literal', echoes the strained relations between the printed page and 'the life of another' in his texts (*W*, 69). On encountering the prose of *Ill Seen Ill Said*, some readers have considered Beckett's creatures not 'quickened', but disturbingly aestheticized. The text, lacking all animating marks of punctuation, and left with merely basic equiparative pointing, has, as Sage puts it 'a Byzantine flatness'.[166] Take the closing words of the opening paragraph: 'There then she sits as though

[165] Samuel Johnson, 'The Vanity of Human Wishes': 'He left a name, at which the world grew pale, | To point a moral, or adorn a tale', *Poems*, ed. E. L. McAdam (New Haven: Yale University Press, 1964), 102.

[166] Sage, 'Innovation and Continuity', 102.

turned to stone face to the night. Save for the white of her hair and faintly bluish white of face and hands all is black. For an eye having no need of light to see. All this in the present as had she the misfortune to be still of this world.'[167]

Brienza asks, after reading this passage, how one is 'to make sense of such forbidding texts where style remains the foremost element', while Lawrence Graver questions 'the significance . . . of the fact that the narrator's struggle to express 'depends on bringing a dead woman back to life, on obsessively charting the last days of her suffering and reproducing her death'.[168] Both critics are, at various levels, questioning the ethics of this aesthetic mastery, concerned for the 'fictional material' at the mercy of its narrator. Hélène Baldwin is another who presses on the point when she writes that 'there is no love in these works'.[169]

One might ask what sort of 'love' Baldwin expects these fictions to yield. Beckett spoke explicitly about his sense of 'ill-narratorship' early in his career, describing his own textual being as both malevolent and victimized: 'a kind of vermin . . . a "skymole" tunnelling in "its firmament in genesis".'[170] Within his text, he is an 'insistent, invisible rat, fidgeting behind the astral incoherence of the art surface'; as Abbott puts it, a 'small burrowing creature . . . busy, threatening, purposive, blind, trapped, buried alive'.[171] Years on, the textual practices of *Ill Seen Ill Said* speak of such painful attachment. The narrator seems all too aware of prolonging the creature's pain. The phrase which repeats itself through the narrative—'All this in the present as had she the misfortune to be still of this world' (*ISIS*, 8 and *passim*)—is, in part, a self-rebuke; it points to the way in which Beckett's fictional 'quickenings and retardings' imaginatively animate a life that is aesthetically pleasing, but no longer worth living. She is 'still of this world' by the author's hand, paralysed in print. Her plight echoes that of Browning's Cleon, 'Alive still', some 250 years after his composition.

[167] *Ill Seen Ill Said* (London: Calder, 1982), 7–8.

[168] Brienza, *Beckett's New Worlds*, 4; Lawrence Graver, 'Homage to the Dark Lady: *Ill Seen Ill Said*', in Linda Ben-Zvi (ed.), *Women in Beckett* (Urbana: University of Illinois Press, 1992), 142–9, at 148; Adam Piette, *Remembering and the Sound of Words* (Oxford: Clarendon Press, 1996), 234.

[169] Hélène Baldwin, *Samuel Beckett's Real Silence* (University Park: Pennsylvania University State Press, 1981).

[170] Abbott, *Author in the Autograph*, p. xi. Abbott cites *Dream of Fair to Middling Women*, 33.

[171] Ibid., p. iv.

Many humanist critics argue that through 'identification . . . literature offers the self the sort of nourishment that is essential for development . . . as Shelley observes . . . "Poetry strengthens that faculty (i.e. the imagination, the capacity to empathize and identify with others) which is the organ of the moral nature of man".'[172] Walter J. Slatoff is an example of such a critic, seeing narrative as 'an occasion for coexistence imaginatively with a fictional person's way of feeling'.[173] Such a desire for 'coexistence' can be taken to an extreme. As Slatoff goes on to admit, the thought of being unified 'into one kind of stuff' carries with it the fear 'of being gobbled up'.[174] Similarly, Beckett's ill-seen texts are critical about the type of moral nourishment that 'identification' with others may provide. Being able to embody the experience of another (an experience equivalent to the cognitive process of simulation), may also be seen in a negative light, as a sort of cannibalism, envelopment, or swamping of another person. One thinks back to the speaker in *How It Is*, craving the 'bits and scraps' that will sustain him. He has an image of being consumed with desire:

suddenly we are eating sandwiches alternate bites I mine she hers and exchanging endearments my sweet girl I bite she swallows my sweet boy she bites I swallow we don't yet coo with our bills full

my darling girl I bite she swallows my darling boy she bites I swallow   (*HII*, 33–4)

There is something unsettling about this image of prandial courtship; the glut of emotion hints at the way in which the pair, consumed with love, are consuming each other. Such hints of cannibalism notions persist throughout *How It Is*, as the speaker has 'no appetite' save for company and emotion:

and if it may seem strange that without food to sustain us we can drag ourselves thus by the mere grace of our united net sufferings from west to east towards an inexistent peace we are invited kindly to consider

that for the likes of us and no matter how we are recounted there is more nourishment in a cry nay a sigh torn from one whose only good is silence or in speech extorted from one at last delivered from its use than sardines can ever offer   (*HII*, 156–7)

---

[172] Marshall W. Alcorn Jr., and Mark Bracher, 'Literature, Psychoanalysis, and the Re-Formation of the Self: A New Direction for Reader-Response Theory', *PMLA* 100 (May 1985), 342–54, at 351.

[173] Walter J. Slatoff, *The Look of Distance: Reflections on Suffering and Sympathy in Modern Literature* (Columbus: Ohio State University Press, 1985), 7.

[174] Ibid. 149.

The way in which imaginative indulgence might teeter between affection, sentimentality, and greed harks back to the Unnamable's fondness for stories: 'Yes, a little creature, I shall try and make a little creature, to hold in my arms, a little creature in my image no matter what I say.' It is a fondness that turns savage: 'And seeing what a poor thing I have made, or how like myself, I shall eat it' (*T*, 226).

For as well as being something 'ever under the control of another', a creature may also be a creature comfort, something to be consumed, and enjoyed; indeed, the sense is stronger in Hiberno-English, where 'creature', or 'craythur', also means 'whiskey'.[175] This sense of the way in which we feed off others finds its way, painfully and reluctantly, to a close in *Ill Seen Ill Said*:

Decision no sooner reached or rather long after than what is the wrong word? For the last time at last for to end yet again what the wrong word? Than revoked. No but slowly dispelled a little very little like the last wisps of day when the curtain closes. Of itself by slow millimetres or drawn by a phantom hand. Farewell to farewell. Then in that perfect dark foreknell darling sound pip for end begun. First last moment. Grant only enough remain to devour all. Moment by glutton moment. Sky earth the whole kit and boodle. Not another crumb of carrion left. Lick chops and basta. No. One moment more. One last. Grace to breathe that void. Know happiness.   (*ISIS*, 59)

This is, like Prospero's epilogue, an indulgence, an extended curtain call, and not an ending. Alerted to the way in which final moments may be savoured, and partings sweet sorrow, the reader is brought face to face with the ethical decision that has haunted them throughout Beckett's texts. As Piette puts it, one is perplexed by the question of whether to give 'the text either a sensuous, lyrical life or a rhetorical and cruel playfulness', or both at once.[176] It is hard to sympathize with this grotesque 'parody of post-prandial thanksgiving'; the undertones of cruelty and of cannibalism touch the limits of human moral assurance.[177] The sense that the readers may have been feasting their eyes, as the narrator licks his chops, casts doubt on the idea that one may ever suffer with those we see suffer. Hunger, it seems, is once again stronger than grief.[178]

---

[175] T. P. Dolan (ed.), *A Dictionary of Hiberno-English* (Dublin: Gill & Macmilan, 1998), 78.

[176] Piette, *Remembering*, 234.

[177] Ibid.

[178] I allude to the tale of Count Ugolini, who, faced with starvation, ate the bodies of his dead children, as recounted in Dante's *Inferno*, 75.

Apparently altruistic acts of identification may, in fact, be narcissistic acts of consumption. But Beckett's writing suggests that something may be salvaged. In revealing how the 'hunger of our imagination' may be self-indulgent, Beckett intimates the ways in which 'exaggerations of love' bring us, physically, and ethically, close to the likes of a creature like Caliban, or Pim, as we 'gorge on his fables' (*HII*, 69). Anthony Cronin finds *How It Is* too overwhelming: it gives, he writes, 'insufficient reward for the pains and difficulties the reader was asked to undergo'.[179] But it is, perhaps, through these 'pains and difficulties' that one finds sustenance, in Beckett's texts. They ask us to reimagine the possibilities and the ambiguities of how we identify with others; to recognize the contempt, as well as the compassion, that these acts may involve.

Writing of Beckett's detachment from his work, Anthony Uhlmann notes that it

> is sent out into the world by the artist, like a child, with its own body... Because it has a separate being... when the work encounters the reader it is not recreated or recomposed by that reader... While the work requires both the writer and the reader... it still has a separate being (just as the child has a separate being from the parents and the others with which it interacts, although it could not exist if these parents and others did not exist).[180]

Not all families let go of each other that easily. While parents and children can interact with each other in ways even stranger than Beckett's world can show us, so writers, works, and readers may find themselves attached and obligated to each other in a manner beyond Uhlmann's imagination. Beckett might once have craved the Proustian '[e]nchantments of reality' when 'the object is perceived as particular and unique and not merely as the member of a family... isolated and inexplicable in the light of ignorance', for 'then and then only may it be a source of enchantment'.[181] 'Unfortunately', for both Beckett, and Marcel, 'habit has laid its veto on this form of perception'. We are, Beckett writes, 'creatures of habit', and a reader of Beckett's work needs to understand what it means to be such a creature, fallen into 'habit[s] of tenderness'.[182]

---

179 Anthony Cronin, *Samuel Beckett: The Last Modernist* (London: HarperCollins, 1996), 538.
180 Uhlmann, *Beckett and Poststructuralism*, 29.
181 Beckett, *Proust*, 22–3.
182 Beckett writes of the narrator's 'habit of tenderness' for his grandmother, ibid. 27.

Understanding is hard, though. Ruby Cohn may be right when she comments that 'Our world "so various, so beautiful, so new" so stingily admitted to Beckett's texts is nevertheless the essential background for appreciation of his work'. Her belief in the ultimate humanity of literature, and in the possibilities for human sympathy through textual encounter, is one such 'habit of tenderness'. It resounds in these words. She echoes (through an allusion to the poetry of Matthew Arnold), Miranda's optimistic embrace of the 'brave new world'.[183] It seems new to her—but one cannot but hear the counterpoint to such optimism in Beckett's work—a sense for the alarming way in which figures from our background, and from other worlds, have a habit of stepping forward, like Prospero, disenchanting and casting shadows over our 'light of ignorance'.

[183] Cohn, *Back to Beckett*, 5. She is quoting the cheerier part of Arnold's 'Dover Beach': 'for the world, which seems | To lie before us like a land of dreams, | So various, so beautiful, so new', *Poems of Matthew Arnold*, 242.

Epilogue: Sympathy Now

> We are wet with sympathy now
> W. H. Auden, *The Sea and the Mirror*

> Mountains, Rivers, and grand storms,
> Continuous profit, grand customs
> (And many of them: O Lakes, Lakes!)
> O Sentiment upon the rocks!
> Geoffrey Hill, 'Elegiac Stanzas'

Writing of 'sympathy now', questions such as 'Who now?' and 'Where now?' (*T*, 293), as Beckett's Unnamable might put it, arise. In many ways, the idea of contemporary sympathy involves just as many difficulties and obstacles as writing about ideas of sympathy from the past does. After all, while the works of other centuries may possess far more than surface strangeness, there is no reason to presume any particular continuity of sentiment based on temporal proximity.[1] In this sense, just as '[n]o one man's English is all English', no one person's idea of sympathy necessarily chimes with another's.[2] The ramifications inevitably extend to relations between individuals and larger groups.

In the last decade, there have been many general claims made in relation to literature and its power to evoke sympathy, and about the relations between the idea of sympathy and empathy and the idea of goodness. In the current climate, the word 'sympathy' is itself used in a fairly loose fashion, often suggesting something nearer to that which is understood by empathy, as in Robin West's assertion that '[l]iterature

---

[1] See Catherine Belsey's criticism of historical readings which 'explain away the surface strangeness of another century in order to release its profound continuity with the present', *The Subject of Tragedy: Identity and Difference in Renaissance Drama* (London: Methuen, 1985), 2.

[2] John Murray, 'General Explanations' to the *OED*, 'Corrected Reissue' (1933), vol. i, p. xxvii.

helps us understand others. Literature helps us sympathize with their pain, it helps us share their sorrow, and it helps us celebrate their joy. It makes us more moral. It makes us better people.'[3] While it would be wrong to see such claims as necessarily signifying a more general feeling about sympathy, they are worth examining for the possibility that they might enter into the fluid circulation of ideas—ideas that in themselves have fluid qualities, changing shape according to the way we attempt to contain them, impossible to hold still.

It is, perhaps, the genre of 'occasional poetry' or 'occasional writing', which brings the notion of contemporary sympathy and its relationship with literature to the fore. The very fact of writing to, or for, an occasion, brings a poet, or novelist, in temporal synch with others. Some writers have taken this task up themselves, in the role of Poet Laureate. Others, such as W. H. Auden, have had such a role almost thrust upon them in retrospect, as was the case when soon after the towers of the World Trade Center fell, lines from his poem 'September 1, 1939' began to be emailed and faxed around the world. The poem, composed after Germany invaded Poland, became, in its own way, 'a poetic anthem' for 9/11, and reports have it that in 2002 a group of drama students at Edinburgh finished a production about the terrorist attack by lighting candles, and chanting these same 'consoling lines of poetry'.[4] Mark Lawson's account of this commemorative event has an ironic tone about it. One senses his uncertainty about the use of poetry 'as' consolation; he draws a veil over the fact that Auden himself disliked the sentiments expressed in the poem.[5] Alongside the extracts of Auden's poetry pasted on the internet, one can find numerous declarations from those either practising reading or criticism, which place emphasis on the role of imaginative writers in the latter part of the twentieth century. Justifying the importance of literary responses to grief, Jahan Ramazani claims that it offers 'a privileged space for mourning', while Alicia Ostriker (who also quotes W. H. Auden's 'September 1') argues that 'the writer's task in times of trouble is . . . first of all not therapeutic but diagnostic'.[6]

---

[3] Robin West, *Narrative, Authority, Law* (Ann Arbor: University of Michigan Press, 1993), 263, quoted in Richard A. Posner, 'Against Ethical Criticism', *Philosophy and Literature*, 21/1 (1997), 1–27, at 4.

[4] Mark Lawson, 'After the Fall', *Guardian*, Friday, 16 Aug. 2002, <http://www.guardian.co.uk/september11/oneyearon/story/0,,782804,00.html>.

[5] See John Fuller, *W. H. Auden: A Commentary* (London: Faber, 1998), 292–3.

[6] See the articles by Jahan Ramazani and Alicia Ostriker, 'Can Poetry Console a Grieving Public', <http://www.poetryfoundation.org/archive/feature.html?id=178621, id=17862.

Novelist Hilary Mantel takes this further. 'Much wickedness', she argues, 'stems from our failure to imagine other people as fully human, as our equals.' She adds that she sees her role as a novelist as similar to (her perception of) the vision of George Eliot—to 'expand our sympathies'.[7] This is a shifty statement. By yoking together the ideas of imagining, imaginatively engaging or possessing 'empathy' for another, and the notion of goodness, it carries with it the neo-Eliotic assumption that reading the work of creative artists can, in some way, help develop these particular imaginative and empathetic skills, and, in an even more mysterious way, lead to fewer acts of 'wickedness'. Ian McEwan hints at something similar in his response to the September 11th attacks in the *Guardian*, writing that '[i]magining what it is like to be someone other than yourself is at the core of our humanity. It is the essence of compassion, and it is the beginning of morality. The hijackers used fanatical certainty, misplaced religious faith, and dehumanising hatred to purge themselves of the human instinct for empathy. Among their crimes was a failure of imagination.'[8]

The phrase that McEwan uses here has become well worn. Looking back on the events of September 11th, Thomas Kean's US governmental report cited a 'failure of imagination' as the principle reason for the failure of security.[9] The question remains, what exactly Kean and McEwan mean by 'imagination' in these cases. The danger with such statements is that they can drift towards merging the idea of imagination and that of goodness, and, to a certain extent, between the upholders of the imagination—our poets and novelists—and the achievement of political peace and unity. Failures of imagination, as Salman Rushdie has subtly explored, can be ways of holding people together, as well as keeping them apart.[10]

---

[7] Louise Tucker, 'Expanding our Sympathies: Louise Tucker talks to Hilary Mantel', in Hilary Mantel, *Beyond Black* (London: HarperCollins, 2005), 7–11, at 7.

[8] Ian McEwan, 'Only Love and then Oblivion', *Guardian*, Sunday, 15 Sept. 2001, <http://www.guardian.co.uk/wtccrash/story/0,1300,552408,00.html>.

[9] See Thomas Kean et al., 'The 9/11 Commission Report', <www.9-11commission. gov/report/911Report_Ch11.pdf>, 339–60, at 339, downloaded Aug. 2007.

[10] Rushdie's narrator is a changeling. Even after the discovery of his true origins, his parents never accept that he might *not* be their child. The narrator attributes this 'to a certain lack of imagination... I remained their son because they could not imagine me out of the role'; 'I was still their son: they remained my parents. In a kind of collective failure of imagination, we learned that we simply could not think our way out of our pasts', Salman Rushdie, *Midnight's Children* (London: Vintage, 1995), 301, 118.

McEwan's intimation concerning the moral powers of imagination, evidenced in his *Guardian* interview, is carried over into his own fiction, in particular his 2005 novel *Saturday*. The novel is a day-in-the-life tale of a neurosurgeon, Henry Perowne, and forms part of the subgenre of 'post-9/11 novels' that include works by Clare Messud, Zadie Smith, and Jonathan Safran Foer.[11] Perowne's profession allows McEwan a certain amount of scope to explore ideas about the physical, chemical, and material nature of mood and emotion, the ways in which the imagination is formed, and the ways in which it might fail us. However, by the novel's close, Perowne is faced with an alternative vision of how our emotions and sympathies work. In a critical scene, he finds himself, and his family, being held captive by a man named Baxter, a man with little formal education and a neurological disorder that causes him to experience sudden mood swings. As Baxter holds the Perowne family at knifepoint, he commands Daisy, Perowne's daughter, to strip naked, and, finding that she is a poet, asks her to read him some poetry— '[s]omething really filthy'. Daisy is in a state of terror but, at the suggestion of her grandfather, she begins to recite something from memory. The poem is Matthew Arnold's 'Dover Beach'. The poem appears to have a peculiar effect on all of those listening, and the aggressive Baxter drops his knife. Arnold, Perowne reflects, 'swung his mood'.[12]

The plot twist is a stretch. The unlikely nature of the situation manages to push McEwan's neo-Comptian idea forwards. However, the stereotypical nature of his characters gives one the sense that this is not only a somewhat heavy-handed attempt to prove that poetry can unify disparate groups, but a case study for the way McEwan thinks things really should work with people and poetry. As Lynn Wells notes, '[i]f there is any kind of moral message, it appears to be that crazy knife-wielding people can be tamed by the beauties of Western literature. I wonder if anybody tried that approach on 9/11.'[13] There is something disingenuous about all this; as Empson notes, the assumption that 'poor

[11] See Clare Messud, *The Emperor's Children* (London: Picador, 2006); Zadie Smith, *On Beauty* (London: Hamish Hamilton, 2005); Jonathan Safran Foer, *Extremely Loud and Incredibly Close* (London; Hamish Hamilton, 2005).
[12] Ian McEwan, *Saturday* (London: Vintage, 2006), 220, 269.
[13] Lynn Wells, 'Review of *Saturday* by Ian McEwan', *Literary London: Interdisciplinary Studies in the Representation of London* 3/2 (2005), <http://www.literarylondon.org/london-journal/september2005/wells.html>.

or low characters' will show us reality is merely 'pastoral machinery dignified into bad metaphysics'.

McEwan's use of Matthew Arnold is not, perhaps, surprising. With its echo of Miranda's 'brave new world', 'Dover Beach' remains an appeal to the powers of the sympathetic imagination in secular crisis. Arnold's remit, as T. S. Eliot claims, has always been to offer a vision of poetry that would supersede the claims of religion, philosophy, and science. By the turn of the last century, he was the ubiquitous figure to whom one turned when consolation was needed. As I. A. Richards argued, 'the most dangerous of sciences is only now beginning to come into action. I am thinking less of . . . mental chaos. We shall be thrown back, as Matthew Arnold foresaw, upon poetry. Poetry is capable of saving us.'[14] After 9/11, one can trace a line of discourse that, if it does not share Richards's fervour, finds itself in tentative step with such Arnoldian claims. It appears, for example, in the 2004 speech given by Martha Nussbaum at Knox College, which argues for the role of the 'liberal arts education, and the liberal arts college' in refining our notions of 'compassion'. One finds it, too, in the claims of Zadie Smith, who believes that 'real empathy makes cruelty an impossibility', and that ' "[w]hen we read with fine attention, we find ourselves caring about people who are various, muddled, uncertain and not quite like us" (and this is good)'. Or in Sue Monk Kidd's assurance that 'fiction creates empathy', which, in turn, offers a 'reconciling force'.[15]

Such statements presume much about the relations between reading, empathizing, sympathizing, and behaving altruistically. Smith's caveat, that one must read 'with fine attention', suggests, however, that there may be better or worse ways to read, in order to develop this 'caring' capacity. Nevertheless, it is hard not to see her statement as implicitly involved in the notion that imaginative reading matter may offer some sort of self-improvement, a substitute for ethical guidance, or a form of social glue. It is, then, one short step to the idea, as Michael Hoffman puts it, 'of poetry, so to speak, in the plural, as a collective mass or

---

[14] T. S. Eliot, *The Use of Poetry and the Use of Criticism* (London: Faber, 1953), 124.
[15] Martha C. Nussbaum, 'Liberal Education in a Time of Global Tension', 9 Sept. 2004, <http://www.knox.edu/x8053.xml>; Zadie Smith, 'Zadie Smith Talks with Ian McEwan, in *Believer: Book of Writers Talking to Writers* (San Francisco: McSweeneys, 2005), 210–39, at 211; Zadie Smith, 'Love Actually', Saturday, 1 Nov. 2003, <http://books.guardian.co.uk/review/story/0,12084,1074217,00.html>; Sue Monk Kidd, 'A Common Heart: A Bestselling Novelist Argues for Empathy through Fiction', *Washington Post Book World*, Sunday, 4 Dec. 2005, 9.

enterprise. Poetry as a certain good.'[16] Recently, one has seen claims for the sympathetic powers of literature, for literature as 'certain good', becoming curiously overblown. Anthologies offer titles such as *Staying Alive, 101 Poems that Could Save Your Life*, and *The Poetry Cure*. Meanwhile *52 Ways of Looking at a Poem: Or, How Poetry Can Change Your Life* or *13 Ways of Looking at a Novel: What to Read and How to Write* (with their titular tributes to Wallace Stevens) seem, similarly, to entertain hopes for the supremacy of fictional imagining and the 'perfectability of self through empathy'.[17] Such promises are often sustained within the dialogues that surround the texts themselves. Padel's review of the *The Poetry Cure* argues, for example, that 'poetry, with its metaphors, can reflect back what we are privately feeling and help us express and bear what is happening to us', while her own account in *52 Ways* notes that '[n]ever . . . have so many published poets been developing new ways of saying things to people in so many different parts of society'.[18] As Peter McDonald notes, 'One question that immediately arises is, *Can this be true?* Another—and a more interesting one—is, *Why are you talking to us like this?*'[19]

One of the main problems with the new wave of neo-Arnoldian thought is the tone that it takes with its audience. Despite there being, as Padel puts it, 'so many different parts of society', she manages to make everyone sound as similar as possible. 'There are a lot of acute, lively, and non-elitist minds out there making poems from the world we live in: from styles of thought and phrase, jokes, events and experiences we all share.' A similar emphasis on 'shared experience' is seen in Jane Smiley's *13 Ways*, which argues that it is the 'quality of commonness'—the unity between reader and writer—that enables literature, especially literature after 9/11, to have such power:

Every novel . . . is a guided meditation on a common thing, common both in perceived the sense of 'mundane' and in the sense of 'shared'—action and reflection as from a particular point of view . . . It is hard to overestimate the

---

[16] Michael Hoffman, 'Sing Softer: A Notebook', *Poetry* (Sept. 2005), 428–38, at 430.

[17] I quote Jerome de Groot, 'Empathy and Enfranchisement', *Rethinking History*, 10/3 (Sept, 2006), 391–413, at 404.

[18] Ruth Padel, rev. of *Apology for Absence* and *The Poetry Cure*, by Julia Darling, *Independent Online Edition*, 29 Apr. 2005, <http://arts.independent.co.uk/books/reviews/article3783.ece>.

[19] Peter McDonald, 'Do You Know Who We Are?', rev. of Shira Wolosky, *The Art of Poetry: How to Read a Poem* and Ruth Padel, *52 Ways of Looking at a Poem: or How Reading Modern Poetry Can Change Your Life, Poetry Review*, 92/4 (winter 2002/3), 99–105, at 100.

importance of this quality of commonness . . . it enables a reader to relax with a novel as with another person, and also to feel as though the novelist might have something to say of relevance to the reader's common life.[20]

In their anxiety to avoid charges of 'elitism', Padel and Smiley assume an easy similarity with their audience. Two things get missed here. The first is the tension implicit in the idea of what is common to all of us; the difficulties of finding a truly shared experience. The second is the fact that in emphasizing the ways in which literary experience may offer a 'non-elitist' opportunity to 'relax', rather than any sort of challenge, these writers manage to sound condescending, or, in the case of Smiley, downright prejudiced, as she argues that 'the commonest bus driver can and often does take an interest in what happens next, and so because the novel requires narrative organization, it will also be a more or less popular form. It can never exclude bus drivers completely.'[21]

The second problem surrounding current arguments about the sympathetic powers of literature is that many commentators appear to rely on the unspoken assumption that an expression of an emotion is innately virtuous; that 'community' is, as sociologist Richard Sennett puts it, 'an act of mutual self-disclosure'.[22] Reflections of our 'private feelings', he notes, are seen as unquestioned good, as in Padel's praise for both 'expressing' as well as bearing what we are going through. Such demands for the expression of emotion are part of much everyday twenty-first-century discourse. Anthony Barnett claims, as a nation, the British people 'are no longer stiff and buttoned-up; we grieve openly, hug each other and believe in talking through our troubles'.[23] Indeed, the absence of such expression can even be perceived as a moral failing. One can see this at work in, for example, the responses to the reviewers of the *London Review of Books*, who offered 'reflections' on 9/11.[24] While one correspondent praised the papers for having offered points of view which demonstrated 'rational detachment and thoughtful reflection, even on very emotional issues', many wrote in to complain about the very absence of expressed emotion, in favour of analytical

---

[20] Jane Smiley, *13 Ways of Looking at the Novel* (London: Faber 2005), 91.
[21] Ibid. 17–18. I refer Smiley to (ex-bus driver) Magnus Mills's Booker-shortlisted *Restraint of Beasts* (London: Flamingo, 1998).
[22] Richard Sennett, *The Fall of Public Man* (London: Penguin, 2002), 4.
[23] Anthony Barnett, *This Time: Our Constitutional Revolution* (London: Vintage, 1997), 116–17.
[24] '11 September: Some LRB writers reflect on the reasons and consequences', *London Review of Books*, 4 Oct. 2001, 20–5.

commentary. Correspondents were accused of 'heartlessness', 'Schaden-freude', and 'patronising insensitivity' in the face of the painful events.[25]

In his critique of this culture of emotionality, which rates 'whether we can personally "relate" to events or other persons, and whether in the relation itself people are "open" to one another', Sennett accurately locates the fact that such expressions of emotion are not necessarily, in themselves, markers of our concern for others. The first, 'he points out', may be 'a cover word for measuring the other in terms of a mirror of self-concern, and the second is a cover for measuring social interaction in terms of the market exchange of confession'.[26] Such an observation is, of course, nothing new, but there is further force to Sennett's argument. He makes a brief but important exploration of the reasons for the desire for openness about emotion: 'the desire to authenticate oneself, one's motives, one's feelings, is', he notes, 'a form of Puritanism'.[27] Sennett recognizes that for writers and readers now, as much as when Browning was writing, much of the desire for emotional exchange comes from a ghostly desire for some sort of salvation.

WHATEVER LOVE MEANS

Of all those writing now, Geoffrey Hill is perhaps the poet who writes with most acuity about the 'gesture[s] of helpless compassion', and hopeless reaching towards faith, that leave their imprint on contempor-ary discourse.[28] Hill's poetry has always offered a scrupulous interroga-tion of, and opposition to, the claims for the 'neo-Symbolist mystique'; the idea that, as Wallace Stevens puts it, '[a]fter one has abandoned a belief in god [*sic*], poetry is that essence which takes its place as life's redemption'.[29] He has equally shown himself to be, like Sennett, suspicious of the 'commodity exploitation of personality'. '[O]ne is right', he notes, 'to distrust the opinion that associates self and self-expression, as if the self-expression were ectoplasm emanating in a tenuous stream from the allegedly authentic self.'[30]

---

[25] Denis McQuail, Letters, *LRB*, 29 Dec. 2001, 4; J. Glenn, Letters, *LRB*, 15 Nov. 2001, 4; Geoffrey O Brien, Letters, *LRB*, 29 Nov. 2001, 4; Guy Deutscher, Letters, *LRB*, 1 Nov. 2001, 4.

[26] Sennett, *Fall*, 10.

[27] Ibid. 11.

[28] Samuel Beckett's figure in *Not I* offers a 'helpless gesture of compassion', in response to the Mouth's stream of words, *CDW*, 375.

[29] Hill, *Lords*, 16.

[30] Hill, 'The Art of Poetry LXX', Geoffrey Hill interviewed by Carl Phillips, Paris Review, 154 (Spring 2000), 272–99, 283.

Hill has an ear for what might, or might not, be said to be common to a writer and his readers, most emphatically in the ways in which we handle the substance of our common tongue, the 'coercive force of language'.[31]

For Hill, there is a clear distinction not only between different senses of what we mean by things that are 'common', but between a scrutiny of the varying meanings implicit in a word and an act of 'common equivocation'. He sees the latter as an assumptive appeal to what is assumed to be the given opinion, or, as he puts it elsewhere, 'a common species of torpor'.[32] For Empson, a writer must always remain, to a certain extent, 'in sympathy' with all members of society, and none—a 'go-between' between different parts.[33] For Hill, '[w]hat we call the writer's "distinctive voice" is a registering of different voices'.[34] Hill himself admits that this act of 'registering' is not without judgement. By 'register', he notes, he 'intend[s] to suggest—balancing between verb and substantive—a (precise) manner of setting down; an entitlement to set down; a device for admitting and excluding'.[35] Such precision allows Hill's poetry to give a view of what it means to read which is, while not necessarily distinct from Smith's notion of 'caring about other people', or Mantel's idea of 'imagining others', one which puts more pressure on the terms in use.

The complexity and difficulty that this involves has sometimes led to accusations that Hill's poetry is, in some ways, difficult or elitist.[36] As his own discussions show, his rigorous notion of the idea of the 'common' is, in its own way, far more sensitive to the variety of 'different voices' than those poets who, in his words (with an echo of Robbie Williams and Nat King Cole), 'Do nothing but assume the PEOPLE'S voice'.[37] The phrase comes from Hill's 2000 collection, *Speech! Speech!*, a book which takes a combative stance with its readers from the start. (The cover shows an engraving by Daumier of an open-mouthed

---

[31] Ibid. 2.

[32] Geoffrey Hill, *Style and Faith* (New York: Counterpoint, 2003), 159.

[33] William Empson and Donald Pirie (eds.), 'Introduction' to *Coleridge's Verse: A Selection* (London: Faber, 1972), 39.

[34] Geoffrey Hill, *The Enemy's Country* (Oxford: Oxford University Press, 1991), 80.

[35] Hill, *Style*, 101.

[36] See e.g. Tom Paulin's attack on his work in *Minotaur: Poetry and the Nation* (Cambridge, Mass.: Harvard University Press, 1992).

[37] Geoffrey Hill, *Speech! Speech!* (Washington DC: Counterpoint, 2000), 19. The line catches the cadence of Duke Ellington's, 'Do Nothing till You Hear from Me', with lyrics by Bob Russell, covered by Nat King Cole, and, most recently, Robbie Williams.

audience, entitled *On dit que les Parisiens sont difficiles à satisfaire*). Given this, and given Hill's reputation, a number of his critics were surprised to find that the collection itself was, in part, 'an oblique threnody' for Diana, Princess of Wales.[38] For many, Diana seemed to be a precise expression of 'the PEOPLE's voice'. A modern Miranda, she was both famously confessional and renowned for her 'genuine compassionate empathy'.[39] For Chris Smith, MP for culture, the death of the 'People's Princess' meant that empathy became general; it offered, he argued, 'a sense of shared identity through shared cultural emotion'.[40] Hilary Mantel adds that Diana's death was seen to 'bring about an emotional convulsion in our national life; it gave rise to a huge, primitive, heartfelt cry of mourning. No one concerned with collective sensibilities could ignore its importance.'[41]

Hill's poem offers something different. It is not simply a 'threnody' for Diana, but also for 'the mass mourning and media frenzy that surrounded her death'—'the funeral sentences | instantly resurrected', as he puts it, touching both on the clutching at cliché, and the need to beatify another. As he reflects on 'her spirit now on this island' (referencing both the British Isles, and the island, surrounded by willows, where her body lies), Hill's poem seems to capture the complexities that surround the issues both of 'collective sensibilities' and 'emotional convulsion[s]', and offers a balance between the desire for contact, and the suspicion of easy gestures towards similarity:

> Whatever of our loves here lies apart:
> whatever it is | you look for in sleep:
> simple bio-degradation, a slather
> of half-rotted black willow leaves
> at the lake's edge.[42]

The island, for Hill, as for Auden and for Shakespeare, stands for isolation. Here again we see a writer struggling to think about the relation between the self and others. Parodic and self-parodic, this is a poem which edges around sympathy, and its relation to what some

[38] See Andrew Michael Roberts, *Geoffrey Hill: Writers and their Work* (Northcote House Publishers: Devon, 2004), 41.

[39] Nicki Gostin, 'Unriddling a Princess', <http://www.newsweek.com/id/45403/page/1/>.

[40] Chris Smith, *Creative Britain* (London: Faber, 1998), 35. As John Carey notes, 'What "cultural emotion" is; in what sense Princess Diana's death represented "culture"; and how dying in a car crash could qualify as a contribution to creativity, are matters Smith leaves unexamined', *What Good are the Arts* (London: Faber, 2005), 44.

[41] Mantel, *Beyond*, 5.   [42] Hill, *Speech*, 18.

might call 'magical thinking' and others might see as belief. This is an allusive poem. Hill's half-rotted willow leaves look back to Yeats, and Keats, and the allusions are sadly used.[43] The echoes act analogously, as if lyric emotion is, like the leaves themselves, 'half-rotted', de-composing. One might be suspicious of such backward-looking. It is certainly out of sympathy with certain current views. As Christopher Lasch argues, 'along with "elitism", "authoritarianism" and "idealism" [nostalgia] now ranks near the top in the vocabulary of political condemnation'.[44] But Hill writes like this not simply to accept, but also to complicate matters of nostalgia and sentiment, and to put pressure on the idea of 'common' sympathy, or what is commonly understood.

One might also, in the end, wonder why the idea of sympathy needs to be put under such scrutiny. Despite apparent 'emotional convulsion[s]', this is an age in which, as Christopher Butler notes, 'a sceptical understanding is dominant', and our emotional responses, are, for the most part 'generous' emotions.[45] Hill seems to recognize this. The phrase '[w]hatever of our loves', is both an echo of Prince Charles's awkwardness on the day of his engagement about whether or not he was in love ('whatever "love" means'), and an attempt at reconciliation.[46] In the end, a 'sceptical understanding' may push us towards the belief that our sympathetic emotions are matters of social construction and object-based desire. This does not take away from the alternative desire, for some, for there to be something more to sympathy than this. Hill's poem acknowledges such matters; the notion of a continuance of love is held, etymologically, within the awkwardness of 'whatever'. It is an equivocal poem about sympathy, without 'common equivocation'. There is, in this island vision, small hope of being '*reliev'd by prayer*'. Instead Hill offers his words up to the judgement of others. Such a poised balancing and offering of possibility speak of humility and generosity, which have something in common with sympathy. They are, perhaps, the closest a writer can come to that ideal.

---

[43] 'By what lake's edge or pool | Delight men's eyes when I awake some day | To find they have flown away?' W. B. Yeats, 'The Wild Swans at Coole' (1917), ll. 28–30, in *Selected Poetry*, ed. Timothy Webb (Harmondsworth: Penguin, 1991), 85; 'The sedge is wither'd from the lake | And no birds sing' John Keats, 'La Belle Dame Sans Merci' (1820), ll. 3–4, in *Poetical Works*, 441.

[44] Christopher Lasch, 'The Politics of Nostalgia', *Harpers' Magazine* (Nov. 1984), 65.

[45] Christopher Butler, *Pleasure in the Arts* (Oxford: Oxford University Press, 2004), 132.

[46] When asked by the Press, on the occasion of their engagement, whether they were 'in love', Prince Charles followed Diana's 'of course' with the qualification 'whatever "love" means', Tina Brown, *The Diana Chronicles* (London: Century, 2007), 124.

Bibliography

'11 September: Some *LRB* Writers Reflect on the Reasons and Consequences', *London Review of Books*, 4 Oct. 2001.

Abbott, H. Porter, 'Beginning Again: The Post Narrative Art of *Texts for Nothing* and *How Is*', in Pilling (ed.), *Cambridge Companion* (Cambridge: Cambridge University Press, 1994), 106–23.

—— *Beckett Writing Beckett: The Author in the Autograph* (Ithaca, NY: Cornell University Press, 1996).

Acheson, James, 'Chess with the Audience: Samuel Beckett's "Endgame"', *Critical Quarterly*, 22/2 (1980), 33–45.

—— and Arthur, Kateryna (eds.), *Beckett's Later Fiction and Drama: Texts for Company* (Basingstoke: Macmillan, 1987).

Ackerley, C. J., and Gontarski, S. E., *The Grove Companion to Samuel Beckett* (New York: Grove Press, 1994).

Agamben, Giorgio, *The End of the Poem: Studies in Poetics* (Stanford, Calif.: Stanford University Press, 1999).

Albee, Edward, *The Zoo Story* (1959), in *The Zoo Story and Other Plays* (Harmondsworth: Penguin, 1995).

Albright, Daniel, *Representation and the Imagination: Beckett, Kafka, Nabokov and Schoenberg* (Chicago: University of Chicago Press, 1981).

Alcorn Jr., Marshall W., and Bracher, Mark, 'Literature, Psychoanalysis, and the Re-Formation of the Self: A New Direction for Reader-Response Theory', *PMLA* 100 (May 1985), 342–54.

Allen, Woody, *Side Effects* (London: New English Library Ltd., 1981).

Allott, Kenneth (ed.), *The Penguin Book of Contemporary Verse* (Harmondsworth: Penguin, 1950).

Alvarez, A., *Beckett* (London: Woburn, 1973).

Ansen, Alan, *The Table Talk of W. H. Auden*, ed. Nicholas Jenkins (London: Faber, 1990).

Arbib, Michael, '"From Mirror Neurons to Understanding": Discussion of Vittorio Gallese's "Intentional Attunement: the Mirror Neuron System and Its Role in Interpersonal Development"', *Interdisciplines.org*, 6 Nov. 2004, <http://www.interdisciplines.org/mirror/papers/1/2#_2>, accessed 27 Aug. 2007.

Arendt, Hannah, *The Human Condition* (Chicago: University of Chicago Press, 1958).

Armstrong, Isobel, *Victorian Scrutinies* (London: Athlone Press, 1972).

—— 'Tennyson in the 1850s: From Geology to Pathology—*In Memoriam* (1850) to *Maud* (1855)', in Philip Collins (ed.), *Tennyson: Seven Essays* (London: Macmillan, 1992), 102–40.

Arnold, Matthew, *Essays in Criticism*, 2nd ser. (London: Macmillan, 1888).

—— *Lectures and Essays in Criticism: Complete Prose Works*, iii, ed. R. H. Super (Ann Arbor: University of Michigan Press, 1962).

—— *The Poems of Matthew Arnold*, ed. Kenneth Allott (London: Longman, Green & Co., 1965).

Ashbery, John, *Selected Poems* (Harmondsworth: Penguin, 1985).

Auden, W. H. (ed.), *The Oxford Book of Light Verse* (Oxford: Clarendon Press, 1938).

—— *New Year Letter* (London: Faber, 1941).

—— *The Enchafèd Flood, or, the Romantic Iconography of the Sea* (London: Faber, 1951).

—— 'Introduction' to *Poets of the English Language: Langland to Spenser* (London: Eyre & Spottiswoode, 1952), pp. xv–xxx.

—— *The Dyer's Hand and Other Essays* (New York: Random House Inc., 1962).

—— *Secondary Worlds: The T. S. Eliot Memorial Lectures Delivered at Eliot College in the University of Kent at Canterbury October 1967* (London: Faber, 1968).

—— *Collected Poems*, ed. Edward Mendelson (London: Faber, 1976).

—— *The English Auden: Poems, Essays and Dramatic Writings 1927–1939*, ed. Edward Mendelson (London: Faber, 1977).

—— *Prose, i. 1926–1938*, ed. Edward Mendelson (London: Faber, 1996).

—— *Lectures on Shakespeare*, ed. Arthur Kirsch (Princeton: Princeton University Press, 2000).

—— *Prose, ii. 1939–1948*, ed. Edward Mendelson (London: Faber, 2002).

—— *The Sea and the Mirror: A Commentary on Shakespeare's* The Tempest, ed. Arthur Kirsch (Princeton: Princeton University Press, 2003).

Auerbach, Eric, *Scenes from the Drama of European Literature: Six Essays* (New York: Meridian Books, 1959).

Auerbach, Nina, *Women and the Demon: The Life of a Victorian Myth* (Cambridge, Mass.: Harvard University Press, 1982).

—— 'Nina Auerbach's Homepage', University of Pennsylvania, <http://www.english.upenn.edu/%7Enauerbac/>, accessed 30 Aug. 2007.

Austen, Jane, *Persuasion*, in *Northanger Abbey and Persuasion* (Oxford: Oxford University Press, 1969).

Austin, J. L., *How to Do Things with Words*, 2nd edn., ed. J. O. Urmson and Marina Sbisà (Oxford: Oxford University Press, 1976).

Babbage, Charles, *Ninth Bridgewater Treatise, a Fragment* (London: John Murray, 1837).

Bair, Deidre, *Samuel Beckett: A Biography* (London: Simon and Schuster, 1990).

Baker, Phil, *Beckett and the Mythology of Psychoanalysis* (Basingstoke: Macmillan, 1997).

Baldwin, Hélène, *Samuel Beckett's Real Silence* (University Park: Pennsylvania University State Press, 1981).

Ball, Patricia M., 'Browning's Godot', in J. R. Watson (ed.), *Browning: Men and Women and Other Poems* (Basingstoke: Macmillan, 1990), 173–83.

Balzac, Honoré de, *Illusions perdues* (Paris: Gallimard, 1974).

—— *Le Colonel Chabert*, introd. Stéphane Vauchon (Paris: Librairie Générale Française, 1994).

Barnett, Anthony, *This Time: Our Constitutional Revolution* (London: Vintage, 1997).

Barrett Browning, Elizabeth, *Aurora Leigh*, ed. Margaret Reynolds (New York: W. W. Norton & Co., 1996).

Barthes, Roland, *Image Music Text*, sel. and trans. Stephen Heath (London: Fontana, 1977).

—— *Roland Barthes*, trans. Richard Howard (London: Papermac, 1995).

Bayley, John, *The Romantic Survival: A Study in Poetic Evolution* (London: Constable, 1957).

—— 'W. H. Auden', in Monroe K. Spear (ed.), *Auden: A Collection of Critical Essays* (Englewood Cliffs, NJ: Prentice-Hall, Inc., 1964), 60–80.

—— *The Characters of Love: A Study in the Literature of Personality* (London: Chatto & Windus, 1968).

—— 'Only Critics Can't Play', in Stephen Spender (ed.), *W. H. Auden: A Tribute* (London: Weidenfeld & Nicolson, 1975), 229–41.

Bearn, Gordon, *Waking to Wonder: Wittgenstein's Existential Investigations* (Albany: State University Press of New York Press, 1997).

Beckett, Samuel, *Comment c'est* (Paris: Éditions de Minuit, 1961).

—— *How It Is* (London: Calder, 1964).

—— *Proust and Three Dialogues with Georges Duthuit* (London: Calder, 1965).

—— *No's Knife* (London: Calder & Boyars, 1967).

—— (trans), *Anthology of Mexican Poetry* (London: Calder and Boyars, 1970).

—— *The Expelled and Other Novellas* (Harmondsworth: Penguin, 1980).

—— *Ill Seen Ill Said* (London: Calder, 1982).

—— *Disjecta*, ed. Ruby Cohn (London: Calder, 1983).

—— *Happy Days: The Production Notebook of Samuel Beckett*, ed. James Knowlson (London: Grove Press, 1985).

—— *The Complete Dramatic Works* (London: Faber, 1986).

—— *'Waiting for Godot' and 'Endgame'*, ed. Steven Connor (Basingstoke: Macmillan, 1992).

—— *Dream of Fair to Middling Women*, ed. Eoin O' Brien and Edith Fournier (London: Calder, 1993).

—— *Murphy* (London: Calder, 1993).

—— *More Pricks than Kicks* (London: Calder, 1993).

—— *The Beckett Trilogy: Molloy; Malone Dies; The Unnamable* (London: Calder, 1994).

Beckett, Samuel, *The Complete Short Prose 1929–1989*, ed. S. E. Gontarski (New York: Grove Press, 1995), 275–8, at 275.

—— *Company* (London: Calder, 1996).

—— *Eleuthéria*, trans. Barbara Wright (London: Faber, 1996).

—— *No Author Better Served: The Correspondence of Samuel Becket and Alan Schneider*, ed. Maurice Harmon (Cambridge, Mass.: Harvard University Press, 1998).

—— *Watt* (London: John Calder, 1998).

—— *Mercier and Camier* (repr. London: Calder, 1999).

—— *Comment c'est et L'Image: Une édition critico-génétique*, ed. Eduoard Magessa O'Reilly (New York: Routledge, 2001).

Beer, Ann, 'Beckett's Bilingualism', in Pilling (ed.), *Cambridge Companion*, 209–21.

Beer, Gillian, 'Darwin's Reading', in David Kohn (ed.), *The Darwinian Heritage* (Princeton: Princeton University Press, 1985), 543–88.

—— *Open Fields: Science in Cultural Encounter* (Oxford: Oxford University Press, 1996).

—— *Darwin's Plots: Evolutionary Narrative in Darwin, George Eliot and Nineteenth-Century Fiction*, 2nd edn. (Cambridge: Cambridge University Press, 2000).

Belsey, Catherine, *The Subject of Tragedy: Identity and Difference in Renaissance Drama* (London: Methuen, 1985).

Benda, Jules, *The Treason of the Intellectuals*, trans. Richard Aldington (New York: Norton, 1928).

Benjamin, Walter, *Reflections: Essays, Aphorisms, Autobiographical Writings*, trans. Edmund Jephcott (New York: Schocken Books, 1978).

Ben-Ze'ev, Aaron, *The Subtlety of the Emotions* (Cambridge, Mass.: MIT Press, 2000).

Berger Jr., Harry, 'Miraculous Harp: A Reading of Shakespeare's *Tempest*', *Shakespeare Studies*, 5 (1969), 253–83.

Bergonzi, Bernard, 'Auden and the Audenesque', in *Reading the Thirties: Texts and Contexts* (London: Macmillan, 1978).

Bersani, Leo, *A Future for Astyanax* (London: Marion Boyars, 1976).

Blackburn, Simon, *Being Good: A Short Introduction to Ethics* (Oxford: Oxford University Press, 2001).

—— 'To Feel and To Feel Not', rev. of Martha Nussbaum, *Upheavals of Thought*, *New Republic*, 24 Dec. 2001, <http://www.phil.cam.ac.uk/-swb24/reviews/Nussbaum.htm>, accessed 30 Aug 2007.

Blakeslee, Sandra, 'Cells that Read Minds', *New York Times*, 10 Jan. 2006, sec. F: 1, 4.

Blanchot, Maurice. 'Où maintenant? Qui maintenant?', *Nouvelle Revue française*, 10 (1953), 678–86.

Bloom, Harold, *A Map of Misreading* (Oxford: Oxford University Press, 1975).

—— *Caliban*, Major Literary Characters (New York: Chelsea House Publishers, 1982).

Boly, Richard, *Reading Auden: The Returns of Caliban* (Ithaca, NY: Cornell University Press, 1991).

Booth, Michael, *The Victorian Spectacular Theatre* (Boston: Routledge & Kegan Paul, 1981).

Booth, Wayne, *The Company We Keep: An Ethics of Fiction* (Berkeley and Los Angeles: University of California Press, 1988).

Borges, Jorge Luis, *Other Inquisitions, 1937–1952*, trans. R. L. C. Simms (Austin: University of Texas Press, 1964).

—— *Collected Fictions*, trans. Andrew Hurley (London: Allen Lane, 1998).

Branigan, Edward, *Point of View in the Cinema: A Theory of Narration and Subjectivity in Classical Film* (Berlin: Mouton Publishers, 1984).

Brater, Enoch, 'The "I" in Beckett's *Not I*', *Twentieth Century Literature*, 20 (June 1974), 189–200.

—— *Beyond Minimalism: Beckett's Late Style in the Theatre* (New York: Oxford University Press, 1982).

Brienza, Susan, *Samuel Beckett's New Worlds* (Norman: University of Oklahoma Press, 1987).

Brodsky, Joseph, *Less than One: Selected Essays* (New York: Farrar, Strauss & Giroux, 1986).

—— *On Grief and Reason: Essays* (Harmondsworth: Penguin, 1997).

Brogan, T. V. F. (ed.), *The New Princeton Handbook of Poetic Terms* (Princeton: Princeton University Press, 1999).

Brower, Reuben A., 'The Mirror of Analogy', in D. J. Palmer (ed.), *Shakespeare: The Tempest Casebook Series* (Basingstoke: Macmillan, 1968), 40–62.

Brown, E. K., 'The First Person in "Caliban upon Setebos"', *Modern Language Notes*, 66 (June 1951), 392–5.

Brown, Tina, *The Diana Chronicles* (London: Century, 2007).

Browning, Robert, *Robert Browning and Julia Wedgwood: A Broken Friendship as Revealed in their Letters* (London: John Murray and Jonathan Cape, 1937).

—— *Dearest Isa: Robert Browning's Letters to Isabella Blagden*, ed. Edward McAleer (Austin: University of Texas Press, 1951).

—— *The Complete Works of Robert Browning*, ed. Roma A. King, vol. iv (Athens: Ohio University Press, 1967).

—— *The Ring and the Book*, ed. Richard D. Altick (Harmondsworth: Penguin, 1971).

—— *The Poems*, ed. John Pettigrew, 2 vols. (Harmondsworth: Penguin, 1981).

—— *Selected Poetry*, ed. Daniel Karlin (Harmondsworth: Penguin, 1989).

—— *The Poems of Robert Browning*, ii, ed. John Woolford and Daniel Karlin (London: Longman, 1991).

Browning, Robert, and Barrett, Elizabeth, *The Letters of Robert Browning and Elizabeth Barrett Browning 1845–1846*, ed. Elvan Kintner, 2 vols. (Cambridge, Mass.: Belnap Press of Harvard University Press, 1969).

Bryden, Mary, 'Balzac to Beckett via God (Eau/Ot)', *Samuel Beckett Today/ Aujourd'hui* 3, ed. Marius Buning (Amsterdam: Rodopi, 1994), 47–56.

—— *Samuel Beckett and the Idea of God* (Basingstoke: Macmillan, 1998).

Buchanan, R. W., *David Gray, and Other Essays, Chiefly on Poetry* (London: Sampson Low, Son & Marston, 1868).

Butler, Christopher, *Interpretation, Deconstruction and Ideology: An Introduction to Some Current Issues in Literary Theory* (Oxford: Oxford University Press, 1984).

—— *Pleasure in the Arts* (Oxford: Oxford University Press, 2004).

Butler, Lance St John, *Samuel Beckett and the Meaning of Being: A Study in Ontological Parable* (New York: St Martin's Press, 1984).

—— (ed.), *Critical Essays on Samuel Beckett* (Aldershot: Scolar, 1993).

Byron, Lord George Gordon, *Complete Poetical Works*, ed. Frederick Page, rev. edn., ed. John Jump (Oxford: Oxford University Press, 1970).

Caesar, Terry, '"I Quite Forget What—Say a Daffodilly": Victorian Parody', *English Literary History*, 51/4 (Winter 1984), 795–818.

Callan, Edward, 'Auden's Ironic Masquerade: Criticism as Morality Play', *University of Toronto Quarterly*, 25 (1965–6), 133–43.

—— *W. H. Auden: A Carnival of the Intellect* (New York: Oxford University Press, 1983).

Calverley, C. S., *Fly Leaves* (Cambridge: Deighton, Bell & Co., 1872).

Carey, John, *What Good are the Arts* (London: Faber, 2005).

Carroll, Noël, *The Philosophy of Horror* (New York: Routledge, 1990).

—— *A Philosophy of Mass Art* (Oxford: Clarendon Press, 1998).

—— *Beyond Aesthetics: Philosophical Essays* (Cambridge: Cambridge University Press, 2001).

Cavell, Stanley, *Must We Mean What We Say? A Book of Essays* (New York: Scribner, 1969).

—— *Disowning Knowledge in Six Plays of Shakespeare* (Cambridge: Cambridge University Press, 1987).

Chambers, Robert, *Vestiges of the Natural History of Creation* (London: John Churchill, 1844).

Chambers, Stephan, 'The Later Prose of Samuel Beckett' (diss. Oxford University, 1985).

Chatman, Seymour, *Story and Discourse: Narrative Structure in Fiction and Film* (Ithaca, NY: Cornell University Press, 1978).

Chesterton, G. K., *Robert Browning* (London: Macmillan, 1967).

Christ, Carol. T., *Victorian and Modern Poetics* (Chicago: University of Chicago Press, 1984).

Cioran, E. M., *The Trouble With Being Born*, trans. Richard Howard (London: Quartet, 1993).

Cixous, Hélène, and Cohen, Keith, 'The Character of "Character"', *New Literary History*, 5/2 (Winter 1974), 383–402.

Cohn, Ruby, *Samuel Beckett: The Comic Gamut* (New Brunswick, NJ: Rutgers University Press, 1962).

—— 'Tempest in an Endgame', *Symposium*, 19 (1965), 328–34.

—— *Back to Beckett* (Princeton: Princeton University Press, 1973).

—— *Modern Shakespearean Offshoots* (Princeton: Princeton University Press, 1976).

—— *Just Play: Beckett's Theatre* (Princeton: Princeton University Press, 1980).

Coleridge, Samuel Taylor, *The Table Talk and Omniana* (London: Oxford University Press, 1917).

—— *Coleridge's Shakespearean Criticism*, ed. Thomas Middleton Raysor (London: Constable & Co. Ltd., 1930).

—— *Lectures 1795 on Politics and Religion*, ed. Lewis Patton and Peter Mann (Princeton: Princeton University Press, 1971).

—— *Lay Sermons*, ed. R. J. White (London: Routledge & Kegan Paul, 1972).

Connolly, Cyril, *The Unquiet Grave* (London: Hamish Hamilton, 1945).

Connor, Steven, *Samuel Beckett: Repetition, Theory and Text* (Oxford: Basil Blackwell, 1988).

—— (ed.), *'Waiting for Godot' and 'Endgame'* (Basingstoke: Macmillan, 1992).

—— 'Over Samuel Beckett's Dead Body', in Clive Wilmer (ed.), *Beckett in Dublin* (Dublin: The Lilliput Press, 1992), 100–8.

—— 'Honour Bound?', rev. of *Cultural Pluralism and Moral Knowledge*, ed. Ellen Frankel Pack et al., *Cultural Studies and Cultural Value* by John Frow, *Honor* by Frank Henderson Steward, *Ethics, Theory and the Novel* by David Parker, *Narrative and Freedom* by Gary Saul Morson, *Times Literary Supplement*, 5 Jan. 1996, 24–6.

—— *Dumbstruck: A Cultural History of Ventriloquism* (Oxford: Oxford University Press, 2000).

Conradi, Peter, *Iris Murdoch* (London: HarperCollins, 2001).

Coover, Robert, *Pricksongs and Descants* (New York: Dutton, 1967).

Cowley, Malcolm, 'Virtue and Virtuosity: Notes on W. H. Auden', *Poetry*, 65 (1945), 202–9.

Critchley, Simon, *Very Little . . . Almost Nothing: Essays on Philosophy and Literature* (London: Routledge, 1997).

Cronin, Anthony, *Samuel Beckett: The Last Modernist* (London: HarperCollins, 1996).

Culler, Jonathan, *The Pursuit of Signs: Semiotics, Literature, Deconstruction* (London: Routledge & Kegan Paul, 1981).

Cunard, Nancy, *These Were the Hours: Memories of my Hours Press, Reanville and Paris, 1928–1931* (Carbondale: Southern Illinois University Press, 1969).

Cunningham, Valentine, *Everywhere Spoken Against: Dissent in the Victorian Novel* (Oxford: Clarendon Press, 1975).
—— 'Fact and Tact', *Essays in Criticism*, 51/1 (2001), 119–38.
—— *Reading After Theory* (Oxford: Blackwell, 2002).
Current-Garcia, Eugene, *O. Henry (William Sydney Porter)* (New York: Twayne Publishers, 1965).
Currie, Gregory, *The Nature of Fiction* (Cambridge: Cambridge University Press, 1990).
—— and Ravenscroft, Ian, *Recreative Minds: Imagination in Philosophy and Psychology* (Oxford: Oxford University Press, 2002).
Dalí, Salvador, *The Secret Life of Salvator Dalí* (New York: Dial, 1942).
Darwin, Charles, *The Voyage of the Beagle*, ed. Kate Hyndley (Hove: Wayland, 1989).
Davenport-Hines, Richard, *Auden* (London: Vintage, 2003).
Davies, Martin, and Stone, Tony (eds.), *Folk Psychology: The Theory of Mind Debate* (Oxford: Blackwell, 1995).
Davies, Paul, *The Ideal Real* (London: Associated University Presses, 1994).
Davies, Tony, *Humanism* (London: Routledge, 1997).
Dearlove, J. E., 'The Voice and its Words: How It Is in Beckett's Canon', *Journal of Beckett Studies*, 3 (Summer 1978), 56–75.
—— *Accommodating the Chaos: Beckett's Nonrelational Art* (Durham, NC: Duke University Press, 1982).
De Graef, Ortwin, 'Browning Born to Wordsworth: Intimations of Relatability from Recollections of Early Monstrosity', in N. Lie and T. D'haen (eds.), *Constellation Caliban* (Amsterdam: Rodopi, 1997), 113–43.
DeLaura, David J., 'Ruskin and the Brownings: Twenty-five Unpublished Letters', *Bulletin of the John Rylands Library*, 54 (1972), 324–7.
Dennett, Daniel, *The Intentional Stance* (Cambridge, Mass.: MIT Press, 1987).
Dentith, Simon, *Parody* (London: Routledge, 2000).
Derrida, Jacques, 'Signature Event Context', trans. Samuel Weber and Jeffrey Mehlman, *Glyph*, 1 (Baltimore: Johns Hopkins University Press, 1977) 172–97.
—— *The Post Card from Socrates to Freud and Beyond*, trans. Alan Bass (Chicago: University of Chicago Press, 1987).
Devane, William Clyde, *A Browning Handbook* (New York: Appleton-Century-Crofts, 1955).
Dickens, Charles, *Bleak House* (London: Oxford University Press, 1948).
—— *David Copperfield* (Harmondsworth: Penguin, 1985).
Donoghue, Denis, *Ferocious Alphabets* (London: Faber, 1981).
Douglas-Fairhurst, Robert, *Victorian Afterlives: The Shaping of Influence in Nineteenth-Century Literature* (Oxford: Oxford University Press, 2002).
Dowden, Edward, *Shakspere: His Mind and Art*, 11th edn. (London: Kegan Paul, 1897).

Drew, Philip, *The Poetry of Robert Browning: A Critical Introduction* (London: Methuen, 1970).

—— (ed.), *Robert Browning: A Collection of Critical Essays* (London: Methuen, 1966).

Dryden, John, and D'Avenant, William, *The Tempest: or, the Enchanted Island, a Comedy* (London: Cornmarket, 1969).

Duchene, François, *The Case of the Helmeted Airman: A Study of W. H. Auden's Poetry* (London: Chatto & Windus, 1972).

Dummett, Michael, *Frege: Philosophy of Language* (London: Duckworth, 1973).

Dupras, Joseph A., 'The Tempest of Intertext in "Caliban upon Setebos"', *Concerning Poetry*, 19 (1986), 75–88.

Durrell, Lawrence, 'The Other T. S. Eliot', *Atlantic Monthly*, 215/5 (May 1965), 60–4.

Eaglestone, Robert, *Ethical Criticism: Reading After Levinas* (Edinburgh: Edinburgh University Press, 1997).

Eddins, Dwight, 'Quitting the Game: Auden's *The Sea and the Mirror*', *Modern Languages Quarterly*, 41 (Mar. 1980), 73–87.

Eliot, George, *Essays and Leaves from a Notebook* (Edinburgh: William Blackwood, 1884).

—— *The George Eliot Letters*, ed. Gordon S. Haight, 9 vols. (New Haven: Yale University Press, 1954–78).

—— *Essays of George Eliot*, ed. Thomas Pinney (New York: Columbia University Press; London: Routledge and Kegan Paul, 1963).

—— *Middlemarch: A Study of Provincial Life*, ed. David Carroll (Oxford: Oxford University Press, 1989).

—— *The Lifted Veil; Brother Jacob*, ed. Helen Small (Oxford: Oxford University Press, 1999).

Eliot, T. S., *The Use of Poetry and the Use of Criticism* (London: Faber, 1953).

—— *Selected Essays*, 3rd enl. edn. (London: Faber, 1969).

—— *The Complete Poems and Plays* (London: Faber, 1969).

—— *The Varieties of Metaphysical Poetry*, ed. Ronald Schuchard (London: Faber, 1993).

Ellmann, Maud, 'Disremembering Dedalus', in Robert Young (ed.), *Untying the Text: A Post-Structuralist Reader* (London: Routledge & Kegan Paul, 1981), 189–206.

Ellmann, Richard, *Eminent Domain* (New York: Oxford University Press, 1967).

Emig, Rainer, *W. H. Auden: Towards a Postmodern Poetics* (Basingstoke: Macmillan, 1999).

Empson, William, *Argufying: Essays on Literature and Culture* (London: Hogarth, 1987).

—— *The Structure of Complex Words* (Harmondsworth: Penguin, 1995).

Empson, William, *The Complete Poems of William Empson*, ed. John Haffenden (London: Allen Lane, 2000).

—— and Pirie, Donald (eds.), *Coleridge's Verse: A Selection* (London: Faber, 1972).

Erickson, Lee, 'The Poet's Corner: The Impact of Technological Changes in Printing on English Poetry, 1800–1850', *English Literary History*, 52/4 (Winter 1985), 893–911.

Esslin, Martin (ed.), *Samuel Beckett: A Collection of Critical Essays* (Englewood Cliffs, NJ: Prentice Hall Inc., 1965).

Evans, Bertrand, *Shakespeare's Comedies* (Oxford: Oxford University Press, 1960).

Evans, C. F., *Explorations in Theology 2* (London: SCM, 1977).

—— *Parable and Dogma* (London: Athlone Press, 1977).

Evans, Stephen C., *The Historical Christ and the Jesus of Faith: The Incarnational Narrative as History* (Oxford: Clarendon Press, 1996).

Everett, Barbara, *Auden* (Edinburgh: Oliver & Boyd, 1964).

—— *Poets in Their Time: Essays on English Poetry from Donne to Larkin* (Oxford: Clarendon Press, 1991).

—— 'Hard Romance', *London Review of Books*, 8 Feb. 1996, 12–14.

Eyre, Richard, 'Sartre and Me', *Guardian Unlimited*, 3 May 2000, <http://books.guardian.co.uk/departments/politicsphilosophyandsociety/story/0,6000,216756,00.html>, accessed 30 Aug. 2007.

Faas, Ekbert, *Retreat to the Mind: Victorian Poetry and the Rise of Psychiatry* (Princeton: Princeton University Press, 1988).

Farrow, Anthony, *Early Beckett: Art and Allusion in 'More Pricks than Kicks' and 'Murphy'* (New York: Whitston, 1991).

Feagin, Susan. *Reading with Feeling* (Ithaca, NY: Cornell University Press, 1996).

Ferré, F., *Language, Logic and God* (London: Eyre & Spottiswoode, 1962).

Findlay. L. M., 'Taking the Measure of *Différance*: Deconstruction and *The Ring and the Book*', *Victorian Poetry*, 29 (1991), 401–14.

Fish, Stanley E., 'Literature in the Reader: Affective Stylistics', *New Literary History*, 2/1 (Autumn 1970), 123–62.

Fitch, Brian T., *Beckett and Babel: An Investigation into the Status of Bilingual Work* (Toronto: University of Toronto Press, 1988).

Foulkes, Richard (ed.), *Shakespeare and the Victorian Stage* (Cambridge: Cambridge University Press, 1986).

Fowler, James Eric, 'The Tempest Legacy: Shakespeare, Browning, Auden' (Diss., Rice University, 1984).

Freud, Sigmund, *Civilisation and Its Discontents*, trans. James Strachey (Harmondsworth: Penguin, 1984).

Fritz Cates, Diana, 'Conceiving Emotions: Martha Nussbaum's *Upheavals of Thought*', *Journal of Religious Ethics*, 31/2 (2003), 325–41.

Frost, Robert, *Collected Poems, Prose, and Plays*, ed. Richard Poirier and Mark Richardson (New York: Library of America, 1995).

Fuller, John, *W. H. Auden: A Commentary* (London: Faber, 1998).

Fuller, Robert C., *Wonder: From Emotion to Spirituality* (Chapel Hill: University of North Carolina Press, 2006).

Gallese, Vittorio, ' "Being Like Me": Self-Other Identity, Mirror Neurons and Empathy', in S. Hurley and N. Chater (eds.), *Perspectives on Imitation: From Cognitive Neuroscience to Social Science* (Boston: MIT Press, 2005).

Genette, Gérard, *Palimpsests: Literature in the Second Degree*, trans. Channa Newman and Claude Doubinsky (Lincoln: University of Nebraska Press, 1997).

Gingerich, Martin E., *W. H. Auden: A Reference Guide* (Boston: G. K. Hall & Co., 1977).

Glover, Jonathan. *I: The Philosophy and Psychology of Personal Identity* (Harmondsworth: Penguin, 1988).

Gontarski, S. E., Fehsenfeld, Martha, and McMullan, Dougald, 'Interview with Rachel Burrows', *Journal of Beckett Studies: Special Double Issue*, 11–12 (1989), 6–15.

Goodall, Jane R., *Performance and Evolution in the Age of Darwin* (London: Routledge, 2003).

Gostin, Nicki, 'Unriddling a Princess', <http://www.newsweek.com/id/45403/ page 1>.

Graver, Lawrence, 'Homage to the Dark Lady: *Ill Seen Ill Said*', in Linda Ben-Zvi (ed.), *Women in Beckett* (Urbana: University of Illinois Press, 1992), 142–9.

Greenberg, Herbert, *Quest for the Necessary: W. H. Auden and the Dilemma of Divided Consciousness* (Cambridge, Mass.: Harvard University Press, 1968).

Grice, H. P., 'Meaning', *Philosophical Review*, 64 (1968), 377–88.

Griffin, Howard, *Conversations with Auden*, ed. Donald Allen (San Francisco: Grey Fox Press, 1981).

Griffiths, Eric, *The Printed Voice of Victorian Poetry* (Oxford: Clarendon Press, 1989).

—— 'And That's True Too', rev. of *Shakespeare's Language* by Frank Kermode, and *Shakespeare* by Park Honan, *Times Literary Supplement*, 1 Sept. 2000, 3–4.

Grigson, Geoffrey, 'Auden as a Monster', *New Verse*, 26–7 (Nov. 1937), 13–14.

Guggenheim, Peggy, *Out of this Century: Confessions of an Art Addict* (London: Andrew Deutsch, 1979).

Gurkin Altman, Janet, *Epistolarity: Approaches to a Form* (Columbus: Ohio State University Press, 1982).

Haffenden, John, *Viewpoints: Poets in Conversation with John Haffenden* (London: Faber, 1981).

Hamilton, William (ed.), *Parodies of the Works of English and American Authors*, 6 vols. (London: Reeves & Turner, 1884–9).

Hancher, Michael, and Moore, Jerrold, ' "The Sound of a Voice that is Still": Browning's Edison Cylinder', *Browning Newsletter*, 4 (Spring 1970), 21–33, and 5 (Fall 1970), 10–18.

Harpham, Geoffrey Galt, 'The Hunger of Martha Nussbaum', *Representations*, 77 (2002), 52–81.

Harré, Rom, *The Social Construction of the Emotions* (Oxford: Blackwell, 1986).

Harvey, Laurence E., *Samuel Beckett: Poet and Critic* (Princeton: Princeton University Press, 1970).

Harvey, W. J., *Character and the Novel* (London: Chatto & Windus, 1965).

Hawlin, Stefan, *The Complete Critical Guide to Robert Browning* (London: Routledge, 2002).

Heaney, Seamus, *The Government of the Tongue: The 1986 T. S. Eliot Memorial Lectures and Other Critical Writings* (London: Faber, 1988).

Hebel, Udo J. (comp.), *Intertextuality, Allusion and Quotation: An International Bibliography of Critical Studies* (New York: Greenwood, 1989).

Hendon, Paul, *The Poetry of W. H. Auden: A Reader's Guide to Essential Criticism* (Cambridge: Icon, 2000).

Herbert, George, *The English Poems of George Herbert*, ed. C. A. Patrides (London: J. M. Dent & Sons, 1974), 191.

Hill, Geoffrey, *The Lords of Limit* (London: Deutsch, 1984).

—— 'A Pharisee to Pharisees: Reflections on Vaughan's "The Night"', *English*, 38 (1989), 97–113.

—— *The Enemy's Country* (Oxford: Oxford University Press, 1991).

—— *Speech! Speech!* (Washington, DC: Counterpoint, 2000).

—— *Style and Faith* (New York: Counterpoint, 2003).

Hillis Miller, J., *The Disappearance of God: Five Nineteenth Century Writers* (Cambridge, Mass.: Belknap Press of Harvard University Press, 1963), 151.

Hoffman, Michael, 'Sing Softer: A Notebook', *Poetry* (Sept. 2005), 428–38.

Hoggard, Richard, *Auden: an Introductory Essay* (London: Chatto & Windus, 1951).

Holland, Henry, *Chapters on Mental Physiology* (London: Longmans, Brown, Green, and Longmans, 1852).

Hollander, John, *The Figure of Echo: A Mode of Allusion in Milton and After* (Berkeley and Los Angeles: University of California Press, 1981).

Honan, Park, 'Eighteenth and Nineteenth Century Punctuation Theory', *English Studies*, 41 (1960), 92–102.

—— *Browning's Characters: A Study in Poetic Technique* (New Haven: Yale University Press, 1961).

Howard, Michael, 'Caliban's Mind', *Victorian Poetry*, 1 (1963), 249–57.

Hulme, Peter, and Sherman, William H. (eds.), *The Tempest and its Travels* (London: Reaktion, 2000).

Hume, David, *A Treatise of Human Nature* (Sterling: Thoemmes Press, 2000).

—— *An Enquiry Concerning Human Understanding*, ed. Tom Beauchamp (Oxford: Clarendon Press, 2000).

Hunt, Lester, 'Martha Nussbaum on the Emotions', *Ethics*, 116 (2006), 552–7.

Hutchings, William, ' "As Strange a Maze as E'er Man Trod": Samuel Beckett's Allusions to Shakespeare's Last Plays', in Anne-Marie Drew (ed.), *Past Crimson: Past Woe: The Shakespeare–Beckett Connection* (New York: Garland, 1993), 3–15.

Huysmans, J. K., *A rebours*, ed. Marc Fumaroli (Paris: Gallimard, 1977).

Hyde, Victoria, 'Robert Browning's Inverted Optic Glass in *A Death in the Desert*', *Victorian Poetry*, 23/1 (Spring 1985), 93–6.

Ibsen, Henrik, *Brand*, trans. Geoffrey Hill, 2nd edn. rev. with introd. by Inga-Stina Ewbank (Minneapolis: National Theatre Plays Series, 1981).

—— *Brand*, trans. Geoffrey Hill, 3rd edn. (Harmondsworth: Penguin, 1996).

Iser, Wolfgang, *The Implied Reader: Patterns of Communication in Prose from Bunyan to Beckett* (Baltimore: John Hopkins University Press, 1974).

Jackson, Richard, *Acts of Mind: Conversations with Contemporary Poets* (Tuscaloosa: University of Alabama Press, 1983).

Jacobs, Alan, *What Became of Wystan: Change and Continuity in Auden's Poetry* (Fayetteville: University of Arkansas Press, 1998).

Jahn, Manfed, 'The Cognitive Status of Textual Voice', *New Literary History*, 32/3 (2001), 695–7.

James, Clive, 'A Testament to Self Control', rev. of *Epistle to a Godson* by W. H. Auden, *Times Literary Supplement*, 12 Jan. 1973, 25–6.

James, Henry, *Notes on Novelists* (London: J. M. Dent, 1914).

—— *Roderick Hudson* (London: Macmillan, 1921).

—— *The Author of Beltranffio, The Middle Years, Greville Fane and Other Tales* (London: Macmillan, 1922).

—— *The Wings of A Dove* (London: Macmillan, 1922).

—— *The Golden Bowl* (London: Macmillan, 1922).

—— *The Notebooks of Henry James*, ed. F. O. Matthiessen and Kenneth B. Murdock (New York: G. Braziller, 1947).

—— *The Complete Tales of Henry James*, xi (London: Rupert Hart-Davis, 1964).

—— *Portrait of A Lady* (Oxford: Oxford University Press, 1995).

—— 'Introduction to *The Tempest*', in Peter Rawlings (ed.), *Americans on Shakespeare 1776–1914* (Aldershot: Ashgate, 1999), 449–62.

James, William, *Selected Papers on Philosophy* (London: Dent, 1917).

—— *The Varieties of Religious Experience* (Cambridge, Mass.: Harvard University Press, 1985).

Jameson, Frederic, 'Postmodernism, or the Logic of Late Capitalism', in Thomas Docherty (ed.), *Postmodernism: A Reader* (Hemel Hempstead: Harvester Wheatsheaf, 1993), 62–91.

Johnson, Samuel, *Lives of the English Poets* (New York: Everyman, 1906).

—— *Poems*, ed. E. L. McAdam (New Haven: Yale University Press, 1964).

—— *A Dictionary of the English Language* (London: Times Books, 1983).

Johnson, Samuel, *Rasselas*, in *Rasselas and Other Tales*, ed. Gwin J. Kolb (New Haven: Yale University Press, 1990).

Joyce, James, *A Portrait of The Artist as a Young Man* (Harmondsworth: Penguin, 1992).

Karlin, Daniel, *Browning's Hatreds* (Oxford: Clarendon Press, 1993).

Kean, Thomas, et al., 'The 9–11 Commission Report', <www.911commission. gov/report/911Report_Ch11.pdf>.

Keats, John, *The Poetical Works of John Keats*, ed. H. W. Garrod (Oxford: Clarendon Press, 1958).

Keen, Suzanne, *Empathy and the Novel* (Oxford: Oxford University Press, 2007).

Keller, John Robert, *Samuel Beckett and the Primacy of Love* (Manchester: Manchester University Press, 2002).

Kelley, Philip, and Coley, Betty, comp., *The Browning Collections: A Reconstruction with Other Memorabilia* (Waco: Wedgestone Press, 1984).

Kennedy, Andrew, 'Mutations of the Soliloquy: *Not I* to *Rockaby*', in Robin J. Davis and Lance St John Butler (eds.), *Make Sense Who May: Essays on Samuel Beckett's Later Works* (Gerrards Cross: Colin Smythe Ltd., 1988), 30–5.

Kenner, Hugh, *The Stoic Comedians* (London: W. H. Allen, 1964).

—— *Samuel Beckett* (London: Calder, 1965).

Kenny, A. J., *Aquinas* (Oxford: Oxford University Press, 1980).

Kermode, Frank, *The Genesis of Secrecy: On the Interpretation of Narrative* (Cambridge, Mass.: Harvard University Press, 1979).

Kiberd, Declan, *Inventing Ireland: The Literature of the Modern Nation* (London: Vintage, 1996).

Killham, John, 'Browning's "Modernity": *The Ring and the Book* and Relativism', in Isobel Armstrong (ed.), *The Major Victorian Poets: Reconsiderations* (London: Routledge, 1969), 153–75.

Knights, L. C., *How Many Children Had Lady MacBeth? An Essay in the Theory and Practice of Shakespeare Criticism* (Cambridge: Minority Press, 1933).

Knowlson, James, *Krapp's Last Tape: A Theatre Workbook* (London, Brutus Books, 1980).

—— 'Beckett's Bits of Pipe', in Morris Béja (ed.), *Samuel Beckett: Humanistic Perspectives* (Ohio: Ohio State University Press, 1983), 16–25.

—— *Damned to Fame: The Life of Samuel Beckett* (London: Bloomsbury, 1996).

Kreilkamp, Ivan, 'A Voice without a Body: The Phonographic Logic of *Heart of Darkness*', *Victorian Studies*, 40/2 (Winter 1997), 211–44.

Kupperman, Joel, *Character* (Oxford: Oxford University Press, 1991).

Lakoff, George, and Johnson, Mark, *Metaphors We Live By* (Chicago: University of Chicago Press, 1980).

Lamarque, Peter, *Fictional Points of View* (Ithaca, NY: Cornell University Press, 1996).

Lang, Andrew, *The Blue Fairy Book* (London, 1889).

Langbaum, Robert, '*The Tempest* and Tragicomic Vision', in *The Modern Spirit: Essays on the Continuity of Nineteenth and Twentieth Century Literature* (London: Chatto & Windus, 1970).

—— *The Poetry of Experience: The Dramatic Monologue in Modern Literary Tradition*, new edn. (London: Chatto & Windus, 1972).

Langdale, Kay, 'God, the Narrator and the Quest for an Aesthetic in Samuel Beckett's Prose Fiction' (D.Phil. diss., Oxford University, 1987).

Lanham, Richard A., *Analyzing Prose*, 2nd edn. (New York: Scribner, 1983).

Lasch, Christopher, 'The Politics of Nostalgia', *Harpers' Magazine* (Nov. 1984).

Lawson, Mark, 'After the Fall', *Guardian*, 16 Aug. 2002, <http://www.guardian.co.uk/september11/oneyearon/story/0,,782804,00.html>, accessed 30 Aug. 2007.

Lazarus, Richard, and Lazarus, Bernice, *Passion and Reason: Making Sense of Our Emotions* (New York: Oxford University Press, 1994).

LeDoux, Joseph, *The Emotional Brain* (New York: Simon and Schuster, 1996).

Lee, Vernon, and Anstruther-Thompson, Clementina, *Beauty and Ugliness and Other Studies in Psychological Aesthetics* (London: John Lane, the Bodley Head, 1912).

Leech, Geoffrey N., *A Linguistic Guide to English Poetry* (London: Longman, 1969).

Lennard, John, *But I Digress* (Oxford: Oxford University Press, 1991).

—— *The Poetry Handbook* (Oxford: Oxford University Press, 1996).

Lepore, Ernest (ed.), *Truth and Interpretation: Perspectives on the Philosophy of Donald Davidson* (Oxford: Blackwell, 1984).

Levinas, Emmanuel, *Levinas Reader*, ed. Sean Hand, trans. Alphonso Lingis (Oxford: Basil Blackwell, 1989).

Lévi-Strauss, Claude, *Tristes Tropiques* (Harmondsworth: Penguin, 1976).

Levy, Eric, *Beckett and the Voice of Specie*s (Dublin: Gill & Macmillan, 1980).

Lewis, C. S., *The Allegory of Love: A Study in Medieval Tradition* (Oxford: Oxford University Press, 1936).

Lewis, David, *On the Plurality of Worlds* (Oxford: Blackwell, 1986).

Litzinger, Boyd, and Smalley, Donald (eds.), *Browning: The Critical Heritage* (London: Routledge & Kegan Paul, 1970).

Loehndorf, Esther, *The Master's Voices: Robert Browning, the Dramatic Monologue and Modern Poetry* (Tubingen: Francke Verlag, 1997).

Lowe, Brigid, *Insights of Sympathy: An Alternative to the Hermeneutics of Suspicion* (London: Anthem, 2007).

Lowell, James Russell, *Among My Books* (London: Macmillan & Co., 1870).

Lowell, Robert, *Collected Poems*, ed. Frank Bidart and David Gewanter (London: Faber, 2003).

Lyell, Charles, *Elements of Geology* (London: John Murray, 1838).

Lytton, Bulwer, *England and the English* (London: Richard Bentley, 1833).

McDiarmid, Lucy, *Auden's Apologies for Poetry* (Princeton: Princeton University Press, 1990).

McDonald, Peter, 'Do You Know Who We Are?', rev. of Shira Wolosky, *The Art of Poetry: How to Read a Poem, Poetry Review*, 92/4 (Winter 2002/3).
—— 'The Dreadful Choice', rev. of *The Sea and the Mirror* by W. H. Auden, ed. Arthur Kirsch, *Times Literary Supplement*, 2 Jan. 2004, 3–6.
McEwan, Ian, 'Only Love and then Oblivion', *Guardian*, 15 Sept. 2001, <http://www.guardian.co.uk/wtccrash/story/0,1300,552408,00.html>.
—— *Saturday* (London: Vintage, 2006).
McGinn, Colin, *Ethics, Evil, Fiction* (Oxford: Clarendon Press, 1999).
McMillan, Dougald, and Fehsenfeld, Martha, *Beckett in the Theatre: The Author as Practical Playwright* (London: John Calder, 1988).
Mantel, Hilary, *Beyond Black* (London: HarperCollins, 2005).
Marcel, Gabriel, *The Philosophy of Existentialism*, trans. Manya Harari (New York: Citadel Press, 1967).
Marlowe, Christopher, *Dr Faustus*, 2nd edn., ed. Roma Gill (London: A & C Black, 1989).
Mascall, E. L., *Existence and Analogy: A Sequel to 'He Who Is'* (London: Darton, Longman & Todd, 1966).
Mason, Michael, 'Browning and the Dramatic Monologue', in Isobel Armstrong (ed.), *Writers and their Background: Robert Browning* (London: G. Bell & Sons, 1974), 231–366.
Mathews, Anne, *Memoirs of Charles Mathews, Comedian*, iii (London: Richard Bentley, 1838–9).
Maynard, John, 'Reading the Reader in Robert Browning's Dramatic Monologues', in Mary Ellen Gibson (ed.), *Critical Essays on Robert Browning* (New York: G. K. Hall, 1992).
Melchiori, Barbara, *Browning's Poetry of Reticence* (Edinburgh: Oliver and Boyd, 1968).
Mendelson, Edward, *Early Auden* (London: Faber 1999).
—— *Later Auden* (London: Faber, 1999).
Mengham, Rod, 'Auden, Psychology and Society', in Stan Smith (ed.), *The Cambridge Companion to W. H. Auden* (Cambridge: Cambridge University Press, 2005).
Mermin, Dorothy, *The Audience in the Poem* (New Brunswick: Rutgers University Press, 1983).
Messud, Clare, *The Emperor's Children* (London: Picador, 2006).
Meynell, Wilfred, 'The "Detachment" of Browning', *Athenaeum*, 4 Jan. 1890, 18–19.
Miller, Betty, *Robert Browning: A Portrait* (London: John Murray, 1952).
Mills, Magnus, *Restraint of Beasts* (London: Flamingo, 1998).
Milton, John, *Paradise Lost*, ed. Scott Elledge (New York: W. W. Norton and Co., 1975).
Monk Kidd, Sue, 'A Common Heart: A Bestselling Novelist Argues for Empathy through Fiction', *Washington Post Book World*, 4 Dec. 2005.

Montesquieu, Charles-Louis de Secondat, *Persian Letters*, trans. C. Betts (Harmondsworth: Penguin, 1993).

Moore, G. E., *Principia Ethica*, ed. Thomas Baldwin (Cambridge: Cambridge University Press, 1999).

Moore, Marianne, 'W. H. Auden', in Spears, (ed.) *Poetry of Auden*, 39–53.

Morand, Paul, *Monplaisir... en littérature* (Paris: Gallimard, 1967).

Morgan, Clare, 'Existentialism in England 1945–1960: The Growth of its Influence on Literature and Art' (D.Phil. diss., University of Oxford, 1995).

Morrison, J. Cotter, ' "Caliban upon Setebos" with some notes on Browning's Subtlety and Humour', *Browning Society Papers*, 1 (1881–4), 489–98.

Muecke, D. C., *Irony and the Ironic*, The Critical Idiom 13 (London and New York: Methuen, 1982).

Muir, Kenneth, *Shakespeare's Last Plays*, ed. Richard C. Tobias and Paul G. Zolbrod (Athens: Ohio University Press, 1974), 32–43.

Murdoch, Iris, 'Against Dryness', *Encounter*, 88 (1961), repr. in Stanley Hauerwas and Alasdair MacIntyre (eds.), *Revisions: Changing Perspectives in Moral Philosophy* (Notre Dame, Ind.: University of Notre Dame Press, 1983), 43–50.

—— *Metaphysics as a Guide to Morals* (Harmondsworth: Penguin, 1993).

Murphy, P. J., 'Beckett and the Philosophers', in Pilling (ed.), *Cambridge Companion*, 222–40.

—— Huber, Werner, Brew, Roly, and Schoell, Konrad (eds.), *Critique of Beckett Criticism* (Columbia, SC: Camden House, 1994).

Nabokov, Vladimir, *Pale Fire* (London: Weidenfeld & Nicolson, 1962).

Nagel, Thomas, *The View from Nowhere* (New York: Oxford University Press, 1986).

—— 'Go with the Flow', rev. of *Truth and Progress* by Richard Rorty, *Times Literary Supplement*, 28 Aug. 1998, 3–4.

Naish, E. M., *Browning and Dogma* (London: George Bell & Sons, 1906).

Niebuhr, Reinhold, *The Nature and Destiny of Man: A Christian Interpretation*, i (London: Nisbet & Co. Ltd, 1941).

Norris, Christopher, *What's Wrong with Postmodernism: Critical Theory and the Ends of Philosophy* (Hemel Hempstead: Harvester Wheatshead, 1990).

Northam, John, 'Waiting for Prospero', in M. Axton and R. Williams (eds.), *English Drama: Forms and Development: Essays in Honour of Muriel Clara Bradbrook* (Cambridge: Cambridge University Press, 1977), 186–202.

Nussbaum, Martha C., 'Liberal Education in a Time of Global Tension', 9 Sept. 2004, <http://www.knox.edu/x8053.xml>, accessed 30 Aug. 2007.

—— *Love's Knowledge: Essays on Philosophy and Literature* (New York: Oxford University Press, 1990).

—— *Poetic Justice: The Literary Imagination and Public Life* (Boston: Beacon Press, 1995).

—— *Upheavals of Thought: The Intelligence of Emotions* (Cambridge: Cambridge University Press, 2001).

Nuttall, A. D., *Two Concepts of Allegory: A Study of Shakespeare's 'The Tempest' and the Logic of Allegorical Expression* (London: Routledge & Kegan Paul, 1967).

—— *A Common Sky: Philosophy and the Literary Imagination* (London: Chatto and Windus for Sussex University Press, 1974).

—— *A New Mimesis: Shakespeare and the Representation of Reality* (London: Methuen, 1983).

—— *Openings: Narrative Beginnings from the Epic to the Novel* (Oxford: Clarendon Press, 1992).

Nystrand, M., *What Writers Know: The Language, Process, and Structure of Written Discourse* (New York: Academic Press, 1982).

O'Brien, Eoin, *The Beckett Country: An Exhibition for Samuel Beckett's Eightieth Birthday* (Dublin: Black Cat, 1986).

O'Brien, Flann (Brian O'Nolan), *The Best of Myles*, ed. K. O'Nolan (London: Grafton, 1987).

O'Connor, Flannery, *Mystery and Manners* (London: Faber, 1984).

Orr, Mrs Sutherland, 'The Religious Opinions of Robert Browning', *Contemporary Review*, 60 (Dec. 1891), 876–91.

—— *The Life and Letters of Robert Browning*, new edn., ed. F. G. Kenyon (London: Smith, Elder & Co., 1908).

Orwell, George, *Inside the Whale and Other Essays* (Harmondsworth: Penguin, 1976).

Ostriker, Alicia, 'Can Poetry Console a Grieving Public?', <http://www.poetryfoundation.org/archive/feature.html?id=178623>.

Otto, Rudolf, *The Idea of the Holy: An Inquiry into the Non-Rational Factor and its Relation to the Rational*, trans. John W. Harvey (London: H. Milford, 1925).

Padel, Ruth, *52 Ways of Looking at a Poem: or How Reading Modern Poetry Can Change Your Life* (London: Vintage, 2004).

—— rev. of *Apology for Absence and the Poetry Cure*, by Julia Darling, *Independent Online Edition*, 29 Apr. 2005, <http://arts.independent.co.uk/books/reviews/article3783.ece>, accessed 30 Aug. 2007.

Parfit, Derek, *Reasons and Persons* (Oxford: Clarendon Press, 1984).

Paulin, Tom, *Minotaur: Poetry and the Nation* (Cambridge, Mass.: Harvard University Press, 1992).

Pearce, Donald, 'A Fortunate Fall: W. H. Auden at Michigan', in Alan Bold (ed.), *W. H. Auden: The Far Interior* (London: Vision, 1985), 129–57.

Pearce, Howard, 'Henry James's Pastoral Fallacy', *PMLA* 90/5 (Oct. 1975), 834–47.

Perloff, Marjorie, 'Between Verse and Prose', *Critical Inquiry*, 9 (Dec. 1982), 415–33.

Phelan, James, *Reading People, Reading Plots* (Chicago: University of Chicago Press, 1989).

Phillips, Adam, *On Kissing, Tickling and Being Bored* (London: Faber, 1993).

Picker, John, *Victorian Soundscapes* (New York: Oxford University Press, 2003).

Piette, Adam, *Remembering and the Sound of Words* (Oxford: Clarendon Press, 1996).

Pilling, John (ed.), *The Cambridge Companion to Beckett* (Cambridge: Cambridge University Press, 1994).

——— and Knowlson, James, *Frescoes of the Skull: The Later Prose and Drama of Samuel Beckett* (New York: Random House, 1980).

Plato, *The Republic*, trans. Desmond Lee (Harmondsworth: Penguin, 1955).

Plutchik, Robert, 'The Circumplex as a General Model of the Structures of Emotion and Personality', in Robert Plutchik and Hope Conte (eds.), *Circumplex Models of Personality and Emotions* (Washington, DC: American Psychological Association, 1997).

Poole, Adrian, *Tragedy: Shakespeare and the Greek Example* (Oxford: Oxford University Press, 1987).

——— *Shakespeare and the Victorians* (London: Thomson, 2004).

Porter, Peter, 'Recording Angels and Answering Machines', *1991 Lectures and Memoirs: Proceedings of the British Academy*, 80 (1991), 1–18.

Posner, Richard A., 'Against Ethical Criticism', *Philosophy and Literature*, 21/1 (1997), 1–27.

Prins, Yoopie, 'Elizabeth Barrett, Robert Browning, and the Différance of Translation', *Victorian Poetry*, 29 (1991), 435–51.

Proust, Marcel, *A la Recherche du temps perdu*, iii, ed. Pierre Clarac et André Ferré (Paris: Gallimard, 1954).

——— *A la recherche du temps perdu*, i, ed. Jean-Yves Tadié (Paris: Gallimard, 1987).

Prynne, J. H., 'English Poetry and Emphatical Language', *Proceedings of the British Academy*, 74 (Oxford: Oxford University Press, 1989), 135–69.

Puttenham, George, *The Arte of English Poesie*, ed. G. D. Willock and A. Walker (Cambridge: Cambridge University Press, 1936).

Quarles, Francis, *Judgement and Mercy for Afflicted Souls, or, Meditations, Soliloquies and Prayers*, new edn. (Philadelphia: W. W. Woodward, 1813).

Quilligan, Maureen, *The Language of Allegory: Defining the Genre* (Ithaca, NY: Cornell University Press, 1979).

Rader, Ralph W., 'The Dramatic Monologue and Related Lyric Forms', *Critical Inquiry*, 3 (1976), 131–51.

Radford, Colin, 'How can we be moved by the fate of Anna Karenina?', *Proceedings of the Aristotelian Society*, suppl. vol. 49 (1975), 67–80.

Ralli, Augustus, *A History of Shakespearean Criticism*, i (London: Oxford University Press, 1932).

Ramazani, Jahan, 'Can Poetry Console a Grieving Public', <http://www.poetryfoundation.org/archive/feature.html? id=178623>.

Ratcliffe, Sophie, rev. of *Samuel Beckett and the Primacy of Love* by John Robert Keller, *Review of English Studies*, 55 (2004), 301–3.

Raymond, W. O., *The Infinite Moment and Other Essays on Robert Browning* (Oxford: Oxford University Press, 1950).

Reed, Henry, 'W. H. Auden in America', in *New Writing and Daylight* (London: Hogarth Press, 1945), 131–5.

Renan, Joseph Ernest, *The Life of Jesus* (London: Trübner, 1864).

Reynolds, Matthew, 'Browning in Meditation', rev. of *The Poetical Words of Robert Browning*, vol. v, ed. Ian Jack and Robert Inglesfield, *Essays in Criticism*, 47/1 (Jan. 1997), 70–8.

—— 'Browning's Forms of Government', in Woolford, *Contexts*, (1998), 118–47.

—— 'Browning and Translationese', *Essays in Criticism*, 53/2 (Apr. 2003), 97–128.

—— 'Seriously Entertaining', rev. of *Performance and Evolution in the Age of Darwin* by Jane R. Goodall, *Times Literary Supplement*, 20 June 2003, 37.

Richardson, Samuel, *Selected Letters of Samuel Richardson*, ed. John Carroll (Oxford: Clarendon Press, 1964).

Rickey, Mary E., 'Rhymecraft in Edward and George Herbert', *Journal of English and German Philology*, 58 (1958), 502–11.

Ricks, Christopher, 'Distinctions', rev. of *Visible Words: A Study of Inscriptions as Books and Works of Art* by John Sparrow, *Essays in Criticism*, 20/2 (1970), 259–64.

—— *The Force of Poetry* (Oxford: Clarendon Press, 1984).

—— *Beckett's Dying Words* (Oxford: Oxford University Press, 1993).

—— *Allusion to the Poets* (Oxford: Oxford University Press, 2002).

Rickword, C. H., 'A Note of Fiction', in *Towards Standards of Criticism*, ed. F. R. Leavis (London: Wishart, 1933).

Rilke, Rainer Maria, *The Selected Poetry of Rainer Maria Rilke*, ed. and trans. Stephen Mitchell (London: Picador, 1997).

Ritvko, Harriet, *The Animal Estate: The English and Other Creatures in the Victorian Age* (Cambridge, Mass.: Harvard University Press, 1987).

Robbe-Grillet, Alain, *Snapshots and Towards a New Novel*, trans. Barbara Wright (London: Calder & Boyars, 1965).

Roberts, Andrew Michael, *Geoffrey Hill: Writers and their Work* (Devon: Northcote House, 2004).

Robinson, Peter, *In the Circumstances: About Poems and Poets* (Oxford: Clarendon Press, 1992).

Rorty, Amélie O., *The Identities of Persons* (Berkeley and Los Angeles: California University Press, 1976).

Rorty, Richard, *Contingency, Irony and Solidarity* (Cambridge: Cambridge University Press, 1989).

Rosen, Stephen, *Samuel Beckett and the Pessimistic Tradition* (New Brunswick, NJ: Rutgers University Press, 1976).

Rushdie, Salman, *Midnight's Children* (London: Vintage, 1995).

Safran Foer, Jonathan, *Extremely Loud and Incredibly Close* (London: Hamish Hamilton, 2005).

Sage, Victor, '*Innovation and Continuity* in *How It Is*', in Katherine Worth (ed.), *Beckett the Shape Changer* (London: Routledge & Kegan Paul, 1975), 87–103.

Said, Edward, *Beginnings: Intention and Method* (London: Granta, 1997).

St George, E. A. W., *Browning and Conversation* (Basingstoke: Macmillan, 1993).

Sartre, Jean-Paul, *Existentialism and Humanism*, trans. Philip Mairet (London: Methuen, 1948).

—— '*On the Sound and the Fury: Time in the Work of Faulkner*, trans. A. Michelson (New York: Collier Books, 1962).

—— *Being and Nothingness*, trans. Hazel E. Barnes (London: Routledge, 2000).

Sawyer, Robert, 'The Shakespeareanization of Robert Browning', in Christy Desmet and Robert Sawyer (eds.), *Shakespeare and Appropriation* (London: Routledge, 1999).

Schachter, Stanley, and Singer, Jerome, 'Cognitive, Social and Physiological Determinants of Emotional States', *Psychological Review*, 69 (1969), 379–99.

Schad, John, *Victorians in Theory: From Browning to Derrida* (Manchester: Manchester University Press, 1999).

Scheinberg, Cynthia, 'Recasting "Sympathy and Judgment": Amy Levy, Women Poets and the Victorian Dramatic Monologue', *Victorian Poetry*, 35 (Summer 1997), 173–91.

Schleiermacher, Friedrich, *On Religion: Speeches to Its Cultured Despisers* (1799), trans. John Oman (London: Kegan Paul, 1893).

—— 'On the Different Methods of Translating', trans. Waltrud Barthscht, in Rainer Schulte and John Biguenet (eds.), *Theories of Translation: An Anthology of Essays from Dryden to Derrida* (Chicago: University of Chicago Press, 1992), 36–54.

Schopenhauer, Arthur, *The Basis of Morality*, trans. Arthur Broderick Bullock (London: Swan Sonnenchein & Co. Ltd., 1903).

Schuman, Samuel, 'Man, Magician, Poet, God—An Image in Medieval, Renaissance, and Modern Literature', *Cithara: Essays in the Judaeo-Christian Tradition*, 19/2 (May 1980), 40–54.

Schwarz, Daniel R., 'A Humanistic Ethics of Reading', in Kenneth Womack and Todd F. Davis (eds.), *Mapping the Ethical Turn: A Reader in Ethics, Culture and Literary Theory* (Charlottesville and London: University Press of Virginia, 2001).

Scruton, Roger, *The Aesthetic Understanding* (London and New York: Methuen, 1983).

Sennett, Richard, *The Fall of Public Man* (London: Penguin, 2002).

Shaffer, E. S., '*Kubla Khan' and the Fall of Jerusalem: The Mythological School in Biblical Criticism and Secular Literature 1770–1880* (Cambridge: Cambridge University Press, 1975).

Shakespeare, William, *The Tempest: A New Variorum Edition of Shakespeare*, ed.
    H. H. Furness, ix (Philadelphia: Lippincott, 1892).
—— *The Tempest*, ed. Sir Arthur Quiller-Couch and J. Dover-Wilson (Cambridge:
    Cambridge University Press, 1921).
—— *The Tempest*, ed. Frank Kermode (London: Routledge, 1964).
—— *The Tempest*, ed. Anne Barton (Harmondsworth: New Penguin Shakespeare,
    1968).
—— *The Tempest*, ed. Stephen Orgel (Oxford: Oxford University Press, 1987).
—— *The Tempest*, ed. David Lindley (Cambridge: Cambridge University
    Press, 2002).
—— *The Riverside Shakespeare*, ed. G. Blakemore Evans, 2nd edn. (Boston:
    Houghton Mifflin, 1997).
Shaw, W. David, *The Lucid Veil: Poetic Truth in the Victorian Age* (London:
    Athlone Press, 1987).
—— *Victorians and Mystery: Crises of Representation* (Ithaca, NY: Cornell
    University Press, 1990).
—— *Origins of the Monologue: The Hidden God* (Toronto: University of
    Toronto Press, 1999).
Shroeder, John E., 'The Mothers of Henry James', *American Literature*, 22/4
    (Jan. 1951), 424–31.
Silver, Carole, *Strange and Secret Peoples: Fairies and Victorian Consciousness*
    (Oxford: Oxford University Press, 1999).
Silverstein, Henry, 'The Utopia of Henry James', *New England Quarterly*, 35/4
    (Dec. 1962), 458–68.
Simon, Alfred, *Beckett* (Paris: P. Belford, 1983).
Sinfield, Alan, *The Dramatic Monologue* (London: Methuen, 1977).
Sisson, C. J, 'The Magic of Prospero', in *Shakespeare Survey*, xi (Cambridge:
    Cambridge University Press, 1958), 70–6.
Slatoff, Walter J., *The Look of Distance: Reflections on Suffering and Sympathy in
    Modern Literature* (Columbus: Ohio State University Press, 1985).
Slinn, E. Warwick, *Browning and the Fictions of Identity* (London: Macmillan,
    1982).
Smiley, Jane, *13 Ways of Looking at the Novel* (London: Faber, 2005).
Smith, Adam. *The Theory of Moral Sentiments*, 6th edn., ed. Knud Haakenssen
    (Cambridge: Cambridge University Press, 2002).
Smith, Chris, *Creative Britain* (London: Faber, 1998).
Smith, Murray, *Engaging Characters: Fiction, Emotion and the Cinema* (Oxford:
    Clarendon Press, 1995).
Smith, Stan, *W. H. Auden: Rereading Literature* (Oxford: Basil Blackwell, 1985).
Smith, Zadie, *On Beauty* (London: Hamish Hamilton, 2005).
—— 'Zadie Smith Talks with Ian McEwan', in *Believer: Book of Writers Talking
    to Writers* (San Francisco: McSweeneys, 2005).

—— 'Love Actually', *Guardian*, 1 Nov. 2003, <http://books.guardian. co.uk/ review/story/0,12084,1074217,00.html>, accessed 30 Aug. 2007.

Sontag, Susan, 'Notes on "Camp" ', in *A Susan Sontag Reader* (Harmondsworth: Penguin, 1982).

—— *Illness as Metaphor and AIDS and its Metaphors* (London: Penguin, 1991).

Spalding, Frances, *Stevie Smith: A Critical Biography* (London: Faber, 1988).

Spears, Monroe K., *The Poetry of W. H. Auden: The Disenchanted Island* (New York: Oxford University Press, 1963).

Stevens, Wallace, *The Collected Poems of Wallace Stevens* (London: Faber, 1984).

Strauss, David Friedrich, *The Life of Jesus Critically Examined*, trans. Mary Ann Evans, ed. Peter C. Hodgson (London: SCM, 1973).

Tandon, Bharat, *Jane Austen and the Morality of Conversation* (London: Anthem Press, 2003).

Tate, Allen, 'The Man of Letters and the Modern World', in *Essays of Four Decades* (London: Oxford University Press, 1970).

Temple Kingston, F., *French Existentialism* (Toronto: University of Toronto Press, 1961).

Thackeray, W. M., *Letters and Private Papers*, ed. G. N. Ray, vol. ii (London: Oxford University Press, 1945).

Tillich, Paul, 'My Search for Absolutes', *Religion Online*, ed. Ruth Nanda Anshen, <http://www.religion-online.org/showchapter.asp?title=1628&C=1619>.

Tracey, C. R., 'Caliban upon Setebos', *Studies in Philology*, 35 (July 1938), 487– 99.

Trezise, Thomas, *Into the Breach: Samuel Beckett and the Ends of Literature* (Princeton: Princeton University Press, 1990).

Trippi, Peter, *J. W. Waterhouse* (London: Phaidon, 2004).

—— 'Essay' in 'Sale 14218: 19th Century Paintings and Watercolours, 14 November 2006', *Bonham's Catalogue*, <http://www.bonhams.com/cgibin/ public.sh/pubweb/publicSite.r?sContinent = EUR&screen=lotdetails NoFlash &iSaleItemNo = 3180526&iSaleNo = 14218 and <http://www.johnwilliam waterhouse.com/>, accessed 30 Aug. 2007.

Trull, Joe. E., 'Women and Other Creatures: The Gender Debate', *Christian Ethics Today* (Apr. 2003), <http://www.christianethicstoday.com/Issue/010/Women %20And%20Other%20Creatures%20%20The%20Gender%20Debate%20 By%20Joe%20E% 20Trull_010_12_.htm>, accessed 30 Aug. 2007.

Tucker Jr., Herbert *Browning's Beginnings: The Art of Disclosure* (Minneapolis: University of Minnesota Press, 1980).

Turner, Daphne, 'Delight and Truth: Auden's *The Sea and the Mirror*', *Journal of Literature and Theology*, 3/1 (Mar. 1989), 95–106.

Turner, Mark, *The Literary Mind* (New York: Oxford University Press, 1996).

Tuve, Stuart, *The Amiable Humorist: A Study of Comic Theories and Criticism of the Eighteenth and Nineteenth Century* (Chicago: University of Chicago Press, 1960).

Uhlmann, Anthony, *Beckett and Poststructuralism* (Cambridge: Cambridge University Press, 1999).

Updike, John, 'How How It Is Was', *New Yorker*, 19 Dec. 1964, 164–6.

Valéry, Paul, 'Poésie et Pensée Abstraite', in *Œuvres*, i, ed. Jean Hytier (Paris: Gallimard, 1957), 1314–39.

Van Ghent, Dorothy, 'The Dickens World: The View from Todger's', *Sewanee Review*, 58/3 (Summer 1950), 419–38.

Vaughan, Alden T., and Vaughan, Virginia Mason *Shakespeare's Caliban: A Cultural History* (Cambridge: Cambridge University Press, 1991).

Wagner-Lawlor, Jennifer, 'The Pragmatics of Silence', *Victorian Poetry*, 35 (1997), 287–302.

Walker, Roy, 'Samuel Beckett's Double Bill: Love, Chess, and Death', *Twentieth Century*, 166 (Dec. 1958), 533–44.

Watson, John B., and Skinner, B. F., *The Behavior of Organisms* (New York: Appleton-Century-Crofts, 1939).

Weil, Eric, 'The Strengths and Weaknesses of Existentialism', *Listener*, 47 (8 May 1952), 743–4.

Weil, Simone, *First and Last Notebooks*, trans. Richard Rees (London: Oxford University Press, 1970).

Wellershoff, Dieter. 'Failure of an Attempt at De-Mythologisation: Samuel Beckett's Novels', in Martin Esslin (ed.), *Samuel Beckett: A Collection of Critical Essays* (Englewood Cliffs, NJ: Prentice-Hall, 1965), 92–107.

Wells, Lynn, 'Review of *Saturday* by Ian McEwan', *Literary London: Interdisciplinary Studies in the Representation of London*, 3/2 (2005), <http://www.literarylondon.org/london-journal/september2005/wells.html>, accessed 30 Aug. 2007.

Weston, Michael, 'How can we be moved by the fate of Anna Karenina?', *Proceedings of the Aristotelian Society*, suppl. vol. 49 (1975), 81–93.

Wicker, Brian, *The Story-Shaped World: Fiction and Metaphysics: Some Variations on a Theme* (London: Athlone Press, 1975).

Wilde, Oscar, *Selected Works*, ed. R. Aldington (London: W. Heinemann, 1947).

——— *The Picture of Dorian Gray*, ed. Donald Lawler (New York: W. W. Norton & Co., 1988).

Williams, D. C., 'Dispensing with Existence', *Journal of Philosophy*, 59 (1962), 748–63.

Willoughby, John W., 'Browning's "Childe Roland to the Dark Tower Came"', *Victorian Poetry*, 1 (1963), 291–9.

Wilson, Daniel, *Caliban: The Missing Link* (London, 1872).

Wilson, R. Rawdon, 'Spooking Oedipa: On Godgames', *Canadian Review of Comparative Literature*, 4 (1977), 186–204.

—— *In Palamedes Shadow: Explorations in Play, Game and Narrative Theory* (Boston: Northeastern University Press, 1990).

Winter, Alison, *Mesmerized: The Powers of Mind in Victorian Britain* (Chicago and London: University of Chicago Press, 1998).

Wittgenstein, Ludwig, *Philosophical Investigations* (Oxford: Blackwell, 1958).

—— *Culture and Value* (Oxford: Blackwell, 1980).

—— *Remarks on the Philosophy of Psychology*, i, ed. G. E. M. Anscombe and G. H. von Wright, trans. G. E. M. Anscombe (Oxford: Basil Blackwell, 1980).

Wolosky, Shira, *Language, Mysticism: The Negative Way of Language in Eliot, Beckett and Celan* (Stanford, Calif.: Stanford University Press, 1995).

Woolford, John, 'Sources and Resources in Browning's Early Reading', in Isobel Armstrong (ed.), *Robert Browning: Writers and their Background* (London: G. Bell & Sons, 1974), 1–46.

—— *Browning the Revisionary* (London: Macmillan, 1988).

—— 'Self-Consciousness and Self-Expression in Caliban and Browning', in id. (ed.), *Robert Browning in Contexts* (Winfield, Kan.: Wedgestone Press, 1998).

—— and Karlin, Daniel, *Robert Browning* (Harlow: Longman, 1996).

Wordsworth, William, *Poetical Works*, ed. Thomas Hutchinson, rev. Ernest de Selincourt (Oxford: Oxford University Press, 1936).

Worth, Katherine, 'Beckett's Auditors: *Not I* to *Ohio Impromptu*', in Enoch Brater (ed.), *Beckett at 80/ Beckett in Context* (New York: Oxford University Press, 1986).

—— *Samuel Beckett's Theatre: Life Journeys* (Oxford: Oxford University Press, 1999).

Wright, Iain, ' "What Matter who's speaking": Beckett, the Authorial Subject and Contemporary Critical Theory', *Southern Review*, 16/1 (Mar. 1983), 5–30.

Yeats, W. B., *Selected Poetry*, ed. Timothy Webb (Harmondsworth: Penguin, 1991).

Zurbrugg, Nicholas, *Beckett and Proust* (Gerrards Cross: Colin Smythe, 1998).

Index